Diversity

Also by Kurt April

KNOWLEDGE MANAGEMENT PRAXIS

PERFORMANCE THROUGH LEARNING: Knowledge Management in Action

THE KNOWLEDGE MANAGEMENT WORKBOOK

e or be@ten: E-Business Redefining the Corporate Landscape

RETHINKING LEADERSHIP

Diversity

New Realities in a Changing World

Edited by

Kurt April & Marylou Shockley

California State University
Monterey Bay

UCT
Graduate
School of
Business
the international
business school in Africa

palgrave
macmillan

ASHRIDGE

First published 2007 by
PALGRAVE MACMILLAN
Houndmills, Basingstoke, Hampshire RG21 6XS and
175 Fifth Avenue, New York, N.Y. 10010
Companies and representatives throughout the world

PALGRAVE MACMILLAN is the global academic imprint of the Palgrave Macmillan division of St. Martin's Press, LLC and of Palgrave Macmillan Ltd. Macmillan® is a registered trademark in the United States, United Kingdom and other countries. Palgrave is a registered trademark in the European Union and other countries.

ISBN-13: 978-0-230-00133-6 hardback
ISBN-10: 0-230-00133-5 hardback

This book is printed on paper suitable for recycling and made from fully managed and sustained forest sources.

A catalogue record for this book is available from the British Library.

Library of Congress Cataloging-in-Publication Data

Diversity : new realities in a changing world / edited by Kurt April & Marylou Shockley.
p. cm.
Includes bibliographical references and index.
ISBN 0-230-00133-5 (cloth)
1. Pluralism (Social sciences) 2. Multiculturalism. 3. Diversity in the workplace. I. April, Kurt. II. Shockley, Marylou L. (Marylou Lorraine), 1943–

HM1271.D582 2007
305.8009'0511—dc22 2006043165

10 9 8 7 6 5 4 3 2
16 15 14 13 12 11 10 09 08 07

Printed and bound in Great Britain by
Antony Rowe Ltd, Chippenham and Eastbourne

To Thelma April, Ronald Vollenhoven, Raymond Shockley, and Sandra Shockley

Contents

List of Tables

List of Figures

Acknowledgements

We have learned over the years that diversity is an "offer." The conscious and purposeful choices we make with regard to the numerous "offers of difference," "stimuli of difference," that happen to manifest themselves in our awareness, as our paths cross different people, ideas and concepts, will determine our actionable responses. More importantly, as we make our socially constructed world views permeable to these offers and stimuli, they shape who we ultimately become (as opposed to what we get). In both our cases, our families have always been, and continue to be at the heart of these offers.

For Kurt: My wife Amanda and son Jordan have, and still continue to teach me about the beauty that diversity brings into one's life, if one chooses it to be so! Huge thanks to my immediate family (Ivan April, Thelma April – in memoriam, Monica Vollenhoven, Ronald Vollenhoven – in memoriam, Tanya Vollenhoven-Brown, Henry Brown, Nathalie Sleenhof, Alexander Sleenhof, Savannah Cochrane-Sleenhof, Nickolas Sleenhof and Chloe Sleenhof) who sustain me, and fuel my desire to continue researching and working towards creating a future that works for them, and many like them.

For Marylou: I continue to marvel at my parents, Raymond and Sandra Shockley, who chose love rather than the social mores of their generation to define their relationship, proving that "racial purity" is truly a xenophobic myth. My "*Ohana nui*" (as we say in Hawaiian) or extended family and friends – Glenn, Debbie, Sharon, Tony, John, Rita, Adam, Alexis, Noel, Constance and Judy – are the greatest cheering section a person can possibly have; to all of them I say, "*na 'au ho 'omai ka 'i*" . . . my heart is grateful.

We are indeed grateful to all of our contributing authors who overcame the challenges of busy schedules, time zones, and dodgy Internet connections in far away places to respond to our demanding requests. To Jacky Kippenberger for taking our project on-board, and her able team – Linda Auld, Rebecca Pash and Mirabelle Boateng, thank you for belief in our project, your editorial insights and for nudging us along. We are also indebted to Kai Peters, CEO of Ashridge Business School (UK), who graciously extended to us the lovely, contemplative facilities of Ashridge – for it was at Ashridge that we crystallized "the ideas of diversity" into a book.

Foreword

This collection is an ambitious attempt to look at diversity from very varied perspectives. It is unique in so far as it is international in scope and contains essays which are academic and essays which are personal. In our modern world the question of diversity is not an extra optional but an every day reality and to make it a reality we do need to win both the hearts and minds of those who have to lead in making it work and getting others to see the potential and benefits of positively engaging with the challenges posed by diversity.

The virtue of this book is that it contains chapters which deal with organizational issues and those which deal with social, cultural and political issues. It, therefore, brings together all the dimensions of diversity in one volume and describes how the debate about diversity has developed. It is important that diversity is discussed in all its dimensions. I believe that this book will provide a very timely and useful material for discussion and bring the considerations of this often emotive subject to a different and more productive level.

This book challenges some of the conventional wisdom and encourages the reader to think about diversity as a multifaceted concept – which in my view is necessary because often diversity is looked at in isolation from other considerations – almost as a sideshow, something to be accommodated or tolerated. Understanding diversity in all its dimensions in today's world is essential, and if we are to prepare for new realities and realize new realities then the approach taken in this book is not only novel but has a lot to offer.

Baroness Usha Prashar

Notes on the Editors

Professor Kurt A. April, PhD University Senate Member and Professor at the Graduate School of Business (University of Cape Town, South Africa), lectures and researches in the disciplines of Leadership, Diversity and Knowledge Management. He also is an Associate Fellow of Saïd Business School (University of Oxford, UK), is a Research Fellow at Ashridge Management College (UK), is a regular Visiting Professor at Rotterdam School of Management (Erasmus University, The Netherlands). Previously, the Academic Director of the Centre for Leadership and Public Values (a collaborative initiative with Duke University, North Carolina, USA), Kurt ran a Leadership Workshop for Harvard Business School (USA) as part of their Making Markets Work program in 2004.

Outside of academia, Kurt is Managing Director of LICM Consulting. Additionally, Kurt is an Advisory Board Member of KMPro (Knowledge Management Professional Society, USA), Member of the Midwestern Organizational Learning Network (USA), Member of the Editors' Forum (SA), Member of the IEEE (USA), Member of the Sainsbury's Fellows Association (UK), Member of the Academy of Management (USA) and Member of the British Academy of Management (UK).

He has been educated at the University of Cape Town (SA), having obtained the following there: PhD (in conjunction with Oxford University, UK where he was the first Sainsbury Fellow in 1998–9 researching "IT Strategy and Sustainable Competitive Advantage in Financial Services Companies"), MBA, Master's degree in Electronic Engineering, Bachelor's degree in Electrical Engineering, Higher Diploma in Education; in addition, Certificate in Japanese Production (Nagoya, Japan), as well as two National Diplomas (Electronic Engineering; Logic Systems) at Wingfield College. Prior to entering academia, Kurt worked in a number of industries: International Defence Industry, Rail Transport, Nuclear Power Generation, Education, Oil and Gas, and Financial Services.

He currently consults, and has consulted on various projects in the areas of Knowledge Management, IT Strategy, Leadership and Diversity to, and behalf of, a range of industries, including: Shell International (Europe, Africa, Asia and USA), SABMiller (SA), De Beers (SA, Namibia and Botswana), Old Mutual (SA and UK), Sanlam (SA), Zurich Assurance (UK), Mithras Consulting (Switzerland and China), Standard Chartered Bank (UK, Singapore, Thailand and Africa), Oracle (UK), IBM (Global), Show Business (UK), AngloGold Ashanti (Global), Impala Platinum (SA), European Space Agency (The Netherlands), Presidential Leadership Programme for SA Government DGs, DDGs and Heads of Department (SA), Department of Labour (Employment Equity, SA), RWE

(Germany), Knowledge Factory (Switzerland and Dubai), NHS (UK), Thames Water (UK), Innogy (UK), Trihelix (The Netherlands and China), EIRIM (The Netherlands), Lufthansa (Germany), and the Cool Group (The Netherlands).

Kurt has published a number of management research articles and papers including two award-winning research papers in electronic engineering journals. He has also authored and co-authored five other books (*Rethinking Leadership, e or be@ten: E-business Redefining the Corporate Landscape, The Knowledge Management Workbook, Knowledge Management Praxis* and *Performance Through Learning*), and has another book due out in 2006 (*Diversity in Africa: The Coming of Age of a Continent*). He is also currently researching a number of other books (stewardship; IT complementarity for sustainable competitive advantage; patterned identity through diverse personal story). Kurt is the Executive Editor and Advisory Board Member to the *Journal for Convergence*, is a reviewer in the leadership discipline for the academic accredited journal, *South African Journal of Business Management*, is an international reviewer in the strategy and knowledge management disciplines for the *Academy of Management* in the US, and is an article- and book-reviewer of the internationally accredited academic journal, *Journal of Management Education* (USA), and is a book reviewer for US-based, *Emerald*.

Dr Marylou L. Shockley, PhD is an Associate Professor and Chair in the School of Business at the California State University – Monterey Bay. She completed her Doctor of Philosophy degree at Oxford University – Saïd Business School. Dr Shockley is also a researcher and consultant whose interests include knowledge management, diversity, social application of IT network technologies, and corporate governance with emphasis on social responsibility.

Dr Shockley has significant experience in the telecommunications industry working for both ATT and Pacific Bell. She was one of the first women selected to participate on the fast track programs at ATT to develop women for senior management. Her career of over twenty five years has provided Marylou with significant managerial and leadership experience in the telecommunications industry. She has led teams as large as 8000 employees at SBC Pacific Bell. Her last position held at SBC Pacific Bell was in charge of one of the company's operating subsidiaries. While in this position, she co-led an industry-wide forum that developed legislation in the US Communications Act of 1996 to restructure the payphone industry.

During her career, Marylou was one of two women selected from Pacific Bell to attend the Stanford Business School as a Sloan Fellow. She has also held and sponsored many community activities which included Board membership in such organizations as Junior Achievement-Bay Area Chapter and *Zyzzyva*, a San Francisco based literary magazine. She acted as a Key Advisor on the development of Pacific Telesis' Corporate Diversity Policy, and was a Senior Executive sponsor and advisor to Pacific Bell's Executive Women in

Leadership education program. She was also voted the "Leader of the Year in 1993" by ACCA, an Asian employee and community organization at SBC Pacific Bell.

While at Oxford, Marylou tutored undergraduate engineering students in organization behavior. She has made the following presentations on research: "Research: a Highway or Labyrinth?" (joint University of Oxford-Warwick Business School Research group), "Research: Qualitative Methods" (Singapore's Ministry of Education Staff); and "Internet Adoption Among Teachers" (Information Technology in Education Association). Marylou Shockley has been a reviewer for the journal *Technology, Pedagogy, and Education*. Some articles written or co-authored by her include: "The Economics of Change: The Role of Innovation and Evolution in Technology Adoption," *BETT Journal*, Spring 2001, 3:1; "How Ready is Your Organisation for Knowledge Management?," *Global Knowledge Review*, September, 2004 co-authored with Kurt A. April; and "IT and HRM: Meeting Minds or Hitting Heads?" co-authored with Dr Peter Cunningham and Kurt A. April (forthcoming).

List of Contributors

Amanda April, a South African is currently a Director of LICM Consulting. She is a University of Cape Town (South Africa) Bachelors and Honours graduate in Social Science, and is completing Masters studies in Criminology and in Commerce (specializing in Executive Coaching). Amanda has worked both locally and internationally. After 11 years of experience in the Department of Social Services, as Chief Social Worker (South Africa), she was responsible for providing expert testimony and case histories to courts throughout the Western Cape. Previously, she played roles as Coordinator of Victim Support Services, Victim Support Counsellor, Probation Officer, Intermediary for Survivors of Abuse, Family- and Individual Counsellor, amongst others. In 1996 Amanda participated in an exchange to Chicago (USA), and during 1998 and 1999, Amanda both worked for the Oxfordshire Children and Families Unit (Witney), as well as taught at Oxford College for Further Education in Oxford (UK). More recently, Amanda has been directly involved in coaching executives from the UK, the USA, Zimbabwe, The Netherlands and South Africa.

Dave Bond previously MBA Director at the University of Cape Town, and holder of dual South African and UK citizenship, is now a faculty member of the RSM Erasmus University in Rotterdam (The Netherlands), where he leads the Personal Leadership Development course across all the MBA programs and is Academic Director of the Global Executive OneMBA. Dave's main teaching, research and publication interests are in communication, learning and personal development, particularly for management development in contexts of diversity and change. Dave's qualifications are in philosophy, politics, critical linguistics and educational development. Before joining RSM, Dave worked freelance in Europe, the UK and Southern Africa as a lecturer, facilitator and consultant to business schools, companies and the non-profit sector, and spent the early years of his career teaching English language and communication to adults, teenagers and children from diverse educational and cultural backgrounds, in South Africa, Zimbabwe, England and South-East Asia.

Tony Burnett, born in Britain, is a Founding Partner of Performance Through Inclusion (PTI) and has a wealth of broad business and diversity experience. He was previously Head of People Development at Guinness UDV Great Britain, where he developed innovative, large-scale leadership and human development programs across the UK and Africa. Prior to founding PTI, Tony was European Diversity Manager at Ford Motor Company. In this role, he was responsible for designing the European Diversity Strategy and business case, as well as designing and delivering diversity training for Ford UK personnel. Tony helps major businesses address their most difficult challenges around "diversity" and "inclusion." In addition to diversity and HR, Tony has over 12 years' commercial business experience covering retail, FMCG and leisure sectors. Tony has a Master's degree in Management from the University of Liverpool.

Vinay Dhamija, born in India, has an MBA from Rotterdam School of Management, Erasmus University (The Netherlands). Currently he lives and works in the UK, as a marketing professional with British American Tobacco responsible for HORECA. During his tenure in ITC Limited, a company rated as one of the pioneers in corporate governance in India, he achieved insights and experience in the best international practices in that field. With five years of experience in India and Europe, in the areas of technology and marketing consulting, he is currently researching the effects of EU enlargement on marketing strategies of FMCGs and sustainability of emerging economies' growth. His other interests include business ethics, corporate governance and social responsibility.

Tony Ehrenreich, a South African, helped dismantle Apartheid in same country, and is Regional Secretary, Western Cape, of the Congress of South African Trade Unions (COSATU), is a Fellow of the Centre for Leadership and Public Values (Collaborative Initiative between Duke University, USA and University of Cape Town, South Africa), and is School Labor Leader-in-Residence at the ILR School (Cornell University, USA).

Joanna Eidsmore an American, completed her Master's degree in communication at San Diego State University (SDSU) in December 2004. While at SDSU, Joanna developed an interest in intercultural communication, specifically in the area of identity negotiation. She focused on how English-as-a-second-language (ESL) students in San Diego County managed their native identity, while being exposed to various cultures in the USA. Upon completion of her degree, Joanna has taught intercultural communication, interpersonal communication, and advanced public speaking at various colleges in San Diego County.

Philomena Essed a Dutch national and previously from the University of Amsterdam, now is Professor of Critical Race, Gender and Leadership Studies, Antioch University, PhD Program in Leadership and Change, in the USA. She is also a deputy member of the Dutch Equal Treatment Commission. She is known for her books and articles on *Everyday Racism*, a concept she introduced in the 1980s and 1990s and for her writings on *Diversity: Gender, Color and Culture* (1996). Recent publications include the (co-edited) volumes *Race Critical Theories* (2002) and *A Companion to Gender Studies* (2005). Her current work focuses on cloning cultures – the injustices of preference for sameness – and on humanizing leadership.

Mario Ghiggino a Brazilian, has been educated at the University of Viçosa, Brazil, where he received a bachelor's degree in Agriculture Engineering.

Later on he obtained a Master's degree in Marketing for Food and Agricultural products at IAMZ, Spain and a MBA/MBI at Rotterdam School of Management, The Netherlands, where he was also given the Langman Leadership Award for exemplifying excellence in professionalism, entrepreneurship, and social responsibilities. Mario has worked in various segments of the food industry as employee and, later on, as a consultant. He used to live in Rotterdam where he owns a consulting company in marketing, product development and trading of food products in Europe, working for South American exporting companies, but currently lives in France. He also contributes articles for Brazilian newspapers and magazines, in issues as business, international marketing, globalisation and self-development.

Cathy Havener Greer an American, is an Attorney-Member of Wells, Anderson & Race LLC, and Heads a team of lawyers and support staff on legal matters for which the company is retained. She encourages the creative approach to analysis of legal problems and assessment of potential solutions, through teamwork and collaboration. In addition she is a member of the Executive Committee of the International Association of Defense Counsel (IADC), an organization of approximately 2400 attorneys involved to membership. IADC is the oldest and most prestigious international association of attorneys representing corporations and insurance companies. As a member of the Executive Committee, she heads various task forces and committees of members engaged in the management of the Association and its programs.

Geert Hofman born in The Netherlands, and a graduate from Rotterdam Erasmus University (economics faculty), has been working as a consultant, coach, facilitator, and trainer throughout The Netherlands and Europe since 1988. His main focus is to increase awareness of individuals and companies about the unexplored potential they have, and the effects unlocking this potential has on personal effectiveness and organizational results. Through his work as a coach and consultant, he shows how individuals can tap into their potential and thus achieve higher personal effectiveness and experience sustained fulfillment. Recently he contributed to the book *Liefde voor Talent* (Love for Talent), in which the notion of the destiny-driven organization was presented.

Jonny Holbek born 1940 in Norway, first studied at the Norwegian Institute of Technology (MS degree in 1966), and later at Northwestern University, United States of America (PhD in 1975). He has been a Professor of Business Administration at the Norwegian Institute of Technology, and at Agder University College (Kristiansand, Norway). He recently retired from the latter to focus, in slow time, upon his two main professional interests: "Integrating frameworks of innovation" and "Innovation in the historical context of Byzantium."

Thor Indridason born in Iceland and currently living in Oxford, was educated in the Universities of Iceland, as well as obtaining his DPhil at Oxford University (UK). A talented musician in his own right, he has worked as a researcher for Trade Unions in Iceland, and written several books and articles on Icelandic and Scandinavian politics and industrial relations.

James Joseph Ambassador James Joseph is Professor of the Practice of Public Policy Studies and Executive Director of the United States-Southern Africa Center for Leadership and Public Values at Duke University. Having served three Presidents, he was nominated by President Clinton and confirmed by the United States Senate in December 1995, and was the first and only American Ambassador to present his credentials to President Nelson Mandela. In 1999, President Thabo Mbeki awarded him the Order of Good Hope, the highest honor the Republic of South Africa bestows on a citizen of another country. Ambassador Joseph has had a distinguished career in government, business, education and philanthropy. From 1982–1995, he was President and Chief Executive Officer of the Council on Foundations, an international organization of more than 1900 foundations and corporate-giving programs. Amb. Joseph also served as Under Secretary of the Interior from 1977–1981 and a Vice President of Cummins Engine Company and President of the Cummins Engine Foundation from 1971–1976. An Ordained Minister in the United Church of Christ, he has taught at Yale Divinity School and the Claremont Colleges where he was also University Chaplain. In 1985, he was a Distinguished Visitor at Nuffield College at Oxford University, and he serves presently as Honorary Professor and a member of the Board of Advisors at the Graduate School of Business at the University of Cape Town (SA).

Simon Kettleborough born in the UK, is a Founding Partner of Performance Through Inclusion (PTI) and specialises in "inclusion strategies." He has spent over half of his career in consulting, with PTI and as a consultant with Arthur D. Little in London. He has worked with private and public sector clients across the energy, financial services, healthcare, engineering, criminal justice, media, automotive, publishing, mining and consumer goods sectors. Simon also specializes in products and diagnostic systems for diversity measurement. He is the main architect of the *InclusionIndex™* diagnostic system, a system that enables clients to track their progress in a number of areas relating to diversity. Before consulting, Simon worked for Diageo in the UK, USA and Asia in various strategic and commercial roles. Simon has a BA (Hons) from Durham University, and an MBA from Warwick Business School.

Harald Knudsen born in Norway in 1943, is a Professor of International Management at Agder University College, Kristiansand, Norway. Beyond his management background, he also has a deep interest in philosophy, arts and ethics. He is actively involved in leadership training and public speaking, and is the author of several books on leadership and philosophy in Norway. He is also a keen jazz trumpet-player, and has developed an original concept of "leadership jazz" with live jazz bands in training sessions. He works extensively around the world, with the bulk of his focus (outside of Norway) on East Africa and Europe.

Soonu Kochar Born in India, Ambassador Kochar has extensive experience in the Indian Foreign Service. From 1978 to 1982 she served as High Commissioner of India to Fiji, a posting that was followed by 9 years serving as Indian Ambassador to The Netherlands, Argentina and France, where she currently resides. In the years previous to serving in the Indian Foreign Service, Ambassador Kochar worked in the Ministry of External Affairs. She was Assistant Director of the International Relations Division at the Commonwealth Secretariat in London (UK), and was Director General of the Indian Council for Cultural Relations in New Delhi (India). Ambassador Kochar is a regular visiting faculty member at RSM Erasmus University (The Netherlands), and presents workshops in cultural relational issues, and electives on geo-politics.

Jennifer Kam Jennifer, an American, completed her Master's degree in communication at San Diego State University in December 2004. She is currently a doctoral student in the Department of Communication Arts & Sciences at The Pennsylvania State University, with a specialization in intercultural and interpersonal communication. In particular, Jennifer is concerned with how Chinese-Americans are portrayed in contemporary US culture. Her other interests include cultural adaptation, masculinity, aging identity, and envy among couples.

Lovemore Mbigi a Zimbabwean, is a Board Member and Visiting Professor at Ivestec School of Management at Rhodes University, and exciting and creative thinker, and storyteller of note (even at the World Economic Forum), specializing in the area of managing transformation – working throughout Africa and in North America. Formerly the Executive Director of Eastern Highlands Tea Estates, Director of the Dorbyl Group, Executive Director of Nampak Management Services and Director of Nampak Corrugated, Lovemore is currently the Executive Director of Rainmaker Consultants, which has offices in Sandton, Johannesburg and in Florida, USA, and specialises in practical solutions to change management and strategic challenges. He holds an MBA degree in Strategic Management from the Northeastern University in Boston, USA, as well as a Master's Degree in Management and Social Science from the University of Zimbabwe. He has taught and been a guest speaker at a number of Business Schools, including UNISA, Milpark Business School, University of Cape Town and Witwatersrand University. A well published author, Lovemore has written three best-selling books – his latest is *In Search of the African Business Renaissance*.

Ken Moore is a highly experienced consultant and trainer who specializes in personal and management development. He has been successfully delivering HR consultancy, coaching and training throughout his home country, the UK, and Europe since 1985. Ken's long-standing interest in integrating meaning and purpose into work-life has led him to spiritual intelligence via psychology, philosophy, metaphysics, emotional intelligence, study of world religions and leadership development.

Keith Morrison born in the UK, has worked in higher education for 25 years, in the UK (formerly at the University of Durham) and Macau, where he currently is a Professor, Vice-Rector and Dean of the School of Arts, Letters and Sciences at the Macau Inter-University Institute. He was formerly at the University of Durham, UK. He is the author of over 100 papers in internationally refereed journals, and 11 books, including *Research Methods in Education (5th edition), School Leadership and Complexity Theory,* and *A Guide to Teaching Practice (5th edition).* He has produced reports and papers for government agencies and officers in several countries, including the UK, the Czech Republic, South Africa, Malaysia and Macau, and has also worked in Hong Kong and Singapore. He is the current editor of the journal *Evaluation and Research in Education.* His fields of work include: management, change and leadership; organizational behavior and change; evaluation and research methods; teacher education; and sociology of education and policy scholarship. Keith has undertaken some 20 consultancy projects for educational organizations, governments and commercial businesses.

Kai Peters, a German-Canadian, is Chief Executive of Ashridge Business School. Prior to joining Ashridge, Kai was Dean, and previously Director of MBA programs, of the Rotterdam School of Management (RSM) of Erasmus University in The Netherlands. Peters serves on Supervisory and Advisory Boards for a number of organizations in the technology and telecommunications sector. He is Owner and was Managing Director (1989–1993) of a company in the German publishing sector, and has worked with both IBM and Volkswagen managing marketing activities. Kai is a frequent lecturer on management education and technology for government, business and academic audiences. He holds degrees from York University, Toronto and University of Quebec in Chicoutimi (Canada), and Erasmus University (The Netherlands).

Marilyn Thomas, an American, is currently a Professor at Menlo College, Atherton, California. She received her PhD in English from the University of Minnesota, and has completed five post-doctoral fellowships: one each at Yale and Cambridge; three at the University of Oxford (UK) where she is an Honorary Member of the Board of Governors of Harris Manchester College, Oxford. Her literary criticism has appeared in numerous journals. An essay on Kierkegaard is anthologized. She is the author of a book on the symbolism of the labyrinth in the nineteenth century novel. She is also the author of a biography entitled *Victorian Conscience: F. W. Robertson.*

Sylvia Vriesendorp born in The Netherlands, now lives in the USA and works as an Organization Development Specialist with Management Sciences for Health (MSH), a non-profit public health consulting group based in Boston, Massachusetts. She is frequently asked to facilitate organizational retreats, team-building and strategic planning exercises all with the intended effect of producing, not only tangible plans but also an improved organizational climate for collective learning. She has facilitated numerous such events, both in the United States and overseas, in English and French, always seeking common ground among diverse stakeholders. Sylvia is a regular presenter at the International Association of Facilitators and the Organization Behavior Teaching Conference (OBTC). Originally trained as a psychologist, her special interest is in how people behave in organizations and the influence of culture and gender dynamics on productivity and morale.

Hongyan Xu, a Chinese national, is currently working in Siemens AG Power Generation (Oil and Gas) as Manager of Global Alliances, responsible for Regional Competency Centre and Joint Venture, Alliances and Acquisitions. Previously she had worked in General Electric Germany (GE) as Project Leader for integrating the Global Supply Chain of a newly acquired business. Before her MBA/MBI at Rotterdam School of Management, Erasmus University (The Netherlands), where she appeared on the Dean's List, she had worked for China National Aero-Technology Import and Export Cooperation (CATIC) in Asia and the Middle East. She achieved her bachelor degrees, with Honours, in Aeronautic Engineering and International Business from Beijing University of Aeronautics and Astronautics in China. After living, studying and working in Beijing, Cairo, Hamburg, Rotterdam, London (Canada) and Cologne, she is currently residing in Düsseldorf (Germany).

Introduction: A Diverse Future

by Kurt April and Marylou Shockley

Simmering caldera

Why do we value bio-diversity and yet look upon social diversity as an "issue"? This is a conundrum, for sure. There are many varied views on socially ascribed diversity; its "issues" are critically debated, passionately held, and politically created. This simmering caldera erupts periodically into movements for human rights and social justice. As a response to these movements, public, civil and private sectors in many countries around the world have been encouraged, either by populist pressure, customer demand, citizen action or public policy directives, to address the issues of diversity in their respective milieus.

Historical context: the aristocracy of the dominant view

Diversity issues are not new. They are instead historically situated. It falls on each generation to debate and wrestle with solutions to promote, or erode, the rights of populist expression – including dissent – as well as the rights of societal and political inclusion. The philosopher John Stuart Mills (1859: 417), for example, wrote about the injustices of his day suggesting that the aristocracy of colour and sex had no place in government:

> For with what truth or rationality could the suffrage be termed universal. . . . To declare that a voice in the government is the right of all, and demand it only for a part – the part, namely, to which the claimant himself belongs – is to renounce even the appearance of principle.

Three observations are worth noting within a situated historical context. First, such struggles to obtain equal participation in civil society, government and the workplace require courage, fortitude and real leadership. They also build upon the experiences of past generations; it means that sharing experiences becomes important. In this book, several articles chronicle recent struggles to obtain equality in society and the workplace. For example, James Joseph in

Managing Diversity: The United States Experience, addresses his own career experiences, as a "rarity" in the organizational contexts in which he found himself at the time – an African-American man in very senior positions, in government, civil society and in business, who led efforts to embed the principles of inclusion in the workplace.

The second observation is that, as a new moral consciousness dawns on people everywhere, backlash and retrenchment are also woven into the fabric of many societies, as guardians of the dominant view grapple with transformation of their worlds. Vigilance and responsible action are needed to set the alarm bells ringing. We have included an article by Jennifer Kam and Joanna Eidsmore, Applying Burlesque Rhetoric to Create Social Change, which addresses the inappropriate use of racial slurs to sell their t-shirts by the retailer Abercrombie and Fitch (A&F). When looking at the websites cited by these authors, the range of reactions are mixed – ranging from "what's the big deal, you're over reacting" to "outrageous . . . how can A&F expect to make money off of racial jokes about Chinese people?"

The third observation addresses the transformation of workplace environments themselves. Where compliance to workplace equity has been mandated by legislative fiat, businesses as well as public sector institutions resort to "coverage of the law" as a form of training. What history shows is that diversity is not a *one-time event*, but an *ongoing practice*. Mario Ghiggino in, Diversity: Ideas to Create Value in the Workplace, illustrates some of the practices to instil respect in culturally diverse, multi-national environments.

The future: from managing to leading diversity

During the last 45 years, notions of equal opportunity for those disadvantaged due to race, gender, disabilities, and life style preferences have evolved from compliance to what is currently referred to as managing diversity. Thomas and Ely (1996) walks us through this recent history in terms of three paradigms – discrimination and fairness, access and legitimacy, as well as learning and effectiveness. They suggest that the discrimination and fairness paradigm was based on the notion of "sameness" in which organizational environments should operate as if everyone was the same, irrespective of gender, race or nationality. There was no room for diversity. Organizations then woke up to the notions that not only were demographics changing, but so were their customers or constituencies. The access and legitimacy paradigm recognized these changing profiles as a competitive advantage, i.e., that niche markets needed niche employees to represent these organizations in their respective communities. Thomas and Ely (1996), through their work with clients, further found an emerging paradigm of valuing diversity under a model of learning and effectiveness. Diverse employees were recognized not only for their experiences as niche market advocates, but also for providing a pool of new ideas and ways of doing things that could spark a creative renaissance in a business. Managing diversity meant "integration" – truly valuing different perspectives, and establishing environments where diverse employees could contribute authentically and holistically without leaving "parts of themselves" at home.

However, not everyone "buys into" these concepts of diversity. Critics like T. J. Rogers, the CEO of Cypress Semiconductor, argue that diversity has become an industry of consultants who have influenced many businesses to become "preoccupied" with diversity. Rogers (1995: 177) feels that, "Businesses do not become great because they manage diversity well; well-managed businesses take advantage of diversity in their workforce." Some argue that diversity might be desirable, but its value to bottom-line performance of an organization is illusive. It is a "trap," according to D'Souza (1997), in which consultants get rich selling "diversity workshops"; in fact, he argues that homogeneous groups work far better and are more efficient.

Some members of the academic community are also troubled by the concept of managing diversity. They are more troubled by the "managing" than "diversity" itself. Taking a communications perspective, Grimes and Richard (2003) have studied the practitioner literature and consultant websites and are concerned about the language that tries to link managing diversity with bottom-line performance. They argue that "managing diversity" is a "managerialist view", not necessarily conducive to promoting interactive communication. In a managerial context, as claimed by Kurt April and Amanda April in their article in this book: Responsible Leadership Ethics, people are viewed as "assets" in favor of capital markets – objects, instruments, like any other to gain competitive advantage. Such managerial blinders can lead to gaps in what is said, and what is practiced, as shown by a study in hospitals by Aries (2004).

"Leadership" rather than "management" defines the future of diversity. First, it takes leadership to integrate diversity into the workplace. Valuing diversity can make it from the mission statement on the wall to the daily practice in meetings and human resource development processes, if senior leaders are willing to invest their time to encourage, champion and reward the participation of employees whose backgrounds are "non-traditional" in terms of the prevailing cultural norm, or dominant consciousness, in their organizations. It also means coming to terms with the complexities that follow in the wake of diversity. One of our contributing authors Philomena Essed, when speaking to Leadership in Question: Talking Diversity, Walking Homogeneity in the Dutch Police Force, discusses how precipitous change is now part of the changing landscape for the Police Force in The Netherlands. What she has found, through her research, is that embedding diversity into the workplace takes time, and more importantly require changes in the mindset of the leaders themselves.

In addition, in a pluralistic world, a "one model fits all" approach to leadership is not viable. Cultural diversity, especially at the international level, forcefully nudges us to consider other models to enrich our thinking about leadership. The "dominant view," in this case mostly driven by US theories of leadership, requires introspective inquiry. Several contributions by authors in this book help expand this inquiry into leadership. Most notably is an essay by Lovemore Mbigi entitled Spirit of African Leadership: A Comparative African Perspective, in which he describes a variety of leadership paradigms. He argues that although these paradigms are culturally shaped, leaders must at the minimum understand the various leadership models espoused around the world if they are to lead their firms effectively in the emerging global marketplace. He challenges leaders to embrace the notion of social learning, through which they can incorporate complementary competencies of other global cultural paradigms.

Diversity as multi-faceted realities

Worman (2005: 27) notes ". . .definitions for diversity are almost as diverse as the subject itself". She describes three types of diversity: (1) "social diversity" which includes demographical profiles: age, race, ethnicity and gender; (2) "value diversity" which includes psychological differences based on personality and attitudes; and (3) "informational diversity" which includes organizational differences in educational expertise, tenure, and function. On a personal level in which diverse employees find themselves in organizational cultures that are alien to their persona, Mamman (1996) explores a series of variables that structures the formal and informal interactions for these employees. Although not defining diversity *per se*, his structure provides the basis upon which managers and human resources staff, representing the dominant culture within their organizations, can (re)design processes and training interventions that incorporate these interactive factors.

At an organizational level, Rijamampianina and Carmichael (2005) use an iceberg analogy to suggest that the primary dimensions of diversity (e.g., race, gender, age, ethnicity, and disability) are above the surface secondary dimensions (e.g., religion, sexual orientation, education, and language), and tertiary dimensions (e.g., beliefs, attitudes, and assumptions) are below the surface. This framework is then used to propose a definition of diversity as, "the collective, all encompassing mix of human differences and similarities along any given dimension" (Rijamampianina and Carmichael, 2005: 110). These authors go on to adroitly argue that diversity impacts organizational processes rather than outcome. What remains a bit troublesome is the often uncritical, all encompassing nature of defining diversity in organizational and socio-political environments. Such definitions have the potential to both "dilute" and create complex structures that diversity could mean anything, and paradoxically, nothing. Many experts opt for holism that integrates the characteristics of diversity with the processes of the business (Rijamampianina and Carmichael, 2005; Thomas and Ely, 1996; Worman, 2005). Others, like Liff and Wajcman (1996) are generally supportive of the diversity direction, but are raising the issue that definitions do count, especially within a legal context, where equal treatment translates to being treated the same irrespective of gender, race, ethnicity or age.

We are willing to accept the ambiguity that no definition of diversity will be without its critics. Indeed such a definition, like a pot of gold at the end of the rainbow, is at best an idealized hope – at least for now. A lack of definition does not preclude us from introducing a framework that enables a healthy discussion of diversity. The framework is shown below as a set of multi-faceted realities. As an analog, facets for example on a gem appear in three dimensional space and change with the perspective of the viewer. So does diversity – it too changes with perspective. However, the gem itself is fluid, morphing with changes in local, national and world views. We, therefore, propose that these faceted realities of diversity are constructed, depending on one's perspective, and will continue to change as world views change. Constructed realities enable the creation of meaning from what is a complex and often chaotic sensory input and experience. Such created realities can pose a risk – the danger of potential misinterpretation as Anderson (1990) points out in his anecdote of riders in a streetcar who jumped to the conclusion that a mom on the tram was a child abuser when in fact she had bandaged her son's head because it was stuck in a pot, helmet-like.

Although everyone is entitled to their own perceptions of diversity, not all of these perceptions or facets of reality are equally meaningful. We as Editors, therefore, have selected authors' contributions which we feel will evoke reflection, and spark critical debate, about various aspects of diversity. Like the anthropologist and ethnographer Geertz (1993), who argues for the legitimacy of thick descriptions as an analytic method, the authors' contributions have been selected for the purpose of providing thick interpretive

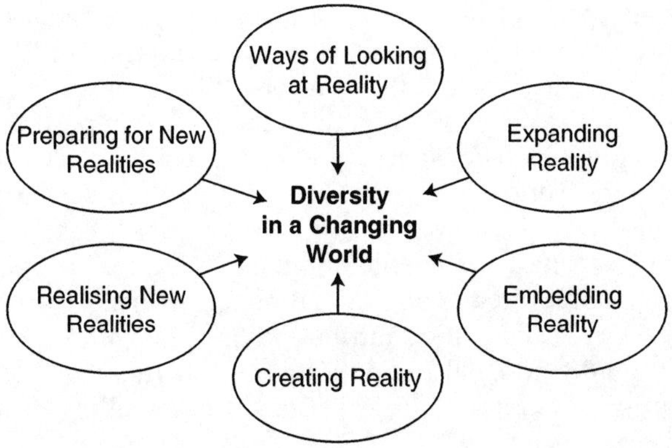

Figure I Diversity: Realities in a Changing World Framework
Source: Authors

descriptions by: (1) revisiting the traditional categories of race, ethnicity, gender, age; and (2) enriching the dialogue to include other realities of diversity.

What's in this book

Several characteristics make this book unique. First, most of the authors have spent time in other countries, other than their country of origin and many are themselves bicultural. Second, the contributions range from highly personal essays to academic papers – written by Ambassadors, academics, senior executives and managers in business, senior managers in government, consultants, union leaders, professional administrators, journalists and students. Evoking reflective inquiry necessitates a range of experiences and thought that not only engages the mind, but the heart and spirit as well. Third, this book is international in scope. Diversity is global, not local or national only. With functions and operations in a given organization increasingly spread around the world, such a collection of multi-faceted perspectives are generally not available.

The six facets in this book are described below; they are organized as six parts:

- *Ways of Looking at Reality*: a survey of some of the current topical issues of diversity is presented. These papers explore the challenges of globalization, rethinking the notions of talent and leadership, and various views of diversity within a local context.
- *Expanding Reality*: the concept of boundaries is explored in this section. These chapters explore the meaning of inclusion, the historical journey to expand the boundaries of inclusion, and the need to protect these boundaries of inclusion from backlash.
- *Embedding Reality*: the challenges associated with integrating diversity principles. Some of the articles take a global perspective, exploring the geo-political aspects of diversity, as well as various structures of governance. Others are more of a "local" view, discussing either historically, or through current intervention, the transformation of organizations.
- *Creating Reality*: the range of diversity perspectives that push the conceptual edges of diversity. The marketplace of ideas creates a rich exchange of mind-expanding concepts. The author contributions encourage us to think about diversity interventions on a continuum scale, from global to local. One paper offers a counterpoint, exploring the attributes of fundamentalism, to capture the notion that not all are believers in diversity.
- *Preparing for New Realities*: the contributions in this section reflect a range of concepts on the personal and philosophical struggles in today's world. Social identity, questions about leadership, and moral responsibility are some of the topics covered.
- *Realizing New Realities*: many of the new realities of diversity require new ways of leading in a culturally diverse world. Leadership is discussed, with

new models presented that challenge the idea that a single model of leadership is culturally appropriate for all organizations in all situations. Some authors also discuss the "distinctiveness" at the national level that should preclude the view that globalization is creating a homogenization of country values and cultures.

Readers may find this collection of contributions unsettling in several ways. By design, some of the contributions in this book push the conventional wisdom about diversity. For example, the paper on Diversity and Corporate Governance by Kai Peters, Kurt April, Marylou Shockley and Vinay Dhamija might be better suited for a strategy or corporate governance book; however, diversity which promotes new ways of thinking is most definitely also part of the organizational landscape. For some readers, the collection may be highly eclectic, stretching their limits of order. Can a paper on National Institutions and the Fate of Diversity: What has Become of Nordic Corporatism? (Thor Indridason) sit comfortably in a book with a paper on Restore Talent and Leadership, (Geert Hofman and Ken Moore)? We, as Editors, say "yes"; though strange bedfellows, both papers make insightful observations about diversity, and both are topical right now on the word stage. Finally, our authors' contributions have been selected to be provocative, not exclusively theoretically dense. For example, the essay by Marilyn Thomas entitled An American in Guangzhou, could easily be dismissed by some as flawed because it is not "objective" – it caters to "tourism"[1] (Silverman, 1993). However, it is our contention that the subjectivity and inter-subjectivity of qualitative insights are equally instructive in creating the "rich pictures" necessary for dealing effectively with the morphous concept, diversity.

Note

1 In his discussion on some of the traps in social research, Silverman (1993:5) describes "tourism" as a potential trap; he says, "I have in mind the 'up-market' tourist who travels the world in search of encounters with alien cultures. Distaining package tours and even the label of 'tourist,' such a person has an insatiable thirst for the 'new' and 'different'."

References

Anderson, W. T. (1990), *Reality Isn't What it Used to Be*, San Francisco: Harper Collins Publishers.

Aries, N. (2004), 'Managing Diversity: The Differing Perceptions of Managers, Line Workers and Patients', *Health Care Management REVIEW*, Vol. 29, No. 3, pp. 172–180.

D'Souza, D. (1997), The Diversity Trap. *Forbes*, 27th January 1997, No. 159, pp. 83.

Geertz, C. (1993), *The Interpretation of Cultures*, London: Fontana Press.

Grimes, D. and Richard, O. (2003), 'Could Communication Form Impact Organizations' Experience with Diversity?', *Journal of Business Communication*, Vol. 40, No. 1, pp. 7–27.

Liff, S. and Wajcman, J. (1996), "'Sameness' and 'Difference' Revisited: Which Way Forward for Equal Opportunity Initiatives?", *Journal of Management Studies*, Vol. 33, No. 1, pp. 79–94.

Mamman, A. (1996), 'A Diverse Employee in a Changing Workplace', *Organization Studies*, Vol. 17, No. 3, pp. 449–477.

Mills, J. S. (1859), *Dissertations and Discussions: Political, Philosophical, and Historical*, Volume 2, London: John W. Parker and Son, West Strand.

Rijamampianina, R. and Carmichael, T. (2005), 'A Holistic Approach to Managing Diversity', *Problems and Perspectives in Management*, January Edition, pp. 109–117.

Rogers, T. J. (1995), 'Managing Diversity – Letter to the Editors', *Harvard Business Review*, Vol. 74, No. 5, pp. 177–179.

Silverman, D. (1993), *Interpreting Qualitative Data: Methods for Analysing Talk, Text and Interaction*, London: Sage Publications.

Thomas, D. and Ely, R. (1996), 'Making Differences Matter: A New Paradigm for Managing Diversity', *Harvard Business Review*, Vol. 74, No. 4, pp. 79–90.

Worman, D. (2005), 'Is there a Business Case for Diversity?', *Personnel Today*, 17th May 2005, pp. 27–28.

Part 1

Ways of Looking at Reality

Editors' Note: Ways of Looking at Reality

by Kurt April

How individuals, organizations, communities and societies navigate the shifting currents of human, organizational, political, social, economic and technical evolutions, and sometimes revolutions, represents significant opportunities and difficulties at the very same time. Transformative movements, not least the advent of, and apparent spreading of, intertwined economic-democracy, make three promises: to provide us with ever-increasing standards of living that are equally desirable and achievable, to periodize and encapsulate the unfreedoms of the past by adopting transparently different and democratic policies, and by implementing institutions and processes that remedy and reconcile the injustices inherited from the past. For the majority of the world, however, economic-democracy has not brought jobs, foreign investment, poverty alleviation, basic infrastructure, economic growth and self-acceptance in a globalized world. No doubt, certain countries and industrial sectors have done well, some extremely well as a result of globalization. But the broad majority of citizens around the world, from a multitude of cultures and ethnic backgrounds and particularly those formerly, and currently, disenfranchised and poor, have not seen significant improvements in their life chances and, in reality, cannot expect to see them in the immediate future.

Something new, something different, some new lenses are required soon if we all are to live in a secure world. It is vital and reassuring, at times, to recognize that the real world is filled with different edges like a diamond, as Sylvia Vriesendorp reminds us in her article entitled: Diversity – A Diamond in the Rough. The real world, in fact, is far messier – more open, variable and changing – than the few paradigms of development on offer, that promote a certain dominant prototype of life. Everyday life and the roles people take on, are forced to take on, choose to take on and cannot take on, provide the rich diversity of scattered light that we need to recognize as sources of variable aspiration and variable balance towards hope. The papers selected for this section were chosen to provide a non-exhaustive "flavour" for the new ways in which the world is coming to see itself, and the tensions and paradoxes it invokes.

As the industrialized world begins exploring Mars, suns of distant planets and the implications of its findings for our globe, most of the emerging world are hoping that they, their countries, and their issues would land up in the "telescopes" of the thinking and planning of the industrialized world – since, as the last Davos event reminded us, the emerging and developing world and particular parts of it, like Africa, parts of Central Asia and Latin America, are not "in their sights." Many individuals and societies have seen upliftment over the past century in their standards of living and, in the Western world mainly, growing material wealth – however, at what cost? At the cost of marginalizing other parts of the world, other societies, other communities and worst of all, marginalization of our own families and friends. Even more worrying, as Hofman and Moore remind us in their article entitled Restore Talent and Leadership, are the well-being effects on individuals, and the misdirected approaches for dealing with symptoms, as opposed to the real causes for the degradation of our well-being, increased family breakdowns, crime increases, increased suicides, increased chronic diseases, increased stress and burnout of younger and younger age groups, and a world in which there is a rising intolerance (bordering on hatred) of "the other," "those who are different" and "those not like us." Is this the promise of development, the future that developing and industrialized countries dreamed of?

Recently, whilst looking through one of the world's largest telescopes in the Chilean Andes on a television program in the USA, the host Alan Alda (of MASH fame) claimed that there was a battle going on out there (in deep space) that will determine the fate of the Universe. He claimed that it was a battle between two great forces – one trying to pull the Universe together, the other trying to push it apart. In this program, Alan joins voices of some of the world's leading astronomers as they try and make sense of the startling and amazing implications of science's latest discoveries: that everything we can see, from the world around us to the most distant galaxies, is only a tiny fraction of what the cosmos is made of. We are told that Dark Matter, the majority of what's out there and still unknown to scientists on earth, pervades space and Dark Energy (repudiated by Einstein though) whistles undetected through our bodies each day – we are told that one day, this Dark Energy will push apart the stars and galaxies so that everything we can see today will have disappeared into blackness. As many folk in emerging and developing economies ponder on the relevance of all of this, they wonder whether such "pushing apart" already exists here on earth, and what the future (not even long-term) may be if we do not do something about it *now*. Herein lies the paradox: as the world squanders billions in money and energy in trying to understand this "Dark Nothingness," of which they can do nothing, and *that which they can do something about* – equality in the world, alleviating hunger, eradicating poverty, celebrating difference, closing the gap between have and have-nots, etc. – *is not seriously entertained or even rigorously thought about.* What is our world coming to when the money spent on cosmetics in any one of the top three industrialized nations can totally eradicate world hunger? As

Wim Kok, previous Premier of The Netherlands reminded us after September 11th, now is the time to do something different in the world. The end-game is simple and obvious – if we continuously ignore the majority of the world, eventually they will take the whole world down. Much that is evidenced and labelled as terrorism and ethnic conflicts we do not believe has much to do with jealousy or religion (perhaps only really at the extreme). We are reminded about the famous statement of Vaclav Hamel (previous Czech President): "I am not an optimist because *I do not believe that everything ends well,* but neither am I a pessimist because *I do not believe that everything ends badly.* I could not accomplish anything if I did not carry hope within me, for the *gift of hope* is as big a gift as the gift of life itself." There are a multitude of opportunities existent if we approach the world through the lens of hope, and if we are willing to suspend judgement on others, on other ways of doing things – in fact, there may be huge opportunities (even financial ones) for those who are willing to take the time to understand "the other" and look through the lens of "the other." In many ways, we have prepared this book, as a gift of hope for a new world – a world that begins to work for all, and in which everyone can be acknowledged in their full humanity.

Scientific revolutions result from the discovery and study of anomalies – phenomena that conflict with prevailing scientific theories. Yet, historically, science has been and still is, resistant to, and intolerant of, anomalies. In both scientific journals and mainstream science magazines today, articles and papers on topics deemed "outside the box" by the scientific establishment are often subject to a form of censorship. This appears to be no different from management practice and theory, social practice and theory, political practice and theory and, generally, human behavior. Unfortunately though, censored humans do not wait to be discovered, they act – often becoming the revolution. Many such revolutions, fortunately, are constructive and positive, and Tony Ehrenreich, in his personal view on globalization, reminds us of the disintegrating consequences of promotion of economic instrumentalism without cognisance for the common good and creating a democratic world that works for everyone – however, in many ways, he signals the integrating growing concern by civil, labour, public and private movements about the motivations of public and private enterprise in the 21st century. The desire and intention to lead a different world are being made explicit from all corners of the globe, and at all levels of society – leadership, it would seem, is no longer only rooted in "positions of leadership" (such as CEOs, CFOs, Directors, and so on; and may not even be found there in many instances), but "new leadership" is found in acting on intention, on purpose, by making to choice to help emerge our collective consciousness.

Perhaps we should all start our own revolutions (or is that called "innovations" in our modern world), and become proactive activists and seek out similar activists, thus becoming activist communities – questioning the dominant paradigms of our world, and being noticed. What are you, the reader, looking at through your telescope – nothingness or a revolution?

1
Diversity – A Diamond in the Rough

by Sylvia Vriesendorp

> We must face life as it is and understand that diversity is its most essential feature . . . Fear of difference is dread of life itself.
>
> Mary Parker Follett 1924 (Graham 1995: 86)

Introduction

What better image to portray the multi facets of diversity than that of a diamond, this unremarkable piece of carbon that, when cut and polished in particular ways, transforms into a jewel that gives a sparkle to life. Diversity, as a biological phenomenon, is simply a fact of life. By "cutting" it and "polishing" it with our joys, hopes and fears, it transforms into something different, ranging from a reason for celebration to a source of trouble and tension.

Thomas Friedman, in his new book *The World is Flat* (2005: 9) describes how the world has gone from a size "large" (when Columbus connected the Old World to the New World) to "medium" (when trade and industrial development took people out of their own communities and exposed them to those from other communities) to "small" (when fibre optic cables and the World Wide Web made connection immediate and instant). And now, Friedman claims, the world is getting flat as the playing field is being leveled. As we are approaching this flatness, the fact of the planet's human diversity becomes increasingly prominent. Traditional and long standing boundaries between sexes, countries, ethnic groups, ages, immigrants and local populations have become too porous to defend. Diversity can no longer be a phenomenon to keep at arm's length, an abstraction to study or philosophize about. Instead it has become "an experience," something that only those who live in very remote and isolated areas can ignore. And for some of us this "bumping into diversity" has been painful some times, joyful at others.

As diamonds can beautify a person but also cut through glass, crown a love affair or bring on wars, so can diversity enhance or destruct. Diversity can pit people against one another when prejudice and fear dominate, or it can start new friendships across boundaries, stimulate rich conversations, bring forth new views and ideas and blend the best parts of groups formerly divided along racial, ethnic, age, or gender lines. Like the diamond industry, diversity has an industry associated with it: diversity consultants who coach and give training that for some evoke images of baring one's soul to total strangers, embarrassment and shame about deeply held prejudices; human resources specialists on equal opportunity; lobbyists to advocate for or stop legislation to protect minorities counts. Whatever diamonds are, thanks to James Bond and the De Beers Company we know they are forever.

Like a diamond, diversity has many facets, each one reflecting back to us a story: about socio-political change, about cultural differences, about organizational attempts to comply or profit from diversity, about communities separated and joined, and finally about powerful personal experiences. What all these stories have in common is the societal and personal struggle that inevitably accompanies the process of questioning, defending and eventually redefining traditional relationships. Treatment of one group by another that was considered normal not all that long ago is now outlawed (discrimination), while other practices considered illegal (marriage between different races) are now legal, and if not welcomed, at least tolerated. I believe there is reason for optimism. We may not be very close yet to a vision of equitable, fair and just treatment of all, but there is movement, culturally, organizationally, and hopefully personally as well.

What are we talking about?

> We see them come./We see them go.
> Some are fast./And some are slow.
> Some are high./And some are low.
> Not one of them/ is like another.
> Don't ask us why./Go ask your mother.
>
> (Dr. Seuss – Theodore Geisel – 1960:14)

With all the debate and activity taking place in the name of diversity, whether it is good or bad for business, or whether it is something to be pursued or not, it is important to keep in mind that diversity *per se* is not the issue. Diversity is a given. This world is populated by men and women, young and old, thin and fat people, rich and poor, even-tempered and bad-tempered people. On this earth we have people with skin colors that range from pasty-white to coal-black, with every shade in between. There are women who love women, men who love men and some who do both. There are men who are really women and women who are really men. There are people who believe in a Divine Presence, by whatever name, and those who do not. There are memberships that people are born with and that are unchangeable, and there are memberships that people choose or are forced into. There are people who can't see or can't hear, or can't do either. There are people who have to make do with less than the four limbs some of us take for granted. Some of these differences are visible, and some are not. Some of the diversity is in our genes, some in our choices, and some is determined by the accident of our birth, who our parents are, and where we were born.

As a psychologist my interest is in exploring the barriers that we set up, consciously or unconsciously, to keep ourselves apart from people who are different. And more interestingly, what happens when we did not know we were different and we find out that we are. Or when we thought we were different and find out later to have much in common? And when is our own uniqueness more important than our belonging to a group, or vice versa, and can we have both at the same time? As a Dutch psychologist who lives in America and works in Africa, I am also acutely tuned into the inevitability of cultural clashes, counterbalanced by the possibility of transcending those, and creating a synergy that we did not think possible. And as a frequent flyer and a student pilot, being high above the ground reminds me of the power of reframing, and looking at something from a different angle. Because it is then that I can see beyond that what is immediately obvious and in my face, and that I can see the larger context in which each encounter is embedded. It is then that I can contemplate the wonderfulness of what I am seeing, wherever I am.

Diversity, and its promise of a richer, nobler life, is one of those phenomena that I can see more clearly from a distance, when I am outside the range of pain, tension and conflict. When I am free from the emotional charges that so frequently obscure what is good, what is right and what is beautiful when people come together. It is easier to talk about diversity, as an interesting socio-cultural, political and historical phenomenon. This I will do first. I will describe in the following pages the journey that diversity took in the United States. It is an interesting story because the United States was the ultimate diverse state from the beginning: immigrants coming into a land already populated by people who had little in common with the newcomers. Each party was, for the other, alien. And over the years more and more "aliens" arrived, making the USA a microcosm of the entire world if we were to simply look at ethnicity or nationality. When I recently became a US citizen, I was surrounded by 200 people, representing some 45 different countries.

Examining the facets – structure of the chapter

Similar to a diamond's facets, I have selected a few to examine up close. A first facet we will explore reflects back to us a short and compact history of efforts in the United States to deal with the diversity that was in its very genes. The emphasis in the final decades of the 20th century, in organizational and national life, on "celebrating diversity" has been the result of a slow reframing over the last few hundred years of the relationships between the diverse populations that make up the United States of America. Essentially, the shift has been one from *not knowing* . . . to *(ab)using and being (ab)used* . . . to *excluding and segregating* . . . to *ignoring and denying* . . . to *tolerating* . . . to *accepting* . . . to *honoring* and finally (although we are not there permanently there yet) to *celebrating* the diversity that is among us.

A second facet highlights some of the organizational and workplace implications that the long, arduous and painstaking legal and regulatory groundwork produced. Part of this discussion relates to the inevitable clashes of culture, and how assertions such as "this is the way we do things around here – adapt!" are giving way to more inclusive ways of working together. As the strict separations between people fade away, people had to learn to recognize the limitations of their mindsets, to avoid retracing the same old territory for ever, as if they never left their hometowns, missing out on all the other wonders of the world outside their garden gate.

The third facet draws our attention to a more subtle manifestation of diversity, namely the way we as individuals are "wired" and interact with the world around us. We may look the same, even come from the same family, but when it comes to thinking and acting, we might as well have come from different planets.

I will close the chapter with examples of some practical applications drawing from my experiences in working in various African, Middle Eastern and South Asian countries with governments and private non-governmental organizations that are involved in public health programs and that have to deal with diversity along all the same dimensions covered in this chapter: societal, organizational and individual.

A societal facet of diversity – the American diversity journey

At a lecture I attended by Elise Boulding, sociologist, long-time Quaker peace activist, Professor Emerita at Dartmouth University in the USA, and former Secretary-General of the International Peace Research Association, she talked of the "two hundred year present." It had a remarkable effect on me, much like seeing the world from an airplane rather than a car. In using the phrase she redefined for me the present from a narrow sliver of time – as in "today" or "now" – to *the time span that is occupied by the people who are living at this very moment in time.*[1] In this conception the present ranges from the moment of birth of the oldest person alive now – plus or minus 100 years ago – to the longest possible lifespan of someone who is born this minute – roughly 100 years from now. Thus the present we live in now extends from about 1900 until 2100. Suddenly one can see the enormous changes that have taken place, and we can see both the enormous progress we have made and the terrible consequences of decisions made early on. This is like looking down from 10 kilometers up in the sky, giving us a more complete picture of the world of today, what made it this way and how we are shaping its future right now.

Such a view, because it shows the consequences of pressured and impatient fixing of problems within a short-term mindset (and the often disastrous long-term consequences), has shifted my pre-occupation with figuring things out and fixing them right now, to seeing and understanding long-term patterns and trends and the small everyday changes that produce them. In exploring the historical journey that Americans have made from fearing diversity towards celebrating diversity, Boulding's notion of a 200 year present gives hope that we will get to our vision of a more equitable, just and fair world, where differences are celebrated and a source of strength, rather than a reason for conflict. Looking at the past makes us realize that from the very first efforts aimed at emancipation (of slaves, later of women), America has moved to a very different place, where "celebrating diversity" is more possible than ever before.

From anti-discrimination to celebrating diversity

A first series of what we could call diversity interventions in the United States took place in the period after the Second World War until the late 70s. At that time the challenge was framed as a problem of discrimination, and the action, or rather re-action, was one of pushing for the elimination of barriers to equal rights. The anti-discrimination stance invariably drew people from non-dominant groups, who had no other means to change the separate and segregated status quo than by engaging in the turbulent and high risk political and community activism that precedes any major societal shift. It is important to remember though that this activism and the resulting legislation build on a foundation that was laid in the beginning of the 20th century by the slow and steady efforts of small pockets of dedicated citizens and activists.

Laying the foundations

In the arena of racial equality, activities intensified with the founding of the National Association for the Advancement of Colored People (NAACP) in 1909. It was formed after race riots in Springfield, Illinois, home of Abraham Lincoln, in the summer of 1908. The riots led to a call to "revive the spirit of the abolitionists," and a new organization was born. In 1910 it melded with "an organization of colored people," formed in 1905 at Niagara and known as the "Niagara Movement" with which it shared a common platform:

> Freedom of speech and criticism. An unfettered and unsubsidized press. Manhood suffrage. The abolition of all caste distinctions based simply on race and color. The recognition of the principle of human brotherhood as a practical present creed. The recognition of the highest and best training as the monopoly of no class or race. A belief in the dignity of labor. United effort to realize these ideals under wise and courageous leadership.[2]

The NAACP is still an active force today on the political landscape and would consider its task far from completed. Its half-million adult and youth members throughout the United States and the world are the premier advocates for civil rights in their communities, conducting voter registration drives and monitoring equal opportunity in the public and private sectors.

Another milestone was the desegregation of schools, which was accomplished, at least legally, with the decision of the US Supreme Court's decision in Brown versus Board of Education, in 1954, after an intense battle between the Brown family and other African American families of Topeka, Kansas, with the support of the NAACP against the Board of Education (Cozzens, 1985).[3]

It took some 50 years to produce many of the cornerstone acts such as the Civil Rights Act (1960 and 1964), the Voting Rights Act (1965), and the Equal Pay Act (1963) that further cemented the foundation on which we are building now.

In the arena of gender equality, the 20th century saw significant changes. Few young women who are now enjoying the fruits of one century of activism could imagine the mindset that our foremothers had to put up with. In a report on the roots of the Equal Rights Amendment[4] movement, Butler and McKenzie remind us where we were only 30 years before Boulding's "current present" began. They refer to one of the many letters that Abigail Adams, wife of the third US President John Adams, who wrote to her husband in 1776: "In the new code of laws, remember the ladies and do not put such unlimited power into the hands of the husbands" (Adams, 31st March 1776, cited in Butler and McKenzie). In a letter two weeks later she writes about John Adams' reply, "I cannot but laugh. Depend upon it, we know better than to repeal our masculine systems" (Adams, 14th April 1776, cited in Butler and McKenzie).

The Equal Rights Amendment (ERA) was first introduced to Congress in 1923, shortly after women in the United States were granted the right to vote, and it was finally approved by the US Senate 49 years later, in March 1972 (Era, 1972). It was designed mainly to invalidate many state and federal laws that discriminate against women; its central underlying principle was that sex should not determine the legal rights of men or women. The text of the proposed amendment stated that "Equality of rights under the law shall not be denied or abridged by the United States or by any State on account of sex" and further that "the Congress shall have the power to enforce, by appropriate legislation, the provisions of this article."[5] It was then submitted to the state legislatures for ratification within seven years but, despite a deadline extension to June 1982, was not ratified by the requisite majority of 38 states.

Like the NAACP in the racial arena, the National Organization for Women (NOW) played a key role in advocating for ending discriminatory practices against women. At the Third Annual Conference of Commissions on the Status of Women in Washington, DC, the failure of the Equal Employment Opportunity Commission (EEOC)[6] to enforce Title VII of the Civil Rights Act prompted the formation of NOW. Twenty-eight women contributed $5 each to help fund its organization. Betty Friedan, author of the *Feminine Mystique*, one of its 28 founding mothers, was elected as NOW's first president. It is currently the largest organization of feminist activists in the United States, with some 500,000 contributing members and 550 chapters across the country.

As we consider the stretched out notion of the present, we can see the fruits of the social, political and legal activism which continue to challenge discriminatory practices that prevent this nation from honoring its diversity. This then is the foundational work, and we are just barely out of Bouldings' "present." There is progress.

Beyond compliance

Of course we know that discrimination does not end when laws and statutes prohibit it. School desegregation and discrimination did not end with the legal decision to outlaw the practices. Honoring diversity, seeing it as an asset, rather than a dangerous source of tension, of conflict, an invitation to chaos or a regulatory nightmare, was an abstract ideal, far removed from real life, especially for people and corporations that managed to live blissfully ignorant of the people that had always been out of sight. Thus, the notion of honoring diversity required a shift away from enforcing the rules (imposing motivation from outside) to developing an awareness of existing racist, sexist and other discriminating attitudes in the workplace, and the identification of strategies to remove those. After all, despite the new laws, certain people did get ahead in an organization and others stayed behind, and it was no coincidence that the people who got ahead resembled most the people who were already ahead, while the people at the bottom of the hierarchy were least like the ones at the top.

From external motivation to a new mindset

After the legal bases were established, organizations had to find ways to comply. This was a process of transforming mindsets, something that is still going on. There is still plenty of lip service paid to the intention of the legislation that was aimed at ending discrimination. People and companies are surprisingly creative in finding ways to comply with the letter of the law while ignoring its spirit; or to present a false image of diversity to the outside world. Present numbers of minorities employed, or sub-contracts to minority-owned firms can easily hide the composition of these numbers (minorities occupying mostly low-level, dead-end positions or sub-contracts for low-level support services). And now with our increased technological capacities we can even tinker with the visual representation of diversity, as a recent report at the diversityinc.com website shows. The University of Idaho was forced to remove a photograph from its Web Site because it had been doctored to offer the appearance of a more diverse student body.[7]

A few companies did genuine attempts to improve the chances of minorities to move out of the menial tasks and up into professional positions. They reviewed their hiring policies and offered educational programs to offset differential access of minorities to the relevant or even highly prized, educational experiences most organizations asked for. The leaders of these progressive corporations (like Polaroid, Connecticut General Life Insurance Company), realized that the tensions that resulted from the lifting of barriers between groups that had not had much exposure to one another, had to be dealt with in face-to-face situations. They began to hire consultants to help them develop some of the early diversity awareness programs. Where the first programs may still have had a bias of limiting or down-playing differences (we can all be great managers, and as long as we follow the rules, we will all be successful), it became soon clear that "the rules" were designed by the white and mostly male middle-aged dominant group. They felt that minorities, who had benefited from equal opportunity action, should actually be grateful for being selected and therefore work hard, keep their nose to the grind, and "not make any trouble." From their vantage point of power and privilege, assimilation had served America well. After all, wasn't it true that the earlier waves of immigrants (mostly from Western Europe) had successfully immersed themselves in the so-called melting pot and had become good Americans? In fact, many senior managers were themselves from such assimilated immigrant stock. Of course, what was left out of this argument was that these early assimilations had come at a high price: people had to give up their language, their culture, their dress, and often change their names. Besides, the early waves of immigrants into American society were essentially white (Irish, German, Polish, Italian, and British).

But the wind of change had begun to blow and the first ripples appeared on the water. In many cases these ripples appeared right away when the consultants appeared at their first interviews. Consultants were no longer middle-aged white males. If the new diversity programs were to be credible and viewed as sincere attempts to change the status quo, senior management realized, the consultants themselves had to present a new face. And thus we came to see teams of men and women, African-American and white (at first) or Hispanic, who were spearheading the early diversity programs. A small breach had been made in the white-male bastion of corporate America.

First wave of programs: changing people

To pay consultants to design and deliver training programs to help improve human relations among a diverse workforce (primarily men and women, African-American, Hispanics, Asians and Caucasians), the organization had to really believe this was a worthwhile investment. Few organizations did so. It is ironic that these companies' investments may have had less impact on their own immediate bottom line, than on the development of a whole new industry (Organizational Diversity and Change Management). The early efforts created a wealth of data that attracted flocks of social scientists who were interested in group relations and dynamics. Originally part of the National Education Association, the National Training Laboratories (NTL) became a hotbed of action to develop and improve human relations. Many of the great names[8] in the American history of Organization Development and Human Relations were in one way or another involved in the period from the 50s to the 80s, in the development of methods and approaches that aimed to help people get along better with one another.

The early intervention programs in some American corporations were often of the "encounter group" variety. These were highly experiential groups of 8 to 12 people who met regularly under the guidance of one or two trained facilitators (human relations experts). Ideally, the facilitator pair represented some of the diversity that was in the group (an African-American male and a Caucasian female for example). Participants were encouraged "to let it all hang out," vent their feelings, and then start the difficult process of listening to and learning about "the Other's" experience of the world. The assumption was that such intimate encounters would change people's attitudes, which would spill over into workplace interactions, and ultimately change stiff hierarchical structures and flatten them into more productive workplaces. NTL's methods and internal dynamics were unconventional and often under attack, but they introduced a new idea into the workplace: feelings, and that what is unsaid, affect the work. The idea is re-popularized, some 30 years later, through the notion of Emotional Intelligence. With the stamp of approval provided by publications from publishing companies of high repute in the business community, the acknowledgment of feelings and how they affect interpersonal relationships, and thus work, is back on the screen in the American corporate world. The necessity of having to deal with feelings eventually became a key argument for organizational interventions that aimed at getting people to talk, across boundaries, across divisions, gender lines, sectors, and communities.

Second wave of programs: alignment of systems and infrastructure

The idea of systems dynamics had been around since the beginning of the century but its language was primarily that of academic physics and cybernetics scientists, and fairly inaccessible and incomprehensible for laypeople. Peter Senge (1990) did much to popularize the concept and made systems thinking into one of his five disciplines. In the work of diversity, and, by natural extension, of organizational change, systems thinking re-focused the work on the structures and systems in which work patterns are contained. The painstaking process of changing people's minds about each other by having them spend intensive periods together proved too long, too unreliable and too tenuous as a strategy to improve relations at work. There were larger forces at work that conspired against fundamental change in how workforces dealt with diversity.

Economic realities

In a less than full-employment economy, when companies have choices on who to hire, there are natural forces at work to minimize diversity (we will explore these more closely when looking at the culture and styles facets of diversity). But in the full-employment economy of Massachusetts in the year 2000, companies had very little choice, and suddenly a whole new group of people who would have had few chances of being hired before, was recruited to work in sales. Diversity was no longer an abstract idea; the economic reality demanded the hiring of people who were, well . . . different from those traditionally hired.

While some companies rose to the occasion and managed to adapt to the new realities by turning this necessity into something that benefited all parties involved, others struggled with a coming and going of sullen teenagers, often minorities, who seemed out of place in fancy stores and malls, ill-prepared and not integrated into the retailer's work ethos and culture, compromising this precious moment of first contact between the customer and the company. Those were the businesses where the corporate functions of training and new staff orientation were caught off guard. Training methods and messages were not reviewed and revised to pull in this group that had always been marginalized. The changes are much bigger than a simple change in language of oreintation manuals. It is one of mindset and of systems and infrastructure that prepare both sides for the inevitable merger between the different groups that, together, make up the workforce of the full-employment economy. But, to be ready, the preparations for this have to happen during times when the economy is not a full-employment one. So how have companies been preparing themselves in the United States?

It is interesting that those companies that realized that diversity was an asset, and that saw the changing of the individual's mindset as the point of leverage, helped bring about the demise of the sensitivity training as a main tool in the "leveling of the playing field." Some business leaders, who had near conversion experiences in the early T-groups (T stands for Training), enthusiastically pushed for getting their own staff trained as T-group leaders. Art Kleiner (1996) describes some of the excesses that happened as a result of unqualified trainers tinkering with the T-group dynamics. All together, these quick fix interventions backfired and ended up discrediting the idea of sensitivity (awareness) training and turning such events into the touchy-feely caricature that they eventually became. In fact, it is only now, some 30 to 40 years later, that the word "touchy-feely" is beginning to fade from the organizational lexicon.

Systems supporting diversity

Thus *systems* and *systems thinking* became the mantra: it was the system and the lack of a supportive infrastructure that trapped people into positions that did not go anywhere; it was systems and procedures that kept women and ethnic minorities from breaking through the glass ceiling. The organizational systems themselves were not supporting the people who came out of their sensitivity training, transformed but not supported. Even when minorities and disadvantaged groups had advocates within the corporate Human

Resource (HR) function, and even if they had the right qualifications, they still needed to find decent low cost childcare, transportation and housing in order to compete successfully with those who did not have to worry about such things.

Enlightened and forward-looking companies realized that a focus on developing organizational systems that encouraged and supported a diverse workforce to develop its skills and talents would benefit all. With the globalization of business, and the breaking down of geographic and spatial barriers, they realized that a multicultural workforce was not just an ideal, but actually a good strategic move. But what to do to get there?

Again, reactions from industry were a mixture of keen strategic thinking, pressures to be "politically correct," or a wish to avoid costly court cases or fines. But sometimes action was triggered by more personal experiences of corporate officers who had had a positive experience with this or that consultant, and the loud cries from established gurus chiding, shaming or prodding corporate leaders to get on the diversity bandwagon, and do something at least. Again a new birth was the result. This time, the simple function of personnel administration that had steadily grown in importance since the middle of the century, turned into human resource management, which then became further jargonized into (high) performance management. Parallel with the increasing complexity of society, the corporate function of Human Resource Management (HRM) began to split off sub-specialties: benefits administration, out-placement services, employee retention, equal opportunity services, training and professional development, recruitment and orientation, diversity programs, etc. There was a market for this sort of thing, and no lack of hungry consultants. Offerings covered the gamut of activities: cultural awareness and competence workshops, training videos on talking, listening, delegating, assessing, evaluating, monitoring, firing and hiring, being assertive, groups, teams in cultural sensitive ways. Companies took their top leadership on outward bound courses to experience leadership, good teamwork, and personal risk taking with the expectations that by doing so together in mixed groups, an appreciation of people's diverse gifts would follow. Consultants came in to overhaul the way staff was recruited, trained, assessed, supervised and, if they have bad luck, out placed. The new systems were to ensure that all people had equal chances, that the company improved its image of a great employer and retainer of minorities, and thus better able to compete in the new market place. This was again a time of movement towards the vision of equitable treatment, fairness, justice and the celebration of differences, albeit grudgingly in some places.

Present promises and challenges for the future

In the United States, slowly a shift took place from a focus on regulatory and legal action (setting up the frameworks), to a focus on educating the individual (diversity awareness and sensitivity training) to the adjustment of structures and systems in institutions and organizations. Currently we can see efforts to acknowledge and appreciate diversity moving along two parallel paths, personal and institutional, with the legal frameworks serving as safety nets or as instigators of change.

Creating inclusive conversations

You may want to make your workplace more diverse because you see it as a sound business decision, independently from your own personal feelings and experiences. Or you may decide that having a diverse workforce and ensuring that the workclimate brings out the best in everyone is your moral responsibility as an employer, whether it increases your bottomline or not. Whatever the motivation, you cannot do this without getting people to talk together about the work they do and how the pieces fit together. This sounds simple and obvious but it is amazing how often this essential method of creating connection between people is left out. Rules and regulations are issued, people are lectured about their rights and responsibilities, sanctions are imposed. Social events may be organized, and people talk together, probably, but not in the way I mean. I refer to conversations about the work that are meaningful and that are done in groups that usually don't have such conversations together. Thus, one of the critical interventions to organize is to create space and opportunity for these cross-boundary organizational conversations to happen. Several methods have been developed to facilitate such conversations.

If one takes a long view, there has been much progress, even though close up it looks like we are not moving forward very much.What was still considered undoable some 15 years ago has fully entered into the language of organizational development: it is now possible to bring together groups as large as 2000 people and plan together the organization's future (Holman and Devane, 1999).[9] The large group approach helps establish the positive side of diversity by "getting everybody improving whole systems" as Marvin Weisbord and Sandra Janoff (Weisbord and Janoff, 1995: 2) call it, and therefore exposing people in a short burst of intensive activity to each other's dreams and hopes for the company or organization, and collectively taking responsibility for the good of the whole, whether it is a community, a church, a school, a factory, or any other organization, large or small, private or public. These events are positive, upbeat and leave, at least for awhile, a strong afterglow and hope that change is indeed possible. They are not Pollyannaish by ignoring that problems and differences exist, they just won't let these paralyze or sabotage organizational inventiveness. Furthermore, the inclusive nature of such events is of course the ultimate way of honoring diversity: nobody needs to be left out because the group is getting too big. Everyone, or at least people from each organizational level, can participate. The promise of the large group events is that they create opportunities to get to know one another in situations that fall outside the normal work environment, without being disconnected from the work (this is not about attending each others' children's birthday parties). The intensity created by working on a series of tasks in constantly changing small group settings allows people to interact in the relative safety of their group and the noisy anonymity of parallel process, with as many as 100 groups "buzzing" along in an atmosphere of hope and optimism.

There has been a significant accumulation of experience with such processes around the world, proving that this is not some new-fangled American or Western invention, which has no real application in cultures that are significant different. Such events have taken place almost everywhere in the world and there is evidence that they have actually worked some magic, at least for awhile, among the employees. Bridges are built, new and unlikely relationships established between people and groups that have only their loyalty to the company in common. And that is a good thing.

The future holds a few challenges for pursuing the use of large group events as a way to cut through boundaries and bring people together to create the future they all want. One challenge is to find ways to continue to nurture and sustain the goodwill and the good feelings that are, invariably, generated by these large group events. Cynicism may disappear quickly during the event, but it returns rather quickly as well when the lights are out again, and immediate changes are not as visible as one had hoped. South Africans know this first hand, as the high of the new South Africa started to fade quickly after 1994 and people impatiently clamored for visible positive change before that year was over. Large warm and fuzzy group gatherings unwittingly raise expectations generated by real or perceived promises of instant change. One urban legend active in the new South Africa "was that everyone who voted for Nelson Mandela would receive a free luxury car in return for their loyalty and support." A Madam&Eve cartoon illustrates the legend (Francis *et al.*, 1997: 92).

Another challenge is to find creative ways to hold such large events without having to spend enormous amounts of money, to find the spaces that can hold large groups, and experienced facilitators that can run such processes and provide the kind of synthesis that is critical to the success of such large, messy and somewhat chaotic events.

Working with individuals

Parallel to these large group efforts was the emergence of the new subspecialty of executive coaching. These are specialists (often ex-HRM people or social workers/counselors) who work intensively with individual top managers to help them become more self-aware, more confident, and by extension (and assumption) more credible and effective leaders.

Executive coaches explore with their clients, on request, their styles of interacting with people who are different. Once a certain level of trust is established, the coach can begin to expose the implicit assumptions and biases that are contained in these interactions and, eventually, the anxieties underlying the behavior. This is a slow process requiring an extraordinary amount of trust and a willingness to really learn. Safety is a major element of the success of coaching. The old saying that it is lonely (and dangerous) at the top is true everywhere, not only in corporate America. Leaders of any kind of organizational unit, anywhere in the world, have this problem. Mistrust caused by jealousies, fear of looking incompetent and being ousted, the unacceptability or inability to reveal doubt, and near total absence of negative feedback make it hard for them to open up and become vulnerable, both prerequisites for learning anything new. It is easy for the chief executive to think that he or she is doing great. "But," as Raymond J. Lane, former president and COO of Oracle says in an interview, "if you don't ask anybody and you don't have any critics, guess what? In this business, you just don't know when you're drinking your own bathwater"[10] (Reich, 2000: 147). Many of these high level executives never get any honest feedback and few ask for it, a perfect recipe for self-delusion. The coach, if credible and trusted, can hold up a mirror in front of the boss and reflect back what he or she has observed about biases and self-inflicted conflict and tension in interpersonal relations. The coach may be the only person who can do that unpunished (and sometimes even that is impossible, and the coach is dismissed!). The realization by the chief executive that he or she is contributing, or even causing some of the tensions and hurdles towards "embracing" diversity, is a first, and giant step, towards creating a work environment in which diversity can fulfill its promise.

De-gendering of professions

A significant number of professions used to be gender typed and many still are. One of the many battles taken on by the National Organization of Women in the United States was that of eliminating a gender bias in recruiting for certain jobs. The Equal Right Amendment is supposed to remedy this. The roots of gender-typing are outdated ideas about what is proper masculine and feminine work, which is based in part on the, supposedly, inferior physical capacity of women. But these ideas are challenged constantly, and at this point it is probably a matter of time (remember the 200 year view of the present). Smoke Jumping,[11] probably one of the most masculine (and dangerous) professions in the USA has seen its professional "brotherhood" invaded by women who have proven themselves just as tough, physically and mentally, as the men. Fortunately, new generations are accepting this as normal. We are seeing the same in other formerly male professions. The invasion of men into traditionally female profession is less obvious. The boundaries of typical male or female jobs remain hard to cross, but for different reasons. For men it is less attractive to cross over into traditional female professions because of the stereotypes and economics. For women moving into traditional male professions may be attractive from an economic point of view but psychologically it is a tremendous challenge. Describing their "invasion" of the upper echelons in academic America, Kathy Kram and

Marion McCollum (1998: 194) raise the issue of the vulnerability/visibility spiral: the more visible a member of the minority becomes as a leader, the more he or she is subject to scrutiny and criticism. Such was the case of Shannon Faulkner whose court case against The Citadel, one of America's premier military colleges, based in South Carolina, led to a Supreme Court ruling forcing the school to accept female cadets or jeopardize its State funding.[12] It was a legal victory for women but the first pioneers paid a high price, being subjected to hazing and other practices that eventually forced several out of the school. Most people who are the first to cross tight borders like this pay a high price. The next wave is made easier by these pioneers.[13]

Such highly publicized – and often polarizing – challenges to the status quo happen less and less as professions are slowly getting de-gendered. Again, a 200 year present has seen enormous changes. Women go into space, women are in the laboratories, women head large computer companies, women sail the world solo and master construction skills. The reverse is not quite happening, but this is probably more a question of economics than mindset. We know that men will take on traditionally female occupations once the pay is good: female chefs tend to become a minority when the cooking is done in high-priced restaurants. Hairdressing is no longer women's work when the hair of the rich and famous needs to be dressed. Seamstresses are women, unless they are the head of large and famous fashion design houses. We have yet to see a surge in applications by men to become daycare providers and nurses.

As a result of the strict division in the past between men's jobs and women's jobs, the promises of diversity still has a long way to go in many workplaces. The people doing the work are too similar in certain respects, the mindsets overlap too much. This is both a good thing and a bad thing. For example, human service agencies have traditionally been staffed by women and were often accused – especially by male legislators and administrators – of being too soft, too ineffective (by their standards) and not business like. At the same time, these agencies turned out to be great nurseries for women to develop their self-confidence and hone their management and leadership skills, and many strong female managers have been added to the world thanks to such opportunities.

In Africa, the internet technology is creating a new brand of young female entrepreneurs. Internet technology, unlike old technologies, is gender-neutral in Africa, and thus created opportunities for anyone willing to work hard and learn fast. John Perry Barlow took a long trip through Africa and wrote "Africa Wired" for *Wired Magazine*. This is what he saw:

> Women are about to take over: Women have been suppressed even more unconscionably all over Africa than they've been in the North, but they also run the economy most places and certainly are more ready to assume

> control of info-tech. Africa is covered with little private telecom centers with phone booths, fax machines, and a few computers for composing official correspondence. These are invariably run by women. Furthermore, I constantly found myself solicited by young women who seemed much less interested in my currency than the information they might extract from me, which they seem to instinctually recognize might profit them more in the long run than will my dollars.[14]

Thus, in Africa, we see that the new technology is reversing the low status position of young African women. They are getting in at the start of the many info-tech outfits. They control fast-growing start-ups and are beginning to make some interesting money. Here is a whole new pool of talent added to the national economy that was until a very short while ago, limited to work in traditional low-paying service-oriented jobs (secretaries, clerks, nurses, childcare providers and teachers).

The curse of political correctness

One of the major challenges is to get past the stage of *political correctness*, or PC as it is usually referred to. The double-edged sword of political correctness is an inevitable and necessary side-effect of the evolution from anti-discrimination legislation to a true honoring of diversity. It is a predictable consequence of the prescriptiveness of the advocacy efforts. When people are told to behave in ways that they feel uncomfortable with at a deep personal level, and when the personal element is not addressed, the result is bound to be unauthentic, even robotic behavior that is apt to misread important cues from time to time and expose the actor as a fake. Of course, the "victims" of PC-ness are usually the past (or still-) dominant group, as they honestly grapple with the new norms, but fail to see the impact of words – no, it's not just semantics! – or behaviors that have so long been taken for granted. How both parties respond to such instances is key: are they willing to explore the mistake and do this in a way that is respectful to both, or is the exchange fueled by a sentiment of revenge for past injustice on one side, and a cynical and disdainful acceptance of the "new order," on the other side?

My experience is that if people are willing to make diversity work, and get to know each other on a more personal level, then they can see past the labels and the masks that people have taken on, and find the common humanity of one another. Then they can also treat the mistakes as such: an opportunity to learn and expand our horizon, see more, understand more, and be more sensitive in our interactions with others. If such an environment gets created, we don't need to worry about making mistakes and have this feeling of walking on eggshells, as so many people currently do.

Bringing an end to this curse of PC is a slow process that demands endless patience and forgiveness. For some, given the things that have happened to them, that is impossible. The healing takes long, and will in some case, take a few generations. We must have that expectation, and then we can move on. This is where the 200 year present can help shift one's gaze.

Continuing the promising work with large and diverse groups, working with individuals to shake loose rigid mindsets and to pass the PC hurdle are some of the obvious challenges on the horizon. How technology, and in particular the internet, will affect the honoring of diversity in the workplace remains to be seen. Certainly, in e-mail conversations we can hide our most visible differences from one another. Our conversations can go on without being hampered by the usual prejudices or biases that would have interfered had we seen one another first. When I co-authored a book with one of this book's editors, we had never met; all we knew about each other were our places of residence and our names. I knew he was a South African male (I could tell from his name). I had no notion of his skin color, his experiences in South Africa before 1994, or his size. When we finally met, he looked very different from what I had imagined. I think I unconsciously assumed he must be looking somewhat like me, because our ideas and thoughts were so similar. Of course, now that we know each other and have developed a friendship I cannot imagine whether it would have made any difference if we had met each other first. Our differences are either a bonus, or they seem totally irrelevant.

A cultural facet – making space for differences

Diversity is not just about racial or gender balance. As mentioned in the opening paragraphs to this chapter, diversity, although frequently used as a synonym for racial and gender balance, is also about differences in psychological make-up, professional background, life experiences, age, sexual orientation and physical characteristics. Because of those differences we belong, either consciously or unconsciously, to different groups. And each one of these groups has its own culture, its own set of values and beliefs that the members of the group take for granted. As the diversity of a group increases, even if it is not as visible as racial and gender diversity, so does the probability of cultural clashes, clashes between ways in which "we do things around here." When a company or organization becomes more diverse, it is, by definition taking in members from groups who do not share a common culture or heritage with the original dominant membership group. Thus, the new members either have to be assimilated into the new culture or the existing culture has to accommodate the newcomers and change as a result. The true and tried historical approach of submerging non-dominant cultures into the dominant one has failed us utterly and provides only a temporary illusion of harmony, until the next outbreak of rebellion. Few people in positions of power who have given diversity a tentative or shy nod realize the enormity of this task of forging a new culture. Few of us have actually done it. But there are some examples around us. If we can become more attuned to the manifestations of culture, we can begin to see those groups that seem to do well, and distinguish them from those that are simply "homogenizing."

In a culturally homogeneous group there is so much implicit contextual knowledge that little needs to be explained. A simple nod, a signal with a thumb, a clearing of a throat may be sufficient to convey entire messages without any explanation. Members of a sub-group or a club have internalized its "way of behaving" and may not be able anymore to describe to an outsider what the unwritten or informal "rules" or conventions are. Members of the group know "how things are done around here." When newcomers arrive on the scene, predictable misunderstandings and confusions are apt to arise, predictable to the outsider, but often not to the insider who is too much embedded in his or her own cultural context. It would be like asking a fish to describe water. From our earliest introduction to the group we learn to decode the signals, the habits, and the behaviors that are shorthand for more complex meanings. This is a simple survival strategy.

To understand the jarring experience of entering into a new culture, we need to simply remember when we ourselves had to do so. This could be an experience of going to another country where another language is spoken, to have dinner with a family that is outside one's own circle of comfort, to enter as a new member into an established club, the first day at a new school, the first dinner with our prospective in-laws. All those experiences hold clues about the feelings engendered by moving into, for us, unchartered territory. Do you remember? The internal conversation in your head, wondering why people do certain things, labeling them as odd or funny or stupid. The questions posed to oneself about what is OK and what is not OK to do. What kind of behaviors would be acceptable and which ones would not.

The cultural facet of diversity is complex because there are so many manifestations of culture all operating at the same time. A Moslem West African female doctor, who is the head of a division in the Ministry of Health has internalized elements of African, and West African culture. She is also the product of a Moslem culture which has some elements of Arabic nomadic culture embedded as well as some notions about being a female and how males and females are supposed to behave in the company of one another. Then there is the professional culture of doctors in which she has been socialized since she entered medical school, and the organizational culture of government and civil service. She is also socialized in the culture of West African women and probably she is a part of her country's urban upper middle class, which has its own culture. Some of these elements overlap and some may be contradictory. If her family is illiterate and lives in a small rural village she probably experiences some intense cultural dissonance and has to do a lot of explaining (why she is not married or has no children, why she has her own bank account, why she is not a nurse, why she doesn't wear a veil). This woman experiences, at a very personal level, the cultural clashes and conflicts that come along with diversity. But she also experiences the richness of the diversity of all these personae that make up who she has become, and would probably not want things to be any different, despite the tensions.

Differences in national culture

When people from one culture get suddenly thrown together with people from another culture, misunderstandings are inevitable as people misread cue cards. The most obvious confusion arises from not understanding each other's language. But culture goes deeper than language. If we look carefully, we will find deeply embedded cultural values that have become such an integral part of the national psyche that we can no longer separate the people from the beliefs. This is where many of the national or ethnic stereotypes have their roots: the serious and disciplined Germans, the industrious Dutch, the entrepreneurial American, Lebanese or Indians, the laid-back Mexicans, the hedonistic Italians, the aggressive Wolof from Senegal, the business sense of the Kikuyu in Kenya, etc.

The stereotypes, whether we like them or not – and they are often not politically correct! – are connected in more or less direct ways to some deeply held beliefs about what is important in life (tasks or people), how predictable things can be (personal choice versus fatalism), how much difference and distance there is between people (egalitarian versus stratified societies), how we work (individual versus collective), and what our horizon is (near future versus long-term view).

In the period from 1967 to 1973, Geert Hofstede (1980), a Dutch social scientist, conducted a series of interviews with some 116, 000 IBM employees from 72 countries. In his foreword to the abridged edition of his findings, Culture's Consequences, Hofstede (1980: 8) writes:

> The Survival of mankind will depend to a large extent on the ability of people who think *differently* to act *together* [my italics]. International collaboration presupposes some understanding of where other people's thinking differs from ours. Exploring the way in which nationality predisposes our thinking is therefore not an intellectual luxury. A better understanding of invisible cultural differences is one of the main contributions the social sciences can make to practical policy makers in governments, organizations and institutions – and to ordinary citizens."

Hofstede identified four dimensions along which national cultures distinguish themselves from one another: high versus low power distance, high versus low uncertainty avoidance, collectivism versus individualism, and masculinity versus femininity. Although Hofstede has been accused of hindsight and of a corporate bias in his findings (he was after all studying values of IBM employees), his findings nevertheless give us some important insights in the relativity of what we hold as "sacred truths." Such national beliefs are much more insidious than those related to an organizational culture because they are so embedded in everything we have been told from an early age that we cannot image another reality.

For example, the tendency to avoid uncertainty is a strong force in American work life. That is why planning is such an important routine in American organizations, as is risk management, or any management practice that is focused on control. When I sit next to someone from a Moslem (Arab or West African) culture in a plane and say, "I hope we will arrive in time at our destination," the response will invariably be "Insha'allah!" meaning, "if it is God's will." For most people from Western Europe and North America that is not an acceptable answer. They would like to arrive at their destination independent of God's will. Much of the acrimonious debate around the investigation of the crash of Egyptair 990 off the coast near New York on October 31, 1999[15] was centered on the meaning of one of the pilot's last words before the crash. Captured on the tape of the black box one of the pilots, alone in the cockpit, repeatedly uttered the phrase "I rely on God" as the airliner plunged towards the water. To the Americans these words meant foul play. For the Egyptians the Americans simply displayed cultural ignorance coming to such a conclusion.

Another one of Hofstede's dimensions is the importance of caring and nurturing versus the aggressive pursuit of accomplishing goals and producing results. Here the Scandinavians sit opposite the scale from the Anglo-Saxons. It is no coincidence that the nurturing professions in Anglo-Saxon countries are of low status and badly paid (nursing, childcare). It is also no coincidence that the Scandinavian countries were the first to establish elaborate support systems and policies allowing women with children to join the workforce.

The fundamental beliefs in the areas mentioned above give rise to a host of more mundane cultural practices, such as how we take our meals: in haste because we have tasks to complete, or slowly because this is a time to spend with our families and strengthen our relationships with one another. Or how we prepare our future: working hard on accumulating money to prepare our "nest egg" when we can no longer work, or spending time with our families because they will take care of us in our old age. Such practices are not just a question of simple preferences, or unconscious habits, they are manifestations of deeply held beliefs about the nature of time, work, human nature and relationships. They are also a typical source of friction and misunderstanding, if not outright hostility, when cultures meet without understanding where the behaviors come from.

As part of a school exchange program, we hosted a young French student at our house for a month. Her English was insufficient to hold any meaningful conversation, so we spoke in short simple sentences. In one of those conversations we gave her permission to help herself to food anytime she wanted. With the risk of over-generalizing, I think that standing in front of an open refrigerator is a very common pose of American teenagers. We have all so gotten used to this that we consider it normal behavior. For the French girl not only was this kind of individualized snacking odd, it felt wrong and she could not get herself to open up the refrigerator at just any time of the day, check around what was there and help herself. The problem occurred when she realized that Americans don't eat at the same times as the French. The French girl expects a meal at 8 or 9 pm, and therefore doesn't eat much at 5.30 or 6 pm, which is when they have their (sit-down) snack. The final (also sit-down) meal of the day in our house is at 6 pm. Thus, the French girl found herself hungry at 9 pm, which would have been no problem if she could allow herself to embrace our habits and breach her own. Throughout her stay, she could not "graze" like her American counterparts did, and she'd rather starve herself than breach a powerful cultural habit that she brought with her from France. This is how strongly our own cultural rules are imprinted in our mind.

Organizational and professional cultures

In organizations culture is often defined as "the way we do things around here." Doctors do things differently among themselves than nurses. Gender cultures and organizational cultures freely weave through professional cultures, creating a complex set of beliefs and dos and don'ts that are not always retraceable to a specific profession, a workplace or whether one deals with men or women. But the result is an elaborate set of beliefs and assumptions that are not necessarily visible to the people on the inside. When a group gets too isolated from others or only interacts with people who hail from the same groups, there is a risk that it keeps on doing what it always has been doing, because that is the most comfortable and the least threatening to its members.

My immersion into this brew of professional, gender and (supra-)national cultures, happened in the late 70s in Dakar, Senegal. As one of a number of young professionals, I was sent out by the Dutch government to take up a position at UNESCO's regional office in Dakar. This was essentially an African organization, not the least because M'Bow, a Senegalese, was the top man at UNESCO at the time. The office consisted of some 50 professionals and support staff, with sharp demarcation lines between those having expert status (the professional staff) and those with support status (clerical and administrative staff). Nearly all experts were older African men, with nearly all the support staff African women (ranging from young to old). And here we were, a bunch of young West Europeans men and women, just out of school, tremendously idealistic, and thinking that we had something to contribute to the development of Africa.

My first error, in this new organizational culture, was to show that I could type. Although I was officially classified as (junior) professional staff, publicly showing my typing capability (two fingers only, but nevertheless skilled at typing), was interpreted by my African colleagues as an acknowledgment that I was willing to type things myself, which therefore reduced my status a few notches down to that of secretary. One of my older African colleagues told me later that that was not a very clever move. I had to refuse a lot of typing assignments after that to re-establish my professional position. Refusing assignment clashed with the image I had of myself as being helpful to others.

There were other jarring experiences. I had moved around in open workplaces, where people freely shared their knowledge and the contents of their bookshelves and filing cabinets. Information was considered public property and only useful if it circulated. In the UNESCO office I was exposed to the concept that information was power, it was scarce, and was to be kept behind lock and key. When my boss traveled, sometimes for several weeks at a time, his office and filing cabinets were locked and he took his keys with him. Essentially work stopped for me and I was left to either twiddle my thumbs or find something else meaningful to do.

As someone with little power, an outsider, a young unmarried woman, and white, there was no way for me to challenge the prevailing culture and its practices *vis-à-vis* information. I could see how it was an obstacle to becoming a more effective workplace. The regional office in Dakar repeatedly lost professionals who treasured the free flow of information and knowledge more than the prestige and material benefits of being employed by a UN agency. I saw it but felt powerless to do anything about it.

As an interesting postscript to this experience, it was only years later that I saw the synergy between the organizational practice of hoarding information and the psychological needs of individuals. Hoarding information has an important psychological benefit for those who have a strong need for being acknowledged and being seen as significant in an organization where they vie with many others for attention (significance), influence (there is so little elsewhere in life) and intimacy. Information can give one an edge. If I have to come to you to get information that you have and I need, you automatically become significant in my eyes. You also have influence (power) over me, which allows you to even demand some sort of intimacy (ranging from "I'll give it to you if you are nice to me," to "I'll give it to you if you sleep with me!"). This is also where sexual harassment rears its ugly head in the workplace. Another phenomenon on the side, like political correctness, that requires our attention as we try to transform organizations into workplaces where we can all enjoy the fruits of diversity in ways that enrich, not diminish, the other.

The three psychological needs for attention, influence and affection, identified by Schutz (1994) and mentioned earlier, provide strong motives for holding on to information and locking one's doors. In a similar pattern, I have seen trainers re-invent the wheel and re-write perfectly serviceable manuals and training curricula because others wouldn't share theirs out of fear that people would "steal" their intellectual property. It is a sad commentary on our world that we need to resort to such unproductive practices in order to get our share of attention, influence and love.

Staying with the familiar

One of Einstein's famous quotes is poorly understood in homogeneous workplaces: "You cannot solve a problem from the same consciousness that produced it in the first place." How often are we not attacking a persistent problem with exactly the same people, the same tools and the same mindset with which we tried to solve the problem before? The real problem is the mindset itself, with all the beliefs and assumptions contained within. A mindset doesn't voluntarily change if it doesn't have to or if there is no one to challenge it. And so we keep on doing things that are essentially variations on a theme.

An individual facet – different drummers, different styles

An often neglected manifestation of diversity is our way of taking in and processing information. Some of us are concrete thinkers. We need to see or feel the data, we want to talk about things that happened in real life, our feelings, the things that have happened to us. We can get very irritated by people who talk abstractly. We want them to get out of their ivory academic tower and talk "real life." They, in their turn, get annoyed with our concreteness, the exceptions we find, the feelings we mention to them. Here is a tension between the little picture and the big picture, the personal and the global, the concrete and the abstract. Similarly, some of us are doers, we like to roll up our sleeves and do what needs to be done, or apply the ideas, or test the instrument, start the computer, put together the construction kit. Others get annoyed with us because we don't even take the time to read the instructions, or think how we are going to tackle something, plan our strategy. When we work together and we don't know about our different styles of working and learning, we can create a lot of conflict. And if one of us is dominant, or one of our styles is the privileged working style of the organization, some of us cannot bring our "gifts" to work. We get frustrated, angry and either quit, if that luxury is an option, or we withdraw and/or sabotage the work of the others, in a vengeful attempt to prove they are wrong. None is a constructive approach and we don't do anyone, including ourselves, a favor. All we do is create an environment in which ulcers and other psychosomatic illnesses thrive.

There are many excellent assessment instruments on the market that can help us understand our differences using neutral language. The realization that the acting and thinking patterns of people who, outwardly, look like us, is often the biggest revelation according to past participants to the leadership courses I have conducted. I often use the Learning Styles Inventory (LSI)[16] or the Myers Briggs Type Indicator (MBTI)[17] to introduce the concept of differences in styles and preferences and have people experience the practical implications of those preferences. The immediate result of an understanding of such differences is the (invisible) diversity in their workgroup, and an increase of tolerance for other people's ideas and ways of working. No longer are differences experienced as direct and frontal attacks on one's competency. The accompanying feeling is almost always one of liberation and the reduction of tension in the workplace. Essentially, what those instruments do is to create a neutral language to describe the contributions and strengths that characterizes each style or type. They help see differences as positive and make it easier for people to understand that it is the diversity of styles and types in a group that gives it its sparkle.

Polishing the gem – practical applications to make diversity shine

A first prerequisite for embracing diversity as an asset and a strategic advantage calls for action at the *societal* level, namely to level the playing field.

A second prerequisite is the transformation that has to happen at a *personal* level. This is, of course, much more difficult to achieve. But if the educational strategy is implemented well, then this one will be easier to establish.

Societal action: education and knowledge dissemination

Any society that recognizes the treasure of its diversity must make sure that everyone can participate in the economic and political life of the country. In South Africa, as in so many other place in the world, this requires a leveling of the playing field which can only be done if the right legal safeguards are put in place, such as anti-discriminatory legislation and the removal of structural barriers to people's active participation in the life of the country. Some of these strategies are systemic or organizational in nature. Education and the creation of equal educational opportunities becomes a cornerstone strategy. Societies that educate *all* of their people, not just a particular sub-group, have, throughout history, been better off than societies that don't. In his comprehensive history of the world, *The Wealth and Poverty of Nations,* Landes (1999) explores the question of why Spain, Portugal and China, all mighty and advanced societies in the 1500s, and Greece and Egypt much earlier, fell into decline and joined the group of lesser developed countries. The role of knowledge and new ideas appears to be critical. All of these country at some point in their history limited education to elites or closed their borders (physically and mentally) to reduce the import of new ideas. The 2002 United Nations Human Development Report for the Arab World (United Nations, 2002) challenged the countries of that region to overcome three cardinal obstacles to human development posed by widening gaps in freedom, women's empowerment and knowledge across the region. The report that was published one year later (United Nations, 2003) comments on the lack of progress and its implications:

> Looking at international, regional and local developments affecting Arab countries since the report [United Nations, 2002] was issued confirms that

> those challenges remain critically pertinent and may have become even graver, especially in the area of freedom. Nowhere is this more apparent than the status of Arab knowledge at the beginning of the 21st century [. . .]. Despite the presence of significant human capital in the region [. . .] disabling constraints hamper the acquisition, diffusion and production of knowledge in Arab societies. This human capital, under more promising conditions, could offer a substantial base for an Arab knowledge renaissance.[18]

According to this report, it is no coincidence that the Arab world lags behind many other countries, except maybe the very poorest in Africa. World history shows that those countries or societies with a strong national identity that opened up their borders, and "risked" the introduction of new ideas (and foreigners) have done rather well for their people.

A political platform or policies that focus on educating minorities acknowledges the complex interplay between opportunities, reduction of poverty and investments in human capital. Such policies also need to take into account the particular dynamics for each disadvantaged group that has kept it from moving ahead. Programs such as Head Start[19] (comprehensive child development programs that serve children from birth to age 5, pregnant women, and their families), special school programs for overcrowded inner-cities schools, teacher incentives to teach at such schools, scholarships and the Equal Rights Amendment are some of the policies and programs that have been put in place to undo the damage inherited from the past. All this is done not only with the aim of reducing inequities, but also to make available to the American economy all talents contained within its borders. Honoring diversity, therefore, is not just a lofty ideal, a moral imperative, but also a matter of investment for economic development. Did not these so-called "poor huddled masses" that entered the United States at the turn of the century, produce many of the entrepreneurs and the businessmen who helped to bring about the enormous economic development that followed?

What marks all these programs is that they are essentially aimed at reducing distance, and creating connections between those who have been different, and disadvantaged (for whatever reason) and the rest of the world. Formal educational structures such as schools, colleges and universities are well positioned to bring the wider world into view, familiarizing their students with people, animals, places and things that were unknown or unfamiliar at first. A slow process of "distance-reduction" has started. Knowledge and experience are the operating factors. When I don't know much about an idea or an object, I will fill the knowledge vacuum with my own notions, heavily colored by my own prejudices and biases, and my (supposedly central) place in the universe. I will use my own yardstick to judge these new ideas and things and apply labels that reinforce my superiority. The more I am exposed to how others label these same ideas or things, and the more direct experience I have with them, the easier it becomes for me to reconsider my initial judgments.

The same happens with people and places. For many people in the United States, Africa is a place of striking natural beauty, wild animals, continuous disaster, civil wars, floods, draughts, corrupt potentates, and pot-bellied hungry children living in straw huts. The idea that Africa also has tall buildings with elevators, computers, internet cafes and children playing Pokemon games is hard to grasp for people who have had no direct experience with the continent or its people. In the absence of any personal connection, and little educational exposure, people fill in the blanks based on their own experience.

The more people are excluded, or excluding themselves, from experiences that widen their horizon, the more they will make up their own reality, a reality that fits their limited and narrow world: otherness is dangerous, not to be trusted, and inferior. As the Bulgarian-born critic Tzvetan Todorov wrote, "The first spontaneous reaction to a stranger is to imagine him as inferior, since he is different from us."[20] This stance is fueled by a basic sense of insecurity and threat, a situation that perpetuates itself because of the inability to embrace the larger world around them. We can see this kind of behavior on both side of the economic and power scale: the embattled white male manager who doesn't dare test his assumptions about people who are not like him, and the person who is part of his country's underclass, and as such remains cut off from educational opportunities. As a result, he too cannot see what is beyond the horizon.

What the early diversity efforts in the United States discovered is that by exposing people directly and intensively to others who were different, in a safe environment, they created connections that required a revision of assumptions. The direct experience with difference (or diversity) created a whole new set of adjectives that often contradicted the old stereotypes ("Hey, this guy is not lazy at all, he is very energetic and dynamic!" Or: "She knows how to keep her cool when under attack, she didn't even cry!" Or, "he is actually very sensitive and insecure!"). The safe environment is of course a critical ingredient in this process. It is the safety that allows people to let go of fear and let their defenses down. And this is what allows new ideas, new conceptions to literally "wash" over the dike and flood the old ideas out.

Although education is presented as a key strategy for accepting, and eventually celebrating diversity, one might point to education as a strategy to solidify biases and prejudices, as used in repressive systems. Here education is used to preserve the status quo, keep people from questioning their reality, and achieve total obedience and compliance. This is of course indoctrination, not education. Education comes from the Latin words "ex" and "ducare", meaning "leading or drawing out." These words imply a gradual exposure, a leading out into the world, making connections with "things out there." That is why education and the sharing of knowledge is a critical prerequisite for honoring diversity.

Personal action: introspection and appreciation

The establishment of links between early childhood experiences and personal maturity later in life is the domain of psychotherapists and psychologists. No one really questions this link. What is less clear is what to do with this information. Some people are aware of how their current behavior is an ineffective response held over from childhood. Those are the lucky ones because they are most likely to seek help in untying the knots and develop new, more effective and mature behavior patterns. Others are less aware and keep operating from a basis of fearfulness, mistrust and anger. Managers confronted with such individuals among their staff can do little to change the past, or demand behavior changes. But they can do something else.

First of all, they can explore their own reaction to the behavior they condemn in others and watch closely how their re-active behavior supports, condones or aggravates the behavior of the other. In the mid 1920s, Mary Parker Follett (Graham, 1995: 81) exposed the two-sided nature of conflict in the workplace, by stressing that, "I can never fight you, I am always fighting you and me. [. . .] response is always to a relation. Employees do not respond to their employers, but to the relation between themselves and their employer." Follett articulated something that we intuitively know but prefer not to emphasize, namely the idea of a "circular response." She compares such interactions to a tennis match, where each player influences how the other will return the ball, which in turn influences how the first player will hit the ball back, and so forth. This is why we cannot change someone without changing ourselves. In the workplace we see this happening when a manager, at wits end, finally resorts to firing the person who refuses to become the person the manager wants him to be. And this is also why the next person we hire may end up exhibiting some of the same undesirable behaviors (after all, if we only alter one half of the equation, we risk getting similar results). The painful message in this is that we *have to* look at our contribution to the problem or conflict if we really want to solve it for good. Douglas Stone and his co-authors (Stone *et al.*, 1999) have provided us with a simple methodology for having difficult conversations so that we can reframe interpersonal conflict in a way that opens rather than closes future possibilities for working together in a productive way.

A second approach is called Appreciative Inquiry. David Cooperrider from Case Western University and colleagues (Cooperrider *et al.*, 2000) have developed and refined over the last 20 or so years a methodology for bringing out the best in individuals, organizations and systems, by weaving together philosophies and insights from various disciplines (sports, medicine, psychology). Through its deliberately positive assumptions about people, organizations and relationships Appreciative Inquiry (AI) rejects approaches to management that are based on finding fault, on finding out what's wrong (the deficit approach). Implied in the method is the assumption that problem-solving is a fundamentally depressing approach that cannot possibly inspire, mobilize and sustain human systems change. It also assumes that we create our reality by naming it: calling something a problem rather than a challenge to our vision depicts a complete different reality, which then triggers off fundamentally different approaches to tackle the issue. The problem-focused, deficit oriented approach creates a feeling of hopelessness, doom, a sense of being overwhelmed. AI starts with a recognition of those factors that bring life to the organization, the system. It recognizes that, despite all the problems, the organization is still alive, that some good work is being done, and that there must be something that is worth being looked at. Then, working backwards from a desired future, problems are seen in a different light, and given a different name: challenges. This is not just a matter of semantics. There is evidence in many different disciplines that how we name things determines how we act. The placebo effect (the measurable, observable, or felt improvement in health not attributable to treatment) is one well-known example of this. From sports and acrobatics we know that the best performances are always by athletes who envision superb performance, not by those who fear making mistakes. From experiments in the classroom we know that what teachers think about their students actually influences their academic success (also known as the Pygmalion effect).[21] On a personal level, many of us also know that this is true. As William James (James, 1956: 62) said, "Be not afraid of life. Believe that life is worth living, and your belief will help you create the fact."

There is an energy generated by this kind of optimistic and hopeful thinking that is contagious and extremely powerful. Some people in the Organization Development field claim that they are really doing "energy work," the kind of work usually associated with various new age and old age touch and massage therapies. I believe this is true. Countless are my experiences, in Africa in particular, where a focus on problems sucked out the energy in the room, in nearly palpable ways. And similarly, when people are asked to articulate their deepest wishes for a program, a project or an organization, the energy in the room swells to make everyone feel powerful and empowered to really take the group where it wanted to go.

Whether this is a coincidence or not, the AI approach has emerged at a time when we realize that the old ways of working together are no longer working. As Donald Schön (1987: 3) writes in the opening paragraph of his book *Educating the Reflective Practitioner*:

> In the varied topography of professional practice, there is a high, hard ground overlooking a swamp. On the high ground, manageable problems lend themselves to solutions through the application of research-based theory and technique. In the swampy lowland, messy, confusing problems defy technical solution. The irony of this situation is that the problems of the high ground tend to be relatively unimportant to individuals or society at large, however great their technical interest may be, while in the swamp lie the problems of greatest human concern. The practitioner

> must choose. Shall he remain on the high ground where we can solve relatively unimportant problems according to prevailing standards of rigor, or shall he descend to the swamp of important problems and non-rigorous inquiry?

The reality of diversity creates the kind of swampy mess that Schön refers to. AI is a tool that helps us to go down there and probe around, until we find a piece of ground we can stand on. In the complexity of our world, the changes in behavior such a descent requires, dictates a complete reframing of how we proceed: we need methods that affirm, that compel, that accelerate learning and assume interdependence. AI offers such an approach, which is particularly relevant to Africa.

Africa, more than any other continent, has been invaded for centuries by people who came to tell the native population what was wrong with them. Worse, Africa's own elite has joined the chorus, cheered on loudly by its own press. A quick glance at some of the major daily newspapers in Kenya will reveal the following pattern: pages one and two are filled with angry stories and pictures. Pages three and four are cynical commentaries on why the country is in such a mess. Pages five and six tell sad stories about poor people having bad luck. It is not until one reaches the sports pages that the clouds are lifted. Not being a sports column reader myself, I found myself busy fighting thoughts of impending doom each day as early as breakfast. And I at least recognized the pattern. What about those who swallow these subliminal messages inadvertently with their morning cup of tea? How could one expect a nation of people to go to work every morning, whistling optimistically as they take on the overwhelming task of "development"? At the same time as I was reading these depressing newspapers in the morning in Nairobi, Moi, President of Kenya at the time, and other African leaders were busy depicting the dismal African scene at the UN millennium summit in New York, wondering why Western companies weren't investing more in Africa. My teenage daughter would say, "duhuhhhh!" She's right, why would they?

Personal change

In a critical account of how "development" is being done in Africa, Robert Chambers names what many of us have experienced first hand, the critical role of self-confidence in enabling power differentials to continue the inequities inherited from the past. "For those who lack confidence and feel insecure, self-doubt can disable. For those who feel confident and secure, self-doubt can be enabling. The insecure, doubting their abilities, may not dare to try and so not learn what they can do. The secure, sharing their self-doubt and embracing errors run the risk of self-righteous complacency. For both groups it helps to recognize that there is a threshold of security and confidence. Above that threshold, self-critical questioning and doubt becomes means to learning and doing better. The challenge for those below the threshold is to gain the confidence to pass above it; the challenge for those already above it is to help others join them." (Chambers, 1997: 203)

The strategy then, for individuals in a corporate setting, is to find ways to pass that threshold of confidence. This is in everyone's interest. Overcompensation is a psychological phenomenon that is painfully familiar to many of us: the insecure boy with low self-esteem becomes the school's bully or the gang leader, the low level powerless bureaucrat who obstructs all our efforts to navigate the system, the harassed secretary who sabotages her boss' work, the marginalized street sweeper, who, when the revolution comes with its new hierarchies, uniforms and weapons, becomes the terror of the movement, settling old scores. These are the people that need to cloak themselves in the external paraphernalia of power to hide the total absence of self-confidence. If such people rise to powerful positions and can command vast resources, we are really in trouble. The Third Reich drama and countless other historic and current dramas convincingly illustrate the phenomenon.

Professor Kurt April from the University of Cape Town (South Africa) and his co-authors (April *et al.*, 2000) propose four meta skills for present day leaders. The assumption is that these meta skills make people into leaders, no matter where they are in organizational or societal hierarchies. The essence of the meta skills is awareness: awareness of self and one's worldview, awareness of hidden and irrational dynamics that operate in groups and between people, awareness of possibilities and dreams, and most importantly, awareness that one's own reality is not necessarily the reality of another. Understanding this opens doors and windows and is the only way to begin to appreciate what diversity brings us.

Meeting differently

As the saying goes, if you keep on doing what you have always been doing, you will keep on getting what you have always gotten. Thus, if there is no diversity in your organization or company, or if diversity is a source of conflict, fear, tension or embarrassment, then the first step is to accept to do things differently. For this one doesn't need to be the Chief Executive. Change can happen at any level. Close to one's own sphere of influence is the best place to start.

Whereas introspection requires little more than a trusted friend, a counselor, a personal journal or the creation of time and space to reflect on what is going on in one's life, appreciative inquiry requires an optimistic nature, an open mind and a few questions with which to start the inquiry.

At your next meeting, have people ask each other any or all of the following questions as a warm-up, especially if you expect fireworks, or if mistrust and tension are considered a normal part of the atmosphere:

> Tell me about a time that stands out for you as a high point in your time here, when you most successfully joined with others in bringing about positive organizational change? Tell me what it was about *you* that made

> this a high point? What values or characteristics or qualities did you bring to the effort that made it so successful? Imagine yourself as a helicopter, hovering above this company/organization. What do you see as the essential "life-giving" elements that sustain us? Looking at the world around you (the industry/sector, the country, the continent, the larger global context), what do you see as macro trends that give you a sense of hope and confidence and that indicate to you opportunities for us to fulfill our mission? Imagine we would all go to sleep and then wake up in the year 2010. What would you like to see around you as you wake up?[22]

When people interview each other, and small groups form to look for themes or patterns in the responses, something happens to a group. A shift in consciousness takes place simply by looking through another window: a view in which our attention is directed past the problems, the obstacles, the cynicism and anger, towards those essential forces that have so far sustained us, and which, if given the necessary attention, can sustain us for another 100 years or so. This is the view that presents opportunities and allows us to dream again. This is also the view that reframes problems as challenges or opportunities to work together in different ways. If there is any view on making diversity work for us, as opposed to tearing us apart, this is where it can be found.

Conclusion

If diversity is like a diamond, it cannot just signify the union between two people, or a sign of individual wealth. The diamond is a symbol for our collective savings, all bundled up into this one sparkling gem that once was an unattractive piece of carbon. It was only after a lot of work of cutting and polishing that it became the gem it now is and that represent such value. The cutting and polishing is the work of learning, sharing, soul-searching, and appreciating, none of them easy tasks. Those who have had more exposure to other groups, other cultures and to different ways of doing things will know about this hard work. For those who are entering this territory for the first time, beware, the ride can be rough. If my own experience in this matter is any indication, no matter how sophisticated we are, how well educated we are, the direct experience of diversity engenders strong feelings, uproots deeply-held biases and prejudices, and at times produces embarrassment and shame that can shake one's very being. But just as the individual, the new global citizen, will increasingly have to incorporate the cultures and biases from other groups than his or her own, so will our organizations, if not sooner because of economic necessity, than later because of the people we hire. No retreat to the good old days (which weren't all that good for others anyway) is possible, as much as we would like to play with this illusion. The path is forward and invites us to include all to enliven our world. We have another 100 years to complete this task in our extended present.

Notes

1 Personal communication.
2 NAACP website: http://www.naacp.org/ [last accessed September 2005].
3 Cozzens, Lisa. "Brown v. Board of Education." *African American History*. http://fledge.watson.org/~lisa/blackhistory/early-civilrights/brown.html (25 May 1998).
4 The Equal Rights Amendment was written in 1921 by suffragist Alice Paul. It has been introduced in Congress every session since 1923. It passed Congress in 1972, but was not ratified by the necessary 38 states by the July 1982 deadline. It was ratified by 35 states.
5 For background on the Equal Rights Amendment and its provisions, see NOW website at http://www.now.org/issues/economic/eratext.htm
6 The EEOC was established by Title VII of the Civil Rights Act of 1964 and began operating in 1965. It is mandated to enforce the principal federal statutes prohibiting employment discrimination, such as Title VII of the Civil Rights Act of 1964, as amended, which prohibits employment discrimination on the basis of race, color, religion, sex, or national origin; the Age Discrimination in Employment Act of 1967, as amended (ADEA), which prohibits employment discrimination against individuals 40 years of age and older; the Equal Pay Act of 1963 (EPA), which prohibits discrimination on the basis of gender in compensation for substantially similar work under similar conditions; the Title I of the Americans with Disabilities Act of 1990 (ADA), which prohibits employment discrimination on the basis of disability in both the public and private sector, excluding the federal government; and the Civil Rights Act of 1991, which includes provisions for monetary damages in cases of intentional discrimination and clarifies provisions regarding disparate impact actions; and section 501 of the Rehabilitation Act of 1973, as amended, which prohibits employment discrimination against federal employees with disabilities.
7 As reported on www.diversityinc.com on 10/4/2000. This website required subscription when last accessed on September 2005.
8 Douglas McGregor, Edward Schein, Edith Seashore, Kathy Danemiller, Warren Bennis, Gordon Lippitt, Kurt Lewin, Lee Bradford, Chris Argyris, etc.
9 Among the most well-known of these processes are Marvin Weisbord's Future Search Conference, David Cooperrider's Appreciative Inquiry Summit, Technology of Participation of the Institute of Cultural Affairs, Lippitt's Preferred Futuring, Kathy Dannemiller's Whole-Scale Change, the Axelrod's Conference Model, and Jacob's Real-Time Strategic Change. A good description of these and other large group processes can be found in Holman and Devane (1999).
10 Also accessible on the web: http://www.fastcompany.com/magazine/39/jobischange.html (last accessed on September 28, 2005).
11 Smoke Jumpers are the people who are parachuted behind fire lines to combat forest fires in the USA.
12 Shannon Faulkner, Nancy Mellette, and three female veterans of the United States armed forces pursued this battle when they sued The Citadel for refusing to admit them to the Corps of Cadets and the former Veterans Day Program based not on their merits as students, but on their gender. They endured a scorched-earth defense by the State of South Carolina and The Citadel to keep all women out of the military college's ranks. After four years, 49 major briefs, over 200 depositions, and 47 days of court hearings, the upshot of this massive litigation was that the State lost, the right of women to equal protection of the laws was vindicated, and female cadets have enrolled at The Citadel since 1996. The Citadel's website now has a picture of a female student prominently displayed on its home page.

13 Shannon Faulkner left The Citadel after being enrolled as the first woman cadet in the history of the academy. The following year, Virginia Military Institute admitted its first class of women cadets. These enrolled as a group and benefited from lessons learned from Shannon's experience, such as the support from mentors. Source: Statement by Assistant Attorney General For Civil Rights Deval L. Patrick on The Supreme Court Decision not to block Shannon Faulkner from Becoming A Cadet At The Citadel. http://www.usdoj.gov/opa/pr/Pre_96/August95/442.txt.html (last accessed on September 30, 2005).
14 *Wired Magazine*, 6.01, January1998.
15 William Langewiesche (November 2001), "The Crash of EgyptAir 990," *The Atlantic Monthly*, Vol. 288, No. 4, pp. 41–52.
16 Hay McBer is the official distributor of David Kolb's Learning Styles Inventory. The instrument can be purchased at http://www.hayresourcesdirect.haygroup.com/ (last accessed on 2nd October 2005).
17 The MBTI is published by Consulting Psychologist Press, Inc. in Palo Alto, California.
18 From the webpage announcing the Report (http://www.undp.org/rbas/ahdr/english2003.html). Last accessed on October 2, 2005).
19 Head Start came out of a task force recommendation in 1964 for the development of a (US) federally sponsored preschool program to meet the needs of disadvantaged children.
20 Quoted in: A. Fadiman (1997), *The Spirit Catches You and You Fall Down*, New York: Farrar, Straus and Giroux, page 100.
21 This refers to a study by Rosenthal and Jacobson (1968) in which children aged six to twelve years from the same school were given an IQ test. Children were then randomly assigned to an experimental or control group. When teachers were told that the children in the experimental group were "high achievers," these children showed significant IQ gains over the course of one year, even though the selection of these children had been done randomly and had nothing to do with their actual IQ scores at the beginning of the research.
22 David Cooperrider, Cape Cod Institute, 2000.

References

April, K., McDonald, R., and Vriesendorp, S. (2000). *Rethinking Leadership*. Cape Town, South Africa: University of Cape Town Press.

Butler, T. and McKenzie P. (no date). "21st Century Equal Rights Amendment Effort Begins." http://www.now.org/nnt/01-94/era.html. Last accessed on September 28, 2005.

Chambers, R. (1997). *Whose Reality Counts?: Putting the First Last*. London: Intermediate Technology Publications.

Cooperrider, D. (2000). Conference "The Professional Learning Network LLC," Cape Cod Institute, Eastham, Mass. Unpublished workshop papers.

Cooperrider, D. L., Sorensen, P., Jr., Whitney, D., and Yaeger, T. F. (eds) (2000). *Appreciative Inquiry: Rethinking Human Organization Toward a Positive Theory of Change*. Champaign, Illinois: Stipes Publishing L.L.C.

Cozzens, L. (1985). "Brown v. Board of Education." African American History. http://fledge.watson.org/~lisa/blackhistory/early-civilrights/brown.html. Last accessed September 2005

ERA (1972). Equal Rights Amendment, Accessed February, 2003, published on the National Organization for Women (NOW) website at http://www.now.org/issues/economic/eratext.html

Fadiman, A. (1997). *The Spirit Catches You and You Fall Down*, New York: Farrar, Straus and Giroux.

Francis, S., Dugmore, H. and Rico (1997). *Madam&Eve's Greatest Hits*. Sandton, South Africa: Penguin Books South Africa.

Friedan, Betty (1963). *The Feminine Mystique*. New York: W.W. Norton & Company.

Friedman, T. L. (2005). *The World is Flat*. New York: Farrar, Straus and Giroux.

Graham, P. (ed.) (1995). *Mary Parker Follett, Prophet of Management; A Celebration of Writings from the 1920s*. Boston: Harvard Business School Press, 1995.

Hofstede, G. (1980). *Culture's Consequences. International Differences in Work-Related Values*. Newbury Park (CA): Sage Publications.

Holman, P., and Devane T. (1999). *The Change Handbook*. San Francisco: Berrett-Koehler Publishers.

James, William (1956). *The Will to Believe and Other Essays in Popular Philosophy*. New York: Dover Publications, Inc.

Kleiner, A. (1996). *The Age of Heretics: Heroes, Outlaws and the Forerunners of Corporate Change*. New York: Currency Doubleday.

Kram, K. E. and McCollom Hampton, M. (1998). "When Women Lead: The Visibility-Vulnerability Spiral", in E. B. Klein, F. Gabelnick, P. Herr (Ed.) *The Psychodynamics of Leadership*. Madison, CT: Psychosocial Press, pp. 193–218.

Landes, D. S. (1999). *The Wealth and Poverty of Nations: Why Some Are So Rich and Some So Poor*. New York: W.W. Norton and Company.

William Langewiesche (November 2001), "The Crash of EgyptAir 990," *The Atlantic Monthly*, Vol. 288, No. 4, pp. 41–52.

Reich, R. B. (2000). "Your Job is Change." *FastCompany*, October 2002, pp. 140–160.

Rosenthal, R. and Jacobson, L. (1968). *Pygmalion in the classroom*. New York: Holt, Rinehart & Winston.

Schutz, W. (1994). *The Human Element: Productivity, Self-Esteem and the Bottom Line*. San Francisco: Jossey-Bass Publishers.

Schön, D. A. (1987). *Educating the Reflective Practitioner*. San Francisco: Jossey Bass Publishing.

Senge, P. (1990). *The Fifth Discipline: The Art and Practice of the Learning Organization*. New York: Currency Doubleday.

Seuss, Dr (pseud. T. S. Geisel) (1960). *One Fish, Two Fish, Red Fish, Blue Fish*. New York: Random House.

Stone, D., Patton, B., and Heen, S. (1999). *Difficult Conversations: How to Discuss What Matters Most*. New York: Penguin Books.

United Nations (2002, 2003). *Arab Human Development Report*. New York: United Nations Development Programme.

Weisbord, M. R. and Janoff, S. (1995). *Future Search: An Action Guide to Finding Common Ground in Organizations and Communities*. San Francisco: Berrett-Koehler Publishers.

2

Restore Talent and Leadership

by Geert F. M. H. Hofman and Ken Moore

Very great leaders in their domains
are known only to exist
Those next best are beloved and praised
The lesser are feared and despised

Lao-Tse, *The Tao Te Ching* (1900)

Introduction

We all seem to be living life in the fast lane. At least in Western societies that seems to be the case. Our schedules are tight, both at work and at home; not just for a short period of time, but structurally.

It is normal when you want to make an appointment with someone that it can only take place in so many weeks. It seems that the only thing that matters is to pack as much action into our schedules as is theoretically possible. If one has room for an appointment, let's say the next day, people can cast a wary eye thinking "Why are they free? Is business bad? Don't they have anything to do?" So, in order to hide this token of underutilization of one's time the best answer can often be that another appointment was cancelled.

Can you remember when you had time to spare, when your diary wasn't packed with back-to-back meetings? Imagine that you are in that situation again. How will you fill the spare time? With more of the same? With something different? Why not stop reading and take 2 minutes now to daydream; let your mind wander through all the things you could do and see if they're the same as what fills your diary. If they are, your overall satisfaction must be high and at the end of your life you'll be able to look back and think "I'm glad I did . . .". If they are not, is your overall satisfaction low and at the end of your life will you look back and think: "I wish I'd . . ."?

Systemic busy-ness – do you want it?

Apparently all this "being busy", or "business" as it's often referred to, does bring some benefits. It cannot be all that bad because, presumably, none of us would prescribe to this lifestyle if it was. For one thing wealth in the Western world has increased dramatically over the last decades. With our increased income we can afford many more material goods and intangible experiences than ever before.

Unfortunately, our general sense of well-being has not kept pace with the increase in wealth – in fact, it has even diminished. For example, the Irish economist Douthwaite, (1999) researched British society from 1955–1988. In this period GDP doubled while at the same time there was an increase in criminality, in the number of divorces and suicides, in absenteeism due to sickness and stress, and in the number of chronic diseases. Where issues of well-being of this nature are addressed, the solutions tend to be surface level, merely addressing the symptoms rather than the underlying causes. For instance, when there are complaints about perceived security in a city, state or country, a typical solution will be to add more staff to law enforcement bodies – put more police on the street. However, does this really tackle the root cause of the problem or increase the sense of security people feel?

Are we working ever harder at earning more money, while at the same time losing the enjoyment and sparkle of life and suffering greater levels of stress and fatigue? Are you postponing the fun and joy of living for a later phase of life – retirement, when you hope to have more time?

Not unexpectedly, this situation comes with a toll. More and more people are tired and burnt-up from this way of life, and stress related complaints are rising dramatically. In The Netherlands, it is reported that 10% of the working population suffered a burnout in 2004, and a staggering 30% claim to feel completely empty at the end of each day (Hupkens, 2005). Similar studies from industrialised countries like Japan, UK, USA, Germany and other countries reach the same conclusion. We, the authors, have found exactly the same trends in the consultancy, training and coaching we do, as well as in our conversations with people from all levels of business. These trends are not only true for individuals, but also for the organisations where they work, and for society as a whole.

Obviously executives face the same challenges, and more. The companies they work for operate in a 24/7 global economy. And demands from shareholders, customers and staff are consistently high. Information travels around the globe at hyper-speeds and is accessible to virtually everyone at a low cost.

The pressures often lead to top management being aimed at profit maximization in the short run, rather than creating true value in the long run – and this is true however profit is defined. Shareholders often show an interest in getting more "value" and in the opportunity for cash in the short term. And they often require the companies whose stock they hold to overperform their already ambitious forecasts. This leads to a systemic consequence: the results must be excellent and preferably greater than expected. Performance on Wall Street seems to have become at least as equally important as performance on main street, if not more so. As a result, there have been several financial scandals which have brought huge organisations, such as Baan Company, Enron, Worldcom and recently Parmalat to their knees and have had strong effects on others, like Ahold. All of those companies reported profits in their profit and loss statements that had not been realised yet, thereby boosting results, company equity and the total value of the company on the various stock exchanges. Unfortunately, the sad news here is that more scandals can be expected. Of course, it would not be fair to put the blame on the executives alone. They too operate in a system where, although an integral part of it, they cannot control the whole.

Being in a leadership position is a risky business (and it's getting riskier), plus one never knows how long one will stay in this position. An action by a staff member on the other side of the world may set in motion a chain of events that cause a CEO, or other senior executive, to step down from their position. Thereafter, to be haunted by criminal law suits, instigated by disappointed shareholders who want their money back. That must be one of the worst nightmares for any executive – from the perspectives of reputation, well-being, identity, confidence and trust.

On the other hand, executives' remuneration has risen sharply to offset those inconveniences, and it has risen to what more and more people think are outrageous proportions. It goes without saying that a valid argument can be made to justify differences in remuneration, especially at executive levels where the risks of career disruption are significantly higher than on the factory floor. However, it has become common practice for top managers to enjoy generous severance packages when they are asked to resign, even when they fail. Of course, the packages have been negotiated and agreed upon by both parties before the appointment but, even so, the growing dissatisfaction with this situation by stakeholders, and the public at large, can no longer be ignored.

In The Netherlands, a society for directors has started a debate on the remuneration of top managers and it is to be expected that this debate will be around for a while. The general line of thinking is that it is unacceptable for top managers to be generously rewarded, through stock options or severance pay, when the (part of the) company they work for is not performing up to standard, and may even be suffering important losses, when sacrifices are asked from everyone else in the company.

The treadmill of quiet desperation

In the working environments described above many people become cynical and start to lose their passion and commitment for work. Men and women who once had ambition, energy and drive begin to see it all fade in the face of intense pressure to perform to progressively higher levels and under increasingly higher workloads. Compare this with the fact that, during the first years of their career, many people derived fulfilment simply from doing their job. They felt, perhaps for the first time, responsible for the important tasks assigned to them. They wanted to be successful at their jobs and worked hard at it, often to the detriment of other aspects of their life. Why does it then go wrong for many of those bright, young hopefuls?

In the late 1980s Halper (1988) published the results of her research into 4126 successful male managers and executives in the USA. The results provide some startling reading:

- Middle managers who said their lives seemed empty and meaningless – 48%.
- Senior managers who said they had neglected their family life in pursuit of professional goals – 68% (50% also said that if they could do it all again they would spend less time working and more time with their family).
- High achievers who felt they had sacrificed their identities and wasted years of their life pursuing material rewards – 60%.
- Successful managers and executives who said they were happy with themselves inwardly and outwardly – 23%.

Although they may lack fulfilment and experience a void in their life, many seniors have what it takes to stay in their position because even though the pressures might be wearing them out, they still have the skills which got them there in the first place. For instance, many executives reach the Board room because of a combination of being able to strongly advocate their position, take tough decisions on their own and motivate others to perform. However, once established at Board level other talents become important: such as, the ability to take a long-term strategic view, the ability to sell compelling visions, political acumen, and the ability to compromise and reach effective consensus with other Board members. It is these new skills (whatever they are for any particular executive or position) that are the person's development potential and it is when these developmental steps are not taken that the likelihood of dissatisfaction and frustration increase.

Viewed from another perspective, the position can be likened to how a plant grows. When plants are in their growing phase they produce carbonic acid. To stop the acid burning them alive they manufacture enough cells quickly enough to contain it. However, when they move out of their growing phase the carbonic acid is still produced, but the plant no longer has the capacity to build enough cells quickly enough to ringfence and contain the damaging effects of the carbonic acid. So, the very process which promoted growth now starts to kill (parts of) the plant.

The lesson for all of us in this analogy is that the skills, mindsets and behaviours we use to reach our next position of responsibility are not the ones which will necessarily bring success in that new dynamic – in other words, we need to be constantly changing and developing to match the new circumstances we find ourselves in. The difficulty is, do people know this and if they do, do they know what to change and how to do it? Halper's (1988) research says, unfortunately not!

There are a growing number of high-ranking executives who want to re-assess their life balance, and involve themselves with what is really important to them at this stage of their life and career. They want a meaning and significance which they cannot find through their jobs anymore, nor through traditional training and development.

Taking all of the above into consideration, it can be argued that a new way of "doing business" is needed; a way that takes an individual's quality of life and dynamic values into account. However, in order to arrive at this new way, we believe a new focus on leadership is required.

New focus on leadership

A new type of leadership in companies is needed from which a new and different way of doing business can evolve. Of course, many great ideas have already been presented and many books have been written on leadership, from Lao-tse's *The Tao Te Ching* (1900) to modern literature on management and leadership. Therefore, we may not be talking of a new focus as in "something that has never been around before" but perhaps aspects of leadership that will be new to the corporate world. Practices that have not yet been adopted by business but can be found, for example, in many spiritual and religious traditions. If adopted by a company, these practices will allow continuity in leadership for the organisation. In traditional (and current) terms this means increasing the useful lifespan of senior executives. Increasing the useful lifespan of executives is worthwhile because it puts companies in a position to reap the benefits of securing the competitive advantage of the wisdom and experience of their seniors over longer periods of time. Moreover, the company will retain the collective, combined experience, skills, tacit knowledge and learning of senior management and avoid the considerable costs, financial and otherwise, of attracting, recruiting and retaining new hires at senior levels.

As the new type of leadership can only start with those who have the position, status and power to influence the organisation as a whole, it must begin at the executive level – and in a way that shows the organisation that they mean what they say. We all have our own stories of Boards that have introduced changes that promise to rocket the company to unprecedented heights of performance, make competitors tremble and give us all greater job satisfaction. But somehow, it is often difficult to see what has really changed in the higher echelons of the company to match the changes enforced on the rest of the organisation. Therefore, any new focus has to be taken up by top managers not purely because it makes good commercial sense, but because it is congruent with what they want to achieve personally. Otherwise, the drive to succeed will not be there and real change will not happen. It really needs executives who have a desire to become leaders in the organisation because it coincides with their life's purpose.

We are not unequivocally equating leadership to a highly paid position on the Board of a Fortune 500 company, and neither are we proposing that Fortune 500 companies lack effective leaders. The leadership we are promoting involves a *personal choice that an individual makes and decides to pursue*, rather than a hierarchical position given by others. What we would call leadership from the inside to the outside, as opposed to leadership from the outside to the inside. Inside-to-outside leadership involves an individual consciously choosing what they want to champion in their life and then adjusting their thoughts, attitudes, behaviours and skills accordingly. Outside-to-inside leadership comes about when a person is promoted into a hierarchical position by others and then begins to adjust their thoughts, attitudes, behaviours and skills to match what they, and others, think leadership is about. We would say that inside-to-outside leadership is part of a self-chosen purpose, and that outside-to-inside leadership is positional good fortune. Therefore, outside-to-inside leaders can be found at any level in an organisation.

The new focus required by leaders can only develop from the inside-to-outside process. And because it is driven by a self-chosen purpose it is completely difference per individual, sustainable by particular individuals, and not dependent on other people's opinions. This is not to suggest, however, that leaders should ignore other's opinions, be closed to alternative suggestions or not be held accountable for their actions. What we are saying is that inside-to-outside leadership as a process is self-sustaining – not that it makes someone perfect!

An example of the difference between inside-to-outside thinking and outside-to-inside thinking can be seen in the issue of company mission statements and values. Many organisations have mission statements and value lists in an attempt to guide and develop company and employee behaviour. In an inside-to-outside scenario it must be asked, how many of the authors of those mission statements and value lists have their own personal mission statement and value list that they behave by? If the individuals in question do not have their own mission statements and values clearly defined, then it is highly unlikely that they will be able to build congruence between what they want to achieve personally and what the company wants to achieve commercially. And if they cannot build that congruence personally, it will be virtually impossible to help the workforce build their own congruence – what will be seen by the workforce as, hollow mission statements and value lists.

In summary, the new leadership focus, as mentioned above, is about diverse people acting according to their self-chosen, different purposes and the sustainable personal development that maintains it, in relation to the context of where they will deploy their talents. It will be argued below that leadership functions on the basis of making right choices from correct considerations from a broader perspective. To explore this we need to take the individual and their unique talents as a starting point.

Leadership development

Two of our foundational premises are that leadership is based on personal development and that personal development does not happen by chance. Another premise we hold to is that we believe that before anyone can lead other people, or organisations, they must be able to lead themselves first.

It can be said that personal development hinges on one question: what do you want? You cannot have everything, but you can certainly have more than you have at the moment. Your potential is an unlimited future. Of course, there are limits but they are usually of quantity rather than quality.

All personal development is conscious and must be aimed towards your answer to what *you have decided you want in your life*. At first, defining what you want may be difficult and short on detail, but it will become clearer as you progress towards it. To use a simple example: if we book a holiday in Hammamet in Tunisia but have never been there before, we cannot know the details of what it will actually be like when we arrive. However, by looking at brochures, talking to people who have been to Tunisia before, comparing it with similar places we have been to, we can develop an idea of what it is like. Once we arrive in Tunisia and begin to travel south to Hammamet, details of the landscape, temperature, local customs and cuisine become clearer.

Development can be summed up in one word: *change*. Change what? *What you believe* and *how you think* – as long as the changes move you further towards what you want. Personal can also be summed up in one word: *you*. The success of your future lies in your own hands. You, not your boss, nor your organisation, nor your customers, will determine how close you come to achieving your self-chosen goals.

Our experience in the fields of executive coaching, training, organisational development and human resources consultancy has led us to formulate a four step process for leadership development – (1) awareness, (2) acceptance, (3) alignment, and (4) activation. We will now expand on these four steps which, we believe, provide a template for a new focus on leadership development. We do not think that this is the only template, nor perhaps the most appropriate for every circumstance, but we do know one thing about it – it works!

Awareness

It is often said that awareness is the bedrock of development because if it is not clear *what* should be changed, and *why* it could be changed, no development can occur. Awareness starts with looking, listening, smelling, tasting, and thinking. As a start, try these questions:

- Name five colours around you.
- How does your left foot feel right now?

- Can you remember five sounds you heard over the last five minutes?
- What state of mind are you in, and did you decide the state or leave it to chance?
- What stimulates your creativity and what stifles it?
- Can you recall the last two instances, and describe and identify why, you lost your temper and said, or did, things you later regretted?
- What does it feel like, physically and emotionally, when you are at your very best, and when you are at your lowest?
- What was the first non-human living creature you saw this morning?

Do not be concerned if you cannot answer all of the questions immediately – most people cannot, unless they were warned to expect them in advance.

Why are we not fully aware of everything all of the time? Being aware means making a conscious notation of what is happening in, and around us. In our age of stimulus overload, that is not something most of us need to do all of the time. As an example: suppose you move to a new house in a new neighbourhood. Everything is new to you and going to work means taking a different route than you are used to. The first time you take this route, you will pay a lot of attention to everything as you do not want to get lost and you will want to make sure you take the most efficient route. The second day it will be pretty much the same because it is still all new. However after, let's say, a year the route will have become very familiar. You will not consciously register anymore where you are driving, and what stores you are passing. The details are all filed away in your memory (unconscious competence), and there is no urgent need to re-register them on every trip.

Being aware allows opportunity for change. For instance, if an individual's left shoulder ached because of the way they sat behind their computer keyboard, it seems logical to assume that they would adjust their position to ease it. Remarkably, many people do not and carry on working day in, day out from the same position. Each day they ignore the ache in their shoulder even though it aches a little more every day. Even when they start noticing it, they will probably rub their shoulder a bit, have a little grimace and carry on working. Eventually, the pain is there all of the working day. In other activities, like walking or watching television, they adjust their posture to minimize the uncomfortability but still the pain persists. Then, one day when a colleague greets them in the lift they *think* they respond in a friendly way. The colleague notices something is not quite right and asks if they're OK – "Fine. Just a sore shoulder" comes the reply, "but that's normal, it's always aching these days". So, instead of re-arranging their computer or seating when they were first aware of the ache the person ignores the body's warning signals and carries on until they accept the permanent ache as a normal, everyday occurrence. This small example shows how it is easy to carry on day-to-day and not be aware of little things which can have a major impact later if not dealt with.

Another example lies in the field of human communication. If a person is not aware of the non-verbal elements in communication, like body language, they are missing out on about 70% of the full possibility of the message. So, even though they may respond to the verbal cues, they may miss the real message being conveyed to them and inadvertently miss an opportunity or offend the other person. Worse still, they may write off the other person mentally and not be open to future messages from that person.

When you are in pain, it is easy to imagine that when the pain gets uncomfortable enough you will do something about it. Or, when you are convinced the set-up of your desk is not productive for you, you will adjust it to where you *can* work productively. In other words, you are aware of the current situation and because it does not fit your desired situation you decide to change it. However, is the same true for your moods, as an example? Are they in your control or do they control you? Are they leading you towards what you want or away from it? Do you believe you are able to adjust your thinking to determine your own moods (as you would adjust a chair for optimum comfort) and if so, do you know what to change and how to change it?

As Goleman (1995) claims in his work on emotional intelligence, and April *et al.* (2000) claim in their work on redefining leadership, awareness is crucial as the first step in any leadership development. Let us now look at the two aspects of awareness: external and internal.

External

External awareness includes the environment and everyone outside of ourselves. The town where we live, our neighbourhood, the house we live in, the office we work in, are all part of the external aspect. Our family, neighbours, relatives and colleagues are also part of it. And let us not forget the weather, which has a strong influence, unique to itself. The influence from our external environment is constant; it is simply always there.

Awareness of our working environment deserves special attention, especially as no company or organisation is identical to another. They all have different missions which give rise to different strategies. These different strategies lead to different practices which in their turn form the different cultures. But there is also a similarity, that stems from the origin of the modern company.

Companies have emerged from specialisation. In prehistoric societies, individual members started performing those tasks with which they could distinguish themselves from the others on the basis of productivity and/or quality. As a consequence they gained more wealth (and presumably well-being as well). In search of further increase in productivity, efforts were combined in order to be able to make use of economies of scale. The process of specialisation continued which led to more, as well as different and new products. More people started working in organised forms (companies) where, due to the ongoing specialisation, they contributed to only a part of an end product. By passing on the benefits of the economies of scale to the end users, products came within reach of all the people. From the initial industrial revolution (mechanisation), we now find ourselves, via a productivity revolution (large scale mass-production) and a management revolution (organisation), in the era of a knowledge revolution.

The increasingly scientific approach to organising work processes, led to further sub-division of tasks into the small, neatly arranged, controllable partial tasks that are easy to monitor at the same time. In Charlie Chaplin's movie "Modern Times", his work was reduced to one single motion at a conveyor belt. It was expected that by analysing movements in minute detail, ideal working methods could be prescribed for all employees. Strict adherence to these rules would lead to maximum efficiency in the manufacturing process. Everything runs on the basis of rigid procedures and is monitored closely and controlled by the next level up the hierarchy. Until the 1940s and 1950s it was believed that any manufacturing process should have shop floor groups of four people: one foreman and three co-workers. This procedural, left hemisphere of the brain approach to organising is still in the genetics of the modern organisation. If possible, we want to know exactly where the company's performance is heading, how it will evolve in the coming quarter, why it's not 100% on track and who is to be held accountable for that. It is only gradually that we can move away from this "genetic lock," in order to design organisational concepts that will better meet the requirements of today. Academics and consultants like Peter Senge, Thomas Davenport, Leiff Edvinsson, Michael Zack, David Gurteen, Nick Bontis, Kurt April and Dan Kirsch demonstrate what inherent mechanisms can fundamentally block organisational learning, how to overcome them and maximize our diverse intellectual capital. One point to remember is that organisational learning can only happen because of learning by individuals.

Although we do not have space to investigate it here, an effective way to broaden awareness of the working environment is to look at systemic behavioural properties in organisations with reference to where they have come from, and the effects they have on day-to-day business.

One of the elements in the heritage of the "scientific" industrial organisation is the preference for standardisation and uniformity over uniqueness. However, there has been relatively little discussion of whether standardisation of machine parts and production processes have brought sufficient benefits.

This "control paradigm" is also now applied to human resources management, although in all areas of human resources management it is proving to be more difficult. Even in the development of executives the control paradigm looks for tools that make their work easier by standardising large parts of it. Most companies are familiar with competency management. In essence, competency management strives to identify behaviour that distinguishes top performers from average performers in a specific field. The theory is that the more the executives imitate the successful behaviour, the more successful they will become. However, an interesting point here is the conflict between uniformity and uniqueness that profiling behaviour highlights. For example, if an executive applies for a certain position, they have to fit a standard profile. Once someone is in a certain job family, as long as they demonstrate the standard uniform behaviour that is linked to each of the positions they want to apply for, they are considered acceptable. Unfortunately, if they demonstrate deviant behaviour, they are unlikely to be accepted and promoted. It may even be considered that certain competencies in their profile cannot be developed to the required levels whereas other competencies the candidate does have may not be measured. The question then arises, what happens to one's individual and unique talents? Will they be recognised and developed or remain undetected and wither?

It would be wrong to claim that competency management is not a valid and useful instrument, because to do so would dismiss the decades of research into what causes people to behave in a certain way. Competency management has proven its usefulness and perhaps it is now time to take it one stage deeper and begin to explore what lies underneath the behaviours. Whatever it is that lies at the core of behaviour – whether called "values" or "motives" or "archetypal talents" – it certainly drives behaviour. It also seems that there is a clear relationship between what lies underneath the observable competencies, and to what extent those competencies can be developed, as we shall see later on is this chapter.

One of the ways to explore these drives and latent competencies in yourself is to consider questions such as:

- Do you feel that you have talents yet to be developed – if so, what are they?
- Is there more you know you can do if only you had the opportunity – if so, how can you create the opportunity?
- Are there activities you enjoyed doing when you were younger and no longer do – if so, why do you not do them?
- Has your career developed in a way that has unleashed hitherto unknown abilities or are you mainly repeating what you learned many years ago – if so, are you satisfied with that situation?
- Do you have a sense of meaning and purpose in your work and is it furthering a cherished cause, or dream – if not, how can you bring these elements into your working life?

Internal

Awareness of oneself often starts by awareness of one's ego. The ego has the typical characteristic of making itself heard at will. It is loud and clearly present once you are aware of it. It will, for example, make you state your disagreement with a person or situation without looking at the broader perspective – simply because *you* do not like it and *you* will therefore decide that *you* will not go along with it. Freud (1971) distinguished the ego, associated with the conscious, rational mind as a secondary process and the id, associated with the body, emotions and the unconscious, as the primary process. He placed the secondary process (ego) as higher and superior to the primary process (id). Zohar (2000: 7) proposes a tertiary process, "... based on the brain's third system, the synchronous neural oscillations that unify data across the whole brain." This tertiary system she calls "spiritual intelligence", or SQ (spiritual quotient). She relates IQ to Freud's ego and EQ (emotional quotient or "emotional intelligence") to the primary process of the id. Zohar's (2000: 7) scientific research suggests that there is evidence for a physiological manifestation of SQ, "providing the self with an active, unifying and meaning-giving centre".

Of course, ego-awareness is in itself neither bad or good. As long as you can oversee the consequences of what it does, and as long as you recognise its "behaviour", there is an opportunity to detach oneself from the ego's process and search for the bigger picture.

Jaworski (1998: 7) refers to leadership as "being" rather than "doing". Taking Jaworski's (1998) concept a stage further, awareness of self opens up interesting possibilities from a (true) leadership perspective. Imagine that your awareness could stretch out beyond the boundaries of your job, your department, your organisation. This would allow "servant leadership" (Greenleaf, 1977) to emerge based on increased self-awareness, where the quest for meaning and significance would start to give increased fulfilment and satisfaction. According to Zohar (2000), a high degree of self-awareness is an indication of a highly developed SQ. Other indications include:

- active and spontaneous flexibility
- inspiration by vision and value
- reluctance to cause unnecessary harm
- recognising connections within and between systems.

Training for awareness

The question is often asked whether one can train awareness. The answer is quite simply: yes! And no preparation is needed, everyone can start right away. Try these exercises to start the process off and to stimulate you own ideas of how to *increase your awareness*:

- When you eat an apple, describe the taste of it to yourself.
- When you drink a glass of wine, try to discern the various flavours and smells that it contains and label each one of them.
- Stop and look around your environment (home, garden, office, car, etc.) every now and again and try to see it with fresh eyes, as if for the first time.
- Spend a whole day noticing how people use their hands, or what their eyes do when they talk, or what their voice sounds like or how different people walk.

- Refuse to express unpleasant thoughts or emotions for a whole day.
- Get up half-an-hour early every day (including Sundays) for a month and write down your thoughts.

These simple exercises will start to increase your awareness and help you wake up and live!

In a different sphere, you might want to increase awareness of the relationship of your Body-Mind-Emotions. You have probably experienced that when you are physically fit, you feel full of energy. You stand more erect, are generally more positive and your thinking is clearer. One remarkable aspect is that the relationship of the three functions can be used to consciously influence your mental and emotional states because each variable influences the other two. If you feel unhappy and start thinking of a situation where you felt very happy, your body posture will change and so will your emotions. Therefore, the Body-Mind-Emotions are an effective instrument to help you implement conscious choices about your mental and emotional state – and that ability begins by improving your awareness of all three functions as shown above.

Acceptance

If, during a workshop, we ask a group of managers who wants to be different, most say they do (albeit in only certain aspects) – there always seem to be things about ourselves that we want to change. If the questions is: who wants to be someone else, hardly anyone says they do. This example points towards the next stage in a development path; *acceptance of what one is and what one can, and cannot, do*. Not acceptance by way of resignation so as not to attempt change, but acceptance of one's position as a starting point for change and development. As a wise man used to say, "Be content with your lot, for your lot is your life (while you work towards an improved situation)".

Acceptance and non-acceptance can lead to a self-image that is not accurate – positively and negatively. For example, it is easy to believe that we can do what we want simply because we exist – such as develop leadership or warrant respect from others (rather than working diligently for both to occur). On the other hand, when given a compliment most of us tend to downplay it. Buzan (2001), the inventor of Mind Maps, reports that when showing participants on his courses how to juggle three balls, he invariably encounters the same reactions from virtually everyone when he compliments them on the fact that they have just learned something which is totally new to them. Most participants tell him that it's not that good, or that it should be much better. Very few participants can accept the compliment in the spirit it's meant, and move on.

Accepting that you are who you are, and the way you are, is important in order to lay the *foundation* for your further development and to make sound decisions on it. You may have to accept that to attain what you want will require specific skills and disciplines, or specific mental or emotional training, which you may not currently have. Therefore, could you accept that just because you are you (and you may have been successful in one sphere so far in your life to the point where behaving differently is rapidly becoming anathema – see the concept of carbonic acid above), it does not mean that everything you want is attainable simply because you want it to be so?

Perhaps the most difficult aspect of development to accept is that it feels awkward. Therefore, before attempting change ask yourself the question "Can I put up with uncomfortability at this point in my life?" If you would rather not, our advice is to postpone any attempt to change and accept that now is not the time to add extra pressure to your life.

Try these exercises to feel, mildly, what we mean:

- Fold your arms so you're comfortable – now fold them in the exact opposite way.
- Take a blank piece of paper and sign your name – now sign it using your opposite hand.
- Brush your teeth tonight with your opposite hand.
- Go for a walk round your garden – backwards.
- Eat a meal with the knife and fork in opposite hands to normal.

If they feel awkward when you do them, remember this is only minor uncomfortability at the physical level. Trying to think differently (perhaps, positively rather than negatively) or refusing to have certain emotions so often (such as anger) can feel very awkward and unnatural.

This *uncomfortability is an integral part of the cycle of change* which works as follows. We mostly live our life by habit so that what we do feels both comfortable and natural – but this also means that we are unconscious of what we are doing as we do it. If we want to develop, we have to become conscious of what we are doing and adjust our behaviour (or thinking or feeling). Unfortunately, this then feels unnatural to us – because it is not what we would normally do by habit. Ironically, this state of unnaturalness is the only time when change can happen and, therefore, means that when change happens it feels awkward or uncomfortable. If we persevere with the new behaviour it begins to feel natural to us after a period of time but now, the new behaviour is conscious because we deliberately decided to do it. This means that even when the new behaviour is installed in our repertoire as a habit, we can become conscious of it (to refine it, for example) when we want because we consciously and deliberately initiated it in the first place.

To illustrate the point, let's imagine that we want to improve our presentation skills and attend a public speaking skills course. Before the course our arms and hands feel natural and we move them as and when required without fuss, albeit automatically without much thought. However, when we stand up to speak in front of the other participants our arms and hands suddenly feel very unnatural and we become highly conscious of them. Conscious to the point where we probably ask the trainer, "What do I do with my hands?" – which is a strange question as we've lived for decades without the need to ask anyone what to do with them. The trainer may give us the advice to simply let them hang loose at our side. "But . . ." we say, ". . . that's not me, it's not natural". Nonetheless, we let them hang loose and after a few more presentations it becomes comfortable. And if we want, we can turn our mind to them to check if they are relaxed or tense, whereas before the course we were not even conscious of the fact we had arms and hands unless they were in pain.

To return to the theme of accepting what one is like, there is a body of work which takes a slightly different perspective on the subject. The Dutch management trainer and researcher Aernout Cohen Tervaert noticed several features during the many training programmes he delivered. He noticed that some people learn certain aspects faster than others; some were not capable of putting into practice what they learned immediately; others accelerated their learning so much that they were used as an example for the rest of the participants. It was clear that this was not a matter of cerebral intelligence because everyone understood what he said, and why it would be beneficial for them. So although everyone was happy with his programmes and his performance as a trainer, he was puzzled by the differences in the participants' responses to the training. When researching the processes during his training, he discovered that not everyone was *capable* of adopting each of the behaviours he explained. His research led him to propose that human behaviour can be seen through the lens of *four archetypes*, with each archetype showing a *preference for a certain behavioural style* and, it appears, a natural capacity to develop this style. *Everyone has all four archetypes somewhere in their behaviour* but we all show a preference for one style over the others in different situations. More specifically each archetype relates to one of four talents for that archetype so that for each person a profile results of four talents. A talent is to be seen as "an urge for self-realisation based on personal destiny expressed in a behavioural pattern that is unique to that specific talent" (Tervaert *et al.*, 2003: 25).

The archetypes are:

- Goal-oriented *Lion.*
- Relationship-oriented *Eagle.*
- People-oriented *Serpent.*
- Task-oriented *Bull.*

By taking your archetypal profile as a starting point, certain steps you may want to take in your life will be easier and feel more natural to you than others. In other words, the archetypes give an indication about where your potential lies.

In Figure 2.1 below, some further properties of the archetypes are listed.

Archetype	**Lion**	**Eagle**	**Serpent**	**Bull**
Energy	Shoulders	Head	Hips	Legs
Orientation	Goal	Relation	People	Task
Social style	Controlling	Persuasive	Supportive	Analytical
Time perception	Future	Here and now	Plasmic	Past
Conflict style	Extraverted Offensive	Extraverted Defensive	Introverted Offensive	Introverted Defensive

Figure 2.1 The Four Archetypes and Characteristics

It is beyond the scope of this text to elaborate in detail on the archetypes but the matrix above may help you see certain trends. For instance, the goal-oriented lion will feel at best in situations where they can set the direction or goals and see to it that the goals are met. Their communication style ensures that they will tell others what needs to be achieved. Trying to imitate this behaviour, without having connection with the lion archetype, will lead to a loss of authenticity that most people around will notice. As a result, the effectiveness of the exposed behaviour will be drastically reduced. For the person involved, it can lead to frustration and disappointment. A goal-oriented lion who has been informed that they have to show care and ask employees how they are feeling will do it in a goal-oriented way, rather than a people-oriented way, like the serpent will.

Alignment

Having decided what you want, where you want to go, and how to start the journey of getting there, you now need to align yourself and your life to the direction you have decided to travel. Alignment can only come from working from the inside-out (see above for explanation). *True alignment needs to be mental, emotional and physical with each requiring different activities to align properly.* When all three align towards your self-chosen purpose, an energy and a synergy occur rather like the extra energy that happens to a piece of iron when it is magnetised. Everything in you will then pull in the same direction and others will notice a charisma beginning to form within you.

To illustrate: if a person wanted to align their life towards "care", they would first need to determine what "care" actually is for them. In this example we will use the definition "the continued anticipation of another's needs". A physical demonstration of this could be that the person regularly waters their pot plants because they know regular watering in a centrally-heated home is essential for the plant's survival. A mental demonstration could be the person anticipating what their child will need to know about how to revise for exams and showing the child how to do it well before the pressure of exams starts. An emotional example could be when the person knows that a close friend has suffered a bereavement and decides to show empathy and support towards that friend to help them through the grieving process.

Activation

Having determined what to change and why to change it, you need to do it! And *keep doing it until your desired state is reached.*

It is one thing to think of a new concept, let's assume a behavioural concept. It is another thing to experience it, let's say in a training environment. It is yet another to personalise it, to imagine how a specific behaviour would work out for you personally and what it would bring. After having decided "what" to change and, more importantly, "why" to change it, it is key to define a strategy to implement it in your life.

For instance you may decide that you want to work on the basis of "respect". It means that you have to work out how you can show "respect" through your behaviour, your interactions, your words and speech patterns, your thought processes, the music you listen to, with the pets in the house, with your family, with those who are out to damage you, with your loved ones. Thinking, feeling and theorising all have their place, but for anything to change things need *activating* – and if you are trying to change, not the things which you normally activate, but different things (behaviours, speech patterns, thought processes, communication processes, as just a few examples), and not just activated for a while, but activated until your objective is achieved.

If the three previous steps have been worked through, this stage is the natural culmination of the process and the first phase of the *new you.* It is here that actual development starts and preparation for a new phase in your professional and personal life begins. It is the start of the journey, rather than the achievement of the goal.

References

April, K., Macdonald, R. and Vriesendorp, S. (2000), *Rethinking Leadership*, Kenwyn: University of Cape Town Press (Juta Academic).

Buzan, T. (2001), *The Power of Spiritual Intelligence*, London: Thorsons/Harper Collins, pp. 64–65.

Douthwaite, R. (1999), *The Growth Illusion*, Dartington, Totnes: Green Books.

Freud, S. (1971), *Group Psychology and the Analysis of the Ego*, New York: Bantam Books.

Goleman, D. (1995), *Emotional Intelligence: Why It Can matter More Than IQ*, Westminster, Maryland: Bantam Books.

Greenleaf, R. (1977), *Servant Leadership: A Journey Into the Nature of Legitimate Power and Greatness*, New York: Paulist Press.

Halper, J. (1988), *Quiet Desperation: The Truth About Successful Men*, Boston, Massachusetts: Warner Books Inc.

Hupkens, C. (2005), *Burn-Out en Psychische Belasting* (25th July 2005, Webmagazine CBS, The Hague, The Netherlands, URL: http://www.cbs.nl/nl-NL/menu/themas/arbeid-inkomen-sociale-zekerheid/arbeidsmarkt/publicaties/artikelen/2005-1738-wm.htm, accessed in July 2005).

Jaworski, J. (1998), "Destiny and Leadership", in L. Spears (Ed.), *Insights on Leadership: Service, Stewardship, and Servant Leadership*, New York: John Wiley and Sons.

Lao-Tse (1900), *The Tao Te Ching*, La Vergne, TN: Lightning Source Inc.

Tervaert, A. C., Spijker, Q. and Hofman, G. (2003), *Liefde Voor Talent*, Utrecht: Het Spectrum.

Zohar, D. (2000), *Spiritual Intelligence: The Ultimate Intelligence*, London: Bloomsbury Publishing.

3

Globalisation: A Personal View

by Tony Ehrenreich

Introduction

Globalisation is a phenomena that has been with us for thousands of years, when human beings for the first time set off across land and sea in search of new areas to occupy. It has more recently, taken the form of first colonialism and then imperialism. The present form of globalisation, however, has a very distinct feature in that it is an attempt to define global relations in a way that benefits a particular group or transnational class, but more about that later. There have been, without doubt, many benefits that have flowed from an ever increasing globalising world, but unfortunately for people in the Southern Hemisphere the more negative features of globalisation outweigh the positives by far. Your location in the debate around globalisation is informed by the impact that it has on your personal circumstances, and in the instance of this chapter it advances the perspectives of working families.

South Africa – a global microcosm

The context of this contribution towards the globalisation debate is from the perspective of working families, working families located within South Africa who have a particular experience of globalisation, not only as it manifests itself today but also the influence that it has had on the transition within South Africa as we moved away from Apartheid.

The changes in South Africa from an Apartheid state to a democratic state, as realised in the 1994 democratic elections, were preceded by extensive negotiations. The balance of power that existed and impacted on these negotiations was a climate of revolution, given expression by the many struggles of people inside the country against Apartheid. The global balance of power, however, had as much to do with the changes in South Africa. The end of the Cold War played a decisive role in changing the environment for negotiations, because whilst the Soviet Union was no longer supporting struggles in Africa, the USA and its allies understood and appreciated the necessity for change – even while the moral abhorrence of Apartheid was presented as the key selling point. It was also true that they realised this was a moment in time in the South African struggle in which it was possible to change the political construct, while still maintaining the economic construct of skewed ownership. Essentially this meant that Black people could get the vote and the old owners of the wealth in South Africa could maintain their positions of ownership. The change in the political construct is an important one, and provides an opportunity for changing many of the other relations that existed, or continue to exist, within South African society. But the manner in which that change unfolded was influenced by the big corporations, like Anglo America and De Beers, who had essentially become multinational corporations with strong allies in the global, interdependent capitalist system. The extent of the relationship between local capital and transnational capital was such that De Beers, a South African diamond mining company, along with the Russian diamond industry controlled the global diamond market.

Whilst, in many respects, the changes in South Africa were far reaching, they were increasingly happening within the construct and the parameters defined by the World Bank, the IMF and the World Trade Organisation (WTO). These changes had all the features of neo-liberalism, and were ensuring that South Africa's integration into the global economy provides opportunities for multinational corporations and the advancement of the global hegemony of capital within South Africa. This agenda for change was imposed on South Africa and embraced by South Africa through the adoption of GEAR, the South African government's macro-economic strategy (Growth, Employment And Redistribution strategy). This strategy was adopted by the South African government in 1996, after speculation in the SA economy had led to a 40% decline in the value of the Rand (ZAR, the South African currency). South Africa was then advised to demonstrate its commitment to macro-economic stability, and ensure global investor confidence. The features of this global set of rules for economic success were:

- Privatisation – which saw the selling off of State-Owned Enterprises to both South African and global capital. Whilst this benefited both local and foreign capital, it severely undermined the power of the democratic state to intervene in the economy and direct it in a way that it ultimately benefited the main constituency of the ANC (one part of the ruling tripartite, the African National Congress[1]). This constituency that the ANC was primarily obliged to serve, and in whose interests they should have been acting, was the poor Black majority.
- The second key feature of GEAR was cutting the country's social expenditure, and subsequent cutting of the country's budget deficit. This led to a cut in state expenditure and reduced the state's participation in the economy – which contributed to the economy contracting in quite a serious way, with thousands of people losing their jobs through retrenchments and

restructuring. A lot of this restructuring was probably inevitable, but it should have been done in a more just way, that critically considered the impact on working families.

- A third key feature was the tariff liberalisation programme, which saw the government dropping South African tariffs even beyond our obligations to the WTO. This, once again, led to huge job losses.
- The reduction of tariffs led to the government having no tools at its disposal in which to intervene in the economy, and defend fledgling new industries. The very tool that the United States of America (USA) and the European Union (EU) used to build their industries after the 2nd World War was not an option for the South African government and other emerging economies. This inability to support industries effectively means that the economy will not move production up the value chain, and the country is destined to remain a commodity exporter that imports high value-added products from the industrialised world.

The net effect of this political transition and the restructuring, was the further impoverishment of working families within South Africa. And if one is to believe the Reserve Bank (central bank of South Africa) then today the bottom 60% of society has seen their income reduced by nearly 70% over the last 10 years. This is both a direct consequence of the effect of globalisation on South Africa, but it is also an indication of the influence that global institutions have over domestic economies.

In South Africa, however, there have been beneficiaries of our reintegration into the global economy, and this has not only been the existing White elite but a new emerging Black elite has benefited to such an extent that today we see the top 10% South Africans being nearly 12% wealthier than they were in 1994.[2] Now whilst this transformation has seen more Black people integrated into the wealthy sector of our communities, it has unfortunately seen that emerging Black capitalist class take on the features of not only domestic capital, but also global capital. This has led to many of the new Black elite being assimilated into the practices and values of global capital, largely dismissing the plight of the poor (not often in their rhetoric, but certainly in their action). How easily they forget that it was the struggles of the African majority that had liberated this land and had as a result thereof opened up all these new opportunities that they today enjoy. This new elite further demonstrates no explicit consideration to Black working families, and are quite comfortable with the *growing* inequalities in the society – not appreciating that these inequalities pose the greatest threat to the future and the country's sustainability, and it is in fact not in their long-term interest to ignore or merely appease the masses.

In the restructuring of both the South African and the global economy there have been those who have benefited and those who have not, and it is because there are beneficiaries that there are those who ardently defend the philosophy that underpins the present form that globalisation takes. The current tension in the world is growing more palpable, almost on a daily basis, as the world both integrates and disintegrates at the same time. Globalisation has provided opportunities for consumers across the world, but whilst it is taking ever increasing numbers of the global population into the group of people who benefit from its diffusion, it also has its darker side which is not often reported. It is this darker side that today sees more people across the world living in abject poverty than at any other time in the history of the world – setting the scene for quite dangerous times in our global history.

Power in setting agendas: slow (r)evolution towards diversity

This present form of globalisation sees the power and the interest of multinational corporations usurping those of the nation state. We have seen how multinational corporations, and the governments who support them, regulate the world in a way that serves their best interests. So today the World Bank, IMF and the WTO defines the agenda of global relations and global governance – they determine "who counts" and "who does not count". This agenda is one of profit maximisation and market domination in ever-shorter time periods, paralleled by the objectification and instrumental use of global peoples, and with blatant, and sometimes masked, disregard for the needs of development and making the globe a more equitable village.

The WTO negotiations has led to greater inequalities in the global trading system – this was recognised in Doha, Qatar[3] where a commitment was made to a round of negotiations that would support development. At this stage the negotiations were still dominated by the USA and the EU who essentially coerced smaller economies into adopting their positions.

In 2003, in Cancun, Mexico however, there was a fundamental shift in the balance of power in these negotiations, where emerging economies led by China, India, Brazil and South Africa led the formation of a group of the G20 countries that insisted on a different trade agenda. The refusal to no longer accept the domination of the agenda by the USA and the EU led to the collapse of that round of negotiations. This rejection of the agenda of the emerging economies is happening at the same time as global social movements are challenging the agenda, and becoming stronger, with greater collaboration across the globe.

This has led to a coalescence of organisations that have committed themselves to challenging the dominance of, and the agendas of, multinational corporations. The World Social Forum and the World Summit on Sustainable Development sees thousands of people and organisations across the world coming together under the slogan of a *"New World is Indeed Possible"*.

The war in Iraq is an example of how the global agenda is being dominated by force, where one country, the USA, can essentially invade any sovereign state without any reason or approval by the United Nations, or in pursuit of their own interests (in this case the oil reserves of Iraq).

Globalisation and the continued and expanded global inter-relations are inevitable, but the present form that it takes is not inevitable and it is this that must be challenged. The continued agenda of globalisation must ensure greater equality across the world and must see an expanded role for organisations like the International Labour Organization (ILO) and the United Nations (UN), in its present form or modified form, in setting the global agenda.

Whilst there is a broad appreciation for the importance of diversity in the national context as a pre-condition for development, there is not yet an appreciation of the importance of diversity across the globe and an appreciation that each country must be allowed to have expression on the global stage. This will not only ensure inclusivity and the hegemony of a global agenda, but it will remove the legitimacy that more radical anti-globalisation groups have.

Democracy has been defined as an important requirement for global integration, and participation in world bodies. This is indeed supported and advanced by all countries of the world. There is a loud and expanding call to ensure that democracy is not seen as synonymous with elections. So, a circumstance where a government has elections for its leaders every five years and essentially does as it pleases in the intervening years, is no longer acceptable. Diverse organisations and people now demand participation in the discourse on policy and governance. The whole idea of social dialogue amongst the social partners is becoming a feature of successful and sustainable economies.

The attempt by many industrialised countries to now roll back the social gains, like the living wage, the forty-hour work week and diminishing health and safety standards is a worrying one. What this represents is a "chase to the bottom", where countries are reducing standards of employment to be able to attract multinational corporations to invest in their economies (a lowest denominator effect). It is this driving down of the standards, enjoyed by working families, that is the root-cause for the growing global inequalities, not only in particular nation states but also between the Northern Hemisphere and the Southern Hemisphere.

Whilst it is true that in the past many of the social democracies of Europe could compel their domestic capital to expand the social wage, and in that way secure decent standards of living and work for working people, multinational corporations based in these social democracies are now part of a global transnational class of companies and people using the World Bank and the WTO to regulate the world in a manner that suits them, and their drive for profit. In this way, they quite cleverly are able to unshackle themselves from any restrictions placed on them by their own countries.

Civil society and globalisation

In this epoch of globalisation it is important to appreciate the new role played by civil society and the voluntary sector. It is civil society organisations that, in the most acute way, give expression to the aspirations of people and raise what are the most crucial questions. There are five key challenges that confront civil society in its engagements:

- The *first challenge* is the challenge of power and power imbalances between different organisations. This is the diversity reflected between single-issue NGO's/voluntary organisations and multimillion dollar organisations that tackle issues at a global scale.
- The *second challenge* is in how civil society seeks to bridge the gap between narrow interests and broader goals. Here it is important to appreciate the centrality of networking and collaboration between the different organisations that operate in this sector.
- The *third challenge* is to ensure that civil society can articulate a coherent vision for a more just and equitable global system. One of the key criticisms that many civil society organisations are confronted with is that they are against everything, but not *for* anything. This would challenge all of us in civil society to define a programme for achieving the vision.
- The *fourth challenge* is one that comes from outside of civil society; this is where many governments charge that civil society is undermining the democratic systems by short-circuiting established procedures of decision-making. This is the desire to reduce the questions of democracy to elections. Civic activism complements democratic practices by drawing citizens more fully into public life and providing the necessary checks and balances.
- The *fifth challenge* is one about legitimacy as well as fostering transparency, representation and accountability within civil societies. There are many who would try and undermine the role of civil society, and that places an even greater challenge on us to ensure that we lead in the areas of good governance.

Clearly the workings of civil society in its ever-expanding challenge for participatory processes are designed to advance those principles that seek a more just world, that works for all (the common good).

Interdependent capital strategies

The new global developments and global order dates back to the world economic crises of the 1970s and took shape in the 1980s and 1990s. It is marked by a number of fundamental shifts in the capitalist system; amongst these shifts are the rise of truly transnational capital and the integration of every country into new, interdependent global production and financial systems. Secondly, there has been a paralleled rise of, and marginal growth of, a new transnational capitalist class, a class grounded in global markets rather than national markets and international wellbeing. In every country of the world, a portion of the national elite has become part of this new transnational elite. Thirdly, the rise of the transnational state – there is an ever increasing network of super-national political and economic institutions to which the nation state is obliged to be more and more accountable, and more fundamentally, take their direction from. It is this transnational state, or transnational mechanism, that has been the key institution imposing the neo-liberal model on the global south. It advances the interest of international capitalists and their allies over nationally-orientated groups. Fourthly, we have seen new relations of inequality in this global society – whilst millions of people have been brought into this system and participate in these new markets, many millions more are more impoverished now than at any other time in the history of the world. This global capitalism has become hegemonic, not just because its ideology has become dominant but because it has the ability to provide material rewards and to impose sanctions. Globalisation is anything but a neutral process, it produces definite winners and definite losers, and therefore has its defenders and opponents. This new construct has made it almost impossible to address local issues removed from the global context.

Under this new brand of globalisation we have seen inequalities increase, as well as the polarisation of the globe. During the 20th century and as a result of mass struggles the world over, society came up with a mechanism for softening the most glaring inequalities of capitalism, the state intervened in the process of production in order to capture and redistribute wealth. Redistribution of wealth was carried out in various ways, including taxes on capital, minimum wages, labour protection, public services and social welfare. This was largely known as keynesianism or social capital in the West. It did not put an end to inequalities, but gave each country a set of tools and a strategy to bring about development – mass popular movements could pressure states to intervene and provide a buffer of social protection from unchecked market forces.

But in the 1980s and 1990s capital adopted a strategy of going global in order to break free from these nation state constraints to profit-making. A new context for global relations was constructed; this so-called Washington consensus ensured worldwide market liberalisation and the construction of a new legal and regulatory super-structure for the global economy. Another consequence of this global strategy was the internal restructuring and global integration of each country's economy. In this way it opened up local markets and all areas of the society to the logic of profit-making, unhindered by the logic of social need. This further led to the national social and welfare systems being dismantled and/or modified, as well as the restructuring of tax systems and privatisation.

Global capitalism is not just about the monopolisation of wealth and resources by minorities. More importantly, it is also about the concentration of power in the hands of these minorities. It is in many respects similar to South Africa where Apartheid was not only about economic control, but also about the monopoly of political power by the minority. The group of eight rich countries (G8[4]) exercises both economic and political control over the globe using institutions at the World Bank, the IMF and the WTO. They make life and death decisions for entire industries and entire countries, yet this transnational state is entirely unelected and utterly unaccountable to those over whom it imposes its dictates.

Crises in global capitalism

In the 21st century the crises in global capitalism can no longer be disguised. The claim that this global capitalism could somehow be made to work for the benefit for poor majorities has proven to be false, and the system has been the subject of a deepening crises since the late 1990s. The first feature of this crisis is *social polarisation*; the system cannot meet the needs of the majority of humanity, and there is expanding poverty, inequality and deprivation. Ironically, certain recent, tragic events in some of the G8 countries, have unveiled its (growing) legacy of social polarisation – some of which are still along race and class lines. The second is a structural crisis of *over-accumulation*. This is brought about by the marginalisation of a significant portion of humanity from economic participation, and has reduced the ability of the world market to absorb world output. This was demonstrated by the crises in Mexico in 1995, the crises in Asia in 1997 and the world recession that began in 2001. The world's apparent two most successful economies, the USA and Japan, are visible examples of the results of over accumulation – the USA, for instance, still has the largest debt to the World Bank, and Japan is still battling, many years on, to make headway of its financial crises. Thirdly, there is a crises of *legitimacy and authority* as millions of people question the legitimacy of the explicit, and sometimes shadowy, systems that regulate the globe. This has led to spontaneous, ever-increasing, organised resistance movements across the world, that appeared to reach its apex at the recent World Social Forum.

Clearly this presents a global crises to which there are three (not entirely mutually exclusive) possible outcomes:

(1) *Global reformism*, based on global keynesianism. This will see a major overhaul of the system where the more reformist section of the World Social Forum will ally with the more reformist wing of the World Economic Forum to push such a project. This is to some extent seen in the current attempts to restructure the global institutions that exist – we see it in the proposals to change the World Bank, the WTO, even the UN, as well as various other institutions. These reforms, whilst necessary, are an attempt to put a plaster on the problem, without meaningfully addressing the root causes of the problem.

(2) The rise of *global fascism/despotism* based on a new war order, founded on military spending and wars to contain the down-trodden. This is already

a feature of the current American administration and its conduct in the Middle East, Africa and South-East Asia – acting in a way that disregards the entire world and its institutions, favouring only its perspective on the world (economic, political, religious, social and technical), and establishing a uni-polar world. This displayed military might is the greatest threat to world stability, and demonstrates the lengths some countries will go to in order to pursue their interests. This attitude from the USA will see it define rogue states as those who do not comply with their economic prescriptions, or their foreign policy dictates.

(3) A *global anti-capitalist alternative* that seeks a fundamental change in power relations, where a radical programme is advanced to respond to the deepening crisis of capitalism. This project is the most dangerous as it poses the greatest danger to world peace and stability, but it is the option that we are increasingly moving towards. The growing instances of terrorism and so-called ethnic clashes will continue to expand, as they attempt to challenge the might of the dominant economic countries in unconventional ways – and they will have support in unlikely allies who, in their perceived hopelessness, have their own issues with the dominant economic countries, led by the USA.

The three scenarios outlined above will advance in different ways given the continued marginalisation of greater sections of global communities and, in the present construct, confrontation, in various and all forms, is inevitable. This confrontation must however be chanelled in a manner that ensures that meaningful and constructive change is possible, that the diverse voices of the world are heard and their diverse interests attended to, without plunging the world into a/multiple war(s) that will have no winner.

In conclusion, it is fair to assume that the current state-of-play is unsustainable, and the future not predetermined. And whilst national struggles are essential, it is equally important to build a global response. The popular mass of humanity must develop a transnational class-consciousness and global political strategies that link the local to the national and the national to the international, and rise up to demand meaningful change – change that works for all.

Notes

1 In South Africa, a new tripartite government, consisting of the African National Congress (ANC), Congress of South African Trade Unions (COSATU) and the South African Communist Party (SACP) took office in 1994 from the National Party (NP), which ran the Apartheid government for many decades.

2 South Africa has a two-tiered economy; one rivaling other developed countries and the other with only the most basic infrastructure. It therefore is a productive and industrialised economy that exhibits many characteristics associated with developing countries, including a division of labour between formal and informal

sectors – and uneven distribution of wealth and income. The formal sector, based on mining, manufacturing, services, and agriculture, is well developed.

3 The November 2001 declaration of the Fourth Ministerial Conference in Doha, Qatar, provides the mandate for negotiations on a range of subjects, and other work including issues concerning the implementation of the present WTO agreements.

4 The G8 stands for the "Group of Eight" nations. It began in 1975 when President Giscard d'Estaing of France invited the leaders of Japan, the USA, Germany, the United Kingdom and Italy to Rambouillet, near Paris, to discuss the economic problems of the day. The group expanded to include Canada in 1976 and Russia in 1998. Unlike many other international bodies, the G8 does not have a fixed structure or a permanent administration – it is up to the country that has the Presidency to set the agenda and organise the annual G8 Summit.

Part 2

Expanding Reality

Editors' Note: Expanding Reality

by Marylou Shockley

Boundaries provide a convenient mechanism by which to structure reality. It gives shape to our world views, social relations, and geopolitical spaces. Without the ability to construct boundaries, we would find the physical realm around us chaotic and undecipherable; we, therefore, create boundaries to order our world. This ability to construct boundaries has enabled us to create complex institutions such as business corporations. We have bestowed "personhood" on corporations so that, among other things, they can be subject to taxes. Through boundaries established by legislative fiat, government regulation, and legal precedent, corporations have thrived as complex institutions who can acquire resources and other businesses just as we can as private citizens. Corporations, as persons, have developed personalities (brand/image), created cultures (sense of purpose/values), become pioneering (research/global expansion) and, at times, lapsed into sinister behavior (greed/fraud). Although corporations, like our governments, have incredible sway over our daily lives, it is we who have created them. We can redefine their boundaries.[1] This is the underlying premise of the chapters that appear in Expanding Reality.

Not only are boundaries constructed and given legitimacy, they are demarcations between "in" and "out" that have profound impact on our identities of who we are *vis-à-vis* others. These identities are powerful. It is what makes for strong cohesiveness in teams. Olympic national teams are good examples of team solidarity. Winning for these teams brings fame, lucrative sponsor contracts and national accolades to those who individually or collectively excel in their sport as part of their country's team. Similar demarcations, though not as visible, create groups in all aspects of social life – many of these groups are institutionalized, e.g., voter blocs, nonprofit associations, social clubs, and companies to name a few. What advocates of diversity are most concerned about is *expanding our realities of inclusion*. They are not "against" boundaries *per se* or institutions constructed through them. Instead these advocates are vigilant, constantly testing a boundary's permeability with respect to gender, race, lifestyle, or religious creed. More specifically, they want to know what criteria – declared or practiced – forms the basis for determining the rights of *full* participation. Full participation goes beyond the notion of entry. It embraces practices, structures, and roles within a group that may create pockets of undue advantage or disadvantage.

The chapters included in this section were selected to emphasize three aspects of expanding the realities of inclusion. First, the struggle for inclusion is contextually historic and experiential in the sense that foundations of inclusion that we take for granted today were, in fact, forged through struggles of the past. Recognizing the contributions from those who grappled with their respective generations' issues of inclusion not only provides us with a sense of gratitude for their hard won effort, but also of hope that boundaries are permeable and can be re-constituted. Second, realities of inclusion in which diverse contributions are recognized require a re-tooling of existing mindsets and capabilities. In order for diversity policies to deliver value, training and changes to existing processes may be necessary. Such fundamental changes require senior leadership commitment that goes beyond declared policies; for example, executives may need to create and support change programs which institutionalize new or revamped cultural values. Third, the final aspect of expanding the realities of inclusion is forward looking, i.e., searching the outer edges of boundaries with a vigilant eye on what still needs to be done. Selected papers supporting this area take the baton from others who have fought to make institutional boundaries more permeable.

Of the four contributions by authors, James Joseph's, Managing Diversity: the United States Experience provides a historical context in the struggle for inclusion. Joseph's essay exudes credibility as "lived experience." He has witnessed, participated, and led much of efforts that characterize the US experience as the American people grappled with the boundaries of inclusion. Joseph identifies three distinct pluralistic paradigms – segregation, assimilation, and egalitarian pluralism. He offers pragmatic advice to leaders on how to organizationally leverage diverse identity group differences to advance learning and success within firms.

With the same intent as Joseph's advice to leaders, Mario Ghiggino in his chapter Diversity: Ideas to Create Value in the Workplace adds to the discourse on diversity by suggesting that employees bring a wealth of talent to an organization that can be classified through an "Agents Model" in which employees are agents of creativity, agents of continuity and agents of change. "Fit" of employees to the right jobs with these agency components brings bottom-line value to the firm. Ghiggino also argues that "ideas segregation" creates barriers within firms – especially those with a global reach – from exploiting the rich diversity of its employees. He posits that it is only through developing effective listening techniques that these barriers are neutralized.

This part ends with two chapters whose theme is active engagement at the societal and firm levels. Tony Burnett and Simon Kettleborough in their paper, New Frontiers for Diversity and Inclusion, urge us to step out of our over-burdened, well-meaning daily environments and expand our notions of inclusion to embrace the plight of others whose lives are defined by poverty. They use a series of five myths to make their case for inclusion in which governments and global business promote a "winning together" approach to interfacing with others in the world. Lastly, Jennifer Kam and Joanna Eidsmore in Applying Burlesque Rhetoric to Create Social Change remind us that retrenchment always lurks at the out edges of boundaries. Corporations such as Abercrombie & Fitch can slip into racial stereotyping, using humor as its defense. Rather than focusing on the "outrage" of such corporate behavior, Kam and Eidsmore tackle the issues of effective communications and alliance building across racial boundaries as a means of maintaining vigilance at the boundaries of inclusion.

Note

1 Even in the most despotic regimes, bounded structures are created to maintain itself. These types of regimes are changeable. The timeframes for change may be much longer than in more democratic regimes.

4

Managing Diversity: The United States Experience

by James Joseph

Introduction

There is much that the USA can learn from South Africa about managing diversity and leading hope. Yet, I share these thoughts on the American experience in the hope that they can be used to help avoid some of the pitfalls that has made US efforts more difficult, and the national conversation unnecessarily explosive and complicated.

A maturing concept

I grew up in the segregated South and worked over the years in all three sectors of our democracy: (1) the private sector driven by markets; (2) the public sector driven by ballots; and (3) the non-governmental sector driven by the institutions of civil society. During the course of the last 50 years, I have seen the American people move through three distinct paradigms of pluralism: the first was *segregation*, an idea that in theory was based on the notion of separate but equal; the second was *integration*, a hierarchical pluralism that sought the assimilation of differences around Euro-American norms; and the third is an *egalitarian pluralism* that seeks to accommodate an un-assimilated diversity.

As a boy growing up during the period of segregation, I studied from hand-me-down books in hand-me-down buildings. The books provided to Black children had been discarded by White schools as no longer fit for use by White students. The buildings in which we studied were also passed on to us after they had been abandoned by White schools as unsafe and unfit for their use. The public philosophy of the time spoke of separate but equal, but while our institutions were rigidly segregated they were far from equal.

Fifty years ago, the US Supreme Court shifted the paradigm from separate but equal to integration, ordering the desegregation of public schools and ushering in a new approach to diversity. I was young and in many ways naïve, but when informed about the Court's decision, I shared the enthusiasm of those around me that this might be a landmark moment in American history.

The 1954 decision was based primarily on arguments that integration would benefit the Black population: providing better facilities and equipment, a stronger curriculum and an environment more representative of the broader population with which African-Americans would now have to both compete and collaborate.

The basic definition of diversity shifted from separate, but equal, to integration: facilitating a black presence, getting African-Americans into the room. This was the colour- and gender-blindness paradigm. The emphasis was on access and assimilation. The previously White institutions were to be more diverse, but the learning culture and the institutional ethos were expected to remain basically the same.

If you fast forward 49 years later, there was another challenge to the prevailing orthodoxy. The arguments in support of diversity in the Supreme Court decision two years ago regarding practices at the University of Michigan reflected a change in the national view of diversity.[1] The emphasis was on the benefit to the larger society, rather than simply the benefit to affected groups. Many businesses filed supporting briefs arguing that diversity contributes directly to the bottom-line. African-Americans and other minorities were now demanding an "unassimilated diversity," a paradigm of egalitarian pluralism rather than the old hierarchical form that regarded differences as deviant.

If the emphasis of the second paradigm was on access and presence, getting people into the room, the present emphasis is on inclusiveness, getting people around the table. R. Roosevelt Thomas, Jr. (1991), a diversity consultant, astutely foresaw the issue in the 1990's by observing that the problem is not just hiring women and minorities in at entry level; it is a problem of leveraging their potential at every level to make a contribution to the business. The new understanding of diversity involves more than simply increasing the number of different identity groups on the payroll.

Diversity – key learnings for business

Thirty-five years ago, I was a rarity in business, a Black man serving as a senior officer of a large transnational business corporation, reporting to the Chief Executive Officer and serving on the Management Committee. My portfolio did not include employment equity *per se*, but I had a mandate to integrate ethics and corporate responsibility into all aspects of the business.

The process we used still has implications for today's efforts to manage diversity. As the first ethics officer in a large American business corporation, we concluded that I would only have the status I needed to get the job done by reporting to the Chief Executive Officer, but we also concluded that I could only be effective if I engaged line managers directly in developing goals and timetables to achieve what we regarded as desirable. While I began with the *appropriate organizational rank*, I worked to ensure that there was not just an understanding of our public commitment, but *ownership throughout the organization.*

Our corporate philosophy on ethics and accountability was *comprehensive in scope and scale.* Our Chairman argued that a *responsible corporation* is one that locates a site responsibly, hires and compensates its workforce responsibly, manufactures a product or provides a service responsibly, sets prices responsibly, distributes the return on investment responsibly, deals with government responsibly and serves its communities responsibly. In other words, the opportunity and *the requirement to act responsibly begin with the decision to do business* and carries over through every aspect of corporate operations.

The second thing I learned during my years with the world's largest producer of heavy duty diesel engines is that *a business corporation is what it rewards and celebrates.* It is not so much what it says in its mission statement, code of conduct or press releases as it is what it compensates its people for being. If employment equity is an important corporate value, the reward system, both performance reviews and compensation, must reflect it. While the practices at Cummins pre-dated by many years recent research on managing diversity, it is interesting to note how similar our philosophy was to that described by David Thomas and Robert Ely (1996) in a recent *Harvard Business Review* publication. We are essentially in agreement on how best to position organizations to *use identity-group differences* in the service of organizational learning, growth, renewal and success:

(1) The leadership must understand that diversity involves more than simply increasing the number of different identity groups on the payroll. There must also be awareness that diversity brings *different perspectives and approaches* to both work and management.
(2) The leadership must recognize *both the learning opportunities and the challenges* that the expression of different perspectives presents for an organization. The organization must be led to see *difference as a benefit* rather than a burden, with leaders focusing on how differences can be used as a source of individual and organizational effectiveness.
(3) A company must dismiss the notion that all of its workers are the same or aspire to be the same, especially the idea that it should operate as if every person were of the same race, gender and nationality. The colorblind, gender-blind ideal may sound good but it ignores reality. *People must be made to feel that differences are valued and respected* rather than suppressed.
(4) The organizational culture must *stimulate personal development* through the careful design of jobs as well as through education and training programs.
(5) The organizational culture must *encourage openness and instil a high tolerance for debate and constructive conflict* on work related matters.
(6) The culture must make *workers feel valued.*

(7) The organization must have a *well-articulated mission* and a *widely understood set of values*.
(8) The organization must *separate the enabling elements of bureaucracy* (the ability to get things done) *from the disabling elements* (those that create resistance to experimentation and over-value consistency and predictability).

Advice to senior management

What advice would I now offer to senior management? I agree with those diversity consultants who emphasize the following guidelines – especially Roosevelt Thomas Jr. (1991):

(1) *Clarify your motivation.* A lot of companies give off mixed or confusing signals about why diversity is important. Some point to government-mandated legal requirements, others to community relations and still a few others to a social and moral responsibility to employ minorities and women. All these can be useful if they lead to success, but I prefer *business reasons*. They are more likely to *provide the long-term motivation*. A diverse workforce is not just something a company ought to have. It is in today's environment likely to be something a company already has. Learning to manage that diversity will make the company more competitive.
(2) *Clarify your vision.* In my experience, the best vision to hold up before the company and to communicate to all managers is an image of *fully tapping the human resource potential of every member of the workforce.*
(3) *Expand your focus*. Managers usually see affirmative action and equal employment opportunity as centering on minorities and women, with very little to offer White males. Diversity must include *not just race, gender, religion and ethnicity, but also age, education, background and personality differences*. Moreover, it is time to see the emphasis on diversity as bringing in people who are *differently qualified* rather than as bringing in the unqualified.
(4) *Audit your corporate culture.* Set goals and objectives and *hold people responsible by periodically measuring performance.*
(5) *Modify your assumptions*, especially the idea that, left alone, the cream will rise to the top. I like the analogy of two people running a hundred yard dash. One has been provided all the support needed to build healthy legs while the other has had one leg deliberately broken. There can be no equal opportunity until the broken leg has been *mended.*
(6) *Modify your systems.* Many people rise to the top because they have an *advocate, a sponsor or a mentor*. The system must be changed so that all work is valued and the *promotion and reward systems works equally well for all employees*.
(7) *Help your people understand that conflict and failure come with the territory.* Managing diversity is not easy. Many institutions are tranquil and apparently at ease before they diversify, but the larger the presence of different

identity groups the larger the instances of conflict. The psychiatrist and writer Scott Peck (1993) says that there are four stages on the way to community. The first is *pseudo-community* where people who are very different are brought together, but for a time they pretend that they are all alike and gloss over differences.

The next stage is an *awareness of differences* that are very important to some of the people in the group. There is a real clash, with some individuals trying to convince themselves that their difference is so important that they must convert others, convince them that they need to assimilate. This is the stage Peck calls chaos. The third stage is one of *emptiness*. People begin to realize the chaos they have created because of their need to affirm the value of their particular difference and they feel regret and even remorse about the conflict this has caused. It is only then that people are ready for *real community*, according to Peck. So conflict must be accepted as one stage on the way to community.

(8) *Continue affirmative action but recognize how it differs from managing diversity.* The concept of affirmative action is greatly maligned in some corners because it is criticized by its stereotypes rather than supported because of its original intent. Let me give you an example of how affirmative action in the United States was intended to work. When I served in the Administration of President Jimmy Carter, our Secretary of the Army received a list of recommendations of people to be promoted to General. As he looked at the list, he said there are no Black officers in this group. Surely, there must be Blacks somewhere in this army who qualify for consideration. He sent the list back and suggested that the organization take a second look and come back again with recommendations. On the second list was the name of a man named Colin Powell who was promoted to General and the rest is history.

The fact remains that diversity is an organizational asset and where you do not have it *you sometimes need affirmative action to get there*. But it is also true that while affirmative action is good at getting a mix of talents in the door, *it takes diversity management to develop the full potential of everyone in the mix*.

So why should companies concern themselves with diversity? Until recently, many managers answered the question with the assertion that discrimination is wrong, both legally and morally. Today in the United States, many managers are stepping up to argue that diversity is good for business. But some well-intended managers still ask "How are we doing on race relations?" The right question, most diversity consultants agree, is *"how do we build a workforce where 'we' is everyone?"*

It is clear that while there may be some things in the American experience that is worth either avoiding or emulating, it is South Africa that has the best chance to demonstrate that diversity need not divide; that pluralism rightly understood and rightly practiced is a benefit and not a burden; and, finally, that the fear of difference is a fear of the future.

Note

1 A good analysis of the Michigan case can be found in Bell, D. (2003) "Diversity's Distraction," *Columbia Law Review*, October, vol. 103, issue 6, pp. 1622–1633.

References

Bell, D. (2003). "Diversity's Distraction," *Columbia Law Review*, October, vol. 103, issue 6, pp. 1622–1633.

Peck, M. Scott (1993). *A World Waiting to be Born: Civility Rediscovered*, New York: Bantam Books.

Thomas, R. Roosevelt, Jr. (1991). Beyond Race and Gender: Unleashing the Power of Your Total Workforce by Managing Diversity, New York: AMA Publications.

Thomas, R. Roosevelt, Jr., and Woodruff, Marjorie I. (1999). Building a House of Diversity: A Fable About an Giraffe and an Elephant Offers New Strategies for Today's Workforce, New York: AMA Publications.

Thomas, D. A., and Ely, R. J. (1996). "Making Differences Matter," *Harvard Business Review*, September/October, vol. 74, issue 5, pp. 79–90.

5

Diversity: Ideas to Create Value in the Workplace

by Mario Ghiggino

Introduction

The merits of diversity, like many other concepts in business, have been discussed widely in the popular press. This chapter presents two basic ideas which managers may find useful as they reflect upon diversity within their organisations. The first idea or concept is that employees bring a diverse range of talents into organisations and the notion of "fit" to the business situation often calls for the successful match of these employees to the "right" jobs. The Agents Model may provide a useful means of considering the notion of "fit". The second concept introduces the notion of "ideas integration" instead of "ideas segregation" in which organisations are tapping into the rich knowledge resources of their work groups – in many cases located globally, throughout the world. The notion of effective listening is introduced as a cultural necessity to institutionalise the receptivity of new ideas. This chapter argues that receptivity of new ideas requires organisations to understand national cultural variations as one means of how employee values are shaped.

Fitting the profile: matching the right people to the right jobs

Business, like all other spectrums of activity, often boils down to whether temperaments and talents are best suited to the environment in which they find themselves. The Agents Model offers a guideline to matching the right business personality to the right situation. Having the right people, at the right place, at the right time is crucial for any organisation to survive and grow. However, how to evaluate companies' needs and assess personal skills in order to achieve this objective?

The current available literature mentions many distinct ways of analysing and describing organisations under different models, as well as assessing employees' uniqueness when evaluating their personality profile and behaviour matches with specific demands necessary to perform a certain activity within an organisation. Buckingham and Coffman (1999) in their book, *First, Break All the*

Rules: What the World's Greatest Managers Do Differently recommend using the following principles which I have summarized:

- Hire for talent (not experience).
- Define the goals.
- Focus on people's strengths (not their weaknesses).
- Find the right fit between strengths and structure.

The Concept of Agents

As a general rule, people can be categorised into three distinct groups: agents of creation, agents of continuity and agents of change. Figure 5.1 shows how these types of agents fit into a company's evolving life cycle.

Agents of creation are entrepreneurs, visionaries, people who start their own business within – or, most of the time – outside established organisations. These agents reply to the following question: "What is there to be invented or reinvented, to be created, to be discovered, to be done that has never been tried before?" They take a revolutionary stand – not agreeing with the status quo. They show focus, energy and commitment with their ideas. They are fast thinkers and equally fast decision-makers, determined to realise their vision, and they succeed as long as they are able to pursue and share this vision with people around. They might work based on a totally new business model or upon existing ones, reshaping them in a new reality.

When they have an idea they believe will work, they go for it, often relying on intuition. Agents of creation are usually intelligent, charismatic and individualistic characters who might almost be called "business artists", since

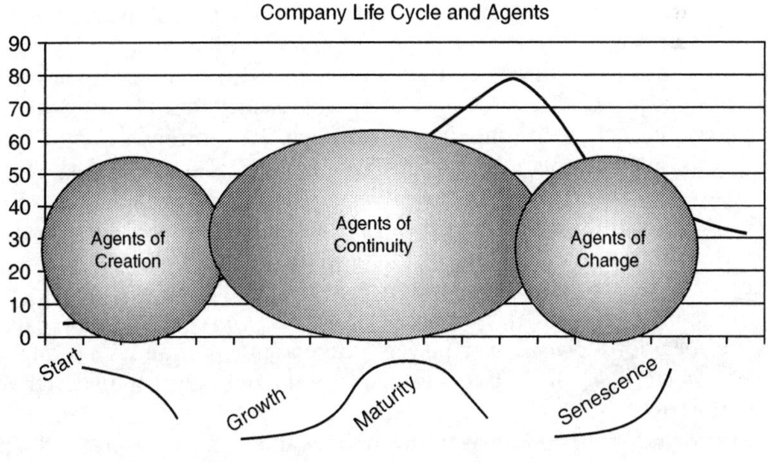

Figure 5.1 Three Agent Types within a Company's Life Cycle
Source: Author

they have a need to direct the show, sell their ideas and, of course, enjoy the spotlight. They are self-confident people who do not fear defeat, but do not like to lose; they like to say they are "ahead of theory" or "beyond explanation" – which they usually are. They are often obsessive people who breathe, dream, marry and love their business.

Agents of creation are often so passionately attached to their original idea that they might be unable to make an impartial assessment about their own company's business model. They look for and are surrounded by people willing to paddle under their orientation, and might not be able to tolerate criticism or realistic assessments of a situation which imply their idea was off track. Sometimes they run the risk of mixing loyalty with homogeneity and do not foster diversity. They also run the risk of being surrounded by adulators and flatterers.

Some of them – like Bill Gates, Anita Roddick, Richard Branson, Michael Dell, Henry Ford, Akio Morita and Pierre Omidyar – turn out to have winning ideas. However, there is a risk attached to running with their brainwave suggestions, since these are often under-researched and impulsive. In addition, agents of creation tend to pass the buck in the event of failure, usually looking for someone else to blame and unable to believe they themselves were mistaken. This might help to explain why 95% of US enterprises do not survive their fifth year! And the Internet's start-up statistics could be even worse.

Agents of continuity are the "real" executives. They are there to reply to the questions: "What has to be done?" and "How can this be done better?" They play the role of evolutionaries. Usually less charismatic than agents of creation, they comprise the big bulk of executives, spanning all positions at the company. They may be blindly obedient or have criticisms of the task at hand, but they ensure that things are put into place according to what has been defined by the agents of creation. They seldom question the company's vision, mission or strategy – at best, they might query an aspect of a particular plan. Nor would they ever voice their reservations at boardroom level. They are put in place to protect the agent of creation's ideas until they blossom and to prevent anyone "changing the seeds". They translate entrepreneurs' vision into action, put controls in place, optimise systems and operations, minimise costs, improve profitability, and manage the show. They are most comfortable with routine, norms, reports, organisation, smoothness and security. They are not sprinters, but stalwart long-distance plodders. Agents of continuity are less interested in innovation than in stability. They are happy to improve or expand on an existing strategy, but resist revolutionary changes. They are operations-focused team players, pushers and optimisers. They might not be strategically brilliant, but – teamed with the right entrepreneur – they can do the trick.

The third personality profile is the agent of change. The question to which they reply is: "What has to be changed now?" They are very similar to agents of creation, but they prefer to revamp and revise whole departments than create entirely new ones. They are seen as the insurrectionists. They might be as fast as agents of creation, but they are less obsessive and more receptive to input from others. Usually they are decathlonists – they know a little of everything, are highly adaptable and can bring diversity to the company.

Agents of change usually come from a small kernel within company. They are the skeptics, rebels, complainers, the nonconformists. They do not agree with the way things are done, and this disagreement can run from mild questioning to entrenched opposition. It is important, however, to listen carefully to their complaints before acting on their suggestions. Their protests could be motivated by a need for a raise in salary or an internal power struggle. Another way to check this is by gauging the complainers' functional activity. "Professional complainers" are generally lazy people, reluctant to shoulder a load of hard work that could be offloaded onto someone else if they are vocal enough in resisting.

Notwithstanding this, agents of change are usually intellectually active and can frequently present research to support their complaints. They are willing to find the data to back their arguments, and they are fact-and/or number-crunchers. They are usually the ones to point out that the budget will not support a proposed new computer system, or that the company's latest product is completely inappropriate to its market segment. They are keenly sensitive to timing, and usually make such comments at the moment of most impact.

Agents of change are not always positioned within the company. They might, for example, come as strategic consultants. In this case, they are particularly difficult to resist, since their observations carry the stamp of authority. Moreover, they might even be manipulated by someone inside the company who needs their strategic support.

Some top strategic consultants can be turned into agents of change by internal executives. IBM's CEO Lou Gerstner is one example. Others are executives who have the autonomy to change the rules of the game. These people are highly intelligent, analytical and passionate to put knowledge into practice. They constantly apply and adapt concepts in different ways, test hypotheses, create scenarios and reinvent the company. Lee Iacocca, Carlos Goshn and Mark Fields are good examples.

These profiles are not mutually exclusive – in fact, most people have elements of two (or all three) within their working style. The challenge is to identify which profile fits an employee or manager, and then decide where that person would fit best in the company structure. A few individuals have enough insight to combine all three of these profiles among their organisation in just the right way to effect dramatic and highly profitable results. Bill Gates and Akio Morita, for example, have re-invented their companies several times because they know how to manage growth and they are prepared to risk changing everything – even things that are working well!

How do these agents work together? Figure 5.2 expands on Figure 5.1 to show the interactions between agents by distances, areas of influence and

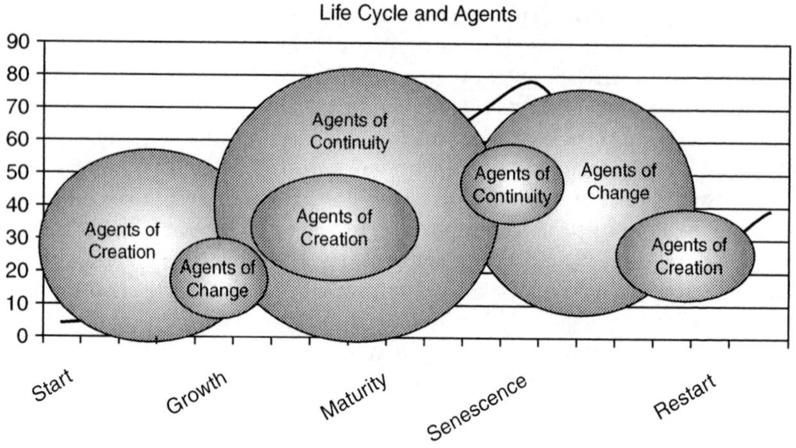

Figure 5.2 Agent Maximum Influence on Organisation's Life Cycle
Source: Author

overlaps. In general, people within a particular profile prefer to work with each other.

However, as the company expands and developments take place which necessitate internal shuffling, it is inevitable that different profiles will find themselves working side by side. In this case, there is a risk of conflict and perceptive managers should be alert to irreconcilable clashes between personalities which can become very destructive, to the company as well as these individuals' morale, if left unchecked.

If this happens, the organisation is in danger of stagnation. It could find itself jammed with unproductive channels in which the inability to communicate leads to excessive bureaucracy, internal politics, paperwork, tension and de-motivation. IBM, Xerox, Sears, Ford, GM, GE and Unilever have all suffered from this symptom. Like a myocardial infarction, the company's veins become clogged and nothing seems to run smoothly.

Agents of change are the first ones to realise that something is wrong in the environment, but they are often not heard because they are outnumbered or those around them are simply too demoralised to act on their advice. However, if they are successful in showing what is happening and top management is able to listen, the company has the chance to take measures to unclog its arteries – either by instituting the necessary procedures or by calling in external help.

Table 5.1 provides some fascinating insights into the dynamics which govern the working relationships of the different profiles. It might also help to explain why consultants have so many difficulties when they decide to join a start-up company! They enter determined to challenge, gather data, analyse and shake

Table 5.1 Working Relationship Characteristics of Different Agent Profiles

	Agents of Creativity	Agents of Continuity	Agents of Change
Agents of Creativity	+Alike at the beginning −Cannot leave the kindergarten +Creation power +Revolution +Daring, bravery	+Necessary for the sake of continuity −Enforcing −"Imposters" −Creativity-killers	−Conflicting positions −Complainers −Too rational −Need strategy
Agents of Continuity	+Structure −Lack of freedom	−Bureaucracy −Too much organisation −Splinter +Foreseeable +Stable +Structured	−Complainers −Risk to stability +Solution to company problems +Diversity
Agents of Change	−Dreamers −Short-term driven −Short-sighted, fanatics	−Bureaucrats −Conformists	−Information paralysis −Analysis paralysis +Strategic thinking

Source: Author

up structures – only to find themselves in a company where they have to paddle to keep their heads above water, with no time for discussion, no time to think, no time to analyse or draw strategies. That is also why it is so boring for entrepreneurial minds to work within a big and stable organisation: they do not have the free space to create, their cash-flow can no longer be written on the back of a paper napkin and they need to follow strict controlling rules. That is precisely the same reason why genuine agents of continuity cannot invade anyone else's areas: they neither have the creative mind as entrepreneurs, nor the aggressively challenging mind-set of an agent of change; they are there simply to make things work.

Table 5.1 also shows why it is so important to have the right people in the right place at the right time in a company. For example, while agents of continuity are bureaucrats and conformists for agents of change, agents of change are complainers for agents of continuity. Healthy companies are the ones where all agents are represented in the right proportions at all times. But what are the "right proportions"? This is not an easy question to answer and much depends on the creative element of management, which has to sense and predict what will be good for the company.

What can be said to help as a general guideline is an assessment of where the department, business unit, company or industry is in its life-cycle and, from there, to decide what is best. Is the company a new venture in a new industry?

If so, it will certainly need very enthusiastic people to be highly motivated by the entrepreneur's ideas and paddle along happily. Is the company forming a new level of management? If so, it is necessary to put people in place to build up the right structures. Is the business sluggish, or has it failed to keep pace with the latest industry developments? If so, an agent of change is necessary.

This business model does not only apply to companies and organisations, but to entire sectors and industries. Agents of creation must be in place to reap margins and create the appropriate structures.

Equally so, agents of continuity are necessary to milk all the possible benefits, while continuously improving and optimising operations. And agents of change are essential in order to act quickly and decisively in the event of a sudden problem or unforeseen development. All three profiles play an indispensable role in the composite picture of a healthy, functioning entity.

For organisations, however, even more important than achieving the right ratio between the agent profiles is ensuring that the overall structure is sufficiently responsive to the changes and interactions within it. In order to determine the appropriate ratios, the analyst must first know the scope of the entity subject to change, which point in its life-cycle it has reached and, finally, which point its related structures have reached in their own cycles.

For example, if the entity subject to analysis is a business unit, it is important to know to what point it has already developed, as well as how this is affected by the point the entire organisation (and the industry) has reached. If the problem being experienced is restricted to the business unit, then it is easier to deduce that agents of change will be most effective in solving it. However, if the whole organisation – or, indeed, the entire industry – is experiencing the same problem, then it would probably be better to call in agents of creation to make sweeping, fundamental revisions which will use new and radical options. On the other hand, if the problem is a temporary reaction a situation which can be rectified, then an agent of continuity would be able to solve it without up-ending the entire business structure and taking unnecessary risks.

Finally, it is important to bear in mind that it is much more costly for a company to change than to create. Revamping a sluggish business is like overhauling an old car or making a very old and rusty aircraft fly. It takes time, patience, fuel and stress. And it will not change the basic nature of the company or industry – it will simply repair or redirect blocked channels within it. As Peters (1994) describes in his book *The Pursuit of Wow!*, this was what inspired Percy Barnevik to restructure ABB in small and competitive units – the attempt to keep the innovative fire burning forever, with constant vibrancy and energetic interaction.

Having examined the agent concept, how can it be applied in a practical way? The first thing that must be determined is: "Is this a viable model to correlate entities and people?" If, for example, some names mentioned in the "List of 25 Rising Stars – Global Leaders for the Next Generation", published in *Fortune* (Powell *et al.*, 2001) are taken as an indicator, it becomes evident that at the most successful new ventures around the world, these "rising stars" are the best fit for the proper task (related to company's life cycle). They know what to do, they know how to do, and they know which talents they would need in order to achieve their businesses' commitments. The reason they succeeded so dramatically in their respective fields of endeavour was that they were perfectly positioned to use their individual talents to best effect. Either their particular skills were identified and harnessed correctly by perceptive managements, who realised what could be gained from doing so, or they themselves were aware of the environments best suited to them, and took measures to find or create those settings.

Another simple "feet-on-the-ground" example can be taken from a small start-up company. At the beginning of the start-up's life-cycle a decision is taken to hire an assistant to work in marketing and sales, as well as help with operational office issues – and, in addition, any new and unexpected issues that might crop up. In short, in a start-up company, roles are very loosely defined and interchangeable. Each employee must be flexible but, at the same time, determined, disciplined, organised and able to paddle with the team to make things happen.

Let us say two candidates present themselves for the job: a shy 22-year-old Finnish 100 m sprinter, with a green belt in karate, who is highly organised and disciplined (as her sporting achievements attest to), with almost no working experience – and a 29-year-old outspoken Canadian girl with widely diverse experience, having worked in many different environments and activities, ranging from homeless people in Ottawa to travel agencies in New York.

The first impression from the CVs and level of activity would seem to suggest that the Canadian girl is more suitable for the position. However, during the interview, both candidates can be assessed using the Agents Model. Knowing where the company is in its life-cycle, knowing the current team strengths and weaknesses, it is easy to work out what is really required: someone organised and disciplined, but who is also energetic and willing to have fun within the environment. As a result, the Finnish girl is appointed – and turns out to be the correct choice for the position.

The Agents Model, like all other theories, is simply an abstraction and cannot satisfy Cartesian requirements of right and wrong. There is a margin for error and experimentation within it, and there is no definite time or format that can be applied as a universal principle. It is important that companies never make decisions arbitrarily by this (or any other) model, since – ultimately – working relationships can never be forced or manipulated. In fact, the Agents Model might be most valuable in helping managers and business leaders understand how and why certain things work in certain ways within a company, and in offering a possible explanation for why promising young executives fail to thrive in certain structures, why entrepreneurs sometimes do not succeed, and why certain individuals flourish or flounder in their jobs.

Learning to listen: beating ideas segregation in the workplace

Many companies nowadays express concern about ethnic/demographic/biometric diversity issues. Yet, at the same time, they disregard one of the most damaging forms of discrimination: ideas segregation. "Ideas segregation" is the opposite of accepting diversification as part and parcel of a company's repository of knowledge. This refusal to acknowledge or respond to diversity manifests itself in discriminatory comments, habits, actions and behaviours towards others. Respect and receptiveness to new ideas, regardless of who they come from, are key to tapping into the repository of knowledge any social organisation carries with it.

In the business world, the need to encourage and manage diversity of ideas is a cornerstone of successful human relations practice; it indicates humility, tolerance, objectivity, creativity and emotional maturity, understanding and self-knowledge in business leaders, and an awareness that the success of the company draws directly on its interaction with those who comprise it.

Despite the hefty budgets corporations and governments dedicate to diversity management programmes, discrimination is still very much in evidence. Recent research conducted by Kochan *et al.* (2003)[1] on American corporations revealed that the effects of race and gender diversity and organisational performance depend on how well a number of intervening group processes (communications, leadership, conflict resolution, etc.) are managed and on several aspects of the larger organisational culture, business strategy, and the demographic make-up of management.

> On the basis of these results, we suggest the need for going beyond the simple "business case" rhetoric of today which would have some believe that just recruiting more diverse employees will automatically result in better business performance. Instead, we suggest that diversity is a reality in today's customer base and workforce. The challenge is both to attract a diverse workforce and to build the skills and organisational capabilities needed to learn – and benefit – from this diversity.
>
> (Quoted from home page of T. Kochan – IWER.)

Hofstede study

While working for IBM from 1967–1973, Dr Geert Hofstede conducted a worldwide study on how values in the workplace are influenced by culture ("culture" here meaning "the collective mental programming of the people in an environment"). Subsequent studies performed by him and his colleagues included a myriad of different behaviour groups in order to validate his early study. Consequently, Hofstede developed a model based on five dimensions which are used to differentiate cultures: power distance (PDI); individualism (IDV); masculinity (MAS); uncertainty avoidance (UAI); and long-term orientation (LTO).

According to Hofstede (1991: 28), power-distance "is the extent to which less powerful members of institutions and organisations within a country expect and accept that power is distributed unequally", while individualism Hofstede (1991: 52) says:

> . . . focuses on the degree to which the society reinforces individual or collective, achievement and interpersonal relationships. A high individualism ranking indicates that individuality and individual rights are paramount within the society. Individuals in these societies may tend to form a larger number of looser relationships. A low individualism ranking typifies societies of a more collectivist nature, with close ties between individuals. These cultures reinforce extended families and collectives, where everyone takes responsibility for fellow members of their group.

In arguing the case for idea diversity, two of Hofstede's dimensions – power-distance and individualism – can be used to compare cultures and the different levels of idea acceptance within and between them. It is also important to examine the degree of business success achieved by these cultures, as well as their adaptability in times of crises. Demographic *versus* behavioural marketing concepts also lend a new perspective to this analysis.

Much has been written about resource-based theory and knowledge management, and both disciplines straddle the crucial area of diversity management within social and corporate structures. Basically, having the right people in the right place, at the right time, with the right knowledge and generating value-adding ideas, is paramount for the success of any organisation. Managers need to build organisational capabilities in order to retrieve and explore knowledge and talent resources hidden within their diverse workforce, thereby elevating the issue of racial barriers to one of multi-cultural strength and potential.

Although there is not a strong enough statistical correlation among these indices to explain the success or failure of any social organisation, it is possible to infer that wealth and well-being are related to Hofstede's dimensions and might illuminate certain dynamics of inter-cultural relationships (see Figure 5.3). When Hofstede's indices are plotted against GDP2 and HDI, it can be concluded that, in general, countries and organisations which foster and tolerate new ideas – represented by individuality and power distance dimensions – are more successful in economic (GDP) and welfare (HDI) terms.[2] It is also interesting to note that 18 out of the 20 highest-ranked countries in HDI are the ones in which individualism is high and power distance is low.

What these countries share is a vision of a democratic society based on strong egalitarian values and respect for the individual. This does not mean to say that there are no discriminatory tensions between groups struggling to defend their own interests, but the extent and frequency of such tensions are controlled – and, to some extent, subdued – by democratic mechanisms.

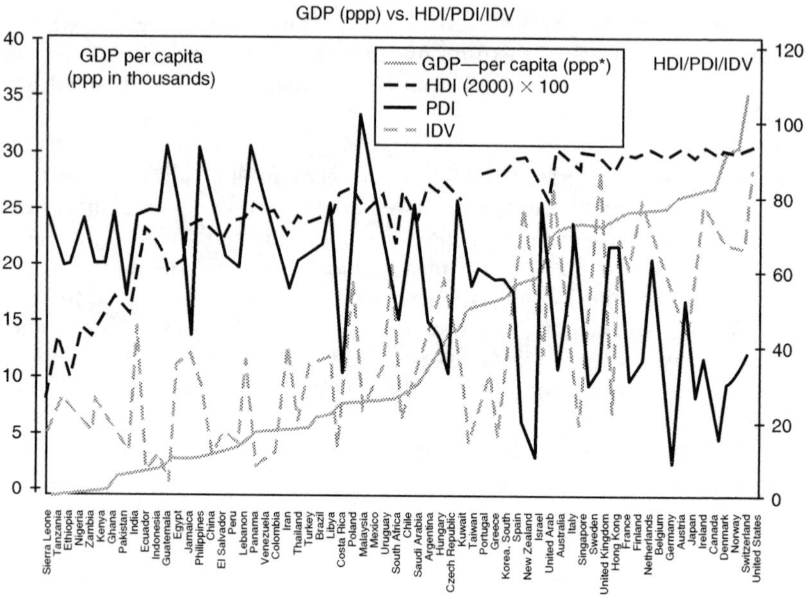

Figure 5.3 Summary of National GDP and Hofstede Dimensions
Source: Designed by Author using the following data sources: (CIA, 2002; Hofstede, 2003; UNDP, 2003)

In low power-distance/high individualism countries, this common vision is negotiated among interest groups (see the Dutch "Polder Model", for example),[3] whereas ruling groups impose their vision on others in high power-distance/low individualistic societies (such as dictatorships).

The effectiveness of a low power-distance/high-individualistic society relies on the balance of power and self-expression among different clusters, and this is provided by democratic institutions and efficient communication among members of a society. Low power-distance (egalitarian) and individualistic (respectful of the individual) behaviours towards others within a social organisation actually raises its level of well-being and economic growth.

Corporations as organic systems: need for value alignment

The lessons learnt from social and governmental structures can be applied to the microcosms of corporations. Every individual within a company holds his or her own set of values, which aligns with or challenges the values of others in the same company. As groups of people find common values and create clusters of affinity, management needs to introduce an overarching vision and framework of rules and limitations which can mould and guide them, leading to greater cohesion and co-operation. If this does not happen, different clusters will become increasingly insular, resenting and distrusting other clusters, and unwilling to share ideas and values with them. Such factionalism within a company polarises the workforce, effectively curtailing the possibility of real interaction and shared commitment to a common goal.

Inevitably, stronger personalities within the different clusters assume leadership/spokesperson roles within them, further alienating the groups from management and sowing further dissent among diverse individuals. It is a vicious – and costly – cycle, which no company can afford. Worse, it leads to the stagnation of imagination, impetus and intellectual receptiveness. The weaker the internal culture of democratic institutions within a company, the worse its level of communication and the greater the risk of uncontrolled, unaligned behaviours from diverse clusters. Ultimately, the victim is the company's vision.

In order to institute values which encourage shared ideas among diverse groups, however, managers need to avoid simplifying employee behaviours as homogeneous. Instead, they should sensitise themselves to different cultural values and learn to contextualise behaviours within them. Like any other organic system, corporations are dynamic entities with interactive components (in this case, human beings). Understanding this interaction is key to comprehending people's different needs, without rationalising or assuming their motives and aspirations.

The challenge facing managers is to align values and goals along the whole social structure, linking these to organisational development rather than to gender or race. However, in organisations where there is high power-distance – and therefore little respect for human beings as individuals – the corporate culture engenders fear and suspicion. As a result, employees become complacent, preferring to silently accept strategies and proposals the organisation puts forward to them, rather than risk possible reprisals by expressing their own opinions.

How, then, can a better environment be created in which ideas are encouraged, generated and shared, regardless of who expresses them?

The following steps are good starting points:

(1) Know yourself and where you are, have your own mission, know your personal values, culture, characteristics and objectives in order to relate better to others around you. Security within one's own identity is a prerequisite to seeing diversity not as a threat, but as a growth opportunity. It is also important to get to know your company's values, culture, objectives and expectations of you and your cluster.
(2) Communicate on all levels, sharing your values and objectives with other people, showing respect for and interest in their approach to issues and remaining open to what you can learn from them.
(3) Let people think! Louis Gerstner, of IBM, once observed: "We can teach employees how to run a machine or develop a marketing plan. What's

killing us is having to teach them to read, compute . . . and to think." (Jones, 1996: 1B) Encourage people to be enterprising, resourceful and self-confident by listening to their views, taking their ideas seriously and responding to their suggestions with respect.

(4) Learn to value diversity: it represents wealth, solidarity and healthy growth.

The need for action

The ILO (International Labour Organisation) recently published a report entitled *Time for Equality at Work* (ILO, 2003) in which it warned that failing to tackle "widening socio-economic inequalities" in the business world is not only a "waste of human talent", but could have "disastrous effects on national social cohesion, political stability and, hence, growth" in the future.

The warning is valid: segregation ultimately results in quantifiable losses for any human society, be it a country, institution or company. Business can no longer afford to ignore cultural diversity issues, or relegate them to abstruse human resources departments to manage. Diversity is potentially the strongest determinant of growth or destruction within a company. By harnessing its wealth of ideas and tapping into its potential resources, organisations are investing in their own future. As ecologists have long known, overall balance within a system can only be sustained if every living being within it contributes to its functioning. Even the smallest and most easily overlooked element is crucial. The whole is never greater than the sum of its parts.

Notes

1 Thomas A. Kochan is George M. Bunker Professor of Management at the MIT Sloan School of Management. In 1993 he was appointed to President Clinton's Commission on the Future of Worker/Management Relations, which investigated methods to improve productivity and global competitiveness of the American workplace. From 1992–1995, he served as president of the International Industrial Relations Association. His Website is: http://ccs.mit.edu/ebb/peo/koc.html

2 GDP2 means Gross Domestic Product – purchasing power parity; HDI refers to UN's Human Development Index. Prepared by various organisations including IMF and the World Bank.

3 The Dutch polder model has become famous in the world. The polder model is the term used for the Dutch model of consensus in which employers, syndicates and the government meet with each other to make agreements about labour. The model of consensus goes back to the Middle Ages, when farmers, noblemen, cities and others needed to collaborate in order to build dykes in order to keep out the water.

References

Buckingham, M. and Coffman, C. (1999). *First, Break All the Rules: What the World's Greatest Managers Do Differently*. New York: Simon & Schuster.

CIA (2002). *World Fact Book*. US Government – CIA. Retrieved December, 2004, from the World Wide Web: http://www.cia.gov/cia/publications/factbook/

Hofstede, G. (1991). *Cultures and Organizations: Software of the Mind*. London: McGraw-Hill International.

Hofstede, G. (2003). *Creating Cultural Competence – Cultural Dimensions*. ITIM. Retrieved April, 2005, from the World Wide Web: http://www.geert-hofstede.com/hofstede_dimensions.php

ILO (2003). *Time for Equality at Work*. Paper presented at the International Labour Organisation 91st International Conference, Geneva.

Jones, D. (1996, March 27). Employers say it's the lack of education, stupid. *USA Today*, pp. 1B.

Kochan, T., Bezrukova, K., Ely, R., Jackson, S., Joshi, A., Jehn, K., Leonard, J., Levine, D., and Thomas, D. (2003). *The Effects of Diversity on Business Performance: Report of the Diversity Research Network*. Institute for Work and Employment Research (IWER). Retrieved, from the World Wide Web: http://mitsloan.mit.edu/iwer/a-main.php

Peters, T. (1994). *The Pursuit of Wow!* New York: Macmillan.

Powell, W., Tomlinson, R., Nee, E., Fox, J., Murphy, C., Stipp, D., Schlosser, J., Taylor, A., Guyon, J., Serwer, A., Rohwer, J., O'Reilly, B., Roth, D., and Sellers, P. (2001, May 14). List of 25 Rising Stars – Global Leaders for the Next Generation. *Fortune, 143*, 140–153.

UNDP (2003). *Human Development Report – Millennium Development Goals: A compact among nations to end human poverty*. United Nations Development Programme – Human Development Report Office. Retrieved April, 2005, from the World Wide Web: http://hdr.undp.org/reports/global/2003/

6
New Frontiers for Diversity and Inclusion

by Tony Burnett and Simon Kettleborough

We have it in our power to begin the world all over again.
A situation to the present hath not appeared since the days of Noah until now.
The birthday of a new world is at hand.

Tom Paine, 1776

Introduction

Since the late 1990s, we have seen a new wave of values-driven business people wake up to the issues of Diversity and Inclusion. We realise that now more than ever, we have an unprecedented opportunity to create the kind of societies and organisations in which we all want to live and work. These are societies and organisations where values are more important than skin colour and where all people have the opportunity to succeed on merit. Environments where being British can be as relevant for Black people as it is for White people, where people are selected because of the gifts they bring and promoted based on what they do and, more importantly, how they behave when they are doing it.

Although oft misused by well-meaning leaders and over-burdened HR managers, the words 'Diversity' and 'Inclusion' are forcing their way into our business rhetoric. Indeed, Diversity and Inclusion are sometimes viewed as synonymous in Britain and Europe, yet our experience tells us that the impact of each as strategic imperatives is markedly different. Diversity may increase the representation of minorities and help achieve ethnicity or gender targets (a practice currently *de rigueur* amongst public sector institutions in Britain) but it will rarely address the societal and organisational factors that lead to the exclusion of many people. Indeed despite the dogged pursuit of diversity in the UK, the London bombings of the 7th July 2005 suggest that some groups still do not feel included. Further, the events in London may even suggest that diversity as a concept has failed. Inclusion may be the solution.

Diversity is often a game of percentages, a game where the rules state that organisations must frantically hire visibly different people in order to hit targets or quotas. Inclusion takes the journey further. Inclusion is about creating environments where all people can prosper and progress irrespective of race, colour, gender, physical ability, age, religion, sexual orientation or belief.

For the doubters and sceptics (of whom there are many), this sounds like a distant dream. For us, this is our *raison d'être*, the drive behind our company and the reason why it is time to stamp on some myths that shackle the progress in this most critical area of business and society.

Myth 1 – Global governance supports a level playing field

In recent times the plight of the Developing World has risen up the political agenda driven by a greater public awareness, due in part to the publicity achieved by high profile celebrities. Left-wing British broadsheet newspapers are packed with stirring articles about the responsibility the Western World has to the Developing World and about the need for an inclusive society. The same newspapers are also bursting with stories about a Britain overrun with asylum seekers and refugees. What they often fail to mention is that migration is absolutely necessary to support the continued growth of the UK economy.

In many ways, Black people in the Western World are fortunate. Whilst they may have many issues, few of them are about sheer survival. However, we have to ask how has the world come to this? How can it be that the wealth on our planet is so unevenly distributed? When you look hard at the issues, the reasons are glaringly apparent. We have a global governance structure that is designed to make developed countries richer at the expense of developing nations. Many people feel that the WTO, World Bank and IMF are puppets of the USA, itself a global superpower that seems to see Planet Earth and Planet America as the same entity. An ineffective and iniquitous approach to global trade, particularly in respect of agriculture, does much to perpetuate the vast chasm between the 'haves' and 'have-nots'.

Taste not, want not

Agriculture is often the main source of income for developing countries, yet due to the subsidies the USA and the EU pay to their farmers, developing nations can often buy Western produce cheaper than their own. The result is widespread unemployment and poverty amongst farmers in developing nations. Recent dialogue between developed nations regarding agricultural subsidies has once again failed to reach any conclusion that will impact positively the plight of farmers in developing countries.

We are told that genetically modified crops will be the salvation of the developing world. Unfortunately, this is seen by many as a myth, as corporations are busy filing for and, in some cases, being awarded patents on basic foods that have been in our staple diets for centuries. Plant varieties have become legally protected intellectual properties and patents have been taken out on the main food crops – rice, wheat, maize, soya and sorghum. Four big companies – Monsanto, Syngenta, Bayer and DuPont – own most of these patents. This may lead to farmers in developing nations having to pay corporations like Monsanto and DuPont for the privilege of growing their own crops. Is this truly creating a level playing field?

Trade not aid

A further disconnect between global governance and inclusion surfaces around the issue of financial aid for developing nations. Free-market capitalism Anglo-American style is *the* aspirational economic model for those countries that have not already embraced it as their own. When a Third World country looks for aid, it is usually only granted with a string of trade conditions attached. One of the common conditions is access to markets for foreign corporations and the privatisation of state-owned companies.

Many countries have seen the devastating effect this can have on both the economy and also upon the labour force. In our practice, as we travel around the world, we have heard and observed first hand many of the impacts of globalisation. For example, in Latin America, after the privatisation of state owned firms, labour unions have been decimated with their members falling dramatically. Under the global rubric of "efficiency" and "competitiveness", countries like Mexico, the Dominican Republic and Chile have experienced significant increases in unemployment, infrastructure service discontinuities for water and power, and less than adequate health care provision.

The ironically named "Free Trade" economic model is seen, by many, as a model for disaster, and it has a huge impact on the lives of the most vulnerable people. Those of us who have food in the refrigerator and clothes on our back, a roof over our head and a place to sleep are richer than 75% of this world. Those of us who have money in the bank, in our wallet, and spare change in a dish someplace we are among the top 8% of the world's wealthy. Exclusion of so many by so few has to stop.

This is not about Diversity, as we know that our world is already extremely diverse, this is an issue of Inclusion. Free market capitalism and the global governance associated with it are exclusive vehicles; juggernauts that run down and obliterate the majority of people on this planet. Some things should surely remain the property of all people; they are instead for sale to the highest bidding corporation.

Myth 2 – It's about race . . . and it's black and white

Out of all the dimensions of Inclusion, race is one of the most difficult areas for White men to understand, simply because it has never been an issue for them. Those White people who bother to comprehend the vagaries of ethnicity (and, frankly, there are plenty who do not) are constantly faced with the stark reality that they have rarely experienced bias emanating from the colour of their skin. Without this experience, it is only an unquenchable thirst for learning, coupled with Daniel Golemanesque levels of empathy that can inspire any kind of insight into what it feels like to be compromised because of colour. Even then, White people are hampered by the eternal handicap of a White view of the world (White consciousness) that has been engrained into them, and the world, since birth.

The reason for this goes back half a millennium. The White man has ruled the House of Race since the Chinese relinquished control and ever since, being White has provoked both obsequiousness and resentment from every other human on the planet. White people are mostly oblivious to the global passport their skin colour bestows upon them. It does not matter in which corner of the world they find themselves, White people have a curiously blind insensitivity to the implications of skin colour. Martin Jacques, of the London School of Economics (LSE), recently commented that he and his Malaysian-Indian wife moved from London to Hong Kong, believing that his wife would feel more included within this global melting-pot of ethnicity. Instead, he was treated with even greater deference, and his wife's understanding of local culture and language was treated with racist contempt. When this is the behaviour we encounter, it is little surprise that White folk are less than switched on to the issues and challenges of colour than they could be.

There is little doubt that White men are in denial (some consciously and other unconsciously) about the impact of racism in our global society and organisations. After all, the dominant group in any societal construct is unlikely to see, much less admit, its own biases and blind spots. However, as the White view of the world is challenged, so the White population is slowly addressing its shortcomings, lack of understanding and shortsightedness. These shortcomings are not a reason to brand White men the enemy, for they are wrestling with prejudices, beliefs and values that are as old as humanity itself. Given time, the world expects them to stop underplaying the presence of racism and to start raising and discussing the issue, as it's an issue that represents a clear and present danger to the future of global Inclusion.

Myth 3 – The best person should get the job

A common question, usually posed by white men, is 'shouldn't the best person for the job get the job?' To an extent, we sympathise with this argument, however it really depends upon your definition of the 'best person'. Taking Britain as an example, no-one can tell us that in a country where 8% of the population is ethnic minority and over 50% of the population is female (Office of National Statistics, 2001), the 98 White men who are Chief Executives of our top 100 companies (Singh and Vinnicombe, 2004) happen to be the best people for the job? In some instances it may be true, however, in many cases they are where they are because of an exclusive education system that values class and wealth above skills and ability.

'Best man for the job' in our society means those who have been privileged enough to reach the start line of the race. Most Black, poor and disabled children never even get to the track. Inclusion is not about reverse discrimination, it is about reversing discrimination; levelling the playing field so all people have access to opportunities.

Myth 4 – Inclusion is a moral issue, not a commercial issue

> Our success depends entirely on our ability to understand diverse consumers' needs. A diverse organisation will out-think and out-perform a homogeneous organisation every single time. I am putting particular importance on increasing the representation of women and minorities in leadership at all levels.
>
> Alan Lafley, CEO Proctor and Gamble (Skapinke, 2001)

Show me the money

Arguably one of the most important aspects of Inclusion often overlooked by organisations is the business case. In other words, how will investment in this area impact the performance of the organisation? Notwithstanding the fact that we are passionate about our business and we do the work we do because we believe in it, we also realise that any action taken by organisations has one of three motivations:

(1) They have to do it, usually for legal or other reasons which threaten the business.
(2) They recognise their moral obligation – this is usually driven by the personal values and commitment of a senior leader.
(3) They see the business benefit – this is often the hardest to prove but will give any initiative the best long-term chance of success. In our experience, if you can show the leadership of an organisation how Inclusion impacts the bottom line, then they are signed up to taking action.

The business case is different for every organisation, but every organisation has one. Most focus on the internal aspects of the business case for Inclusion such as recruitment, development of staff and the transfer of knowledge and learning around the organisation. However, a good business case is just as clearly linked to the way a business operates in the external environment with its customers and suppliers, as well as its ability to do business on a global stage (see Figure 6.1).

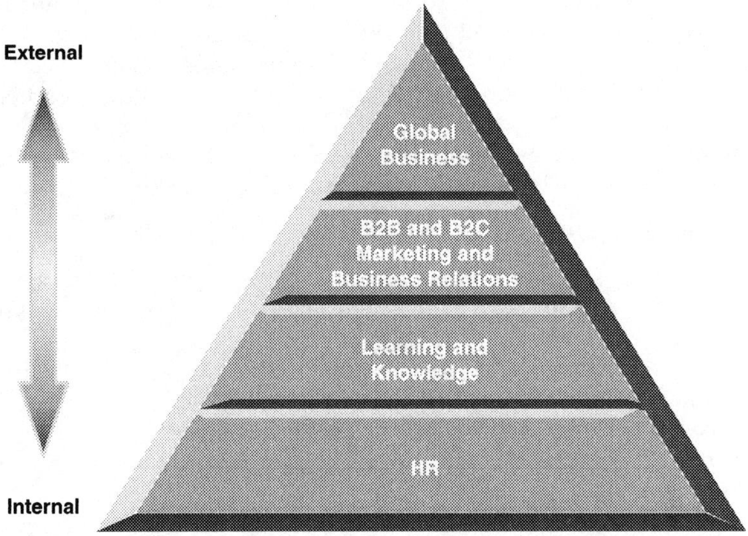

Figure 6.1 The Business Case Pyramid

A robust business case will also help organisations overcome one of the main barriers to Inclusion, which is the apathy of the majority population, usually White male and often in middle management. This group is often indifferent or even hostile to Inclusion, not because it does not value it but because this group does not understand Inclusion, and therefore sees it as a threat. The business case clearly shows everyone why Inclusion is as important for the 'majority' as it is for Black people, women, gay and lesbian people and people with disabilities.

One of the stark business case issues we will face in the next ten years is the ageing population. Quite simply, Europe is getting older. Between now and 2010 we will have approximately 15 million more 'over forties' and 15 million fewer 'under forties' (Employers Forum on Age, 2005). This will significantly impact the way organisations manage their employees and serve their customers. Age is not a Black or White issue, or a disabled issue or a gender issue, it is an issue for everyone. After all, we are all getting old.

Race is again hitting the headlines in Britain. Extreme right-wing parties, and even moderate right wingers, are citing the increasing numbers of asylum seekers and refugees as reasons why the White population is experiencing poor public service levels and soaring taxation. The shocking events of the 7th July 2005 have served as a licence for many to turn the race clock back by 20 years in terms of how race is debated, and the language that is acceptable when engaging in such a debate. What the press does not share, however, is any educated commentary around the business case for race. For example, Indian boys and girls are our highest performing groups in primary and secondary education, and their success is continued when it comes to employment and career advancement (Office of National Statistics, 2001). We also know that boys from Caribbean descent are less likely to achieve ultimate success in the education system, despite being amongst the top performing groups at age seven (Muir and Smithers, 2004). In other words, education is inclusive for some, but not for others.

Hole in the workforce

The hard business case facts about race and immigration across Europe are simple. People are living longer and having fewer children, meaning that the working age population of Europe will decrease significantly over the next 20 years. The only groups that are bucking the trends are second generation Asians and Africans, who are younger. As this trend develops, our workplaces and societies will see more faces-of-colour. The challenge for societies and governments is how we become inclusive so all people are treated with the same respect and dignity as one another.

Given these trends, many European countries will have significant shortages of labour over the next 20 years. Realistically, the only way these shortages can be filled is by labour from outside the EU. That means immigration. The most recent members to sign-up to the EU will undoubtedly fill some of this surplus, but more talent will also come from outside the Union.

The exclusion zone

Britain and Europe can address potential labour shortages by ensuring all groups have the opportunity to succeed. Many people now believe that women enjoy the same opportunities as men. Unfortunately, women are still paid, on average, one quarter less than men. They are still far less likely to progress to Board level positions in Britain and across Europe, and are still subject to unacceptable levels of harassment in the workplace (Equal Opportunities Commission, 2005).

People with disabilities are still largely ignored, despite accounting for around 10% of the UK population. When able and willing to work (and most are), they are five times more likely to be unemployed than any other group in the UK. With only 7% of disabled people needing wheelchairs and 70% of disabled people not born with a disability (Disability Rights Commission, 2005), organisations are blatantly ignoring a richly talented group of individuals.

So, our population is decreasing and people are having fewer children. We are living longer and therefore more likely to become disabled. Yet still we live in a Europe that provides an assault course for those professionals who are not White, young middle-class, able-bodied men. The statistics prove the case. Notwithstanding the tragedy of this message from both a moral and a legal perspective, commercially, it's a mindset that is costing our economies billions.

Myth 5 – Inclusion boils down to good HR Management and some training

Organisations that are really serious about Inclusion take a systemic approach. Inclusion is not just about awareness training, it needs to address all areas and tackle the internal (employee) issues as well as the external (customer/supplier) interface. The organisation-wide systemic approach needed for success is the reason we implore organisations to separate the Inclusion function from HR. In some organisations, HR processes and practices that are sometimes exclusive can compromise Inclusion.

There are four enablers that must be put in place for an organisation to accept Inclusion:

- *Get leadership buy in,* with a strong, robust business case. If leaders see that Inclusion is a key business imperative, it will be much easier for them to get buy in from the majority population.
- *Grow your culture,* by creating the internal environment where all people can flourish. This is where good training plays a major role, but organisations must be clear about why you are training people and the desired training outcomes. This is not measured with 'happy sheets' at the end of a workshop; it's about what happens differently in the organisation as a result of the training.
- *Have inclusive values,* making sure they spell out how people should expect to be treated in your organisation. Review performance against the values and take action to reward good behaviour, whilst clearly penalising unacceptable behaviour without exception. Non-values driven behaviour needs to be addressed at the most senior leaders, as well as on the 'shop floor'.
- *Get the dialogue right,* providing clear messages about Inclusion to the organisation with consistent dialogue. Remember, it's not Inclusion if briefings constitute merely sharing and celebrating the percentage of Black people who now work for the organisation. If your communication creates fear rather than opportunity, you turn off the very people you need to make change happen.

> Dad once looked down at an assembly line of women and thought 'these are all like my own mom – they have kids, homes to take care of, people who need them'. It motivated him to work hard to give them a better life because he saw his mom in all of them. That's how it all begins – with fundamental respect and empathy.
>
> Bob Galvin, CEO speaking of his father, founder of Motorola
> (Pearl Academy, 2005)

References

Disability Rights Commission (2005). Retrieved November 2005, from the World Wide Web: http://www.drc-gb.org/

Employers Forum on Age (2005). *Age: The Facts*. Retrieved November 2005, from the World Wide Web: http://www.efa.org.uk/age/business

Equal Opportunities Commission (2005). *Sex and Power – Who Runs Britain?* EOC, January 2005.

Jacques, M. (2003). 'The Global Hierarchy of Race', *The Guardian*, September 20th, 2003, URL: http://www.guardian.co.uk/print/0,3858,4757714-103677,00.html, accessed on March 30th, 2006.

Muir, Hugh and Smithers, Rebecca (2004). 'Black boys betrayed by racist school system', *The Guardian*, Tuesday September 7th, 2004, Retrieved February 2006, from the World Wide Web: http://education.guardian.co.uk/raceinschools/story/0,,1433024, 00.html

Office of National Statistics (2001). *Census 2001*. Retrieved November 2005, from the World Wide Web: http://www.statistics.gov.uk

Paine, Thomas (1776). *Common Sense-Appendix*. Retrieved February 2006, from World Wide Web: http://www.bartleby.com/133/5.html

Pearl Academy (2005). Retrieved November 2005, from the World Wide Web: http://www.pearlacademy.com/consultant/archives05.htm

Singh, Val and Vinnicombe, Susan (2004). *The Female FTSE Report*, Centre for Developing Women Business Leaders, Cranfield University-Bedfordshire, UK: Cranfield School of Management.

Skapinker, Michael (2001). *Proctor and Gamble Promote Diversity*. London: Financial Times, February 6th.

7

Applying Burlesque Rhetoric to Create Social Change

by Jennifer Kam and Joanna Eidsmore

Introduction

This paper focuses on three articles written in response to clothing company Abercrombie & Fitch's new t-shirt line, which depicted Asian American caricatures that promoted negative stereotypes. The company removed the t-shirts from stores after receiving an overwhelming number of calls and e-mails from predominately Asian American college students. Although Abercrombie & Fitch took the t-shirts off the shelves, students and Asian organizations protested against the company, demanding more action to ensure that a similar event would not occur. In particular, this chapter first concentrates on the ways in which three college students use Burke's (1984: 4) concept of burlesque humor in their articles. Next, we address how the rhetors use burlesque argumentation as a tool to save face. Third, we examine what we can learn from the limited audience of Asian Americans and how that can hinder the effectiveness of the burlesque arguments. Fourth, we then look at how the use of burlesque in these three articles was ineffective in producing a more dramatic and long-term transformation. Finally, we point out some required modifications of burlesque in order to advance social change. A closer examination of the three articles indicates how these student writers use burlesque to reprimand Abercrombie & Fitch, thus shedding light on the need to reshape society's moral values related to minorities, specifically, the stereotyping of Asian Americans. In understanding the burlesque strategy, rhetors will have a better chance of creating a long-lasting difference when challenging the social responsibilities of major institutions, which often go unquestioned.

Applying burlesque rhetoric to create social change

On the 18th April 2002, the clothing company Abercrombie & Fitch removed its new t-shirt line from all of its 311 stores throughout the United States, only one week after being released. The company based its decision on an overwhelming number of calls and e-mails from predominately Asian

American college students who accused Abercrombie & Fitch of selling shirts that promoted negative Asian stereotypes (Kang and Kato, 2002). Specifically, the t-shirts had Asian cartoon characters with slanted eyes and conical hats that trivialized the struggles Asian immigrants encountered during the late 1800s and early 1900s when they had to work in subservient positions because of discrimination (Leutzinger, 2002).

In particular, one shirt satirized Asian men in the laundry business with the slogan, "Wong Brothers Laundry Service: Two Wongs Can Make it White." Another shirt depicted an Asian man dragging a rickshaw with the slogan, "Minimum Wage: Rick Shaw's Hoagies and Grinders. Order by the foot. Good meat. Quick feet." A third shirt had a Buddha caricature on it with the lines, "Buddha Bash: Get Your Buddha on the Floor," while another shirt had an Asian bowling caricature with the lines, "Wok-N-Bowl: Let the Good Times Roll: Chinese Food & Bowling." Lastly, a shirt portrayed a smiling Asian caricature with the slogan, "Pizza Dojo, Eat in or Wok Out" (Kong, 2002).

As a response to the t-shirt logos, over 100 college students from California's bay area started the initial protests on the 18th April 2002, which was the day Abercrombie & Fitch announced to the public the t-shirts' removal from store shelves (Kong, 2002). Protests followed in cities nationwide throughout April, while the Organization of Chinese Americans and the Japanese Americans Citizens League joined the college students in the fight against Abercrombie & Fitch. They wanted more from Abercrombie & Fitch than simply taking the shirts off the shelves. Protesters demanded a formal advertised apology from the company's CEO in all major media outlets and in Abercrombie & Fitch stores. In addition, protesters requested that the company:

> . . . Hire a consultant team to deal with minority issues. Develop an educational campaign to encourage diversity. Unconditionally refund everyone who returns the shirts to the stores. Create positive images of Asian American models and employees to represent diversification
>
> (Knight, 2002: 1)

In an effort to force Abercrombie & Fitch to fulfill these demands, protesters stood in front of stores with signs that read "Hell no, racist fashion has to go!" "Clothing designers beware: Don't mess with Asian Americans," "Racist marketing is not funny," and "Honk if you're not a Fitch bitch" (Tow, 2002: 1). In response to the protest, Abercrombie & Fitch's public relations spokesperson, Hampton Carney, from New York based firm Paul Wilmot Communications commented, "These T-shirts were designed to add humor and levity to our fashion line" (Knight, 2002: 1). He further claimed that the company did not intend to affront Asian Americans and then offered an informal apology. The company, then, merely pulled the t-shirts off the shelves and issued Carney's informal statement.

To this date thus far, the public recognizes the New Albany, Ohio-based clothing company as one that gears its merchandise towards the 18–22 year old age group, and at the height of its controversy, Abercrombie & Fitch successfully sold the offensive t-shirts for $24.50 (Gilonna and Goldman, 2002). Ironically, the student uproar failed to cause the company much damage; its stock increased by 54 cents the day after Abercrombie & Fitch declared its removal of the t-shirt line (ElBoghdady, 2002). Consequently, people rushed to buy the shirts before the company completely pulled them from the store shelves, and the auction website e-Bay removed the t-shirts after one sold for $500 (Chow, 2002).

Abercrombie & Fitch, however, is no stranger to controversy. The company encountered similar responses when it released its 1998 catalog, titled *Drinking 101* that provided recipes for alcohol mixes. Since the company has an underage marketing target, its catalogue elicited an angry response from Mothers Against Drunk Driving who demanded removal of the catalogue. Additionally, Abercrombie & Fitch introduced a quarterly catalog with models in sexually suggestive positions, which created a stir over its apparent promotion of underage sex (Lee, 2002). In response to the Asian American protests against the t-shirts, Abercrombie & Fitch remained quiet and never agreed to Asian American protesters' demands. Public attention died down, and even though protesters remained unsatisfied, media attention dissipated while Abercrombie & Fitch escaped serious consequences (Khan, 2002).

This chapter primarily focuses on the rhetoric of college students who protested and wrote articles for university newspapers, expressing their frustration with how Abercrombie & Fitch handled the situation. These students' argumentative style incorporates humor as a tool to strengthen their points, gain support, and tempt Abercrombie & Fitch to concur with their demands. In addressing argumentation techniques, Aristotle's *The Rhetoric* suggests the use of humor to strengthen one's points, while causing the opponent to appear foolish (Aristotle, 1932: translated). Moreover, humor is beneficial when an individual wishes to divert the audience from creating opposing points (Lyttle, 2001). Whether intentionally or not, students applied humorous methods, such as irony, overstatements, and rhetorical questions to vilify and scorn Abercrombie & Fitch.

Graesser *et al.* (1989) define various types of humor. Irony occurs when the statement's actual interpretation is the opposite of its intended interpretation. Overstatement is an exaggeration of the situation at hand, while Leggitt and Gibbs (2002) describe a rhetorical question as one that is blatantly untrue in a specific situation. Altogether, humor allows the audience to identify with the rhetor, assuming they have similar values and beliefs (Meyer, 1997). However, humor that the student rhetors use in their arguments against Abercrombie & Fitch has a darker and more negative tone. This paper will argue that this dark humor is a form of Burke's (1984) burlesque rhetoric that we will discuss shortly.

Throughout history, the definition of burlesque encountered many transformations in its application to poetry, theatre, English literature, and more recently, rhetorical criticism (Appel, 1996). As people's interpretation of humor changed over the centuries, the definition of burlesque changed accordingly. The name burlesque, then, comes from the Italian word, *burlesco*, which is derived from *burla*, a joke. In the 17th century, artists considered burlesque as the opposite of satire in that burlesque was not hostile or bitter. To characterize burlesque, Bond (1932: 3) researched its application in 18th century English poetry. He defined burlesque as the, "use or imitation of serious matter or manner, made amusing by the creation of incongruity between style and subject." The intention of burlesque was not to destroy but to merely laugh at the subject's idiosyncrasies (Clinton-Baddeley, 1947).

In the 20th century, Burke (1984) introduced a more beneficial characterization of burlesque, defining it as a tool of rhetorical genre and a frame of rejection. Burke's definition is all encompassing and more applicable to current social issues and events. Specifically, characteristics of burlesque rhetoric include irony, sarcasm, overstatements, and rhetorical questions to shed light on and evoke change in society's immoralities and injustices. Burlesquers, consequently, make an "attempt to reduce or bring down to size high-placed persons, entities, or ideas" (Appel, 1996: 270). Rhetors of burlesque emphasize the negative qualities or actions of the opponent in an effort to challenge social or historical circumstances (Moore, 1992). With burlesque rhetoric, one mercilessly emphasizes the subject's negative acts through exaggeration. An illustration of burlesque is a caricature within a political cartoon that has exaggerated physical features, resulting in an absurd image of the subject. Furthermore, burlesquers do not consider their opponents' mentality and reasons for their actions. They leave their opponents no room for explanations (Bostdorff, 1987). In addition, burlesquers exclude their opponents from morality and nobility (Appel, 1996). Burlesque rhetoric, therefore, accentuates the subject's immoral behavior and reduces the subject's image with the main purpose of instigating social change (Carlson, 1988).

Within the communication field, research in burlesque rhetoric is scarce. Bostdorff (1987) looked at political cartoons, suggesting that cartoons inevitably use burlesque in order to effectively make their points. In addition, Carlson (1988) studied how mere comedy was ineffectual at promoting social change for women writers in the late 19th century America. As a result, women writers resorted to burlesque rhetoric, using satire to reject traditional ideas of women. Moore (1992) analyzed the burlesque rhetoric as a response to the 1988 nomination of Vice President Quayle, thus making him appear foolish and feminine. In one article, Appel (1996) analyzed the burlesque rhetoric of conservative politician William F. Buckley, Jr. during the 1930s. According to Appel (1996), Buckley used hudibrastic, a subgenre of burlesque, to respond to the presidential election of liberalist Franklin D. Roosevelt and his promotion of the New Deal movement. Throughout these articles, the authors (Bostdorff, 1987; Carlson, 1988; Moore, 1992; Appel, 1996) apply Burke's (1984) definition of burlesque to examine its effects on social movements. Similarly, we use Burke's idea of burlesque rhetoric to understand effective argumentation; however, the consideration of a limited, controlled, and cross-cultural social protest, such as the Abercrombie & Fitch controversy, has been excluded from past studies on burlesque.

While the Abercrombie & Fitch t-shirt incident sparked a variety of responses, the focus of this chapter is on rhetoric that implements burlesque humor to strengthen arguments. More specifically, we looked at three articles by college students, particularly, Brooke Wilson (2002) from San Francisco State University, Kevin Lee (2002) from the University of California, Berkeley, and Natasha Khan (2002) from the University of Pittsburgh.

Wilson's (2002) article, "Make It White: Abercrombie & Fitch and Selling Racism as a Lifestyle," is a student response posted on *Youth Radio's* website, a company based in Berkeley, California that runs commentaries on various bay area radio stations and newspapers (Youth-Radio, 2002). In her article, Wilson (2002), a Cinema and Journalism major from San Francisco State University, discusses the past history of Abercrombie & Fitch as a company that markets towards upper class Caucasian college students by including blonde haired, blue eyed models in its advertisements. Wilson further addresses the protest against Abercrombie & Fitch's t-shirt line by implementing satire, overstatement, and irony to mock the company.

In addition to Wilson's (2002) response, we focus on Lee's (2002) article, "Pimped by Abercrombie & Fitch: How the Whiter-Than-Thou Clothing Giant is Selling Asian Self-Hate and Shame," which he wrote for an online Asian American newsletter based in UC Berkeley called *Hardboiled*. The newsletter addresses current events, education reform, community leaders, and Asian American rights. In Lee's article, he also applies satire, irony, overstatement, and rhetorical questions to enhance his arguments against Abercrombie & Fitch. Throughout his article, Lee (2002) provides an in depth description of the company's past controversies, marketing angles, other students' opinions, and reasons why the t-shirts are offensive.

The last article we looked at by Khan (2002), "A Commercial Mockery of Religion," came from an independent student newspaper from the University of Pittsburgh called *The Pitt News*. Khan's (2002) article also applies irony, satire, and rhetorical questions, which enable her to condemn Abercrombie & Fitch. Furthermore, Khan questions whether the same circumstance would take place with other ethnic or religious groups.

A thorough examination of the three articles indicates how these student writers use burlesque to reprimand Abercrombie & Fitch, thus shedding light on the need to reshape society's moral values related to minorities, specifically, the stereotyping of Asian Americans. However, the burlesque rhetoric present within the articles only worked temporarily; the main protests and uproar only lasted from April through May 2002. Consequently, Abercrombie & Fitch never issued a formal apology or succumbed to the protesters' demands.

By looking at the articles and the overall outcome, we notice that the uproar lasted a short time because the audience was limited to Asian Americans. Bostdorff (1987) states that the addresser must create arguments that apply to the audience's beliefs, values, and attitudes. Asian Americans were the target audience of the articles and already shared similar attitudes with the rhetors about what the shirts depicted. Because the company did not trivialize any other ethnic groups, those groups did not share the same viewpoint as the Asian Americans protesting the t-shirts. As a result, other ethnic groups only created a small portion of the audience partially due to the failure of the rhetors to draw them in. The lack of support from the out-group, therefore, resulted in only a minor change in attitudes, temporary awareness of the problem, and little concern over the solution. With in-groups and out-groups, people tend to prefer their "own group, [their] members, and [their] products and a tendency to derogate another group, its members, and its products" (Forsyth, 1999). Accordingly, Asian Americans make up the in-group, resulting in the exclusion of other people, thus creating an out-group.[1] By limiting their audience, the writers use of burlesque humor, even if an effective tool, failed to provide the strength that would give their arguments a lasting effect. Consequently, the rhetors' burlesque humor only assisted in the days immediately following the t-shirts' release and removal.

The discussion of burlesque humor in argumentation is important because of the way it enhances persuasion; understanding the proper use of burlesque may allow one to successfully combat negative stereotyping and create social change. The Abercrombie & Fitch t-shirt controversy is a perfect example of why researchers need to learn the potential influence of burlesque rhetoric, so that people may argue more effectively. The danger in allowing a situation like Abercrombie and Fitch's t-shirt fiasco to go unquestioned is evident in the reactions to the t-shirts; specifically, the vice chairman of Stanford's Asian American Students' Association said, "It's really misleading as to what Asian people are. . . . the stereotypes they depict are more than a century old. You're seeing laundry. . . . being trivialized" (Strasburg, 2002: A–1). With a corporation's frightening capability of creating negative perceptions in the fashion that Abercrombie & Fitch did, critics must evaluate the ways in which burlesque rhetoric strengthens arguments so that they may quickly combat those perceptions. While burlesque humor did not create a long-term social change in the Abercrombie & Fitch controversy, studying where it failed can enhance the understanding of more effective techniques to improve society's morals.

With a deeper consideration of the three articles related to the Abercrombie & Fitch t-shirt controversy, we first apply the burlesque spirit to the rhetors' use of humor in the articles. Next, we address how the rhetors use burlesque argumentation as a tool to save face. Third, we examine what we can learn from the limited audience of Asian Americans and how that can hinder the effectiveness of the burlesque arguments. Clearly, Abercrombie & Fitch understood that the depictions on their t-shirts were inappropriate. However, the use of burlesque in these three articles was ineffective in producing more dramatic and long-term transformation. Finally, we point out some required modifications of burlesque in order to advance social change.

A burlesque attack on Abercrombie and Fitch

The three college students who wrote articles about the Abercrombie & Fitch t-shirt controversy employ the burlesque spirit by including irony, sarcasm, overstatements, and rhetorical questions, thus reducing the company's image. According to Burke (1984), burlesquers humiliate their opponents, causing them to appear foolish, ignorant, and insensitive. In her article, "Make It White: Abercrombie & Fitch and Selling Racism as a Lifestyle," Wilson (2002: 1) criticizes the company's morals and intelligence by sarcastically stating, "Just do us all a favor and maintain your Anglo-Saxon superiority complex. Then, at least the rest of us know what we're dealing with and we can dutifully put you out of business by not shopping at your stores." Here, Wilson employs sarcasm and overstatement to exaggerate the company's possible outcome if it continues to maintain a reputation as a Caucasian-favoring business and therefore, an Asian-trivializing business as well. Her burlesque rhetoric is sharp and heartless, which creates a dark and bitter tone that shows her lack of concern for Abercrombie & Fitch's success. In applying the burlesque spirit, Wilson (2002) also demoralizes Abercrombie & Fitch by characterizing the company as one that engages in racial stereotyping.

Toker (2002) maintains that a rhetor of burlesque reveals problems and injustices within society. Accordingly, Wilson draws on humor's cutting effects to point out how Abercrombie & Fitch possesses the power to avoid severe punishment. Furthermore, through ironic sarcasm, Wilson disagrees with the protesters' request for an increase of cultural awareness in Abercrombie & Fitch's hiring process and marketing strategies. Arguably, she depends on the audience's ability to identify with her ethics and sarcasm when she states: "If you are going to be blue-blooded, wealthy suburbanites, then go with that image and stick with it as opposed to trying to convince the rest of us that you are really about the respect and admiration of all people." (Wilson, 2002: 1)

While Asian American protesters argue for diversity in Abercrombie & Fitch, Wilson advises the company to maintain its predominantly Caucasian image. Her sarcastic statement, therefore, helps portray as absurd the company's belief that Asian Americans could find humor in the t-shirts. However, Abercrombie & Fitch's public relations representative Hampton Carney contends that, "We poke fun at everybody, from women to flight attendants . . . Irish-Americans to snow skiers. There's really no group we haven't teased" (Cho, 2002: 2). In short, Wilson uses the burlesque spirit to degrade

Abercrombie & Fitch's perceived elitism and highlight the company's ignorance. Since Abercrombie & Fitch finds nothing wrong in trivializing other groups, Wilson uses the company's indifference as another way to ridicule it.

According to Burke (1984), burlesquers have no interest in their opponent's motivation or rationalization; moreover, they do not wish to understand their opponent's mind. Consequently, these three student rhetors are only partially successful in their use of burlesque arguments. Specifically, Khan (2002) mocks Abercrombie & Fitch's attempt at humor by providing her own sarcastic new t-shirt design. She creates an obviously gaudy and sacrilegious depiction, "Take your average solid-colored T-shirt and then add a comical cartoon Jesus 'bling blingin'. . . . No doubt, some major clothing line is going to pick up my design" (Khan, 2002: 1). Although Khan's ridicule of the t-shirt designs adds amusement to her argument, she merely addresses Abercrombie & Fitch's actions and not their reasons for them. By acknowledging and then refuting the company's reasons behind distributing the t-shirts, Khan would have a stronger case, leaving a lasting impression on the audience. A burlesquer like Khan, however, rejects the use of logic and reasoning, thus, taking humor to an excessive level in his/her arguments (Bostdorff, 1987).

While entertaining, the arguments within these three articles excessively focus on making the company appear ridiculous and absurd rather than attempting to understand the mindset behind the creation of the t-shirts. Lee (2002) does not concern himself with the more important issue of why and how someone thought producing these t-shirts was acceptable. In his article, Lee (2002: 4) utilizes sarcastic overstatements such as: ". . . they [Abercrombie and Fitch] ignore the plights of laundrymen of years ago: to be subjugated to countless abuses working in degrading positions because racism provided a glass ceiling so low they can barely limbo their way across town."

Because the t-shirts were offensive and Abercrombie & Fitch rejected protesters' demands, Lee uses sarcasm to shed light on the company's immoral behavior. While he correctly focuses on the reasons why the t-shirts were offensive and how Asian Americans felt about them, Lee keeps in line with the burlesque spirit. Nevertheless, he needed to learn more about Abercrombie & Fitch's reasoning and psyche. Abercrombie & Fitch claimed that the company tested Asian Americans' approval of the t-shirts before their release, but Lee did not address this pre-test (Tow, 2002). In maintaining the burlesque characteristic of not attempting to get inside the opponent's mind, Lee fails to argue from all points of the controversy.

Burlesque's application to face-saving

As the three student writers of the Abercrombie & Fitch t-shirt controversy manage the burlesque spirit within their arguments, they are able to criticize the company while defending their own image. According to Dews *et al.* (1995: 364) "irony provides a way for a person who has been wronged to criticize the offender in a way that reflects well on the speaker." For this paper, we consider all humorous forms, such as sarcasm, overstatement, and rhetorical questions as tools of burlesque that have the same face-saving quality as irony. By using burlesque to criticize Abercrombie & Fitch, the rhetors are able to reprimand the company without it having a negative effect on them.

In his 2002 article, Lee particularly demonstrates how rhetorical questions can shame Abercrombie & Fitch, while maintaining a positive face and attaining Asian Americans' support. He questions the company's absurd depictions of Asian Americans as a passive group easily duped; "Do they see a mass of consumers full of self-hate and self-loathing that they will latch onto any negative stereotype of themselves and parade it around town like a yellow minstrel?"(Lee, 2002: 5). Consequently, saving face occurs when individuals are aware of the need to defend their image when it is threatened, and in defending their own image, they will likely threaten their opponent's (Brown and Levinson, 1978). In his article, Lee saves face by using rhetorical questions to attack Abercrombie & Fitch's image, thus, restoring his own, along with other Asian Americans.

According to Ting-Toomey and Oetzel (2001), an individual maintains his/her face by making an effort towards the resolution of a conflict. In the case of the t-shirt controversy, the rhetors use face-work strategies to eliminate negative stereotyping. Furthermore, face-work allows them to oppose or confront another individual and to defend their persona. In addressing the protest against Abercrombie and Fitch, Khan (2002: 1) defends Asian Americans with a sarcastic and caustic statement against the company's portrayal of minorities, "The fact is that you never should have been entrusted with the capacity to comment – humorously or otherwise – about communities you know nothing about." By putting down the company's intelligence and inability to understand other cultures, Khan constructs a righteous and moral image for Asian Americans as well as herself. As she forms burlesque arguments with sarcasm, Khan reveals Abercrombie & Fitch's mistakes and ignorance through the application of face-work.

A limited audience hinders burlesque rhetoric

Since the t-shirt controversy surrounding Abercrombie & Fitch revolved around its depiction of Asian Americans, Asian Americans obviously make up the majority of the protesters and the audience of the three rhetors. As mentioned earlier, the Organization of Chinese Americans and the Japanese Americans Citizens League joined Asian American college students in the protest; accordingly, Asian Americans submitted many of the written responses to newspapers and online discussion boards. Although the president of Seattle,

Washington's Organization of Chinese Americans (OCA) claimed that the protest was "for all minority groups and all Americans" (Knight, 2002: 1), the article was from *Northwest Asian Weekly*, which limits the accessibility of the article to mostly Asian Americans. In a further effort to gather an audience of Asian Americans, the executive director of OCA planned to e-mail several thousand Asian Americans, encouraging them to send complaints to Abercrombie and Fitch (Kong, 2002). Clearly, the main audience for the three articles is Asian Americans, which creates an in-group-out-group effect where people in the in-group tend to favor and converse with their own members. As a result, the in-group of Asian Americans creates the exclusion of other groups, gaining support from only a limited audience.

While the three student rhetors employ humor to create burlesque arguments that reduce Abercrombie & Fitch's reputation, communicating mainly to an audience of Asian Americans hinders their efforts to establish a permanent social change. Bostdorff (1987) reveals that humor has an aggressive nature; when a person is hostile or afraid, he/she may respond with humor. Burlesque, as used by rhetors, acts to convey rejection in correspondence with the students' attacks against Abercrombie & Fitch. Furthermore, the rhetors must include attitudes, beliefs, and values that correspond with the audience to increase the humor's persuasive effects. The rhetors share many of the same experiences with the target audience of Asian Americans who are part of the in-group. Therefore, the Asian American audience experience the rhetors' intended emotions and meaning. The case against Abercrombie & Fitch, as a result, creates an "us against them" attitude, Asian Americans against all other ethnic groups. The lack of support from all ethnicities left Asian Americans on their own, creating only a short-term effect. In sum, the three college students direct their rhetoric at Asian Americans to take action against Abercrombie & Fitch, which in turn would hopefully stimulate the company to take social responsible action. Abercrombie & Fitch, then, is the target of the burlesque campaign, while Asian Americans make up the primary audience.

To further emphasize how the limited Asian American audience harmed the rhetors' burlesque arguments, we examine how little support protesters had and how Abercrombie & Fitch benefited from the controversy. During the time of the protests, CNN took a nationwide poll asking Americans whether the t-shirts were offensive. With a ratio of 2:1, Americans did not believe the shirts were offensive (Chow, 2002). Additionally, Lee (2002) claims that the media made Asian American protesters appear as an emotional, whiny, and bothersome group of minorities. The media portrayed Asian Americans as overreacting, and the only outcome of their protests was an informal apology from Abercrombie & Fitch's public relations spokesperson and the removal of the t-shirts. Consequently, Abercrombie & Fitch had:

> . . . their name on the top of minds of consumers, they have strengthened the edgy, rules-skirting persona of the brand. They're beyond the

> confines of multiculturalism and political correctness, and have joined the fashionable ranks of folks like Howard Stern, who has in the past called Asians "eggrolls" on the air
>
> (Lee, 2002: 5).

Not only did Abercrombie & Fitch escape serious repercussions, they obtained an increase in public attention and brand recognition. Because of the limited audience, the rhetors and the protesters did not receive enough support from equality-seeking Americans. The lack of voice and strategy ultimately led to the quiet demise of the issue.

Although the student rhetors worked towards establishing social change by using burlesque arguments to reprimand Abercrombie & Fitch, their efforts ultimately failed at achieving a long-term transformation. One of the problems with burlesque arguments is that they often are "partial not only in the sense of partisan, but also in the sense of incompleteness" (Burke, 1984: 55). The burlesque arguments merely address a limited aspect of the controversy and failed to acknowledge other underlying elements surrounding the release of the t-shirts, such as the out-group or reasons why Abercrombie & Fitch released the t-shirts. In the case of the t-shirt controversy, "the incident was not heavily publicized and that was the end of the story" (Khan, 2002: 1). The use of burlesque, therefore, simply offers rhetors a chance to release tension, which only provides evanescent satisfaction (Carlson, 1988).

How burlesque rhetoric creates social change successfully

As the initial uproar against Abercrombie & Fitch took place, the rhetors of burlesque introduced a need for social change by demanding more cultural awareness within the media and businesses. The use of mere comedy and light humor was not powerful enough to evoke substantial support and reaction; as a result, rhetors resorted to the darker and more degrading form of humor by emphasizing rejection through burlesque (Moore, 1992). Accordingly, Appel (1996: 296) suggests that "Burlesque rhetoric may emerge when comic social distance fails to effect change, comic role-players fall short of the mark, or historical shifts in political, social, or scientific orientation occur." As a reaction to Abercrombie & Fitch's ill-fated display of Asian American stereotypes, rhetors attempted to rectify the situation through spiteful and heartless humor, which one could argue the company deserved.

In this instance, the burlesque strategy merely assisted in the initial uproar to allow those within the anti-Abercrombie & Fitch audience to vent their frustration. However, in order for the rhetors' endeavor to be successful, they needed to expand into the out-group. The burlesquer must create identification with all groups (Carlson, 1988). In *A Commercial Mockery of Religion*, Khan (2002) makes the mistake of excluding members of the out-group and differentiating between Asian Americans and other groups, thus, creating greater separation. Khan (2002: 1) creates a blatant division between Asian Americans and other ethnicities in stating, "Yet if they [the t-shirts] had been black or Jewish stereotypes and jokes on those t-shirts, would Abercrombie & Fitch have gotten off so easily?" She uses a rhetorical question to point out that businesses would be less likely to attempt similar negative stereotyping with other minority groups. Khan also creates a greater division because she suggests that other groups would have greater power and influence to reprimand Abercrombie & Fitch. Conversely, Khan would be better served by having other minority groups identify with Asian Americans through their past experiences of discrimination. Burlesque, then, loses some effectiveness without support from everyone. Not only must burlesque rhetors identify with an audience that includes groups other than the ones specifically affected, they must also create change that benefits and suits the needs of others (Carlson, 1988). Unfortunately, Carlson does not include an explanation of how a rhetor can be all-inclusive. While creating identification with all groups is appealing and making the attempt is worthwhile, the task is difficult to complete and perhaps impossible to fully obtain. Convincing others to join in support of the rhetor's arguments does not only require empathy, understanding, and identification with similar values and beliefs, but the rhetor must suggest changes that positively affect out-groups as well.

Conclusion

The burlesque strategy Wilson (2002), Lee (2002), and Khan (2002) relate to their arguments worked to enhance them; however, they were not strong enough to persuade Abercrombie & Fitch to reconsider how its corporate decisions affect society. Although the student rhetors claimed to include a diverse audience, they failed to ask other ethnicities to draw upon similar experiences and to identify with Asian Americans. Instead, their burlesque tactics resulted in further separation between the in-group and out-group. Using burlesque rhetoric draws attention to the need for a moral change in society and for righting social wrongs. However, the three rhetors as well as the protesters only obtained a fleeting satisfaction with short-lived media attention.

In light of this analysis, burlesque humor is beneficial and persuasive at times, yet the rhetor should first determine a useful strategy. Specifically, the burlesquer must speak to members from the out-group as well as the in-group, create solutions that satisfy both groups, and address all aspects of the argument – including understanding the opponent's reasoning. Knowing how to weave humor into argumentation enables rhetors to identify with the audience and to make use of the similar values, beliefs, and attitudes to make an impact. In the future, understanding the burlesque strategy will allow rhetors to make a long-lasting difference when challenging the social responsibilities of major institutions, which often go unquestioned. If a large corporation is somehow prevented from escaping the consequences of a major transgression, then other businesses and even media may reconsider how they depict various ethnicities. Hopefully, this would ensure that similar offensive acts do not occur again. Admittedly, this burlesque effect on American companies appears idealistic and unobtainable; nevertheless, even the smallest change makes a difference.

Note

1 A threaded conversation appears at Adam Tow's (2002) website in which a variety of comments are made on Abercrombie & Fitch controversy. The idea of racial affiliation is indeed an underlying view; i.e., "in" and "out" groups. The tenor of some of the comments is chilling, showing that many still feel that this was an "overblown" incident by sensitive Asians. Tow's hosted dialogue is another avenue of communication effectiveness; unfortunately, it is beyond the scope of this chapter.

References

Appel, E. C. (1996). Burlesque drama as a rhetorical genre: The hudibrastic ridicule of William F. Buckley Jr. *Western Journal of Communication, 60*(3), 269–284.

Aristotle. (1932). *The Rhetoric* (L. Cooper, Trans.). New York: Appleton-Century-Crofts.

Bond, R. P. (1932). *English burlesque poetry 1700–1750*. Cambridge, MA: Harvard University Press.

Bostdorff, D. M. (1987). Making light of James Watt: A Burkean approach to the form and attitude of political cartoons. *Quarterly Journal of Speech, 73*(1), 43–59.

Brown, P., and Levinson, S. (1978). Universals in language usage: Politeness phenomenon. In E. Goody (Ed.), *Questions and politeness: Strategies in social interaction* (pp. 56–289). Cambridge: Cambridge University Press.

Burke, K. (1984). *Attitudes toward history* (3rd ed.). Berkeley: University of California Press.

Carlson, A. C. (1988). Limitations on the comic frame: Some witty American women of the nineteenth century. *Quarterly Journal of Speech, 74*(3), 310–322.

Cho, C. (2002, April 19). *Stanford students protest clothing line for stereotypical images*. Retrieved June 25, 2003, from the World Wide Web: http://daily.stanford.edu/tempo?page=content&id=7998&repository=0001_article

Chow, A. (2002). *APAs to Abercrombie: It's not over yet; Racist t-shirts are gone, but activists demand more sensitivity*. Retrieved June 25, 2003, from the World Wide Web: http://www.asianweek.com/2002_04_26/news_abercrombie.html

Clinton-Baddeley, V. C. (1947). *The burlesque tradition in the English Theatre after 1660*. London: Methuen & Co.

Dews, S., Kaplan, J., and Winner, E. (1995). Why not say it directly? The social functions of irony. *Discourse Processes, 19*(3), 347–367.

ElBoghdady, D. (2002, April 19). T-shirts' ethnic joke flop: Abercrombie halts sales as Asian groups protest. *The Washington Post*, pp. E-1.

Forsyth, D. R. (1999). *Group Dynamics* (3rd ed.). Belmont: Wadsworth Publishing Company.

Gilonna, J. M., and Goldman, A. (2002, April 19). Retailer to pull line of t-shirts that mock Asians. *Los Angeles Times*, pp. B-1.

Graesser, A. C., Long, D. L., and Mio, J. S. (1989). What are the cognitive and conceptual components of humorous text? *Poetics, 18*(1–2), 143–163.

Khan, N. (2002, October 10). *A commercial mockery of religion* [University of Pittsburg-Student Publication]. Retrieved June 25, 2003, from the World Wide Web: http://www.pittnews.com/vnews/display.v/ART/2002/10/10/3da4f67c4ef95

Kang, C., and Kato, D. (2002). Offensive t-shirts pulled. Abercrombie & Fitch. *San Jose Mercury News*, pp. 1-C.

Knight, C. (2002). Two Wongs do not make it right. *Northwest Asian Weekly, 21*(18), 1.

Kong, D. (2002, April 19). *Abercrombie & Fitch pulls t-shirts, but Asian Americans still protest.* SF Gate.com. Retrieved June 25, 2003, from the World Wide Web: http://www.sfgate.com/cgi-bin/article.cgi?file=/news/archive/2002/04/19/ state0328EDT0021.DTL

Lee, K. (2002, May, 2003). *Pimped by Abercrombie & Fitch: How the whiter-than-thou clothing giant is selling Asian self-hate and shame.* UC Berkeley – Student Publication. Retrieved June 25, 2003, from the World Wide Web: http://www.hardboiled.org/5.5/55-08-af.html

Leggitt, J. S., and Gibbs, R. W. (2002). Emotional reactions to verbal irony. *Discourse Processes, 29*(1), 1–24.

Leutzinger, M. (2002, April 23). *Abercrombie & Fitch recall t-shirts after protests.* Retrieved June 25, 2003, from the World Wide Web: http://www.dailyprincetonian.com/archives/2002/04/23/news/4999.shtm

Lyttle, J. (2001). The effectiveness of humor in persuasion: The case of business ethics training. *Journal of General Psychology, 128*(2), 1–9.

Meyer, J. C. (1997). Humor in member narratives: Uniting and dividing at work. *Western Journal of Communication, 61*(2), 188–208.

Moore, M. P. (1992). "The Quayle quagmire": Political campaigns in the poetic form of burlesque. *Western Journal of Communication, 56*(2), 108–124.

Strasburg, J. (2002, April 18). Abercrombie & glitch: Asian Americans rip retailer for stereotypes on t-shirts. *San Francisco Chronicle*, pp. A–1.

Ting-Toomey, S., and Oetzel, J. G. (2001). *Managing intercultural conflicts effectively.* Thousand Oaks-CA: Sage.

Toker, C. W. (2002). Debating "What ought to be": The comic frame and public moral argument. *Western Journal of Communication, 66*(1), 53–83.

Tow, A. (2002, April 19 2002). *Abercrombie & Fitch Protest.* A. Tow's website. Retrieved June 23, 2003, from the World Wide Web: http://www.tow.com/photogallery/20020418_abercrombie_protest/

Wilson, B. (2002). *Make it white: Abercrombie & Fitch and selling racism as a lifestyle.* Retrieved June 23, 2003, from the World Wide Web: http://www.youthradio.org/lifestyle/020424_abercrombie.shtml

Youth-Radio (2002). *About Us.* Youth Radio. Retrieved July 13, 2003, from the World Wide Web: http://www.youthradio.org/about/outlets.shtml

Part 3
Embedding Reality

Editors' Note: Embedding Reality

by Kurt April

Many have sought to understand the dynamism of modern life through the lens of "generic constructivism." Complexity, multi-leadership and multi-management, around the globe, are not only poorly understood, but very poorly implemented – and, unfortunately, the true and maximized benefits of good intentioned public and private processes and systems are never fully realized. It was Bennis who wrote: "Leaders do the right things, while managers do things right" – in the modern world both are needed in an integrated manner (we can't have one without the other). In this part of the book, the authors deconstruct the myriad of paradigms, perspectives, cultures, traditions, approaches and its underlying discourses across the world: the dispositions discourse, the contextualizing discourse, the subjectivity discourse, the narrative and dialogical discourse, the process and systems discourse. Too often, dominance of one paradigm over the other leads to partial success and even failure.

Where the process of setting objectives and achieving results is inconsistent, and where the intentions are not aligned across teams or departments, stovepipes are reinforced, dominant paradigms win out the day, and cross-cutting issues do not get resolved. As a whole, organizations become more bureaucratic, less able to change, not necessarily because their parts are individually badly organized, but because there is not adequate communication and alignment *between* the parts *and* between organizations and their environment (including stakeholders). This same issue arises at every level – from nation, to province, to district, to locality, to organization, to person. Effective processes provide feedback loops, linking policy, strategy or objectives to measures, and link measures to actions that people care about, to ensure that intended results are produced and key objectives are delivered. Keith Morrison, in his chapter on complex change and, in particular, the monopolistic position of Companhia de Electricidade de Macau (CEM) – the company which provides electricity to Macau – describes experiences (not dissimilar to many utilities and even public sector organizations around the globe, which are facing, and have faced, deregulation) where multitudes of committed and professional employees are striving to deliver modern services with inadequate management systems and processes. Keith clearly articulates the effectiveness of current CEM leadership who understand how to action their intentions, and leadership who are convinced that preparation for a new external situation begins by changing the internal environment of an organization. However good the people and committed the leadership, though, if the systems and processes that organize them does not work, the organization will not be fully effective. The weakness is in the ability to translate compelling vision, policy and objectives into the programs and projects that deliver results/outcomes "on the ground" – both inside the organization, as well as with stakeholders. And if people, on an individual level, are not willing to renegotiate their identities, they too will not be fully effective.

Exponential increases in everyday complexity and the speed of change, enabled through techno-scientific changes and transparent and efficient management techniques, accelerate the pace at which new regional, and transnational, opportunities and risks emerge to challenge us all. Well implemented systems, practices and ways of thinking about embedding the burgeoning global realities jointly seek to embed visionary leadership ideas, good management practice and achieve key objectives for sustainable and effective communities, organizations, societies and countries. Authors of this part of the book propose various reasoning architectures to make explicit those areas and practices where stumbling blocks can be removed, for disseminating best practices and for sharing knowledge. We are encouraged to not only think systemically about organizations, but more importantly of organizations as the processes of people "relating to each other" and "interacting with each other over time." Hongyan Xu, in her article Chinese Culture: Its Impact on Knowledge Sharing, succinctly describes the way in which Chinese people relate to each other, and how time-honoured traditions and philosophical legacies permeate the everyday lives of Chinese people. Hongyan presents her article as an offer to the Western world – a gift for possible enrichment of Western perspectives and practices, particularly in knowledge management and knowledge distribution, through a deeper understanding of harmony, encouragement of a learning attitude, appreciation of wisdom and accumulated knowledge, respect for elders and those who have gone before, the respect for people's capabilities in various aspects of their lives, the seeking of shared intent and Guan Xi, and the continuous practice of dialogical identity. She does however caution that some of the dimensions of Chinese culture, such as hierarchy consciousness, subtlety, indirect hinting and conversational accommodation, lengthy time-based trust particularly of outsiders, alienation of "others" and acceptance before questioning, have the potential to problematize knowledge sharing capability.

In China, emotional intelligence, social intelligence and spiritual sensing, manifested through sensitivity to interpersonal relations, cooperation and the desire to avoid conflict, are perceived differently than in the Western and

Northern world. These highly developed sensing and intelligence capabilities have the potential to act as facilitators of change-through-people, as opposed to the predominance of change-through-systems in the West (and proposed for developing regions by the West over the last 50 years).

Ambassador Kochar presents a geo-political view of diversity across the planet, unpacking the dominant religious and cultural influences on political, business and everyday life. The individual's contextual role and choice are examined within the historical and cultural social practices and action, and the individual is challenged to focus on how s/he cognitively engages, individually, in the construction of knowledge from collective social construction. If done well, the opportunity exists for individuals, organizations and many parts of the world to leapfrog much of the parochial approaches currently practiced. The overall message of this part is that the world may expand its "reality," by listening more carefully to different voices, dissenters, resisters and "others" who may reveal important messages, and this could be critical to the effectiveness and speed for embedding "expanded reality." Organizations in emerging economies and/or transitional societies, in fact, have the opportunity to leapfrog organizations in other industrialized nations, by implementing joined-up governance and service delivery from the start. We use the term "leapfrog" to mean overtaking industrialized nations – as opposed to playing "catch-up" – to take a position of primacy, by both recognizing and living out what is really going on in the world now and capitalizing on its wealth of advantages, e.g., demographics and inclusive diversity, national and humankind's history, multi-cultural heritages, geographical location, motivation for change, best practice reconciliatory stance and transformation, and the world's roots in spirituality – this is why some pundits avoid using the word "developed" vs. "developing" countries because it presupposes that countries like South Africa, China, India, countries in Latin America and other emerging and transitional economies and societies are not more developed in certain human competences than industrialized nations. There is thus much for all to learn, in the spirit of collaboration in order to co-create not only a liveable future, but a desired one (a future inclusive of all).

One particular type of parochialism is unpacked by Cathy Havener Greer, in which she discusses the unintended consequences of precedent, stability and continuity in the rule of law in American legalistic society, in her article: American Legal System Diversity: *Stare Decisis* in a Changing World. Cathy posits that the legal profession itself, including the judiciary as well as attorneys, are key players in maintaining social stability, and therefore serve to embed continued discrimination, especially of women, in the legal profession in the USA. She raises some worrying consequences of a continued status quo, namely, biased legal treatment of American citizens, the dilution of democracy, perpetuation of conditional/privileged law and degradation of the desire to serve.

In fact, the one-dimensional legalistic approach to governance is the brunt of critique offered by Kai Peters, Kurt April, Marylou Shockley and Vinay

Dhamija, in their chapter Diversity and Corporate Governance. By broadening and expanding the dominant, control approach through engaging both external and internal checks and balances, they argue that organisations will achieve the desired transparency improvement and governance strengthening – by highlighting key barriers. By comparing practices, structures and policies in both industrialized and emerging economies, Peters, April, Shockley and Dhamija illuminate potential grey areas of accountability and transparency that breed corruption, and loss of knowledge-competencies.

Reading this part of the book will make it obvious to the reader that plural constructivism is a needed philosophy, and an essential managerial/leadership competency. "Reality" in modern cultures actually takes the form of a conglomerate of multiple realities, a conceptual landscape of socio-cultural-political-religious worlds. As was the case with ancient cultures, through their lived experience our authors posit that these modern worlds or frames emerge and are embedded through varied narrative themes, oral myths, stories, dialogical identities and symbols.

8

Complexity Theory and the Electricity of Life: A Chinese Perspective

by Keith Morrison

Introduction

Management and leadership literatures have frequently stood charged with naive, unprincipled faddism and an atheoretical basis for judgements (e.g. Micklethwait and Wooldridge, 1997). This chapter provides a counter to this charge. It reports some of the outcomes of research which was undertaken from September to December 2002, at the Companhia de Electricidade de Macau (CEM) – the company which provides electricity to Macau.[1] The research used interviews, questionnaires, the *Organizational Culture Inventory* (Cooke and Lafferty, 1989; Szumal, 1998), documentary analysis, case study and observational data to gather a picture of the organizational cultures at CEM. The chapter first reports some key features which were found at CEM, and then 'theorizes' these, in part with reference to the local Chinese cultural characteristics. Complexity theory is seen to be very fitting in analyzing the situation at CEM, and CEM provides a very powerful example of complexity theory at work in an organization.

The Macau Special Administrative Region is a small enclave of China. Until December 1999 it had been under Portuguese administration for 450 years; after that date it reverted to China and operated on the 'one country, two systems' policy, akin to that of its close neighbour, Hong Kong. In many ways it is an interesting mixture of East and West. With a population of around 470,000, and occupying only some 27 square kilometres of land space in all at the Pearl River Delta, it heads the list of the most crowded cities in the world. The population is growing, with an influx from mainland China (50% of residents were born in China, in figures given for 1991 (Yuan, 1997)). Macau has a higher Chinese proportion of the population (98%) than its larger neighbour Hong Kong, and the cultural affiliation to China is strong.

The Companhia de Electricidade de Macau (CEM) is the sole provider of electrical energy in Macau. Whilst most of its employees are Chinese (*c*. 95% of its *c*. 750 employees), many of its shareholders are from Portugal and Western Europe, and, indeed Portuguese expertise is visible in the make-up of its senior management team and Heads of Departments. As is common for utility companies in many developing countries, CEM has a concessionary contract with the local government that assures it of a monopolistic position in the production, transmission, distribution and supply of all the electricity in Macau, i.e., in all aspects of electricity. Demand for electricity is rising in Macau significantly, not least with the upturn in the economic market since the Asian economic crisis of the 1990s and the major economic boom that Macau is experiencing – amongst the fastest growing economies in the world; Macau's major source of income is from tourism and gambling, and tourists are returning to Macau in their millions (1.5 million per month at the time of writing) after the slump in the previous decade, bringing increased demand for electricity, and CEM has commenced several significant development projects to meet the demand.

The external environment for change

The external environment of CEM is poised to change. The concessionary contract which it has enjoyed for many years is due for review within the next decade, and deregulation may result. In the cold wind of a deregulated market, with the possibility of all aspects of the electrical energy provision being put out to competitive tender in Macau, and with several possible providers of electricity being close at hand (e.g., in mainland China and Hong Kong), CEM is having to position itself carefully in advance of the review of the concessionary contract in order to meet a changing external environment. Developments in mainland China (and Macau is separated from the mainland by only a very short isthmus) mean that the Chinese electrical grid is very close, and developments in the fuel storage facilities in the neighbouring Pearl River Delta district of Shenzhen, a special economic zone of China, mean that the pressure for survival on CEM will be great; too easily it could be absorbed into, or lost to, mainland providers.

The likely impact of deregulation has already been felt elsewhere in Macau: another large market in Macau – the telephone service – was deregulated in 2001, and other providers have now come into what was for many years a monopoly company. In this case the existing local provider cut its staffing drastically, and the effect of this did not escape the notice of CEM staff – they realized that they must change, or risk massive staff reductions and loss of business to new players.

The internal environment at CEM

CEM has a developed and mature sense of social responsibility; it has a policy of non-redundancy, and this served its employees very favourably in the downturn of the economy in the 1990s. Further, it is known as a "good" employer in Macau, offering many benefits to its employees, for example in salary and income (which are considerably higher than in other local industries and employment), health and medical benefits, in pension arrangements, and in the provision of free electricity for its employees. The beneficent situation is reflected in the fact that employees stay for a long time at CEM – there are very many who have been with the company for over 20 years, the median length of employment at CEM is 18.2 years, and the average age is 43.6 (Companhia de Electricidade de Macau, 2000). Whilst this means that there is a rich experience on which to draw, it also raises issues of career development, reskilling, and the difficulties in changing employees' mentality in order to anticipate and prepare for changes.

Further, with income assured (and business currently comes very easily to CEM rather than CEM having to go looking for it), with company performance being benchmarked to, and meeting or even exceeding, the best practices in international companies, and with a degree of comfort in the Macau situation, employees have enjoyed stability, guaranteed employment, and a 'good life' at CEM. Further, with many of the workforce in their 50s and early 60s, many staff will retire before the review, or possible expiry, of the concessionary contract comes into operation, so their need to change seems limited. Coupled with a policy of non-redundancy it is clear that Senge's (1990: 57) view that 'yesterday's solutions are today's problems' carry some force in the recent history of CEM.

As a monopolistic provider, and with income rising and profits assured, it would be easy for a company to sit back and enjoy its comfort. Not so at CEM. Acting judiciously and prudently, the company is already taking steps to prepare for the future, and it recognizes that internal cultural change is an essential ingredient of change. Given the possible changes in the external environment, CEM has already begun to prepare itself for a new external situation by changing its internal environment. It has done this in several important ways:

(a) Since 1999, CEM has installed a *Culture of Efficiency* project, with rotating project leadership to ensure that the project remains fresh, and this project has made considerable inroads in improving internal communication, openness to change, flexibility, efficiency gains, and introducing an appraisal system. Employees are aware that long-standing practices and the status quo will change; awareness of the need for change is high.

(b) Some *efficiency gains* have been made inasmuch as, when staff retire, they are not always replaced. The workforce dropped from 835 in 1995 to 748 in 2000, a drop of 10.4%, at a time when demands on the company, and its supply to the local population, were, and are still, increasing.

(c) CEM has taken many steps to *promote cross-departmental projects, teamwork and communication*. Indeed, on its own initiative, it has established a new department of Safety, Health, Environment and Quality, and it is clear that its remit will touch all employees and departments at CEM.

(d) CEM has actively sought to move from *being simply a utility company to being a service provider*, with the intent to serve well both its internal and external customers. Indeed in 2001 it introduced a new company logo as an emblem of rebranding the company – from one which simply related to its customers by an electrical cable link, to networking and providing all-round quality service. Put simply, it has moved its mentality from monopolistic 'producer capture' to a consumer-driven, partnership service provider.

(e) CEM has brought in leading international consultants to advise on steps to be taken to inject yet further *preparations for a devolved and deregulated market*. These are complemented by a strong sense that change must come from within, i.e., that individuals must change their mentality, that group and company behaviour must change, and that, whilst external consultants might be useful in suggesting pathways for development, *in fact* it is individuals within the organization who will carry forward these changes by changing themselves.

(f) CEM has *undertaken a review* of its organizational cultures and an evaluation of its *Culture of Efficiency* project, and customer satisfaction surveys, with the intention of using these as stepping-off points for future internal cultural developments. Important amongst developments here is the *fostering of employee participation and speaking out actively*.

(g) CEM has engaged in a *vigorous building programme* so that it can meet its stated 'big audacious goal' of 'being seen as one of the best suppliers of electricity in Asia' (Companhia de Electricidade de Macau (CEM), 1999: 3). It continues to invest considerable sums of money in building a new power station on reclaimed land on one of the islands of Macau, at Coloane, and in ensuring that it meets internal environmental standards.

(h) the *leadership of CEM*, in the form of the CEO, has been, himself, a *model of change*, both in substance and in process, moving the company forwards with the projects outlined here, and, himself, opening up communication and decision-making to a wider range of participants.

(i) whilst there are several strategies at CEM to prepare it for an unpredictable future, and whilst the company is clear in its strategic development, the *planning for the future is deliberately open* rather than fixed and static, enabling the company to reorganize itself in anticipation of, and response to, emergent priorities and issues, whilst still being able to keep its eyes firmly fixed on the impact of the deregulated market. It combines uncertainty about the future with an ability to respond to different contingencies that emerge as the future is realized.

(j) CEM has made *provision for identifying training needs* which are linked to in-house and sponsored external provision, so that development is complemented by support and so that the local workforce is developed from within. CEM has recognized that, in the near future, it will seek to reduce the number of ex-patriate staff, and the move to 'bring on' local employees into management and senior management positions has already begun. Indeed it had already reduced the number of its ex-patriate staff from a figure of 67 (8.6% of its total workforce) in 1990 to 38 (5.1%) in 2000.

(k) Linked to training and development is the notion of *continuous improvement*. At present this is being seen in individualistic terms. By furthering the development of cross-functional and cross-departmental teams, CEM has been extending the continuous improvement mentality to groups and teams, realizing the full notion of *kaizen* from Japanese organizations, in which continuous improvement is practised, often by multiple, small, incremental changes, and which is undertaken by teams (Morrison, 1998: 53).

(l) CEM has been running an *appraisal system* for some years, and this is designed to provide *feedback to employees*. Further, the development of a database on employees enables career development, with concomitant training provision, to take place. Hence feedback has the potential to be rich, informed and linked to a strategy of development.

(m) CEM has been making significant strides in *inducing a new mentality* into its workers, in which risk and an unseating of comfort figure highly. Here a shift is taking place from simply encouraging employees to take risks, to employees recognizing that if they do not take risks for improvement then this is counter to the company will. Further, and not in a conflictual sense, CEM is successfully developing a clear awareness in its employees that the future is likely to be uncomfortable and that, therefore, they should learn to accommodate discomfort.

(n) CEM has recognized that it must be *proactive in its relations with the public*, hence *networking* is not simply a 'one-way street', from the outside in, but involves the company reaching out into the public. For example, it has placed high quality customer service at the top of its agenda, with an intention to 'reach total customer satisfaction' (Companhia de Electricidade de Macau (CEM), 1999: 3) and has commissioned customer satisfaction surveys with focus groups, 'customer panels' and consultants' reports. It signed a contract with the local Jockey Club (a large concern in Macau) for maintenance and repair work, leading to amplification of services, to mutual benefit. It established a *Customer Liaison Committee* to network with representatives of social and professional organizations in Macau, and it set up an internal help desk and an external call centre for customers. CEM has established a new department of Safety, Health, Environment and Quality, in order, in part, to improve to customer service and environmental quality, and it is part of the ISO 9000 and ISO 14000 certification programmes. Its environmental protection work has involved the creation of a sludge incinerator in 2001, a lubricant oils treatment system at one of its power stations, oil booms at its power plants, and significant emission control and cleaning mechanisms.

It is also liaising with other overseas companies (e.g., Singapore Power Automation and Efacec Oriente (Macau)). It is linking with a local University for training and part-time student employment. It is installing a second inter-connection with the electricity network in the neighbouring mainland Guangdong province. Clearly CEM is making several moves to relate to its external environment.

(o) CEM has installed a *system of performance measurement* for its senior employees, so that achievement, performance and 'bottom-line thinking' are addressed even more fully.

(p) CEM is taking active steps to furthering its concern for people, and the *development of a people-centred culture* within its organization. It recognizes that change is effected by *people*, and that people are a major resource for the organization.

Clearly CEM is being very proactive in making considerable internal changes in order to meet the demands of a turbulent, unpredictable external environment, i.e., fulfilling the 'law of requisite variety' (Ashby, 1981; Hatch, 1997: 90) which states that the variety within the organization or system must be, at least, as great as the variety within the environment.

The local Chinese culture

In describing the situation found at CEM, care must be taken to avoid stereotyping; in this case the phenomena reported are described strictly through the comments given by employees at CEM, most of whom (87% of participants in the research) were local Chinese. The Chinese culture within CEM articulates with the mutually potentiating and reinforcing wider Chinese cultural characteristics of obedience, hierarchy, seniority, conformity, collectivity, deference, consensus, face, avoidance of confrontation, and the acceptance of differentials of power.

Obedience, hierarchy, respect for seniority, and conformity

One of the interesting issues at CEM is the culture of the local Chinese employees, who make up the overwhelming majority of the CEM workforce. The 'Confucian heritage culture' celebrates respect for seniority, acceptance of, and deference to, authority, compliance, obedience, non-challenge to authority (Rozman, 1991: 30), and a sympathy with hierarchical, command-and-control management. It is rare for a good son, argues Confucius (*Analects*, I: 2) who is 'obedient, . . . to have the inclination to transgress against his superiors' (Lau, 1992: 3). A man, Confucius suggests, is 'schooled who shows deference' (Lau, 1992: 5), and 'if a man is correct in his own person, then there will be obedience without orders being given' (*Analects*, XIII: 123) (Lau, 1992: 123). Acceptance of inequalities of power is a 'cardinal relationship' (Bond and Hwang, 1986: 216).

Voicing out by, or critique from, subordinates goes against deep-set cultural norms; rather, deference, silence and acquiescence are a feature of the local Chinese culture and the local Chinese employees at CEM. As Berlie (2001: 1) remarks, 'the Chinese society is relatively secret'. In Chinese culture and at CEM, some subordinates are reactive, accepting, dependent (Rozman, 1991: 30), indeed expecting, the mandates of bosses and managers – the job of the bosses, perfectly legitimately, is to boss. Employees commented that the Chinese culture was to keep quiet and accept the decision of their superiors, even if they privately thought the decisions were not good. As Redding and Wong (1986: 280) suggest: 'the cultural preference for harmony, at least on the surface, means that dissatisfactions . . . are unlikely to be brought out into the open'. Complaints were very rare at CEM, and employees did not wish to, or seek to, offend their bosses. Indeed Chinese management behaviour is a 'distinctly more autocratic approach than that found in the West, especially in the contexts of sharing information with subordinates and allowing them to participate in decision making' (Redding and Wong, 1986: 279).

The local Chinese culture, within and outside CEM, is of conformity and orderliness (e.g., role behaviour and compliance); one employee indicated that people did not feel comfortable in suggesting different things, and preferred to receive, rather than to initiate. This rendered 'thinking out of the box' and problem-posing a difficult proposition at CEM. Indeed comments were received that the majority of the local Chinese did not want to 'open their minds'. Many of the steps that CEM has taken, outlined above, were beginning to break this deep-seated cultural phenomenon; it is a cultural norm, not merely a company matter. So great was it that some comments suggested that the best way forward, given the impending retirement of many employees in the next few years, would be to adopt the Chinese custom of waiting out the situation to solve itself in the fullness of time, rather than confronting people, as an advisable way forward.

Consensus, collectivity and being right first time

The local Chinese culture (within and outside CEM) of seeking consensus and harmony (often allied to 'deference, compliance and cooperativeness' (Redding and Wong, 1986: 287)) was profound; people would seek cooperative behaviour, rather than trying to create problems. This could be both an inhibitor and facilitator of change. On the one hand it could lead to inertia; on the other hand, moves towards cooperation and developed interpersonal relations – 'the soul at work' in a company (Lewin and Regine, 2000) – augur well for change, as they embrace the cooperative teamworking principles which are advocated for companies to keep up with change and innovation. Indeed collectivism and interrelatedness, rather than individualism, are hallmarks of Chinese culture (Hawkins *et al.*, 2001), particularly when coupled to loyalty and obedience (Hofstede, 1980; Bond and Hwang, 1986: 215–23; Salili, 1996: 86; Hau and Salili, 1996; Wu, 1996: 23). Confucian collectivist culture is characterized also by hierarchical social relationships (Ho, 2001: 99). Associativity is a key characteristic of Chinese culture (*Analects*, XVIII: 6) (Lau, 1992: 185); as Confucius says (*Analects*, II: 14): 'the gentleman enters into associations' (Lau, 1992: 15). Indeed Zohar (1997: 110) writes: 'in Chinese culture, I am defined by my relationships . . . and thus the boundaries of my own identity are quite ambiguous and contextual'.

The Confucian heritage culture principles of effort, diligence (Hau and Salili, 1996: 126–8), dedication (Rozman, 1991: 28–9) and doing a very good job – being absolutely sure of all the procedures involved before doing a job (seeking to be 'right first time'), contrasted to the comments received at CEM that Westerners may plunge into a job with more confidence than expertise. Confucius (*Analects*, I: 5) suggests that it is important to 'approach your duties with reverence and be trustworthy' (Lau, 1992: 3), and 'a subject should serve his ruler by doing his utmost' (*Analects*, III: 19, in Lau, 1992: 25). Given these Chinese characteristics, the signs for maintaining and developing quality and efficiency were powerful. Indeed Watkins and Biggs (2001: 7) suggest that diligence, conformity to group norms, and the preparedness to spend a long time on uninteresting tasks, are significant Chinese cultural features. Self-actualization and ego needs are more prevalent in Western cultures, whereas social needs predominate in Chinese culture (Redding and Wong, 1986: 285).

As a high reliability organization in some aspects of its work, e.g., production, supply, distribution and transmission of electricity, CEM has to ensure an error-free environment in some areas of its activities, and indeed it sets itself the target of 'zero seconds of interruption' in its mission statement Companhia de Electricidade de Macau (CEM) (1999: 3). The culture of reliable, error-free work through conforming to given procedures, was strong and positive at CEM.

'Face'

'Face work' (Bond and Hwang, 1986: 225; 243–9) is a central aspect of wider Chinese culture. Maintaining, saving, enhancing and gaining one's own and others' face are not only important but key elements in themselves, but are also in maintaining differences of power and status. There was an acknowledged feature at CEM that the local Chinese people would rather not, and rarely did, expose themselves to the risk of 'losing face'. Face-saving, face-gaining, face-giving and face-receiving are important aspects of the local Chinese culture. Reputations can be very fragile, and 'face is a fragile commodity' (Faure and Ding, 2003: 91). On the one hand, in CEM this could act as a brake on change, as it made for defensive and self-protective cultures which were inimical to change. On the other hand, at CEM it fostered a culture of harmony and cooperation that could be turned to advantage in developing the interpersonal aspects of change. As Redding and Wong (1986: 286) remark, 'face-related behaviour is important for maintaining social harmony, and collectivist societies must be sensitive to social mechanisms for maintaining harmony'. Emotional intelligence, a significant aspect of effective management, leadership and employee behaviour, could be fostered through the 'face' mentality in the local Chinese culture.

Avoidance of confrontation

Another important aspect of the local Chinese culture that was found at CEM was the desire to avoid confrontation. As Bond and Hwang (1986: 221) argue, 'Chinese . . . attach a great weight to the anticipated reactions of others'. On the one hand this can bury problems rather than surface them, and it can enable poor practice to go unchallenged. However, on the other hand, it makes the *will* to change very powerful. Employees at CEM *want* the company to thrive, they *want* to work well, and they *want* to cooperate. They prefer harmonious and consensual relationships to aggressiveness and conflict, and many of them have a strong sense of company loyalty. Indeed they prefer to try to solve matters themselves, locally and often informally, rather than 'troubling the boss'; here are the seeds of self-organization within, and across, departments in order to 'get the work done'. Associativity, rather than, for example, confrontation and fighting, is an important Chinese cultural trait (Bond, 1994); associating also links with the emphasis given to informal networks (sometimes family networks). Indeed social relationships are an important dimension of work relationships in this Chinese culture, both within and outside CEM.

Given these characteristics, it was unsurprising to find some defensive cultures at CEM (where people act to protect themselves and enhance their own status and security), and the presence of three particularly strong organizational cultures, derived from the *Organizational Culture Inventory* by Cooke and Lafferty (1989) and Szumal (1998):

- the 'perfectionistic' culture, in which persistence and hard work are valued, as are the avoidance of error and the desire to keep on top of everything and complete it to the last detail;
- the 'conventional' culture, where members are expected to conform, follow the rules, make a good impression and avoid confrontation;
- the 'avoidance' culture, taking few chances, lying low, and waiting for others to act first, and emphasizing consistency and reliability.

Many aspects of the local Chinese culture sit comfortably with command-and-control, hierarchical management, and indeed the style of management of CEM in the 1980s and early 1990s was of a command-and-control style. Defensiveness, self-protection and 'in the box' thinking may be one corollary of this, and this was reinforced by relative departmental isolation. When the external environment was stable, these management practices succeeded in rationalizing and improving the efficiency and performance of CEM to high quality levels. These practices run deep, particularly with long-serving employees. To try to accommodate an environment of turbulence, unpredictability, and maybe a proclivity to an unstable future, CEM has been pursuing several strategies to reduce top-down, perlocutionary (directive) communication which seeks simply to enact the predetermined agendas of senior managers, and to replace these with illocutionary communication – setting agendas, consulting and speaking out. CEM has taken several bold steps to work with local Chinese culture, but not to let it be an obstacle to change.

Theorizing the changes at CEM

What have we learned about CEM here? CEM provides a very striking positive example of complexity theory at work (c.f. Waldrop, 1992; Lewin, 1993; Kauffman, 1995; Stacey, 2000). Complexity theory is a theory of adaptation and development in the interests of survival (Morrison, 2002). New internal systems emerge through the interaction of internal and external environments; the theory is one of 'emergence through self-organization', feedback and learning. Linear, mechanistic models of management no longer apply, and networks and dynamical, ever-changing systems and turbulent environments are the order of the day. Put simply, 'complex adaptive systems' (Waldrop, 1992: 294–9), or, as Stacey (2000: 368) terms them, 'complex responsive processes', scan and sense the external environment and then make internal adjustments and developments in order to meet the demands of the changing external environment. This is the 'law of requisite variety', or 'law of requisite diversity', which states that internal flexibility, change and capability must be as powerful as those in the external environment. In these, according to complexity theory (Morrison, 2002), adjustments, organizational learning, internal leadership, order without hierarchical control, self-organization, distributed leadership and emotional intelligence, loose-tight coupling, organizational alignment, teamwork, positive organizational cultures and climates, and communication figure very highly. CEM is an organization that, deliberately or not, is adhering to several principles of complexity theory. It is doing this in several ways.

First, it is sensing its external environment by gathering intelligence about that environment (McMaster, 1996: 10), and it is responding to the present and anticipated environmental changes by changing its internal environment. CEM is interacting with its environment, reaching out into it, and networking extensively with that environment; it is changing its internal and external environments and the dialogical, communicative processes involved in this, both proactively and reactively. Organizations, people and environments co-evolve (Cohen and Stewart, 1995; Kauffman, 1996; Stewart, 2001). Changes and new orders are *emergent* through interaction within and between internal and external environments (Casti, 1997), and CEM has developed systems for feedback from employees and the outside world, which are linked to the provision, storage, and communication of rich information.

Second, CEM is changing itself, metamorphosing irreversibly, from a utility provider to a fully-developed, high quality service provider. It is changing itself through auto-catalysis, i.e., self-propelling itself into change, rather than waiting for external events to happen which impel change, with order evolving from within rather than from without (Cohen and Stewart, 1995: 265). It is changing its internal practices through self-organization, moving from a hierarchical, departmentally territorial, previously closed organization, to an open organization that is marked by an information-rich environment, cross-departmental and multifunctional teams, and an emphasis on efficiency, performance and internal as well as external customer service. CEM is operating on the principle that self-organization occurs through feedback and communication (Marsick, 2000: 10). Hence it is developing internal and external networking systems – connectedness (Youngblood, 1997: 27; Wheatley, 1999: 10). In doing so it is developing organizational alignment (Wickens, 1995) within a loosely coupled organization (Johnson, 1999: 32).

In this process CEM has been enhancing its internal, cross-departmental communication systems and practices, to both speed up communication and to ensure that 'the message' reaches its intended audiences completely and without distortion. It is promoting internal connectedness and external connectedness (Morrison, 2002: chs. 5, 7). To further this, CEM has inaugurated several projects which are designed to generate a climate of change and innovation. CEM is seeking to develop the capabilities, creativity and proactivity of its employees – moving to the 'edge of chaos', wherein the greatest creativity lies. Complexity lies at the 'edge of chaos' (Lewin, 1993). CEM has established a new department of Safety, Health, Environment and Quality, which, very astutely, not only touches all the internal departments of the organization, but also touches the external environment. This is a pivotal new department at CEM.

Third, CEM is developing a climate of risk, a degree of discomfort with the status quo, and moves to break cultures of conformity, stability, compliance, defensiveness and negative, closed, self-protection. It is developing distributed leadership and distributed control in the devolution of some important aspects of decision making to Heads of Departments and senior managers (c.f. Lewin and Regine, 2000: 30; Johnson, 2001: 78–9). CEM is breaking with grand plans and simplistic teleological models of strategy development and implementation, preferring to set up the *conditions* to anticipate and respond to emerging changes within an overall indication of what might be on the horizon. CEM is evolving into a dynamical, 'complex adaptive system' to replace a mechanistic, static organizational system. As April (1997: 26) remarks, 'a butterfly which flies in a straight line without zigzags – will fall prey very fast'. In this process CEM is deliberately creating disturbance and disequilibrium in the minds of employees in order to activate development processes. As April (1997: 9) remarks, 'systems *need* disequilibrium in order to survive'.

Fourth, it has been creating a clear new identity (of service and excellence) which is reflected in its 'rebranding' exercise and the inauguration of a new company logo. CEM is engaged in *autopoiesis* – the creation of a unique and autonomous identity (Kelly and Allison, 1999: 28; Wheatley, 1999: 20) – which is an important feature of complexity theory, as species survive by finding their own specific niche (their own 'fitness landscape' (Kauffman, 1995)) in the environment. CEM has emerged into a streamlined, efficient, customer-oriented company, with its employees moving to a preparedness for change through a change of mentality, as well as change in practices. By moving towards a person-centred organization, CEM is developing the 'soul at work' in a large company (Lewin and Regine, 2000). Indeed Stacey *et al.* (2000: 188) suggest that thinking of an organization as a system has to be replaced by thinking of the organization as the *processes of people relating to each other and interacting with each other over time*. Here emotional intelligence, manifested through sensitivity to interpersonal relations, cooperation and the desire to avoid conflict, could act as a facilitator of change-through-people.

In pressing the organization to change and innovate, CEM is moving toward 'self-organized criticality' (a feature of complexity theory, in which organizations propel themselves, through self-organization, away from stability, to the 'edge of chaos' – a point at the boundary between maximum diversity and chaos, where irreversible change is unavoidable). The movement towards greater degrees of complexity is a movement towards 'self-organized criticality' (Bak and Chen, 1991), in which systems evolve, through self-organization, towards the edge of chaos (Kauffman, 1995), and where creativity and innovativeness are at their peak (Karr, 1995: 3; Morrison, 2002). Stacey (2000: 395) suggests that a system can only evolve, and evolve spontaneously, where there is diversity and deviance (Stacey, 2000: 399) – a salutary message for command-and-control leaders who exact compliance from their followers. Similarly Fullan (2001: 42) suggests listening carefully to dissenters and resisters, as they may have an important message to convey and they may be critical to the effectiveness of change, and build in difference; leaders must not simply have like-minded innovators. This may be difficult in the local Chinese cultures of harmony and consensus, reported here.

Conclusion

Clearly CEM is facing an uncertain time, despite massive expansion with the tremendous growth in the Macau economy. Internally the large numbers of older staff may be a 'brake' on rapid change, and, with the discussion of the future of the concessionary contract still some years away, it may be difficult to engender a climate of urgency in the older employees, as they will retire before the expiry of the concessionary contract. CEM is taking clear, decisive steps to prepare for the future. Whether it can effect those changes quickly is debatable, hence there is wisdom in CEM's decision to move early. Maybe, in fact, adherence to the Chinese culture of 'wait it out and it will all come right' is a useful way forward in respect of its older employees.

Several aspects of local Chinese culture are seen as facilitating change at CEM, for example: the emphasis on positive interpersonal relationships and the thrust for harmony, collectivity and associativity, the desire for perfectionism first time, and the protection of face. On the other hand, these selfsame features, together with the deeply-ingrained Confucian heritage culture of acceptance of hierarchy, conformity, silence, deference, command-and-control and authority-driven management, and the reluctance to surface problems, could act as important inhibitors to change at CEM. As has been suggested here, CEM is striving to press for the unseating of stability, the development of risk cultures, and the creation of turbulence to meet the incipient demands of a complex, turbulent future.

CEM rightly recognizes that the solution is one of networking and developing relationships in the wider community. This resonates well with the local Chinese culture of developed networks, relationships, and associativity. It recognizes that customers are more than simply a matter of being joined by an electrical cable link; clearly other potential service suppliers may only be a cable link away from Macau in a deregulated market. Through self-organization and internal change, internal and external feedback, information and communication, and the interaction of internal and external environments, CEM is changing itself, and newer, higher forms of organization are emerging. A vigorous pursuit of development, innovation, and change in mentality and practices, is preparing employees to operate in a turbulent environment. Organizational and individual learning and feedback are leading to change and the emergence of newer organizational forms. This has necessitated both working with, and adapting, the local Chinese cultures and environments. That is the challenge of complexity for complex, dynamical and adaptive organizations. CEM is alive, and the spark of life is powerful.

Acknowledgements

Thanks are due to the former Chief Executive Officer and his colleagues at CEM for their permission to use material from the research on organizational cultures undertaken at CEM, and for their kind and extensive cooperation in this project. Thanks are also due to the other members of the research team: Ho Kit Sam, Shirley; Li Yuan, Frank; Ngai Sou, and Vong Iao Mei, Myriam, for their extensive involvement in this project.

Note

1 The research was conducted during these four months of 2002; to contextualize parts of the research, reference is made in this paper to two earlier documents of 1999 and 2000, produced by the Companhia de Electricidade de Macau. Full bibliographic details of these documents are provided.

References

April, K. (1997), *An Investigation into the Applicability of New Science, Chaos Theory, and Complexity Theory to Leadership, and Development of Guiding Principles for the Modern Leader and Organisation*, Research Report, Cape Town: Graduate School of Business, University of Cape Town.

Ashby, W. R. (1981), *An Introduction to Cybernetics*, 3rd Edition), New York: Harper and Row.

Bak, P. and Chen, K. (1991), Self-Organized Criticality, *Scientific American*, January, Vol. 264, pp. 46–53.

Berlie, J. (2001), *Macau: a Multi-Community Society*, Paper presented at the Conference, *Macau on the Threshold of the Third Millennium*, Instituto Ricci de Macau, 15th December.

Bond, M. H. (1994), *Beyond the Chinese Face: Insights from Psychology*, Hong Kong: Oxford University Press.

Bond, M. H. and Hwang, K. H. (1986), 'The social psychology of the Chinese People', in M. H. Bond (Ed.), *The Psychology of the Chinese People*, Oxford: Oxford University Press, pp. 213–66.

Casti, J. (1997), *Would Be World*, New York: John Wiley and Sons.

Cohen, J. and Stewart, I. (1995), *The Collapse of Chaos*, Harmondsworth: Penguin.

Companhia de Electricidade de Macau (CEM) (1999), *Performance Management System, CEM Policy* 27th July, 1999, Macau: Companhia de Electricidade de Macau.

Companhia de Electricidade de Macau (CEM) (2000), *2000 Relatório Annual (Annual Report)*, Macau: Companhia de Electricidade de Macau.

Cooke, R. A. and Lafferty, J. C. (1989), *The Organizational Culture Inventory*, Michigan: Human Synergistics International.

Faure, G. O. and Ding, Y. F. (2003), 'Chinese culture and negotiation: Strategies for handling stalemates', in I. Alon (Ed.), *Chinese Culture, Organizational Behaviour and International Business Management*, Westport, CT: Praeger, pp. 85–98.

Fullan, M. (2001), *Leading in a Culture of Change*. San Francisco: Jossey-Bass.

Hatch, M. J. (1997), *Organization Theory: Modern, Symbolic and Postmodern Perspectives*, Oxford: Oxford University Press.

Hau, K. T. and Salili, F. (1996), 'Achievement goals and causal attributions of Chinese students', in S. Lau (Ed.), *Growing up the Chinese Way*, Hong Kong: Chinese University of Hong Kong Press, pp. 121–45.

Hawkins, J. N., Zhou, N. and Lee, J. (2001), 'China: balancing the collective and the individual', in W. Cummings, M. T. Tatto and J. Hawkins (Eds.), *Values Education for Dynamic Societies: Individualism or Collectivism*, Hong Kong and Australia: Comparative Education Research Centre and Australian Council for Educational Research Ltd., pp. 191–206.

Ho, I. T. (2001), 'Are Chinese teachers authoritarian?', in D. A. Watkins and J. B. Biggs (Eds.), *Teaching the Chinese Learner: Psychological and Pedagogical Perspectives*, Hong Kong and Australia: Comparative Education Research Centre and Australian Council for Educational Research Ltd., pp. 99–114.

Hofstede, G. (1980), *Culture's Consequences: International Differences in Work-Related Values*, Beverly Hills, CA: Sage.

Johnson, K. B. (1999), *The Development of Progressive and Sustainable Human Complex Adaptive Systems: Institutions, Organizations and Communities* (URL: http://www.wam.umd.edu/~nafikiri/webcomplex.htm, retrieved 26th June 2001).

Johnson, S. (2001), *Emergence*, London: Allen Lane, The Penguin Press.

Karr, B. (1995), *Complexity Theory and Rhetorical Invention* (URL: http://english.ttu.edu/courses/5361/papers/paper1_karr_420.html, retrieved 26th June 2001).
Kauffman, S. A. (1995), *At Home in the Universe: The Search for the Laws of Self-Organization and Complexity*, Harmondsworth: Penguin.
Kauffman, S. A. (1996), *Investigations: The Nature of Autonomous Agents and the Worlds They Mutually Create*, Lecture 1 from the series: *Search for a Possible 'Fourth Law' of Thermodynamics for Non-Equilibrium Systems*, URL: http://www.santafe/sfi/People/kauffman/Lecture-1.html, retrieved 12th November 2000.
Kelly, S. and Allison, M. A. (1999), *The Complexity Advantage: How the Science of Complexity Can Help Your Business Achieve Peak Performance*, New York: McGraw-Hill.
Lau, D. C. (1992), *Confucius: The Analects*, Hong Kong: Chinese University of Hong Kong Press.
Lewin, R. (1993), *Complexity: Life on the Edge*, London: Phoenix.
Lewin, R. and Regine, B. (2000), *The Soul at Work: Listen, Respond, Let Go: Embracing Complexity Science for Business Success*, New York: Simon and Shuster.
Marsick, V. (2000), 'Learning Organizations', cited in V. Marsick, J. Bitterman and R. Van Der Veen (2001), *From the Learning Organization to Learning Communities toward a Learning Society*, Information series no. 382. ERIC Clearinghouse on Adult, Career and Vocational Education, ED-99-CO-0013, Ohio State University, Columbus: Ohio, URL: http://ericacve.org/docs/marsick/marsick3.pdf, retrieved, 4th February 2001.
McMaster, M. D. (1996), *The Intelligence Advantage: Organizing for Complexity*, Newton, Massachusetts: Butterworth-Heinemann.
Micklethwait, J. and Wooldridge, A. (1997), *The Witch Doctors*, London: Mandarin Paperbacks.
Morrison, K. R. B. (1998), *Management Theories for Educational Change*, London: Paul Chapman Publishing.
Morrison, K. R. B. (2002), *School Leadership and Complexity Theory*, London: RoutledgeFalmer.
Redding, G. and Wong, G. Y. Y. (1986), 'The psychology of Chinese organizational behaviour', in M. H. Bond (Ed.), *The Psychology of the Chinese People*, Hong Kong: Oxford University Press, pp. 267–95.
Rozman, G. (Ed.) (1991), *The East Asian Region: Confucian Heritage and Its Modern Adaptation*, Princeton, NJ: Princeton University Press.
Salili, F. (1996), 'Accepting personal responsibility for learning', in D. A. Watkins and J. B. Biggs (Eds.), *The Chinese Learner: Cultural, Psychological and Contextual Influences*, Hong Kong and Australia: Comparative Education Research Centre and Australian Council for Educational Research Ltd., pp. 85–105.
Senge, P. M. (1990), *The Fifth Discipline: The Art and Practice of the Learning Organization*, New York: Doubleday.
Stacey, R. D. (2000), *Strategic Management and Organisational Dynamics*, 3rd Edition, Harlow, England: Pearson Education Limited.
Stacey, R. D., Griffin, D. and Shaw, P. (2000), *Complexity and Management: Fad or Radical Challenge to Systems Thinking?*, London: Routledge.
Stewart, M. (2001), *The Co-Evolving Organization*, Rutland, UK: Decomplexity Associates Ltd, URL: http://www.decomplexity.com/Coevolving%20Organization%20VU.pdf, retrieved 22nd March 2002.
Szumal, J. L. (1998), *The Organizational Culture Inventory Interpretation and Development Guide*, Michigan: Source Publishing LLC.
Waldrop, M. M. (1992), *Complexity: the Emerging Science at the Edge of Order and Chaos*, Harmondsworth: Penguin.

Watkins, D. A. and Biggs, J. B. (2001), 'The paradox of the Chinese learner and beyond', in D. A. Watkins and J. B. Biggs (Eds.), *Teaching the Chinese Learner: Psychological and Pedagogical Perspectives*, Hong Kong and Australia: Comparative Education Research Centre and Australian Council for Educational Research Ltd., pp. 3–23.

Wheatley, M. (1999), *Leadership and the New Science: Discovering Order in a Chaotic World*, 2nd Edition, San Francisco: Berrett-Koehler Publishers.

Wickens, P. (1995), *The Ascendant Organization*, Basingstoke: Macmillan.

Wu, D. Y. H. (1996), 'Parental control: psychocultural interpretations of Chinese patterns of socialization', in S. Lau (Ed.), *Growing up the Chinese Way*, Hong Kong: Chinese University of Hong Kong Press, pp. 1–28.

Youngblood, M. (1997), *Life at the Edge of Chaos*, Dallas, Texas: Perceval Publishing.

Yuan, D. Y. (1997), 'Age-sex profiles of Asian migrants in Macau', in R. Ramos, D. Rocha, R. Wilson and D. Y. Yuan (Eds.), *Macau and its Neighbours in Transition*, University of Macau and Macau Foundation, pp. 429–35.

Zohar, D. (1997), *Rewiring the Corporate Brain*, San Francisco: Berrett-Koechler Publishers Inc.

9

Chinese Culture: Its Impact on Knowledge Sharing

by Hongyan Xu

Sharing of knowledge

Knowledge sharing is not about a mechanical distribution of packages of data or shifting information from one place to another. Rather, knowledge is a commodity, which is often only transferable in personal exchanges between individuals (Nonaka and Takeuchi, 1995; Spender, 1996). Thus, it is crucial to discuss knowledge sharing practices in a "people" context, i.e., to examine the theories and techniques of knowledge sharing in a particular culture environment.

Most of the world's leading knowledge management gurus and institutes originated in the West, resulting in noticeably Western-oriented concepts and ideas in contemporary knowledge sharing. With a profound history and a wonderful and colourful civilization, China, on the other hand, has always been mysterious to the Western world. How then could the Chinese culture impact knowledge sharing practices? What are the elements unique in Chinese culture that would help in the distribution of knowledge? And to what extent does the Chinese culture pose a challenge to Western knowledge sharing ideas, and practices?

Chinese culture

Hofstede (1980) conducted an extensive project capturing the fundamental essence of culture, which put forward the idea that values of certain cultures are relatively stable over time. The Chinese, for longer than any other ethnic group, have carefully developed their culture in a 5000 year-evolution. Certain historical events have significantly influenced the shape of Chinese culture, notably the 2000 years empire and the constant absorption of invaded ethnics. Without any doubt, the backbone of Chinese culture originated from deep-rooted Confucian philosophy, preaching the values of loyalty, righteousness, friendship, filial piety, and the importance of education.

The uniqueness of Chinese culture has drawn wide attention from the West. Bond and Wang (1986) identified four values indigenous to Chinese culture: (1) *Confucian work dynamism* (ordered relationships, thrift, protecting your face and respect for tradition); (2) *integration* (tolerance for others, harmony with others, non-competitiveness, trustworthiness, and filial piety); (3) *humanity* (kindness, forgiveness, compassion, patience, courtesy, and patriotism); and (4) *moral discipline* (moderation following the middle way, keeping oneself disinterested and pure, having few desires, and adaptability).

The Chinese value harmony, respect and generosity within, above all else, a disciplined, ordered society. They avoid public attention and exhibitionism. Moreover, the Chinese are highly group-orientated and place a strong emphasis on collective identity. History has taught them that there is safety in obscurity, and that surrendering their personal/individual visibility to a group protects them from political turmoil and victimization.

Enablers for knowledge sharing

The Chinese group-oriented culture, by its very nature, provides the basis for promoting knowledge-sharing. In many ways, the West's struggle with knowledge sharing has been attributed to individualism (April and Ahmadi-Izadi, 2004) and instrumental independence. Other unique aspects of Chinese culture are equally beneficial to encouraging shared knowledge, particularly the enabling forces of collectivism and harmony, respect for knowledge and learning, as well as the unspoken rule of Guan Xi.

Collectivism and harmony

The Chinese culture is collective-orientated (Hofstede, 1980), which encourages interrelationships and interdependency. The Chinese are brought up with the idea that the groups' needs take precedence over those of an individual. Thus, the Chinese tend to define their identities in terms of their relationship to a group such as the family, school or employer. This mentality influences Chinese management styles in organizations, and makes an employee more willing to help others and share their knowledge. For example, Chinese companies, particularly state-owned organizations, adopt a parental attitude to their employees, taking care of the personal and community concerns.

The responsibilities taken on by the employer range from small issues, such as organizing groceries, laundry, a company car, and holidays, to bigger favours such as arranging for housing, schooling of children, finding a job for an employee's spouse, and even helping to choose a husband or wife.

It is quite common for employees to regard the organization they work for as a big 'family', and there is no clear separation between private and professional life. Such a culture is conducive to building trust among colleagues, thereby facilitating the socialization process in knowledge sharing.

The Chinese believe people should maintain harmony inwardly, and keep balance with an outside world. They cherish peace and abhor conflict. From the long tradition of avoiding confrontations, the Chinese tend to tolerate and appreciate differences. Cotterell and Morgan (1975) claim that a capacity to retain diverse viewpoints, at the same time, is a notable feature of Chinese thought. This ability to suspend judgement on others fosters an inclusive and tolerant social environment that could encourage the spreading of different ideas, innovation, multiple mental models and comfortableness with uncertainty.

Respecting knowledge and learning attitude

In traditional Chinese social hierarchies, scholars and learned people were always ranked at the top of society, with parallel social prestige – well above businessmen and land-owners. Knowledge is highly valued, as a result, the ethos among Chinese students is one which prizes intelligence, diligence and academic competitiveness. Respect for, and the high social value of, knowledge thus fosters a life-long desire for continuous learning. Chinese learning, in many respects, has no boundaries, quite opposite to the "not invented here" syndrome, noted in Gorelick *et al.* (2004), and so often encountered in Western organizations. *Among any three people walking, I will find something to learn for sure* (Confucius, 500 BC).[1]

People have different capabilities and abilities, have predispositions for different ways of learning, and therefore have different expertise in different areas of life, and they deserve to be accorded respect, regardless of their functions, or the industries, in which they work. Equally important, and while quite different from to many Western approaches but surprisingly similar to African, Latin American, native American and native Oceanic cultures, Chinese people are also expected to learn from their natural environments at all times, from plants, animals and the fluctuation of the elements.

There is a strong impetus to accumulate knowledge, share it and enhance it. Indeed, the habit of continuous learning and accumulation passed from generation to generation, building up the "absorptive capacity" (Van den Bosch *et al.*, 1999) of the knowledge recipients in China.

The unspoken rule of Guan Xi

Guan Xi has become a familiar term in Chinese society. Although it is worth questioning whether Guan Xi is a phenomenon limited to China, or equivalent to notions of *sereti* (the extent of one's domain of influence as a direct consequence of the "authenticity" with which one approaches life and others) in Africa, it is still the "unspoken rule" governing and explaining everything in China. Guan Xi, in fact, has significant implications for knowledge-sharing.

The Confucius social hierarchy, i.e., the five relationships of (1) emperor-subject, (2) father-son, (3) husband-wife, (4) brother-other siblings and (5) friend-friend, describes a natural networked Guan Xi web of relationships in the Chinese social fabric. Underpinning this structure, is the wisdom passed from one generation to another, from friend to friend, colleague to colleague and community to community. Again, not unlike the oral traditions of wisdom sharing in many native cultures such as those found in most of Africa, native America, Aboriginal Australia, and so on (a dialogical identity based on shared intent). This wisdom is not only limited to the professional and tactical skills, but also including knowledge gleaned from personal experience, life-skills, relationship dynamics, business and social etiquette, etc. It encompasses all facets of interpersonal skills, emotional sensing, social savvy and social intelligence, and the soul.

Guan Xi today has even broader applications, referring to the relationships between people and organizations, which implicitly indicates assurance, understanding, and mutual obligation (Ahmed and Li, 1996), "you scratch my back, and I'll scratch yours". In promoting the concept of knowledge-sharing, Guan Xi can serve as a powerful information gathering and distributing mechanism. In the Internet age, the web-based virtual community extends the accessibility of Guan Xi, and increases the opportunity to build knowledge sharing networks. There are numerous knowledge-sharing websites in China – for example, any keywords relating to "exams", "certifications" or "learning" entered in a search engine, will provide a multitude of valuable resources, including "short cuts", "tricks", "tips for passing exams", "what to concentrate on", "where to go for help", "particular individuals who are known to assist others", and so on. Those websites are typically set up by one person or several individuals, but are strongly supported and resourced by entire communities.

Challenges for knowledge sharing

In a multi-levelled, complex cultural environment such as in China, knowledge sharing practices can also diverge into opposite directions, so that certain cultural factors, which ordinarily can serve as enablers in certain circumstances, can become hindrances in others. Such stumbling blocks include hierarchy-consciousness, subtle communication, group solidarity, loyalty to family and organization, and the educational dictum to "accept before (and/or without) questioning".

Hierarchy-consciousness

The Chinese emphasize social hierarchical structure and, as such, they are taught from an early age to "know their position", "know their place" and resist acting beyond the boundaries. Seniority and rank are thus the determining factors in the knowledge-sharing chain. Information is generally passed from parents to children, boss to employee, manager to subordinate and teacher to pupil. Although this is gradually changing (boundary permeability) as younger generations acquire more education and exposure to Western, Southern, and Northern cultures, there is not yet enough flexibility in the general Chinese culture to facilitate boundary-breaking.

Another concept related to the social hierarchy is "face", which represents respect, reputation and pride. The Chinese greatly value their status in society, the impression they make on others, their public image and their decorum. As a result, they are often inhibited in sharing knowledge if this will risk their social standing, or perceived dignity. The junior staff may be afraid to challenge the ideas and opinions of their older colleagues, as this may be seen as insolence or lack of respect. This might lessen the creation of positive results and innovative ideas through "creative friction".

Subtlety

The Chinese communicate in a complicated and delicate way. In their eyes, Western body language, such as outstretched hands and pointed fingers, can be perceived as threatening or a lack of self-control. The Chinese favour indirect hinting and an accommodating conversational style, non-confrontational, non-provocative, restrained and graceful, while still conveying the full meaning and force of the message (Pang *et al.*, 1998). A spoken sentence can have many different meanings and subtexts, which is why the Chinese are cautious in their choice of words. However, such circumspection can result in ambiguity, reserve and misunderstandings.

Since the Chinese are used to avoiding sharp, direct comments and feedback, they tend to express themselves cryptically, or poetically. Politeness is crucial, and anything too candid is seen as vulgar and offensive. When they have to give negative answers, they normally start with something positive. Thus, it is not surprising to hear Chinese saying "yes, but ..." rather than a direct "no". This can be very confusing and difficult for other cultures to comprehend, and can hinder proper communication.

Trust and sharing inside the group

The Chinese are highly group-orientated, with a strong "them" vs. "us" mentality. They prefer to seek advice from those inside the group, and are suspicious of outsiders. Trust is hard-earned; normally it can only be developed through a long-term interaction with constant probing. However, once gained, the trust becomes the "passport" to access the Chinese community networks. Differences will then be understood and tolerated; certain mistakes will even be forgiven. Communication inside the group flows freely and unhindered, whereas, influenced by the distrusting nature, communication with outsiders is always handicapped. As a result, newcomers and foreigners may feel alienated in China or around Chinese people, and find it difficult to develop deep friendships and effective social circles. Naturally, this also damages knowledge-sharing networks between Chinese and other cultures.

Accept before questioning

The education system in China emphasizes memorizing and repeating knowledge, rather than original and creative ideas or independent thinking.

Children are told to regard what their teachers say as the "golden rules", "authoritative" and "indisputable", even regarding personal issues. It is not uncommon in Chinese schools to hear the comment: "don't ask why, remember it." Thus, the Chinese are ready to accept theories without skepticism. Back in China, Chinese students are under heavy workloads and tremendous pressure to secure limited places in a top university. Creativity, especially personal indulgent creativity, is not encouraged, and time spent on issues unrelated to improve one's grades is frowned upon. It will probably still take decades before unbridled curiosity and non-conformism are fostered and encouraged in Chinese schools and Universities, which will in turn promote a truly dynamic, interactive knowledge-sharing process infiltrating Chinese trade and industry.

The future

The Chinese must leverage the strengths of their culture, while at the same time avoiding the potential damage of other factors. There are ways of overcoming the dichotomies of their tradition. For example, appreciating that disagreement and constructive dissent may be positive ways to generate more ideas; developing self-awareness of closed mental models and the power of diverse perspectives in extending one's mental models; advocating open and straightforward discussions; changing the education system to encourage original thinking; and becoming more receptive to outsiders and foreigners. For this to happen, though, it will be necessary for knowledge-sharing to become a national issue, with input and encouragement at State level.

China, a country undergoing tremendous reform and development, is in the stage of merging centuries-old tradition with the influences of the Western world, and no doubt in time to come, with the influences of the Southern and Northern worlds, to shape a modern Chinese cultural identity. It will be a long and difficult process, but one that is rich in opportunity for both the Chinese themselves and those eager to tap its ancient wisdom. The global business community may yet find a unique and exciting reservoir of insights and ideas coming from the Far East.

Postscript

The standpoint of this article was based on my experience of working for a large state-owned enterprise in China, which has been strongly influenced by the traditional Chinese culture. Large multinational corporates, on the other hand, have its own deep-rooted company culture, for example the GE way and the Siemens process house. The knowledge-sharing practices would have to incorporate both the company and the local culture.

There is also a risk of over-emphasizing the Chinese culture impact. The Chinese culture is a part of the environment where a business breathes in and out, but it does not decide the health of a business. For business leaders, defining organization, communicating targets and setting incentives to reinforce the expected behaviour are critical for fostering knowledge-sharing, as for any other business initiatives. A well-defined knowledge-sharing model has the potential to work across all the cultures: that is the beauty!

Note

1 Confucian saying, translated into English by author.

References

Ahmed, P. K. and Li, X. K. (1996), "Chinese culture and its implications for Sino-Western joint venture management", *Journal of Strategic Change*, Vol. 5, October Issue, pp. 275–286.

April, K. and Ahmadi-Izadi, F. (2004), *Knowledge Management Praxis*, Kenwyn: Juta Academic.

Bond, M. H. and Wang, K. H. (1986), "The social psychology of the Chinese People", in M. H. Bond (Ed.), *The Psychology of the Chinese People*, Oxford: Oxford University Press, pp. 213–266.

Cotterell, A. and Morgan, D. (1975), *China – An Integrated Study*, London: Harrap.

Gorelick, C., Milton, N. and April, K. (2004), *Performance Through Learning: Knowledge Management in Practice*, Burlington, MA: Elsevier Butterworth-Heinemann.

Hofstede, G. (1980), "Motivation, leadership and organization: do American theories apply abroad", *Organizational Dynamics*, Vol. 16, No. 4, pp. 4–21.

Leung, T. K. P. and Wong, Y. H. (2001), "The ethics and positioning of Guanxi in China", *Marketing Intelligence & Planning*, Vol. 19, No. 1, pp. 55–64.

Nonaka, I. and Takeuchi, H. (1995), *The Knowledge-Creating Company: How Japanese Companies Create the Dynamics of Innovation*, New York/Oxford: Oxford University Press.

Pang, C. K., Roberts, D. and Sutton, J. (1998), "Doing business in China – The art of war", *International Journal of Contemporary Hospitality Management*, Vol. 10, No. 7, pp. 272–282.

Spender, J. C. (1996), *Organizational Learning and Competitive Advantage*, London: Sage, pp. 56–73.

Trompenaars, F. (1993), *Riding the Waves of Culture*, London: The Economist Books.

Van den Bosch, F. A. J., Volberda, H. W. and de Boer, M. (1999), "Coevolution of Firm Absorptive Capacity and Knowledge Environment: Organizational Forms", *Organization Science*, Vol. 10, No. 5, pp. 551–568.

10
Geo-Political Diversity

by Soonu Kochar

Introduction

Geography is a predeterminant of human destiny. Through the ages, the history of different peoples and races has been shaped by their environment – the climate, the terrain, water resources, etc., influence racial characteristics which become the roots of distinct cultures. It is no chance that the earliest civilizations were founded in the riverbeds and valleys of the Nile, the Euphrates, the Indus and the Yangtze, which became cradles of highly developed cultures; whereas, hilltops and mountains were chosen in areas of dense forest. The sacred centres of the Mayas and the Incas rise above the dense vegetation of the Amazon and equatorial America. These ancient civilizations vanished and the people who now inhabit the valleys of the Pharaohs, or the sites of ancient Babylon and Mesopotamia have no real links with these early cultures. Only in India and China have the lines of continuity been maintained by a strong oral tradition and the preservation of the cultural boundaries.

Culture denotes the essence of civilizations. Like race, language and religion, it is a group manifestation and consists of these three elements as well as some others. In an increasingly global society, while ideology, governance, business, education etc., are becoming trans-national, culture remains distinctive and even more divisive. Hence for smooth interaction between nations and peoples, an awareness of the variations in cultures makes for better understanding and better relationships. But, to understand different cultures, we must go to their respective roots – and these are embedded in religion.

A *Tour D'Horizon* of cultural variations

Europe

Let us start with Europe. It is a patchwork of various distinct cultures, bound by the glue of Christianity. It's distinct features are:

- A common heritage of Judeo-Christian values.

- Graeco-Roman laws.
- Renaissance humanism, empiricism and liberalism.

Till the dawn of the modern age (1600 AD), the Church was an all-pervasive influence in the life of the people, and yet the Church also has been divisive. The first separation of the Church of Rome from the Eastern Orthodox part, came in the second half of the fifteenth century, surprisingly, by an order of Sultan Mehmet II, then ruler of the Ottoman Empire, after he conquered the Byzantine capital in 1453. He freed the East Orthodox Church, from obedience to Rome and granted independence by a decree.

The Reformation, which started in different years in England, Germany and Switzerland etc., was a product of the 16th century. What emerges today out of these divisions within the Church are distinctly different cultures which divide Protestant northern Europe (Scandinavia, Germany, Denmark, The Netherlands and Britain) from Latin Europe (France, Spain, Portugal, Italy as well as Celtic Ireland) and the Central European Catholic countries (Poland, Hungary, Austria, the Czech Republic, Slovakia, Slovenia and Croatia) from Eastern Europe (Russia, Greece, Rumania, Bulgaria, Serbia and the former Slav and Caucasian Republics of the old Soviet Union) who belong to the Eastern Orthodox Church.

Language and race have also contributed to these cultural variations. Some Eastern European countries use the Cyrillic script while the rest of the European languages spring from Latin. Race also plays a part. While the blanket definition for European is White Caucasian, there are distinct characteristics, moulded by climate and environment:

- The Anglo-Saxon and Teutonic races with very fair complexion, blonde hair and blue eyes.
- The Latin races with a Celtic streak – more swarthy, darker hair and sharper facial features.
- The Slavs with colouration which is fair or dark, but very distinctive features – high cheek bones derived from their Central Asian ancestors etc.

This by no means implies that there is no *melange* of races or religion within the countries. Indeed there is. Germany and The Netherlands, while primarily Reformist, have Catholic majorities in the south.

Today, when Europe has embarked upon this unique experiment of unification, it is amazing how often and strongly cultural differences assert themselves. At the core of Europe-building is this constant tension between national identities versus European unity. It is foremost when enlargement of the Union is under consideration. When the European Community was first enlarged in 1973 by the admission of Britain, Denmark and Ireland, France reluctantly conceded because President Pompidou was secretly worried about Chancellor Willy Brandt's Ostpolitik and chose enlargement westwards rather than eastwards, however strong Gallic intentions were to keep the British out. Again, at the next stage, the conservative government in France resisted the admission of the poorer members of Southern Europe, until the Socialists came to power. President Mittterand readily agreed to accept "The Meds", i.e., Spain, Portugal and Greece, because he found that the European Community was weighted in favour of the Anglo-Saxons. Earlier reluctance of the European Union to admit the countries of Central and Southern Europe was not only because of their financial situation. It also had something to do with race. The Scandinavians – Sweden and Finland – as also Austria were readily accepted in 2000, while Poland, Hungary and the Czech Republic were left knocking on the door.

Moreover, Europe also has its pockets of Islam. Turkey is Islamic, though secular. Reluctance to admit Turkey into the EU has this as one of the unmentioned reasons. Albania, Bosnia, Kosovo and Azerbaijan are also Islamic, and their faith has caused friction with their Christian neighbours, like Serbia and Armenia respectively. It is the force of circumstances and American pressure, that has made the European Union reluctantly agree to the admission of ten more countries including most of the erstwhile Communist block in the future.

The United States of America

The United States of America are often described as a melting pot of European and Native American cultures, with more recent additions of Asian and Hispanic variations, as well as vibrant Afro-American and Afro-Caribbean cultures. It is a nation built by immigrants which still has an open door policy. Newcomers tend to aggregate; hence there are ghettoes of Poles, Irish, Italians, Greeks, etc., who migrated after the first wave of settlers who came mainly from Britain, France and Germany. But by the second or third generation, they have integrated. They have become Americans in speech, handwriting, mindset, etc. The first immigrants came largely to escape religious persecution in Britain, France, and Germany, etc., to have the freedom to practise their faith. Their Puritanism as well as their urge for freedom still inspires the American way of life, and were the well spring of American Law and the American Constitution. Later immigrants came for economic reasons – to escape poverty or even famine the Irish and the Italians for example, or latter day persecutions from Nazi Germany and Poland, etc. The Jews came driven out earlier after Stalin's pogroms in Russia and later from Hitler's Germany; the Armenians wanted to escape Turkish tyranny.

For similar reasons, the Chinese, the Japanese, the Vietnamese and the Koreans came and settled along the west coast of America. Migrations peaked between and after the World Wars as people who had lost their homes came to build a new life. Asians from the sub-continent and South East Asia came largely as students and became successful professionals. And all along, there were migrants from Mexico and other Central American countries coming in, seeking employment and a better life. America is a success story of immigrants. The remarkable fact is the sea-change which transforms them into Americans – not by way of looks, colour, etc., but in the way they think and behave, and identify themselves with their new homeland.

While Christianity is the predominant faith, it abounds in a variety of denominations, not existing in the old countries. It is also a strong impulse in the lives of the people in the American heartland, rural communities and what is often called Middle America. The African-American population, no less zealous, has added a new vibrant dimension to their Church with soul music, the Blues and mass exuberant celebration of their faith. While Judaism was the second most important religion, today Islam has overtaken it. It is a growing religion in the inner cities and particularly among the deprived, which is a danger sign.

Thus, American culture, even if its roots are in Europe, has these added values and is reflected in their governance, way of doing business, life style etc. It is not surprising that there is a clash of cultures when there are cross-Atlantic mergers and acquisitions. The common points of departure between the US and Europe are over capitalism, social services, regulatory authorities, citizens' rights, etc.

Asia

In its vastness, variety and even mystery, Asia as a continent and another quilt work of cultures, is only now becoming comprehensible to the West. Asia is the cradle of old civilizations as also of the important religions of the world. You cannot put a date on the birth of Hinduism, certainly the oldest of living religions. There are traces of its rituals found in the excavations of Mohenjo, Daro and Harappa, scattered across the valleys of the Indus River that date back to 5000 BC. The Aryans who came soon after from Central Asia and settled in the valleys of Hindustan contributed the Vedas and later the Puranas and the Upanishads, which remain the embodiment of the Hindu religion. The lines of continuity stretch until today, maintained by a resilient oral tradition. Hinduism is confined to India and Nepal and the island of Bali – where it was taken by merchant settlers – and nowhere else. This is because it is not a proselytizing religion. Hinduism is a way of life. You are either born a Hindu or you seek your salvation from gurus and sages. But the search has to be your own.

Buddhism, born as an offshoot of Hinduism 2500 years ago, had an identified Master in the Buddha (he never claimed to be a Prophet). His teachings spread from India northeastwards, into Tibet, which became its centre, over to China, Japan and Korea; south-eastwards; to Myanmar; Thailand, Vietnam, Laos and Cambodia; and further southward to Sri Lanka, Malaysia and Indonesia, etc. Buddhism did not become the religion of the majority in the country of its origin, i.e., India. The challenge it posed revitalized, and even led to a reformation of, Hinduism.

In the Far East, Buddhism co-existed peacefully with Confucianism, Taoism, and Shintoism. These three began as philosophical systems, but later took on the form of a cult or religion. Confucius was a great philosopher and teacher like the Buddha who lived from 551–479 BC in China. His teachings also embrace governance, business relations, employer-employee interaction and even conduct of martial arts. To this day, it pervades the Chinese mindset, even under the veneer of Communist dogma. Confucianism spread to Japan, Korea, and Vietnam, etc., during the heyday of the Chinese Empire. It influences relationships in the family and the workplace, teaches a work ethic, moderation, frugality and balance in personal habits and behaviour. It imposes duties and a code of conduct on the leader, as well as the led. It is an important factor in understanding business relationships in South-east Asia's Chinese communities.

Taoism is another philosophical system, founded by the Chinese philosopher Lao-Tze who was born in 604 BC. It has become a religious system combining Taoist philosophy with magic and superstition and the worship of many gods. Taoists believe in re-incarnation and non-violence, and recommend vegetarianism.

Shintoism is more homespun and is confined to Japan. It is actually a nature and hero cult, which has become the indigenous religion of the country. It denotes ancestral worship, Emperor worship and nature worship. It also became the cult of heroism, of the Samurai and the Ronins. It propounds a sense of honour, which has to be saved, if necessary, by suicide.

These Eastern religions/beliefs are older and different from the Semitic religions. They are more pantheistic, the concept of Mother Earth and a Life Force is more important than the idea of Man's descent from Adam and Eve. And re-incarnation is a strong belief in respect of afterlife.

Finally, there is the impact of *Islam*. Islam became a dominant religion from the 8th century onwards, and spread from the Arabian Peninsula in all directions. It is an aggressively proselytizing religion, which has been spread by the sword rather than preaching. For nearly six centuries, Islamic empires formed a mosaic from Morocco to China, and included North Africa, the Middle East, Spain, the Balkans, the Caucasian region, Central Asia, Iran, Afghanistan and Northern India. From there, Islam spread southwards to Malaysia and Indonesia (replacing Buddhism), and as far as the Philippines. It has contributed to world heritage noble architecture, calligraphy, miniature painting as well as to science and mathematics, and has its own system of medicine.

Africa

Before the advent of the Europeans, Africa was an inclusive tribal society. There was cannibalism. But there was also a primitive kind of social structure. Animism – worship of the elements, plant life, etc. – was the predominant form of religion. The Europeans brought Christianity and imposed their own norms of social behaviour, mainly by force. They carved up territories into different states for administrative convenience, without consideration of common language, custom or tribal affiliation etc. Some of Africa's problems today, especially the internecine warfare witnessed between Congo, Rwanda, Uganda and Zimbabwe in central Africa and Sierra Leone, Guinea and Liberia, as well as Nigeria in the west, arise out of these divisions to some extent. Islam came into Africa from the North. Today it is the fastest growing religion in Africa.

Australia, New Zealand and the Pacific Island States

Australia and New Zealand were settled primarily by the British in the 19th century, who brought with them their Victorian values and notions of racial superiority. Australia actually started as a penal colony, and a place to banish no-good sons and adventurers etc. New Zealand was discovered by a Dutchman – Abel Tasman – but also became an English colony of farmers and sheep breeders. Today, both these countries are at a crossroads, and are trying to come to terms with their geo-political reality.

The island states of the Pacific are still isolated from the rest of the world. They are mono-crop economies. They are also the last bastions of Christianity. All denominations co-exist among the tiny populations of these states. Although distance separates them from each other, they still have some common customs from the pre-Christian past, e.g. their kava ceremony for welcome and for festivals, their offerings of pig fruit and flowers and the rhythm (and the monotony) of their songs and dance. They lie in the backyard of Australia, which has the predominant position in their economy, education, even defence. The exceptions are the French Outre Mèr territories of New Caledonia and French Polynesia. The economic importance of these islands lies in the future, when deep-sea exploitation of the seabed will become a technological reality.

Latin America

The countries of Latin America display a unique homogeneity of culture and lifestyle. The cementing factors are the Spanish language, the Catholic Church and common history. These countries, south of the Rio Grande, were largely settled by Spanish conquistadors (the Portuguese in Brazil) who have an experience of international trade that goes back four centuries. As a matter of fact, freedom to trade and to draw upon the technical and financial resources of the industrial world was one of the mainsprings of their independence movements that were successful 150 years ago.

Today, the Latin people, especially those of Central America and of the Amazon and Andean regions, are a mix of these Spanish and Portuguese settlers and the indigenous people. Further south, in the countries of the southern cone, the population is largely European, as the natives were largely decimated. There have been later migrations between and after the World Wars of other Europeans – Italians, Dutch, English, French, and Swiss etc.

Argentina, Paraguay and Chile became safe havens for the Nazis. There are also Japanese and Korean settlers and even Arabs from Syria and Lebanon.

While the melting pot effect of the US is not so discernible, by language, religion and lifestyle, Latin American culture has a distinct cultural identity. This makes political cohesion easier. The Latin American countries have their own political confabulations and in international fora they often vote as a block. These countries have close relations with the USA in terms of trade, investments and education etc., but their cultural and emotional ties still remain with Europe.

Now we look at the basic tenets of the four important religious systems and the distinct cultural manifestations that flow from them.

The Judeo-Christian values

- One God – all men (women) are equal before Him.
- Ethics, a sense personal sin responsibility, penance, redemption.
- Clear separation of the Church and the State in most countries (exception, the UK).
- Today, honest dissent is accepted.
- Today, the Church accepts the spirit of empiricism, enquiry, humanism, even agnosticism.

Its impact on governance

- Provides foundation of Rule of Law and jurisprudence.
- Accepts different systems of governments.
- Preference for democracy and human rights.
- Tendency of Christian nations to impose these on others.

Its impact on business

- These values provide the matrix of International Law and Code of Business followed worldwide as well as of: Corporate Law, Accounting Systems, and Jurisprudence.
- These systems have been adopted even in non-Christian countries.
- The exceptions are some Islamic countries and Communist or erstwhile Communist countries.

Islamic fundamentals

- One God – Allah!
- Five Prophets – Adam, Abraham, Moses, Jesus, Mohamed.
- Day of Reckoning.
- Regimented way of life.
- The five pillars:
  - Testimony – Allah!
  - Prayers – daily, five times a day.
  - Zakaat – charity – a percentage of income.

  - Pilgrimage – Haaj.
  - Fasting – Ramadan.
- Prosetylization – a duty.
- Kaafir – a pagan, an infidel, to be converted, conquered or killed.

Its impact on governance

- All people are created equal rejects monarchy.
- The Mosque and the State are one.
- Laid down principles of daily living.
- The "Shariah" or Koranic Law must govern every facet of life, including government, commerce, etc.
- Jihad – two interpretations: an inner struggle between good and evil to defeat evil within self; take up arms against the oppressor, the infidel, the enemy of the faith.
- Martyrdom – Promise of Paradise.

Its impact on business

- More and more Islamic countries are adopting the "The Shariah" or the tenets of the Koran as the law of the land, civil, criminal or corporate.
- The "Shariah" also impacts banking, e.g., the Koran prohibits enjoying interest on investment, but permits sharing of profit and loss out of investment.
- Also a different system of jurisprudence.

Hinduism and Buddhism

- Belief in cycle of life, death and re-birth, e.g., transmigration of souls. The belief in Karma – you pay for the sins of this life in the next.
- Respect for all forms of life – reluctance to kill.
- Doctrine of "Ahimsa" or non-violence.
- The four stages of life: youth – family man – old age – "sanyasi-renunciation" striving for "moksha" – salvation.
- Fatalism.

Impact on governance

- The ruler and the ruled have each their code of conduct and responsibility.
- Peaceful co-existence between nations.
- Non-interference in the affairs of other nations.
- Peaceful settlement of disputes between nations.
- Women's participation.

Impact on business

- A network of Asian globalism from the 7th to 14th century. Trade followed the spread of Buddhism.
- Family-oriented businesses, from generations to generation.
- Cultural rigidity in labour markets.

- Wide spectrum of business practices followed: from bazaar bargaining to secret, sophisticated negotiations.
- Hierarchical systems – deference to superiors.

Confucius and related value systems

- Ancestral worship.
- Respect for parents, elders, superior rulers, and authority.
- Ethics of hard work, obedience, thrift.
- Harmony in society.
- Sense of honour.
- Sense of status.
- Sense of shame (saving "face" is very important).
- Suicide to save honour, or out of shame, is acceptable.

Its impact on governance

- The ruler can be a benevolent dictator, or like a patriarch of the family.
- He must maintain discipline.
- Obedience and fidelity is due to him.
- Failure or dishonour merit death.

Its impact on business

- Basis of so-called "Asian values".
- Tough negotiators.
- Deference and loyalty in employer-employee relationship.
- Businesses kept within family, clans and community.
- Different outlook on bribery and corruption.
- Prevalent "cronyism".

Five major cultural groups in the non-Western world

Japanese society and business

For centuries, Japan has been a feudal society and a closed one. Europeans first came to Japan in the 16th century for trade and evangelism. The Portuguese, the English, the Dutch established their trading posts. The Jesuits came with their customary zeal, including St. Francis Xavier. But the Japanese did not like this trespass on their own faiths, and the Portuguese were driven out. The English did not find the trade profitable, and left. Only the Dutch remained at the southern tip of the country, as Calvinism does not indulge in conversions.

Thereafter, Japan grew deliberately inward-looking and remained so until the mid-19th century. It was a very creative period when Japanese art flourished, e.g., the Kabuki theatre, miniature paintings, calligraphy etc. and the production of the finest pottery and ceramics belong to this period. But Japan also missed out on the Industrial revolution and other changes taking place in the outside world. In 1853, Commodore Perry sailed into Tokyo Bay and demanded trading rights practising gunboat diplomacy – which succeeded. This was Japan's first opening to the West.

Political changes also took place in Japan. The Meiji Emperor was installed and Japan embarked upon rapid modernization and industrialization and built up an efficient modern army, navy and airforce that tempted it to embark upon military adventures in China, Korea, and other neighbouring countries, and eventually to declare war against the Allies during World War II. After its surrender in 1945, when Japan came under American Occupation, that became its second opening to the world. Thereafter, Japanese society adopted Westernization in all aspects, even if it was just skin deep. This evolution that took place in Japan has an impact on Japanese lifestyle, business practices and politics today.

Japanese society even today remains insular, male-dominated, conformist and traditional to the core. Long years of uncertainty, upheavals and natural calamities that Japan is prone to, have made the average Japanese cautious about risks, Spartan in habits, reluctant to use credit, with a great propensity for savings, and steadfast to his employers. Japan is one of the most densely populated countries in the world. Hence, a shortage of space and a cramped environment has led to a code of very polite manners and formal behaviour. The Japanese indulge in a lot of bowing, for example. It has also made the Japanese very adept at the art of miniaturization. Thus, miniature paintings, miniature craftsmanship, the bonsai, the pattern of Japanese gardens and Japanese inventions like the transistor, the walkman, the micro-chip, etc., arise out of this paucity of space.

However, the times are changing. While after the war, the Japanese readily embraced Western clothes and some Western habits, the traditional core remained the same. But now, driven by the changing economy, global pressures and their internal setbacks, modernism is catching up especially on the periphery. Like everywhere else, the young people are embracing the Anglo-American way of life, not merely in their clothes, their food and drink or their leisure pursuits, but also in their mode of work. They are no longer interested in being "salariman" like their fathers, and devote themselves to serving in large conglomerates like Mitsibushi or Yamarichi till they retire. They want to set up their own businesses or go into journalism or the arts or cinema or make their own music. This has created a generation divide. The older generation call the young "shinjiniruis" or "creatures from another planet". So pervasive is this generational change that even in politics, within the stolid, all embracing Liberal Democratic Party which has ruled Japan for almost half a century, the newcomers (often the sons of older members) who want changes, are derisively called "the bonbon boys".

Moreover, there is now feminine assertiveness. Women are working outside their homes more and more. Even if there are few women at the top, women are making their way into various areas of public life. Most of these young women revel in their freedom, hence they refuse to marry young or have large families. Divorce and abortion are available in Japan and their numbers are rising. But there are few illegitimate births as that is still not socially acceptable. As a result, the birth rate is alarmingly low and Japan has one of the fastest greying populations in the world. This is further accentuated by the fact that the Japanese do not accept immigrants, nor naturalization. The purity of the bloodline is still important in Japan.

Japanese politics and business are dominated by clannishness, cronyism and consensus. The country still remains a loose connection of feudal groups knit together by a powerful sense of communal loyalty. It is clannishness and commitment now devoted to the workplace, which has made for the strength of Japanese enterprises. The pursuit of economic growth was the over-riding priority in Japan's economic policy in the post-war era. The close cultural and institutional links between the politicians, the bureaucrats and businessmen/entrepreneurs, what is called the Iron Triangle, was the bedrock of Japan's phenomenal success. Yet, after years of prosperity, when corruption filtered in, the same linkage became the cause of the persistent economic downturn. This crony capitalism is at the root of Japan's present economic woes. And the LDP persists in its old ways, resisting structural reforms.

The other cultural factor that is typical, all-pervading, in the Japanese system is decision by consensus, whether in politics, governance or in business. It does not however mean a democratic way of consultation by a vote or referendum. In Japanese style of management, decisions often percolate up from the middle or the bottom level towards the top; they are not arbitrarily handed down from the top. Hence, to build consensus, middle managers have to practice the delicate art of 'nemawashi' or tending to the roots.

The three components of Japanese management are stakeholder capitalism, consensus-based decision-making and closed labour system of in-house trade unions. There is life-time employment and promotion by seniority, not merit. This worked well, when the economy was growing. But in the present circumstances, this has to change across the board.

The typical Japanese institutions which still control the economy are as follows:

- Zaibatsu – family – dominated business groups with historical associations organized around a holding company;
- Keiretsu – network of larger business houses connected with affiliated companies;
- Sogo Shosha – spearhead many international activities of Japanese firms with which they are affiliated – their intelligence network is comparable to CIA or KGB.

In this scenario, it is very difficult for foreign firms to penetrate the market. Japan is an open market, but a closed society. After constant pressure form USA and Europe, Japan has lowered its tariff barriers to become negligible.

Yet, protectionism works with an invisible hand. Culture and taste are the biggest barriers. Then of course, there are bureaucratic and regulatory obstacles and a very subtle and intricate distribution system that is weighted against imported goods.

The Japanese consumer is a captive of the system. Culture and taste limit the choice of Japanese people. They often pay a much higher (premium) price for local products than imported ones, e.g., rice. The Japanese are also very service-oriented. They even prefer to pay a higher price for good service. On the other hand, the service industry in Japan is incomparable, as that again is a part of their culture.

The Japanese have a very good work ethic derived from the Confucian influence. They work hard, they are punctual, they rarely strike. They are proud of their self-control and comportment. In family life, they are the providers, the bread-winners – that's all. It is the wife who really manages the finances, the budget, children's education, holidays, festivals, etc. The man of the house is often absent, working hard or sometimes carousing, getting drunk is the only way to let off steam in a high-pressured society. Here lies the dark side of the Japanese character. Years of bottling up emotions, gives way to either going berserk or committing suicide.

The Japanese are also group-oriented. They want to belong and to conform to their group. That is how luxury goods do well in Japan. If one buys a Hermes tie or a Rolex watch, all will follow. Peer pressure is tremendous. Saving face is an obligation to yourself and your family. Therefore suicides increase when companies fail and there is a downturn in the economy. Unemployment, bankruptcy, failure at school or in business are often preludes to suicides.

In direct contact, the Japanese are sensitive to body language – eye contact, firm handshake, correct posture, proper courtesy, proper manners, etc. Otherwise, their subconscious registers their primal disdain for a "ganji" – a pejorative for a foreigner.

Impact of Chinese culture

Communist China

Today, China is an extreme case of a country in flux. It has been a Communist system for 50 years, strictly following the Marxist-Leninist ideology under the totalitarian regime of Chairman Mao. However, since the change of the regime in 1978, China has gradually been changing under the more pragmatic Deng Xioping. Realizing the havoc wrought to the economy, and especially to agriculture by the Communist methods, Deng introduced what he called *"Socialism with Chinese characteristics"*. What it actually means, is that Deng set free the economy from the State-controlled Communist system. He allowed possession of land and a free market in agriculture. Then he opened the long-shut doors to foreign trade and investments. He even established free trade zones for foreign manufacturing plants and industries. Over the next three decades, the economy has been moving towards a free market. Deng's successor, Jiang Zemin, has kept up the momentum of reforms, but gradually – "crossing the stream by feeling the stones" as the Chinese saying goes. After the recent Party Congress, even businessmen and entrepreneurs, once called "enemies of the people" by doctrinaire Communists, can now join the Communist Party, "as they also have a contribution to make to the nation". This opening has had spectacular results; China's GDP doubles every 8 years, foreign investments keep pouring in, and China has even become a member of the WTO (World Trade Organisation) – pretty much a market economy now. Yet there is still the shadow of Tiananman Square, where a peaceful demonstration, in favour of democracy, was ruthlessly put down by tanks in 1989. China is at a crossroads – unable to follow the Maoist path any longer, but still shackled to the Communist Party, and unable to move forward towards full democracy yet (albeit Western-styled understanding of democracy).

However, revolutions, Nationalist or Communist, have not impacted the core of China, which, almost alone among modern states, has a continuous history of statehood and culture going back into antiquity. It is not the oldest civilization, but the lines of continuity stretching from the ancient to contemporary times are more significant. The legacy of traditional China hinges on social attitudes, the style of politics and in culture, the arts and in rural life. Moreover, for nearly 2000 years, despite foreign invasions, the territorial integrity of China has been preserved.

For 2000 years the Chinese lived in the belief that they were the Middle Kingdom, the centre of civilization, superior to "The Barbarians" of the West. To some extent, it was correct. Until 1200 AD, China was more advanced in its inventions and technology than any contemporary state in Europe. The Chinese made paper, and invented the printing machine, gunpowder, the water clock, hydraulic water distribution system for irrigation, etc., besides excelling in creative arts. This belief in their superiority became a conviction when the Koreans, the Japanese, the Vietnamese, etc., acknowledged the superiority of the Chinese civilization and adopted their script, their customs and Confucian ideas.

However, this belief was rudely shaken during the Opium Wars (1838–42 and 1856–60) when the Manchu dynasty suffered a crushing defeat inflicted by the British and French expeditionary forces, and had to conclude humiliating and inequitable treaties. While China did not become a colony exclusively of one power, the British, the French, the Germans, and the Russians carved out their areas of influence. Japan attacked China twice. After the first Sino-Japanese war of 1848, China lost Taiwan and the Penghu Islands and relinquished its privileges in Korea. It had already lost Hong Kong and Macao to the British and the Portuguese respectively, as well as its sovereignty over Tibet.

This résumé of history is important to the understanding of China's attitudes and behaviour today. The Chinese have a long historical memory, a fanatical pride in their history and a different measure of time. They are a race to whom history has taught patience, as well as detachment. When Edgar Snow (the only American writer given access to Chinese leadership in the 1950s and the 1960s) asked Chou-en-Lai, the Prime Minister whether in his opinion the French Revolution had an impact on China, Chou's reply after much thought was: "It is too early to tell".

The Chinese have not forgotten the humiliation inflicted on them during the Opium Wars. They bear a universal grudge, primarily against the West as well as against the Japanese. They do not accept the consequent loss of territory. Hence, they have border disputes with at least four large neighbours and sea-claims disputes with several in South-East Asia. The "Leith motif" of China today is to recover its lost status in the world. Hence every key issue is scrutinized from the prism of this motivation.

In Mao's China, drab uniformity and the "mantras" of his little Red book, replaced religious beliefs, creativity in arts, individual entrepreneurship and the Chinese fondness for colour and pageantry. Athletic sports were preferred to traditional martial arts, the opera and drama became tools of party propaganda. The Cultural Revolution was anything but cultural. And Mao's infamous dictum: "Let a thousand flowers bloom. . ." did not mean an exuberance of new ideas, but a plethora of party political dictates. Authority was in the hands of the Party echelons. Decisions were handed down. Regimentation was the way of life.

After the relaxation allowed by Deng, over the decades China has become a more normal society. A new generation of consumers are availing of the variety of goods, foreign and local now on the market. The old religions and even superstitions are re-surfacing. So are the bad habits of concubinage, kidnap, etc. The inborn entrepreneurial spirit of the Chinese bourgeoisie is back, and paltry capitalism is thriving even in small towns and rural areas in the southern regions of China. With that, comes also the revival of the "guan xi factor".

"Guan xi" means "connections or relationships" – a very practical economic instrument of business dealings. China is not a rule-based society. There is no adequate legal system to protect property rights, support contracts and ensure quality of corporate governance. Hence the guan xi factor is important to China. Transactions are based on relationships not contracts. You check out a prospective partner/manager/client on the relationship network. If he cheats, you can again deal with him through the same network – by blackballing, seizing his assets or his wife or child or getting him beaten up. Therefore in China and amongst Chinese overseas, business must involve only close family, extended family or friends or people from the same village/locality.

Guan xi also means building "cosy" relationships with your bank manager, local party boss, municipal and state authorities – the gatekeepers of power.

As a matter of fact, Guan xi is not confined to Chinese culture, but aspects of it are manifest all over Asia. However, as a result, corruption also has increased in China.

Largely to comfort foreign investors, China is trying to switch from such relationship-based corporate governance to rule-based governance, as in any Western-oriented country. This accelerates the proclivity for corruption. The transition from state-owned, egalitarian poverty to no-holds barred capitalism; from relationship-based to rule-based governance has created fertile soil for widespread corruption. To add to that, the reforms which privatized State-owned enterprises led to downright looting by venal managers. Corruption has tainted the Politburo also – President Jiang Zemin and PM Zhu were also rumoured to have been touched by its ever growing hand.

Rhongji were committed to root out corruption. They made some examples by public hanging of corrupt high-placed officials. But corruption is entrenched, and cannot be so easily eliminated.

Other widespread, remarkable changes are wrought in Chinese education and intelligence pursuits by embracing the new information technology. E-mail has suddenly opened the world to Chinese users. The Communist Party can no longer insulate the people from the ideas of the outside world. After 50 years of regimented thinking, young Chinese are opening their minds to vistas of opportunity they did not know existed. Many are wanting to go abroad for further education (also because the demand for good higher education in China currently outstrips the ability of the University system to supply), and also to be part of the burgeoning "global citizenery". Many are beginning to see the shortcomings of their age-old system. The traditional pride intervenes nonetheless.

The young people in China, like everywhere else, are embracing American music, clothes, food and lifestyles, which again is causing a generation gap. The Party watches warily. One movement, the Falong Gong – which has taken full advantage of the Internet, is however heavily dealt with. The Chinese authorities fear cult movements, which have destabilized governments in the past. Hence the severity meted out to this apparently peaceful movement – stability and ongoing sustainability of the nation are key priorities of Beijing.

The overseas Chinese

There are historic reasons for the Chinese diaspora. First, people migrated solely to countries in Indo-China and South-East Asia to escape from poverty and famine, which were endemic in the 19th and 20th centuries when China was so unsettled. Second, during the same period, the British and the French took Chinese people as indentured labour to work in their plantations in South-East Asia and Polynesia. Third, at the beginning of World War II and after the fall of Nanking during the civil war, the well-to-do merchants and professionals fled to Hong Kong, then a British colony and on to Singapore,

Indonesia, Malaysia and the Philippines, and a large majority followed General Chang-Kaishek to Formosa, later re-named Taiwan. There are Chinese settlers also along the West coast of USA. Unlike international custom, whereby immigrants often take on the nationality of, and integrate into, their chosen homeland, China claims her sons and daughters wherever they are. Hence the notion of a Greater China is a real goal for China, and within the Chinese diaspora.

Wherever they settle down, the Chinese are very hard-working, enterprising people (not overtly seeking to be noticed). They start with small businesses-laundries, restaurants, groceries and gradually build themselves up as entrepreneurs, financiers or brokers. In South-East Asia, the Chinese also cornered gambling dens, casinos and real-estate businesses. From these, they have grown into big business in the countries where they have settled. Over the last few decades they have gained control of most of the commerce. In the Philippines, for example, the Chinese community is just 1% of the population, but controls half of the stock market. In Indonesia the ratio is 4% and 75% respectively. In Malaysia it is 32% and 60%. In Thailand, they control half the total wealth. Thus, these 51 million overseas Chinese in South-East Asia control an economic spread worth US$ 700 billion, and their combined wealth is in the region of US$ 3.5 trillion.

Yet, this is a different kind of capitalism – "the bamboo network" of Chinese family businesses which stretch across South-East Asia. They have provided 70% of overseas investments in mainland China. Now they are pushing into Vietnam, Cambodia, Laos and Myanmar. But these exponents of Asian capitalism are very chameleonic – they conceal more than they reveal; their total assets are never published. Politically, they try to keep a low profile. This secretiveness springs from a visceral sense of insecurity, the inborn fear of an outsider who can be targeted or kicked out. This fear is not unjustified, considering how often Chinese communities have been attacked in Indonesia for example. This leads to other characteristics, e.g., they keep a portion of their wealth liquid in cash or gold. They do not trust outsiders. Even within the family, only the patriarch has absolute control and the total picture of the business. Sons, nephews, cousins, in-laws are included in the business and climb the ladder by their loyalty, not proficiency. Outside managers are taken for their expertise; but after deep scrutiny more because of their reliability than brilliance. But they can never make it to the top. That remains a weakness of the system. When a patriarch dies, the business wobbles. Sometimes it is split up, sometimes it runs into losses. Yet often it is rescued by some other members of the clan. That is an unwritten code – to help each other hailing from the same town, or district, in mainland China.

Entrepreneurial deals are struck between families and clans. Often money to start a new business is provided by the clan members. Each large family or clan, or people hailing from the same district, has its own area of business. Loose entrepreneurial networks are based on "trust". Deals are often clinched just by a handshake. Often small industries spring up making paper flowers, or transistors or garments, make money and then disappear. This nimble-footedness and network-building is another feature of Chinese businesses. The real strength of Chinese capitalism lies in its network of fast moving companies and their capacity to cope with change and uncertainty.

The other important aspects are the much-toted "Asian values", which are cited as reasons for their spectacular success. They consist of family and clannish loyalty, a rigorous work ethic, diligence, discipline and deference for employers, a proclivity for savings and personal frugality and a contempt for Western "profligacy" and "excess". Here again the "guan xi factor" prevails. Reciprocity of favours done/received is most important in relationships. Saving "face" is also very important.

Hence in dealing with Chinese businessmen, a few anecdotal illustrations can be useful. The Chinese are tough negotiators. Often the whole truth is very difficult to ascertain upfront – one has to reveal one's true intentions over time before deep trust is engendered. Frontal confrontation is best avoided, particularly in public or among peers and work colleagues.

To do a deal with a Chinese business, you need more than board room meetings to be "accepted". They would be lavish with their hospitality and often expect you to spend a day or two together. Because thus they can better judge you. This is more so, if they are hiring you. Your diplomas are important. But they want to judge your character, comportment etc. They may even set small traps for you to see how you behave in stress. If you are invited by a Chinese to a Chinese restaurant, let your host order your meal and honour him by consuming it to the last grain (even if you do not like it). Chinese liquor is very potent. But they expect you to drink a lot. Hence make an excuse beforehand, and totally refrain. No half measures are possible.

Unlike so-called well-bred Europeans, the Chinese like to show off their wealth in dress, jewellery, etc. Hence, if you want a deal, wear smart clothes, an expensive watch, a first class ticket in your breast pocket and lavish gifts. Again, the Chinese are very status-conscious. If your bank or company wants a big deal in mainland China or Taiwan or Singapore, make sure your CEO makes at least one visit. When China was opening its banking sector, eight French banks – the very cream of French banking applied, but only two got the licences. Those two whose PDGs had bothered to go to Beijing. It is always difficult to get a first deal, sometimes you could be talking for two to three years. But once it is clinched and the results are satisfactory, a relationship is established. It is plain sailing in the negotiations of deals that follow, because, the Chinese also do not like to change their partners.

You have to be correct and polite in your dealings with the Chinese. The last thing they want to see is any hint of arrogance or impatience. Patience is the name of the game. The Chinese are never in a hurry. And if you show you are hard-pressed for time, they will take advantage of you or view you as needy. They will spin out the negotiations to wear you out. It is a game of chess. And the Chinese have played it for centuries.

The Islamic world

The Islamic world spreads from Morocco to Iraq, as the Middle East where Arabs are the predominant race (exception is Israel) and Sunni Islam is prevalent. Adjacent to Iraq, is Iran – the centre of Shia Islam with Afghanistan and Pakistan next door (both Sunnis). East of India lies Bangladesh and further South, Indonesia, Malaysia, and Brunei which are also Sunnis, but their fervour is moderated by mingling with Hindu and Buddhist influences. In Europe, Turkey and Albania are Islamic, besides Kosovo and Bosnia. Amongst the ex-Soviet Republics, Azerbaijan and the five central Asian Republics – Uzbekistan, Tajikistan, Kazakhstan, Kyrghistan, and Turkmenistan are Muslim (Sunnis) but here Islam is diluted by half a century of Communist Control and vodka drinking. Moreover, there are Muslim communities almost the world over, the second largest being in India.

Islam has also enriched the world with a great civilization: the splendour of its monuments, landscape gardens, calligraphy, paintings and poetry, refinements in cuisine, mode of behaviour and style of living are legendary. Spurred by their belief and the vigour of their faith, the tribes of Arabia rode out in all directions, spreading the new faith more by the sword than by the Book and established empires which stretched from Morocco to China. Islam held sway in Spain for nearly five centuries and Cordoba became a center of Islamic learning. It was a Muslim scholar here who first translated the classics of ancient Greece and Rome. The Caliphates of Baghdad and Damascus were known for their system of governance; Samarkand and Bokhara in modern Uzbekistan were also fabled centres of learning. This culture has also contributed to science, e.g., algebra, astronomy, certain systems of medicine, etc. The splendour of the Moghul Court in India was admired and written about by European travelers of the 16th century.

But eventually, these empires decayed. European nations were establishing their own empires. Revitalized by the Industrial Revolution which provided superior technology and weaponry, they carved up Islamic territories as they pleased and installed puppet dynasties who served their bidding. In Egypt, Libya, Jordan, Iraq, Saudi Arabia, Iran and the Sheikhdoms of the Gulf as well as in Morocco, Tunisia and Lebanon, British and French power had predominance. To add to the humiliation and shame inflicted by the lost wars of the 18th and the 19th centuries, was the imposition of Israel in their midst and the ignominious defeats suffered during each war the Arabs fought with this tiny new nation.

Today, the adherents of Islam have a fractured psyche. On one hand, the memories of a great civilization haunt them, on the other the humiliation of defeat and their present poverty and deprivation anger them. The traditional Islamic schools (Madrasahs), which were real centres of culture and learning in the past, are now partly controlled by semi-educated and bigoted Mullahs and have thus become the breeding ground for extremists, fundamentalists and terrorists.

The Islamic world is also not monolithic. Apart from the major division between Sunnis and Shiahs, there are a variety of sects, usually persecuted by the two major ones, who have historically fought each other. except for Iran, the Shiahs are in a minority in other Muslim countries and are often ill-treated. They are evenly divided in Lebanon. Syria has the peculiarity of an Alawite (Shia) ruler in a largely Sunni country. Nor is the fanaticism and religious fervour uniformally present in all countries. Egypt, Iraq, Syria, Tunisia, Morocco and Jordan can be termed as moderate and even striving to become modern, even though they are plagued by Islamic extremists. Saudi Arabia, Iran, Yemen, Sudan are orthodox and fundamentalist. Turkey is modern and secular, though it has recently elected an Islamist party to form the government. The Islamic Republics of the old USSR are moderate, as the actual control still rests in the hands of the same Communist Leaders.

However, in the last two decades, there is a distinct trend towards Islamization of even moderate States. The Shariah or Koranic law has been adopted, by some, because of the pressure of the Orthodox in countries which were hitherto striving towards modernization, e.g., Pakistan, Oman, UAE, Nigeria, etc. Even moderate countries like Indonesia and Malaysia are making concessions to the Shariah, e.g., women are now increasingly wearing head scarves again. It is certain that the Islamic world is in a ferment. The incidents of September 11th has changed it, as much as it has changed the USA.

To do business in Islamic countries, you require prior knowledge of their customs and habits. You have to deal with them, taking into account the type of government, society, attitude towards the West, towards non-believers, etc.:

- In radical states which have overthrown those Kings or Emirs who were clients of the West and are now Republics like Egypt, Syria, Iraq and perhaps Algeria, business is dominated by the public sector. Hence you require skills to deal with bureaucrats and state control. You require both patience and tact. You have to be discrete, while entertaining or gratifying.
- In monarchies like Morocco, Saudi Arabia and the Gulf Emirates, business is often concentrated in the hands of, or around, the ruling family. Hence, you must learn to gather palace rumours/gossips and establish conduits for gratification. It requires ingratiation, a lot of bowing and scraping, gifts for every occasion, also entertainment of the right people.
- In countries which are switching over to the Shariah or the Koranic law, it is a different ball game. The Shariah imposes different rules for banking, arbitration, contracts, jurisprudence and justice. Yet, there is pragmatism. They are quite ready to sign contracts on neutral territory so that the Shariah does not strictly apply. But you have to be vigilant that it does not

come to the notice of the religious Police, e.g., in Saudi Arabia, Iran, etc. Business dealings are invariably opaque. Corruption is a way of life. Yet caution is most necessary and passing of a bribe should always be through an intermediary who is a local.

For dealing with countries in the Middle East, you have to develop sensitivity to Arab manners and customs. It is less so East of India.

- Breaking bread together is a great ice breaker. However, in a traditional Arab household or even business house, everybody eats with his fingers out of the same huge plate. You have also to join in. Women will seldom be present, though they may serve the meal. That is the custom from Azerbaijan to Indonesia.
- Even on neutral ground, or when you are entertaining Arab guests, avoid pork and liquor.
- Always respect the Ramadan and the Eid festivals.
- There is, in some parts of the world, a great deal of hypocrisy about use of liquor. Some Arabs drink huge quantities, and even in countries where there is prohibition, e.g., Saudi Arabia, you may be asked to supply a few bottles. This has to be very tactfully handled. Laws are very strict in Saudi Arabia about importing liquor, or drinking in public, and you may be jailed for any violation. The same applies to pornography. Even magazines like *Elle* or *Cosmopolitan* can be confiscated if there is a bathing suit on the cover.
- In your dealings, never use the left hand, avoid minimal dress.
- Negotiations are formal, often convoluted. Often deals are struck outside the conference room, at a convivial dinner.
- An Arab's word is his contract.
- It is a strictly patriarchal society, and power is concentrated at the top. There are of course variations between the countries, but the common denominator is distrust even within the brotherhood.
- Women are certainly at a disadvantage.

On the other hand, many particularly the bureaucrats, are often educated in the West. They may pretend to be humble or dumb but will trip you up. Yet, Arabs can also make staunch friends and reciprocating an act of kindness is a commitment of faith to them.

The Indian sub-continent

India is a country rich in cultural variety and baffling contrasts. It is home to many races which have mixed and mingled over centuries. It has 14 languages and 200 odd spoken dialects. All the major religions, besides Hinduism, have thrived here. St. Thomas the Apostle brought Christianity to India, before it was accepted in Rome. Legend says he is buried near the city of Madras in the South. India has an amazing capacity to absorb different cultures and Indianise them. In the graceful sculptures of the Buddha of the Gandhara School in the North, there are distinct influences of the Grecian style, reminiscent of the Greek satraps, left behind to rule by Alexander the Great.

The 7th century was the golden age of Hindu art and architecture, as well as of poetry, drama and literature. Mathematics, astronomy, alchemy, plastic surgery and ayurvedic system of medicine (based on herbs and plants) flourished. So did trade with countries of South-East Asia (which all bore Sanskrit names then) and East Africa. There was a flourishing Asian globalism around the Indian Ocean.

The waves of Muslim conquerors who poured in through the Himalayan passes (after 1000 AD) from century to century did plunder and kill and destroy the marvellous temples and libraries, but they too settled down and were absorbed. The magnificent Moghuls added their style of architecture, miniature painting, landscape gardens and refined manners and cuisine to an already rich culture. Today, North India has some splendid examples of Moghul architecture, including the peerless Taj Mahal which Indians consider a proud heritage of their composite culture. But in the South, beginning with the wondrous Buddhist cave carvings and murals of Ajanta and Ellora (400 BC–1100 AD) to the glorious temples of Madura, Mahabalipuram (200–400 AD) and Konarak in the East (1100–1200 AD), as well as the pristine beauty of the Jain temples in the West (1700–1900 AD), are glorious celebrations of the cosmic nature of Hinduism. One can view the whole panorama of the evolution of Hinduism by looking at the rich carvings inside, and outside, these temples.

India has gone through many vicissitudes since. At the time of Independence, India had back-slid into poverty and social ills. It had become a country of poor, illiterate masses, obscurantist and divisive religions, hardly any industry and prone to famines. When the British left, British India was segmented. Burma (Myanmar) and Ceylon (Sri Lanka), both with a separate identity also became independent, while India itself was divided according to the predominance of the Hindus and the Muslims into two separate states – India and Pakistan. The latter makes conscious efforts to link itself to other Islamic States in West-Asia, yet by dint of language, music, films and cuisine, it feels the pull of its Indian heritage. As elsewhere in the world, it was an untidy partition which created more problems than it solved, and has left behind an open wound in the case of Kashmir.

Through the centuries, despite all the turbulence of its history, India has maintained its cultural identity from Kashmir in the north to Kanya-Kumari, its southernmost tip. The lines of continuity go back almost to pre-history and are maintained by a rich oral tradition. Hence also India's excellence in crafts, handed down from generation to generation. To some extent, the caste system, much misunderstood, much maligned and much exploited, has something to do with this preservation of skills through generations.

Such a complex cultural heritage becomes both a source of pride and joy, as well as a burden and a roadblock, in the progress of India towards modernity.

If the past, however rich and enlightened, becomes a point of reference for the present and the future, it becomes a handicap. As such, so many of the attitudes or positions India takes flow out of this habit of looking back. Indians regret that Britain prevented them from participating in the benefits of the Industrial Revolution and subsequent technological changes. It is therefore a national commitment not to miss out on the new scientific and technological innovations, to become completely self-sufficient and self-reliant. India consequently went in for full-scale industrialization and spent millions on acquiring proficiency in various sectors, including nuclear technology, space research, information technology, bio-sciences, etc., to be entirely self-sufficient, and to keep abreast with new and emerging technologies. This "economic nationalism" was sometimes carried to an absurd extent. It often becomes a disadvantage for foreign investors and entrepreneurs. India has been very selective in the technologies it imports. This "swadeshi" syndrome has been an obstacle to rapid growth.

It is the memories of a glorious past which pushed Indian leaders to play an active role in world affairs, to re-claim the old lead in Asia, and to contribute the concepts of non-alignment, peaceful co-existence amongst nations and to modern international relations. As a matter of fact, during the worst stages of the cold war, India often played a facilitator's role much larger than its actual power. In the causes it championed, India was often ahead of its times. By positioning itself on the moral high ground, India made itself irksome, but time has borne out the validity of India's stand on many difficult issues of those times. On the other hand, the Kashmir issue became a pawn in the superpower rivalry. India's non-alignment was viewed as crypto-communism by the USA with whom Pakistan had an alliance. Hence India came to depend on the USSR for political support and purchase of weapons. For that reason, India has been selective of her trading partners, also preferring the more independent Europeans like France.

The breadth and scope of Hinduism creates a very complex mind-set which accepts paradox at the core of being. That creates a peculiar ambivalence on moral or social issues which the West finds so baffling. For example, Westerners visiting India, for the first time, are overpowered by the pressure of the numbers, the strong smells, the cacophony of sounds and the kaleidoscope of sights India presents. They are both attracted and repelled. They are shocked by the poverty, the misery, the disease and the squalor juxtaposed with Mercedes cars and gold clad ladies utterly oblivious to the obvious deprivation. And yet the poor wear smiles, children are playing or singing – there is no class war or revolution about to happen. This is the result of the all-pervading belief in Karma which makes such acceptance, and such indifference, compatible.

Similarly, the caste system, legally and intellectually totally discredited, still pervades the subconscious and shows up in people's reflexes towards each other. Yet the good thing is that everybody knows their place in society and a sense of where they belong, which creates a certain kind of social stability. The good thing also is that the past rigidity is gone. There is some mobility between castes, in terms of education, economic interaction, even marriages. Foreigners often ask whether caste would impact their relationships with Indians. It does not. Since Independence the Indian government is obliged to ensure practice of "positive discrimination" in favour of the hitherto deprived castes, but that has also created a new set of problems.

Hindu thinking also encompasses both individualism and pluralism at the same time. Pluralism is manifested in the infinite number of gods and goddesses in the Hindu pantheon. But this is for the masses, the simple-minded who need embodiment to understand abstract concepts. But for the thinker and the real seeker, the Sublime One is timeless, formless, limitless – the Creator, the Preserver and the Destroyer all rolled into one – the centre point of all Cosmos. The soul who seeks enlightenment follows a difficult, and even dangerous, path, shedding all earthly ties including loved ones, quitting civilization, practising a regime of asceticism over years before finding Enlightenment and ultimately, only the lucky few, the embrace of the Divine – Moksha, i.e., escape from the entrapment of rebirth. As a result, Hinduism is rather egoistic. It is your personal salvation which matters, not the salvation of humanity. You are responsible for your own space. For example, bathing is very important but allowing the dirty water to flow into your neighbour's yard is not your concern. This is further reflected in a number of daily habits, for example, you give alms to a beggar because it is good for your salvation, but you may not be personally bothered about rooting out the core reasons for why people do beg.

On the other hand, Hinduism is the most tolerant of religions. It has allowed space not only for the religion of the conquerors who came, i.e., Islam, but for others who came seeking asylum, e.g., Zoroastrians driven out by Moslem conquerors of Iran; Christianity came with the early preachers, who founded the Syrian Christian Church and acknowledged the Patriarch of Antioch and Catholicism brought by the Jesuits in the wake of the Portuguese traders. As a matter of fact, India has a Jewish community still thriving in the South. For that reason, though predominantly Hindu and despite the "partition" effected on religious grounds, India's leaders opted for a secular state giving equal rights to all its citizens, irrespective of caste, creed, religion or sex. These rights are enshrined in the Constitution. As a result, though Pakistan was created as a homeland for the Muslims of India, half of them remained in India. Today, the Muslim population of India is larger than Pakistan's entire population.

Finally, there is the significant impact of the British rule in India on the cultural life of the people. Today, more people speak English in India than the entire population of Britain. There is now an accepted genre of English Indian literature. Besides, British law, jurisprudence, accounting system and Westminster style of government adopted and Indianised, there is an impact on the mindset of the people – perhaps not on the masses, but on the intelligentsia, which while striving to be independent of colonial vestiges cannot help but think and behave otherwise. This is changing of course, and British values are disappearing. India, of course, is a vibrant economic democracy which, with all its shortcomings, is a part of the national ethos.

Doing business in India is both easy and very difficult. There are fewer cultural barriers. Even though they may dress differently and be outwardly traditional, the Indians you have to deal with have very Western mindsets. Understanding each other is much easier than in many other parts of Asia. India offers a good infrastructure of intellectual assets, e.g., lawyers, accountants, economists, computer experts, bio-scientists and chemists, doctors, and engineers. This asset has particularly proved fortuitous with the Internet revolution. India has become the back-office to much of world business. Yet, Indian businessmen also often have a hidden agenda. While they share common values of corporate ethics, they can be ambivalent, in terms of corruption. There is a certain streak, at least among some business communities, that it is "macho" to pull a fast one on your adversary, even to cheat. This is squared up, without any sense of guilt, as a manifestation of "karma" – we have settled outstanding accounts of the previous life. However, the same equanimity prevails when the person himself is cheated, and has no other recourse. Similarly when accidents occur or calamities take place, nobody thinks of suing. It is all put down to fate and to karma.

The biggest obstacle of course is India's web of intractable bureaucracy and vested interests which choke enterprise and initiative, and keep away foreign investors. Yet, business does thrive and those who persist reap handsome profits, Indians are from necessity a very thrifty people, with great propensity for savings. From the housewife to the entrepreneur, they want to see value for their money. In any negotiations, whether in the private or the public sector, Indians will always try to bring the price down. To any ambitious businessman, India is a challenge worthy of taking up. But it is not for the faint-hearted.

Latin America

South America is a clearly defined geographical continent whose 13 independent countries aspire towards a collective identity as Latin America. Its culture shaped by European settlements that began 450 years ago, is more homogeneous than that of Europe or Asia. This cultural affinity is based on a common language, religion and shared past experience. With the exception of Brazil where Portuguese is spoken, and the three Guyanas – English, French and Dutch – Spanish (or Castilian, as it is called here) is the spoken language and a unifying factor, as also a shared European tradition and Latin lifestyle. Latin America is 90% catholic. The church and the State are separate, yet the church plays an important, if sometimes a dubious, role in public life.

Here was the first manifestation of an Atlantic globalism, when Spanish (and Portuguese to a lesser extent) conquistadors conquered this region and established trading posts. They, however violently subjugated the local people, imposing on them their own language, religion and cultural habits. Many died as a result of the wars, and many from the new diseases which the conquerors brought with them. This region has also given birth to earlier civilizations. The sacred centres of the Incas and the Mayas in Mexico, Guatemala, Peru, and Bolivia – their crafts and their jewellery show that a highly evolved culture flourished here. The wind-swept ruins of Machu Picchu perched at 16,000 ft in Peru are considered one of the wonders of the world. These civilizations vanished before the newcomers arrived, the pre-Colombian art and treasures left behind are a contribution to world heritage. Unfortunately, the indigenous folk who inhabit these countries now, have little linkage with their past.

These countries, though classified as "developing", have 400 years of participation in international trade. Hence, their economies have acquired, through their contacts with Europe and the USA, a sophistication not yet evident in Asia (Hong Kong and Singapore are the exceptions). As a matter of fact, freedom to trade and to draw upon the technical and financial resources of the industrial world, was one of the mainsprings of their Independence Movements which were successful 150 years ago. All ten of them have fought some sort of wars of liberation against Spain and Portugal respectively. Thus each Republic has its own hero or heroes and martyrs, who are still revered and commemorated (St. Martin – Argentina; Artigas – Uruguay; O'Higgins – Chile; Zapata – Mexico; Simon Bolivar – Bolivia, etc.).

The Latins are very susceptible to demagogy. The "Caudillo" tradition is very strong. Juan and Evita Peron (Argentina), Perez and Chavez (Venezuela), Stroessner (Paraguay), Fujimori (Peru), Castro (Cuba), etc., have held their people in thrall by their speeches and promises, often without honouring many of them. Unfortunately, Western-styled democracy has hitherto not flourished here. Instead Militarism, Marxism and Populism are an integral part of the Latin tradition. The army is politicized and wields power either by direct military rule or pulling strings behind a façade President. During the Cold War period, it suited US strategy to support military dictators all over Latin America, so long as they could root out Marxism and keep the USSR out. This became more accentuated after Cuba and Nicaragua went Communist. Most of these dictators were mediocre rulers who spawned cruel and corrupt governments. Hence the people suffered. Young people who rebelled or expressed liberal ideas just "disappeared". The memory of these practices are vivid, and the USA, given its parallel strategies in the Middle-East is viewed and spoke about with disdain.

It is true that Marxism has always lurked among the peasants, as on the campuses. But it was largely home grown. In Colombia and Peru, Marxist revolutionaries claim to be freedom fighters. In these countries where power and riches are concentrated in the hands of a few and the rich-poor divide is a gaping chasm, Marxism finds a fertile soil.

Latin America escaped the horrors of the World Wars, insulated by distance. At the end of World War II, some of these countries, e.g., Argentina were amongst the richest in the world. Their trade was mainly with Europe and the USA. Boosted by their income, the larger countries went in for large infrastructural projects for which they borrowed liberally from commercial banks in the USA and Europe. But by the 1970s, their exports started falling. The European Community's Common tariffs hit them hard. They however, continued borrowing, in the hope that injection of capital would bolster growth. But that did not happen. The oil crisis of 1973 had also hit them hard. As a result they slipped into a debt trap and hyper inflation. Eventually, they found substitute markets, but the falling commodity prices did not help. The Latins were simply not geared to meet world competition in manufacturing. Their costs were too high, protected by high tariff barriers. Import substitution and foreign exchange conservation seemed the only answer. Yet they could not balance their budgets. Hence, Latin Americans have lived lurching from one financial crisis to the next, some more dramatically like Argentina – others less so. Chile has been the only exception.

While some of their troubles are due to outside factors, some blame has to rest on the Latin character. Richly endowed by nature and still underpopulated, the Latins have been spared, the vicissitudes that the Asians went through during and after World War II. They lack their fortitude, their sharp edge of competitiveness for survival, their proclivity for savings and their distrust of borrowing. But they share with the Asians, the habit of corruption. The blame largely rests with some of their leaders, who as dictators ran cruel and corrupt regimes and lined their own pockets. In South-East Asia, the leadership may be corrupt but it has always been business-friendly and committed to enrichment of the country. Even Suharto, whose corruption was legendary, was responsible for the growth of the Indonesian economy.

Along with a common culture, the Latins also share three major ills – corruption, endemic debt and drugs. Drugs have torn apart the fabric of civil society in Colombia and some of the neighbouring countries, while the rest are not immune. Unbridled corruption has brought the once proud people like the Argentines to their knees. It would appear that the Latins can never escape the vicious cycle of debt and corruption.

The end of the cold war brought a change of regimes in Latin America. American explicit policy changed also, supporting democracies instead of dictatorships. For the first time in their history, during the last decade, democratic governments have taken charge in most countries, except, some would argue, Venezuela and Cuba. With the new spurt in globalization, the Latins embraced market-oriented economies rather enthusiastically. But they were the first to suffer the setback of free financial markets and the fickleness of global investors, as their currencies fell in a domino effect after the crash of the Mexican peso in 1994. While Mexico was pulled up by its affluent partner in NAFTA and is once again doing well, the rest are still struggling.

The Latins do have some beguiling qualities. They have a zest for life. They love having a good time. Though their music is always plaintive, they are exuberant dancers – whether in a market square or in a nightclub. They are more Mediterranean in their habits than American. They put on a brave face. They always dress as well as they can. People on the streets of Lima or Santiago or Buenos Aires look more elegant than in New York. They also have rather an old-fashioned habit of respecting the privacy of their leaders, their friends and the honour of the family. To some extent, the upper class preserves the norm of European society of an earlier century. The world associates Latin America with a "macho" tradition. Superficially it is true. But the women are not subservient at all. In fact, women are the rock of the family. Small businesses from a village grocery store to fashionable boutiques, travel agencies, even banks often have women in charge. The richest person in Latin America was actually a woman entrepreneur some years ago. They are also a very hospitable people.

In Latin America there also is a tradition of family-controlled conglomerates, which dominate the private sector. In some ways, they resemble family business in Asia. First, the extended family ties are strong. It is safer to rely on close relatives than on strangers. Often there is no clear-cut separation between family interests and business interests, and there is a certain flexibility about providing jobs for relatives, arranging convenient work schedules, handling of expense accounts and safeguarding the family prestige. For that reason, these family firms are very secretive about their operations. The typical Latin firm remains a hierarchical dictatorship where information is closely guarded, and outsiders are suspect. These family firms were willing collaborators in the protectionist and interventionist policies of their governments. They also encouraged keeping capital-intensive industries in the public sector, whose output such as cement or steel or power would benefit them. They are also more comfortable on their own home ground, instead of becoming multinationals. Instead they have diversified both horizontally and vertically. And they take full advantage of the weakness of their legal systems.

Things, however, are changing and most family firms will claim they have professional managers (certainly well-off family members have been educated, more and more in business, management and leadership disciplines, at the world's ivy league Universities, typically in the USA and Europe). They are also shaping up to meet global challenges and spreading out elsewhere, e.g., Bunge y Borne, an old Argentine family firm, now has a base in Brazil, and is registered in the Bermudas. Another is the Grupo Corso in Mexico, and Luksic in Chile.

Foreign multinationals which are prolific in Latin America are taking advantage of the economic groupings that are taking shape, to locate their facilities not country-wise but according to availability of raw materials, easier access, labour, etc., to achieve economies of scale. Moreover, the wave of privatizations across the continent during the 1990s were advantageous to foreign multinationals. But privatization has not at all been popular, because it has caused a lot of pain to the public, and lined the pockets of ministers and bureaucrats.

One good sign is that democracy, however flawed, is taking root in Latin America. People are voting with their feet as demonstrated in Argentina, Brazil and recently in Venezuela. As stated previously, there is a peculiar love-hate relationship with the USA. In return, the USA's policy also alternates between interference and benign neglect, neither of which pleases Latin Americans. In some ways their ties with Europe are stronger, especially with Spain, Portugal and Italy. The Latins go to the USA to do deals, to hide their cash, to educate their children; they go to Europe because of the pull of the old country, for holidays, for cultural satisfaction, for expanding their identities, and for renewing their roots.

Some illustrations of differing cultural attitudes

Sense of time

Sense of time varies dramatically amongst different cultural groups: in the USA, time is money. Punctuality is mandatory. Late arrival can cost you the job. But in Latin America, time is elastic. "Mañana" is the buzzword. For business appointments or even a social engagement, count two extra hours, before losing your patience. In Europe, sense of time varies from the north to the south. In Protestant Europe, i.e., Scandinavia, Holland, Britain, Germany and Switzerland, punctuality is sacrosanct. Tardiness is frowned upon. But in Latin countries, there are varying degrees of tolerance for the unpunctual – from fifteen minutes in France up to an hour in Spain and Portugal. In Greece, as an example, it could even be two hours. In Communist Europe, punctuality was ensured by fear, but with democracy, habits are getting more slack. Time gets more elastic as one goes eastwards. The Arabs are generally quite ambivalent – even about keeping appointments. The secretary of a bureaucrat with whom you have an appointment, can tell you after you have reached his office, that it is cancelled. "Monsieur est fatiqué" and that is a good enough excuse. Sometimes, this is deliberately done to convey a message. In Asia with the exception of Japan, again time is variable. But, in communist China, time becomes a powerful instrument to bring psychological pressure on the adversary.

Sense of space

The availability of space or the lack of it, conditions the attitudes of people. In USA, the abundance of space, creates a sense of expansiveness. Everything is big, king-size. The sky is the limit for ambitions, achievements, etc. The reverse is true in countries like Holland or Japan, where space is limited. People learn to make do with small things and cramped space. No wonder the Japanese are good at miniaturization and the Dutch at growing flowers wherever space is available – even between runways at Schiphol airport.

Attitude towards money

In USA, the dollar is king. It is always a race to riches, and American capitalism is geared to making profits. True and actioned social responsibility very rarely come into it. The yardstick is money. If a young girl in America is told: "you look like a million dollars!"; she will be flattered. In France, it will be considered as very bad taste. In Europe, there is a certain deprecating attitude towards money, which is to some extent also hypocritical. Well-bred people do not flaunt their money. Old money is discreet. Only the "*nouveau riche*" spend ostentatiously. In Calvinist-puritan countries, money is never wasted. The Dutch, the Swiss, the Scots, for example, are very parsimonious. Yet for good causes, e.g., charity, church, schools, etc., they will give generously. In Latin Europe, money is to be enjoyed. The French, the Spanish and the Italians love the good things of life, and spend on them. But they are stingy on charity. No wonder, the highest amount of aid to poor countries comes from the Scandinavians and the Dutch. The same habits of Latin Europe, are reflected in Latin America. As a result, they become prone to debt, national and private. Islamic attitude towards money is different. The Koranic law governs both the acquisition, investment and the way to spend money. A part of the income must go to charity regularly. Interest is frowned upon. Money is for good usage, not for self-indulgence. And yet, the oil-rich, Arab Sheikhs are often the most wanton and wasteful and indifferent to the plight of their poor. In Asia, money is respected. Long experience of hardship, calamities and poverty make the Asian people both thrifty and conscious of the value of money. They therefore have a great proclivity for savings, even hoarding. This also makes them good bargainers and negotiators. For the sake of "face" and "standing" in the community, Asians may splurge on weddings or funerals, but they will haggle over a kilo of fruit.

Accounting systems

While Western accounting systems are basically the same, there are nuances which are different. In Britain, Holland, and Denmark, for example, accounts are always open and upfront and any jiggery-pokery is therefore easy to detect. In the USA, on the other hand, the accounting methods have scope for "imaginative" manipulation and the sting is always in the fine print of the most innocuous-looking contracts. In France, the accounting system is in the same straightjacket of the Code Napoleonic. The German system is strict and closed – they only open their books to their in-house banks. In Asia, the Japanese system is deliberately opaque and provides pockets for hiding away profits. In China, the system is totally Chinese, and therefore one of the handicaps Western business faces. In the rest of Asia, depending on the colonial heritage, countries follow either the English or the French accounting systems. However, these are manipulated to suit individual agendas. Keeping two sets of books, hiding profits in a pyramid of front companies – the system called "Chinese boxes" are common in East, South-East and South Asia.

Negotiations

The Americans are straightforward, but tough. They will always wear name tags, prefer to be on first name terms, and be correctly dressed – but they will go hammer and tongs, produce a barrage of data and can even resort to bullying. They will always have a big team and try to cow down opposition. But if you remain firm, they will back off. The British are always correct, relaxed and put their case forward with precision (but it is often difficult to read their true intentions, as in parts of Asia). Their sense of humour enlivens tense moments, but they can use barbed wit, either out of mischief or to rattle you. The Dutch and the Scandinavians are open, direct and even blunt. But they have no hidden agenda. French negotiations are like a minuet. They build an argument with typical Cartesian logic, which for unaccustomed ears becomes too involved and is often confusing. They are meticulous, legalistic and want everything down on paper. The Arabs negotiate in a convoluted manner. But a deal is often struck, not in the boardroom but at the dinner table, or in a private chat between the leaders of the two teams. There is often a secretiveness in their dealings. Most Asians, of Chinese, Indian, and Vietnamese descent, are hard bargainers and always push hard to reduce the price. The Communist Chinese however always have a political agenda. If the Party is well-disposed towards your country and they want your product, the deal will go through at one sitting. On the other hand, if political relations have soured, perhaps because of your country's vote in the UN, you will be given a very rough time. They will spin out the negotiations going round in circles, trying your patience or they will throw you out, e.g., Alcatel had a good relationship in China. They were building their second plant in Shanghai, when Dassault sold some fighter aircraft to Taiwan. Alcatel were brusquely told to pack up and leave. The Russians and Eastern Europeans are also very tough negotiators. They come very well-prepared. They can be manipulative. It is not easy to win with a people whose pass-time is playing chess. The Japanese again are tough negotiators. They always work in a team, with the real authority in the team often not overtly disclosed. They are very formal in dress, comportment and speech. They come well-prepared and never lose a point. Under the veneer of politeness, they are hard as rock.

Advertising

Multinational companies often make the mistake of using a successful "ad" from one country in another. This can be best illustrated by a few anecdotes:

- Rover had a popular "ad" showing their multiracial work force around one of their more recent models. It worked well in the UK, in the Commonwealth countries, but not in Eastern Europe because there exists a certain racist streak in Eastern Europe that is borne out of ignorance, i.e., that Black men are not as competent as their White counterparts.

- Versace, the famous Italian designer, specially designed very elegant sandals for the Middle-Eastern market. There was some calligraphy in Arabic embroidered on the instep. It caused riots in South Arabia, Egypt, etc., and the shopfront windows of boutiques were smashed. Inadvertently, the word embroidered on the shoes – an unclean item – was "Allah".
- Renault presented their Xantia model with some fanfare in Mexico. But the Mexicans did not warm towards it because Xantia in their country means an "ogre", "a devil".
- The Benetton "ads" which often deliberately want to shock to gain attention in a particular market were considered offensive in South Africa and even in Rome.

Advice for designing ads in a global world is simple – take into account local folklore, myths, century-old stories, values, cultural nuances, local humour, etc., and use local models/symbols. For example, in the Middle East, human form is taboo. In India, "ads" even with Gods and Goddesses do well.

Value systems

Value systems are complex and vary enormously within different cultures. While Western values are supposedly universally accepted, it is not really so. In Asia, particularly in East and South-East Asia, people will lie blatantly to save "face". And if you force the issue, you lose that particular contact or relationship. People will not directly disagree with you, or directly contradict you. They will say "yes" when they mean "no". This is a "problem" European or American experts face when they are training local people. They will pretend to accept the advice, but do exactly as they have always done. Honesty also has many complex variations, and is variously understood and practised.

Corruption

While all countries are prone to corruption (Western understanding of corruption is now published on a scale by Transparency International), the difference is in degree and cultural interpretation. There is a very fine line between custom and corruption. In principle, all countries condemn corruption, but the threshold of tolerance varies. In Western-styled democratic countries and open societies, corruption is sniffed out by a vigilant press, and is prone to punishment by an independent justice system. Corruption also exists, and is practised, widely in USA and in European countries and while the resulting wastage of resources may ultimately have to be paid for by the taxpayer, corruption is not understood to disrupt the normal life of the people and sooner or later is exposed. At the other end of the scale, are the totalitarian, despotic governments, for example prevalent in certain pockets of Africa, where corruption is so wile as to cripple the economy and scar public life. African despots like Mobutu, Abacha, Arap Moi, or more recently, Mugabe have treated the state coffers as their personal treasury and their armed guards as their personal thugs. Yet, African societies are tolerant and submissive before a leader, the Big Man, and people are often too scared to rebel. This is now gradually changing, and such leaders are being targeted by the African Union and Commonwealth structures. In Communist regimes, corruption was there amongst the higher echelons and the habit continued with Yeltsin, Meciar, Kuchma and Nazarbaev – but now the people are beginning to question, if not rebel, against corruption. In Russia, corruption power has sifted from the State to business mafias. All over Asia, corruption is accepted as a fact of life from Japan to Jakarta. The difference is that unlike certain African leaders, Asian leaders like Suharto, Roh and Li Penh, while corrupt did not impede the economic growth of their respective countries. Indeed, the economies flourished under them and the people kept quiet. But as soon as there was economic slowdown, the people have rebelled, as in South Korea, Indonesia, and the Philippines, and turned out these leaders. In all Arab countries, corruption exists and is accepted as a way of life. In Latin America, especially during the cruel dictatorships, corruption was a cancer which had spread at all levels of society and contributed to economic disasters, which countries like Argentina are facing. In India and Pakistan, corruption is more at the middle and lower levels of bureaucracy and amongst political leaders. It impinges on the daily life of the people, and turns off foreign investors and businessmen.

Conclusions

Since the end of the World War II, there have been dramatic changes in the demography of nations. Hitherto, the USA was the only country settled by significant numbers of immigrants which kept an open door. Though Australia was also settled by immigration from Britain, it tried very hard to remain that way. But the flood of refugees from Nazi Germany and Eastern Europe opened the doors to selective immigration. With the end of the European empires, the "mother" countries had to accept immigrants from their former colonies. The advent of a more humanistic society in European countries encouraged asylum-seekers from persecuting regimes. But the most attractive magnet was employment and the chance of a better life which attracted economic migrants from less developed countries. European countries on the other hand, depleted by war and migration of their young people to the USA, Canada or Australia were happy to have these Asian and African migrants as factory workers, transport workers, and cleaners, etc. More recently, because of the shift from manufacturing to service/knowledge industries, the lack of sufficiently talented and qualified people in Europe, better healthcare systems for keeping people healthy longer and living longer, and the declining birth rates all over Europe, most countries in Western Europe now have a very polyglot population (which is destined to grow in time). There is as yet no "melting pot" effect as in the USA, and it is uncertain whether Europe wishes to have the "melting pot" phenomenon (being torn between an understanding of the benefits of diversity – "being allowed to be different", and the need to bring in to control perceived "outlying groups" in the name of security – "integrating to sameness"). There are tensions between the nationals and the newcomers in nearly all these countries. But intolerance comes often from the failure on either side to understand and appreciate each other's culture, and intention. Tensions also arise out of misconceptions like "newcomers take away jobs". Several studies have proved, however, that is not so. Some input of fresh blood is always healthy for any society, and in Europe's case with a "greying" of their populations (in Italy a negative birth rate) and the paralleled labour shortages, it is needed/a necessity. Some parts of Europe, like the UK, France and The Netherlands have long histories of immigration (albeit with mainly smaller slices of "preferred" parts of the world, and some "not so preferred"), and therefore have some experience around the key issues – however, the "newer" states within Europe, like the Balkan and Eastern European sectors, have little to no experience or understanding around these issues and it, no doubt, will become issues of tension in the near future.

The immigration issue is not peculiar to Europe. In Asia also, there is migration from the more poor nations to their less poor neighbours. Malaysia tries to stave off migration from Indonesia, and the Philippines and Singapore from all its neighbours. Bangla Deshis and Sri Lankan Tamils migrate to India. Borders are very porous between Vietnam, Cambodia and Laos. Filipinos, Pakistanis, Bangla Deshis and Muslim Indians migrate to the Gulf. The Islanders of the South Pacific states flood Australia and New Zealand, while Far Eastern Asians are also attempting migration to Australia and New Zealand. In this Japan is an exception, and does not accept migrant settlers or give them citizenship. The purity of the bloodline is important. At best, where needed, like in the factories of Sony, Japan prefers to use descendants of Japan – for example, from Brazil and the Philippines. On the other hand, Japan has a fast-ageing population also, and a negative birth rate. Hence, Japan has to do some hard thinking about this demographic crisis looming in the future.

In Africa also, there is a floating population of migrants from one country to another, for reasons of war, persecution, drought, economics, flood or famine. Economically well-off, and politically stable, countries in Africa, like South Africa, Kenya, Botswana, Egypt and Morocco, are key destinations for migrant Africans, and these countries even attract foreigners such as Europeans (mainly), Latin Americans, Asians (mainly Indian, but growing Chinese populations) and Taiwanese who are looking for better economic conditions, business opportunities and/or better lifestyles. More recently, Americans, in particular, are entering Africa – either for experience in the "developing world", diplomatic missions and/or business opportunities (partially engendered by African-Americans search for "rediscovering" their roots and "soul homes"). Since boundaries are artificial, migration in certain parts of Africa is attracted by kinship and tribal links across the borders.

It is true that immigration are a political, economic, and social hot potatoes in most countries. Some politicians (encouraged by most of the "under class" in their countries) want to send migrants back to where they came from – but the tide cannot be reversed, particularly in our current form of globalization. A positive approach is to promote better inter-cultural relations between different communities at schools, clubs, in homes, the workplace, and by participation in sports. So that new-styled "assimilation" and "inclusion" can eventually take place.

11

American Legal System Diversity: *Stare Decisis* in a Changing World

by Cathy Havener Greer

Traditional principles

The American legal system was founded on the principle of *stare decisis et non quieta movere*, i.e., to adhere to precedents, and not to unsettle things which are established. While this principle of precedent, stability and continuity is intended to govern the rule of law in our society, in many ways it is a principle that is descriptive of the legal profession itself. To the extent that the legal profession, including the judiciary as well as attorneys, is seen as a key player in maintaining social stability, it is also a profession that is often regarded as traditional and resistant to change.

An emphasis on tradition has kept many in the legal profession from embracing change and welcoming diversity. Although the United States Supreme Court recently recognized that the "benefits [of diversity] are not theoretical but real, as major American businesses have made clear that the skills needed in today's increasingly global marketplace can only be developed through exposure to widely diverse people, cultures, ideas, and viewpoints,"[1] the statistics demonstrate that the legal profession remains more than 90% white, while the general population of the United States is approximately 70% white.[2] In addition to the challenge of racial and ethnic diversity in the legal profession is a continuing challenge to the progression and retention of women lawyers.[3]

Why is diversity important in the legal profession?

In holding that the University of Michigan Law School has a compelling interest in attaining a diverse student body, the United States Supreme Court in a split decision, authored by Justice Sandra Day O'Connor, acknowledged that "In order to cultivate a set of leaders with legitimacy in the eyes of the citizenry, it is necessary that the path to leadership be visibly open to talented and qualified individuals of every race and ethnicity. All members of our heterogeneous society must have confidence in the openness and integrity of the educational institutions that provide this training . . . Access to legal education (and thus the legal profession) must be inclusive of talented and qualified individuals of every race and ethnicity, so that all members of our heterogeneous society participate in the educational institutions that provide the training and education necessary to succeed in America."[4]

Not only is it important for the leadership of the citizenry, including the legal profession, to include talented and qualified individuals reflecting the diversity of society itself, concerns of a lack of diversity in the legal profession reflect concerns about the quality of justice rendered (McDonough, 2003). As noted by the EEOC in its report, "If race, gender, and social class are determinants for entry into the profession and for the attainment of certain positions within the profession, it may apply that these same attributes affect the sorts of treatment individuals will receive by legal institutions, in part because they do not have access to lawyers who share a similar social background."[5]

Certainly to the extent that an attorney or a judge is limited by his or her own background from understanding the perspective of a client, an opposing party in litigation, or that party's attorney, or a witness, as a result of race, ethnicity, gender, or religion of the person, the quality of the attorney's representation and the quality of justice may suffer. To that end, diversity in the ranks of attorneys and members of the judiciary is critical to the goals of providing equal access, equal opportunity, and equal rights in the United States.

There is no question but that the landscape of the legal profession changed dramatically with the enactment of the Civil Rights Act of 1964, 42 U.S.C. §2000, *et seq*. (Title VII), which outlawed discrimination in employment based on race, gender, national origin and religion. Obviously, the legal imperative provided by this Act made more transparent the hiring of women and people of color by law firms and other employers both public and private. Although the Act covers virtually every aspect of the employment relationship from hiring through compensation and training to discipline and termination, the Act applies only to employers with 15 or more employees. Significantly, partners of a law firm are not counted as employees,[6] but associates of a law firm are employees and consideration for partnership is a "term, condition or privilege" of employment in a law firm and covered by the Civil Rights Act.[7]

Many law firms have come to the realization that diversity within the ranks of their employees and partners is in the financial interest of the firm as a reflection of the heterogeneous nature of American society. As increasing numbers of women and people of color move to employment, and particularly management positions in governmental organizations and corporations, lawyers in law firms representing those entities are called upon increasingly to demonstrate the same commitment to diversity that is made by their clients.

Finally, for more altruistic reasons, diversity is in the best interest of the legal profession because of the special powers, rights, and opportunities afforded to attorneys in American society. Many people are called to the practice of law because of a desire to serve, whether in the defense of a client charged with a crime in the best tradition of Atticus Finch, the principled lawyer of *To Kill A Mockingbird* or in a civil matter in which potential damages could devastate the viability of a business or an individual. Others are drawn to law because of the opportunity that it affords to remedy injustice and challenge inequities within society through litigation or legislation. Still others recognize law as a vehicle for the creation and development of business opportunities for clients small and large. In the opinion in the University of Michigan Law School case, the United States Supreme Court noted that "Individuals with law degrees occupy roughly half the state governorships, more than half the seats in the United States Senate, and more than a third of the seats in the United States House of Representatives." See Brief for Association of American Law Schools as *Amicus Curiae* 5–6. "The pattern is even more striking when it comes to highly selective law schools. A handful of these schools accounts for 25 of the 100 United States Senators, 74 United States Courts of Appeals judges, and nearly 200 of the more than 600 United States District Court judges."[8]

At their best, lawyers play a significant role "in designing and activating the institutional mechanisms through which property is transferred, economic exchange is planned and enforced, injuries are compensated, crime is punished, marriages are dissolved and disputes are resolved. The ideologies and incentives of the lawyers engaged in these functions directly influence the lived experience of Americans, including whether they feel fairly treated by legal institutions" (Nelson, 1994).

Because of the roles that attorneys play and the influence they exert throughout American society, it is critical that the legal profession is comprised of people from diverse backgrounds reflecting the genders, races, ethnicity and religions of our heterogeneous society. The vitality of the profession and the quality of justice depend on diversity from admission to the bar through the early professional years to the senior partner or general counsel level and to the judicial appointment or election.

How diverse is the legal profession?

Since the passage of the Civil Rights Act in 1964, law school enrollment has reflected the expanded opportunities for legal employment for a person who achieves a juris doctorate and gains admission to the bar. From 1982 to 2002, the percentage of women receiving law degrees in the United States increased from 33% to 48.3%. The percentages for African-Americans receiving law degrees in that same period changed from 4.2% to 7.2%, for Hispanics from 2.3% to 5.7% and for Asians from 1.3% to 6.5%.[9]

Similarly, the representation of women and people of color in law firms has shown a substantial increase. In its seminal report on Diversity In Law Firms, 2003, the U.S. Equal Employment Opportunity Commission studied the employment trends in large law firms, defining those firms as firms with 100 or more employees and required to file EEO-1 reports annually. In addition to information derived from the EEO-1 reports and various publications and articles, the EEOC Report relied on data sources including the Current Population Survey, a national monthly survey of approximately 60,000 households which identifies information on employed persons by detailed occupation, sex, race and Hispanic origin and the EEOC relied data provided by the American Bar Association and the Law School Admission Council. The EEOC Report presents extensive documentation about the changes from 1975 to 2002 in the representation of women and people of color as legal professionals in the firms with 100 or more employees. During those 27 years, the number of women legal professionals employed in large law firms increased from 14.4% to 40.3%. Percentages of African-American legal professionals increased from 2.3% to 4.4% with the percentages for Hispanics and Asians increasing from 0.7% to 2.9% and 0.5% to 5.3% respectively.[10]

Although these numbers demonstrate a dramatic increase for entry to the law and in law firm employment, a profound disparity continues to exist at the highest ranks of the legal profession. Significantly, although the EEOC Report shows that large law firms have increased substantially the employment opportunities for women and people of color since 1975, the number of women and people of color becoming partners at firms of 100 or more employees has apparently not kept pace with the percentages of those populations entering the firms. For example, the EEOC Report notes that the percentage of women legal professionals in 1982 reported by law firms of 100 or more employees was nearly identical to the percent of women receiving law degrees in that year. By 2002, the employment of women legal professionals in the same category of law firms is eight percentage points below the percentage of degrees conferred on women by law schools.[11]

The EEOC identifies a number of characteristics of a law firm that appear to influence the proportion of minority and female professionals. According to the report, both the proportion of women and the proportion of minorities are significantly higher in firms with more than one office. Additionally, the size of firm, that is, total number of attorneys, location, prestige and earning rankings appear to influence the proportion of minority legal professions at least at the rank of associate or entry level.[12]

Because the Equal Employment Opportunity Commission is the authorized agency for civil rights enforcement, the Commission's assessment of the significant civil rights issues in law firm employment is instructive. The EEOC has investigative powers over employers whether as a result of a Charge of Discrimination initiated by an individual or as a result of the Commissioner's own initiative. The EEOC may also seek to enforce the Civil Rights Acts by filing a lawsuit in court against an employer separate from the private right of action that an individual possesses to file a lawsuit.

The progression of a lawyer in a private law firm from associate to partner or shareholder can have a significant impact on income, status in the profession as well as community, and lifestyle. The Commission report notes

"In large, national law firms, the most pressing issues have probably shifted from hiring and initial access to problems concerning the terms and conditions of employment, especially promotion to partnership. In smaller, regional and local law firms, questions about the fairness and openness of hiring practices probably still remain, particularly for minority lawyers."[13]

Although discrimination and promotional opportunities within law firms of 15 or more employees is subject to the jurisdiction of the Equal Employment Opportunity Commission for enforcement of the provisions of the Civil Rights Act, the decision to make an associate attorney a partner remains subject to many variables and is often based on subjective as well as some objective factors. For that reason, lawsuits by persons not promoted to partnership and lawsuits initiated by the EEOC against firms for failure to promote, are rare.

A recent study of women lawyers in the state of Colorado indicates that women attorneys have made little progress in the past 10 years, now earning only 60 cents for every dollar a male lawyer makes at a similar point in his career in contrast to 59 cents earned by every woman in 1993 for every dollar earned by a male lawyer (Reichman and Sterling, 2004). The study also confirms that women are not promoted as quickly as male lawyers and are far more likely to leave the legal profession, either as young associates or as senior members of their firms. For those women who left the legal profession, the study found that the women did not leave employment altogether but found work outside of the legal profession in what was described as a more hospitable environment.

Other studies indicate that the more hospitable environment may be in the public sector. A 1995 study reported that 20.7% of white women lawyers were employed by the government or the judiciary compared to 7.6% of white men.[14] That study also confirmed higher percentages for African-American and Hispanic lawyers in the government and the judiciary than in private law firms at 43.8% and 37.5%, respectively.

Opportunities for women and minority lawyers in the corporate world pose some of the same challenges to entry and advancement as does practice in a private law firm. According to the Minority Corporate Counsel Association, in 1993, 43 women served as general counsel to the Fortune 500's legal department. Fifty-six percent of those women were hired between 1996 and 2000.[15]

To the extent that private law firms have been seen as paternalistic with a culture that was historically not inviting to gender or racial diversity, the number of women lawyers and lawyers of color opening their own practices, pursuing government employment or joining corporate legal staffs appears, to be increasing. Statistics for law firms with fewer than 15 employees are not readily available.

How to remove obstacles to diversity in the legal profession?

Many organizations of attorneys, companies and law firms have adopted policies or programs to foster and advance gender, racial and ethnic diversity in the legal profession. Those include the American Bar Association, the Association of Corporate Counsel, the Minority Corporate Counsel Association and the Association of Legal Administrators. The American Bar Association identifies six goals in its program to advance racial and ethnic diversity in the legal profession: (1) create awareness in the legal profession about the value of diversity; (2) ensure that minority students are adequately prepared to pursue a legal career; (3) increase the number of minority students who attend and graduate from law school; (4) increase the number of minority students who pass the bar exam; (5) increase the recruitment of minority lawyers; and (6) increase the retention in advancement of minority lawyers.[16] The Minority Corporate Counsel Association has created a Diversity Self-Assessment Tool for law firms as well as corporate legal departments (Bohannon *et al.*, 2003).

The success of all of these programs requires a true understanding on the part of lawyers, law firm administrators, and corporate executives on the need for diversity. The legal profession, through all of its constituent parts, can only become more diverse if individual lawyers truly embrace the concept that fostering an environment of multiple races, ethnicities, religions and genders, is the right thing to do and is in their best interest and that of their clients. A commitment to diversity requires the active participation and commitment of people throughout the legal organization. A passive acceptance of a diversity plan without a concurrent review of the culture of the organization is recognized for its expediency or insincerity as merely tolerating diversity. A law firm's culture may need to change or be enhanced by exposure to people with different perspectives than that of the prevailing culture and that will succeed only if the people in power embrace those changes and embrace and foster diversity at all levels of the organization and through clients and vendors with whom the firm does business.

Mentoring programs can be particularly important in easing the entry of a woman or person of color into what has traditionally been a white male firm or corporation. Mentoring is equally important after an attorney of color or a woman attorney has become established in the organization so that the diverse professional can continue to progress and develop in his or her career. As noted in the EEOC Report, recruiting for diverse attorneys at the entry level does not transform the organization unless those diverse attorneys have real opportunities to advance and develop to the highest professional levels of the organization.

Americans are often criticized for their unilateral and ethnocentric approach to world issues. If the legal profession in the United States cannot increase the opportunities for qualified women and racially and ethnically diverse lawyers, the opportunities for those professionals in the global marketplace will be severely limited. The complexities of modern society and of our institutions compel thoughtful and creative approaches and solutions that can come only from an appreciation and understanding of diverse perspectives.

Notes

1 *Grutter v. Bollinger*, 539 U.S. 306 (2003), the decision of the United States Supreme Court in case challenging the consideration of race and ethnicity in admissions decisions of the University of Michigan Law School.
2 ABA Leadership Office of Diversity Initiatives (URL: http://www.abanet.org/leadership/diversity.html).
3 "Diversity in Law Firms", U.S. Equal Employment Opportunity Commission Report, 2003, pp. 4, 6.
4 *Grutter v. Bollinger*, at 123 S.Ct. at 1241.
5 "Diversity in Law Firms." U.S. Equal Employment Opportunity Commission Report, 2003 Executive Summary, pp. 7, 9–11.
6 *Hishon v. King and Spalding*, 467 U.S. 69, 104, 104 S.Ct. 2229 (1984).
7 Richey, C. *Manual on Employment Discrimination Law and Civil Rights Action in the Federal Courts at 1:24*, West Group.
8 *Grutter v. Bollinger* at 2341.
9 "Diversity in Law Firms." U.S. Equal Employment Opportunity Commission Report, 2003 Executive Summary, pp. 7, 9–10.
10 "Diversity in Law Firms." U.S. Equal Employment Opportunity Commission Report, 2003 Executive Summary, pp. 6–10.
11 "Diversity in Law Firms." U.S. Equal Employment Opportunity Commission Report, 2003: 7.
12 "Diversity in Law Firms." U.S. Equal Employment Opportunity Commission Report, 2003 Executive Summary, pp. 12–17.
13 "Diversity in Law Firms." U.S. Equal Employment Opportunity Commission Report, 2003: 17.
14 Pane, R. and Nelson, R. (2003), "Shifting Inequalities: Stratification by Race, Gender and Ethnicity in an Urban Legal Profession" (1975–1995) (unpublished manuscript cited by "Diversity in Law Firms", United States Equal Employment Opportunity Commission Report, 2003, p. 3).
15 "Women General Counsel in The Fortune 500" (http://www.mcca.com/site/data/inhouse/womenattorneys/cover0500.htm); Minority Corporate Counsel Association, 2003; See also Weisberg and Moore (2001), "Women in Law: Making the Case", *Perspective*, New York: Catalyst, p. 1.
16 American Bar Association Resource Guide: Program to Advance Racial and Ethnic Diversity in the Legal Profession (URL: http://www.abanet.org/leadership/recmenu.html).

References

Bohannon, A., Giovannini, M., Fitzgerald, P., Robitaille, N. and Richardson, V. (2003), *Diversity & The Bar®* (URL: www.mcca.com/site/data/magazine/coverstory/1003/diversityselfassessment1003.htm).

McDonough, M. (2003), "Damaging Disrespect," *ABA Journal*, Vol. 89, pp. 56–61 (citing Nelson, R., *Partners With Power: The Social Transformation of The Large Law Firm*, Berkley: University of California Press).

Nelson, R. (1994), "The Futures of American Lawyers: A Demographic Profile of a Changing Profession in a Changing Society," *Case Western Reserve Law Review*, Vol. 44, pp. 345–406.

Payne, Monique R. and Nelson, Robert L. (2003), Shifting Inequalities: Stratification by Race, Gender, and Ethnicity in an Urban Legal Profession, 1975–1995 (unpublished manuscript cited in U.S. Equal Empl. Opp'y Comm., *Diversity in Law Firms*, 3 (2003)).

Reichman, N. and Sterling, J. (2004), *Gender Penalties Revisited*: 6, at http://www.cwba.org/pdf/GenderP

Weisberg, A. and Moore, M. (2001), "Women in Law: Making the Case," *Perspective*, New York, p. 1.

12
Diversity and Corporate Governance

by Kai Peters, Kurt April, Marylou Shockley and Vinay Dhamija

Introduction

In the broadest sense, the purpose of corporate governance is to ensure that listed companies are fair and honest with their range of stakeholders. These stakeholders include shareholders, employees, customers and society at large.

A corporate governance framework, from this perspective, would be a wide-ranging system of internal and external checks and balances which policies and advises organisations to different degrees depending on their levels of engagement with, and relationship to, the company.

In reality, attempts to look at corporate governance from this broad perspective are few and far between. Instead, corporate government legislation and corporate governance thought, encompassed in the popular and academic literature, focuses predominantly on a very narrow view of corporate governance. This view is concerned with the rights of shareholders in corporations, and within that group, primarily with the rights of institutional investors.

This view of corporate governance defines its primary task as addressing the agency problem whereby a firm's ownership is separated from a firm's management. By taking this stance, the underlying assumption is that the prime stakeholder in a company is the provider of capital.

This chapter seeks to rebalance the debate around corporate governance by attempting to expand the definition of the corporate governance from a narrow focus on shareholder protection to *include the broader range of stakeholders*, and to map what such an *internal and external scrutiny framework* may look like.

First, a review will be provided of the shareholder view in a variety of countries around the world, including both industrialised and emerging markets. Thereafter, the shareholder view will be considered as one element within the broader framework of scrutiny. We believe that a purely financial, institutional approach does not do justice to the needs of society. Some small steps are being taken to redress this imbalance. In the corporate social responsibility field, there are initiatives to take a triple-bottom line, and social process perspective to take account of involved financial, social and environmental responsibilities. What has not been developed in that area is a diverse view of what scrutiny could look like, both formally and informally, should a real stakeholder view be taken.

The financial community view of governance: its spread

Mallin, Mullineux and Wihlborg (2005) introduce a recent article on development in corporate governance in the UK, with two definitions of what corporate governance is. Sir Adrian Cadbury, who chaired the 1992 Report of the UK Committee on the Financial Aspects of Corporate Governance (Cadbury, 1992a), defined corporate governance in a more recent (Cadbury, 2002:11) book as the 'system by which companies are directed and controlled'. The OECD defined it as 'a set of relationships between a company's management, its board, its shareholders and other stakeholders' (OECD, 2004). Corporate governance also provides the structure through which the objectives of the company are set, and the means of attaining those objectives, and monitoring performance are determined.

The reforms arising from the Cadbury Report focused on board room control. Audit committees were to be implemented to scrutinise the accounts, a nominations committees to ensure board member appointment clarity, and there were to be three non-executive directors on the board to ensure a balance of dependence and independence. Cadbury noted in an interview after completing the report, 'the committee was asked to address only the financial aspect of corporate governance, with a view to restoring confidence in reporting and auditing practice' (Cadbury 1992b: 23).

Following on from Cadbury, further high level committees continued along this vein. Greenbury (1995) focused on executive renumeration, Turnbull (1999) focused on internal controls and risk management, and the 2003 revisions to the 1998 Combined Code focused, on the one hand, on the company and, on the other, on institutional investors, who should regularly engage with the company in 'a dialogue based on the mutual understanding of objectives'.

In the United States, the early nineties saw the publication of the Treadway Commission Report of the Committee of Sponsoring Organisations. It is indeed quite revealing that in a country where, for example, Audit Committees were mandated by the New York Stock Exchange as early as in 1973, a Blue Ribbon report in 1999 was found necessary to explore ways of improving the effectiveness of Audit Committees. Following a flurry of scandals, US legislation culminated in the Sarbanes-Oxley Act of 2002, which focused on internal controls, audits, and legally binding statements from corporate officers. Sarbanes-Oxley has generated a costly compliance culture which affects not only US firms, but also affects international firms who have shareholders in the United States, or who do business in, or with, the United States.

Canadian initiatives on corporate governance, spearheaded by the Toronto Stock Exchange (1994; 1999), led to the publication in 1994 of the provocatively titled report, *Where were the Directors?*, which was itself the subject of a 1999 review of compliance and implementation in *Five Years to the Dey*, appropriately named after the chair of the earlier 1994 committee.

This two-pronged approach to corporate governance has taken place in a range of countries around the world. Corporate governance is defined primarily in terms of the rights of shareholders in companies. By looking at India and South Africa, one can note the spread of these formalised systems.

Early corporate developments in India were characterised by the managing agency system that did not separate ownership from management. It gave birth to not only dispersed equity ownership, but also to the practice of management enjoying control rights disproportionately greater than their stock ownership. The turn towards socialism in the decades after independence denoted by the 1951 Industries (Development and Regulation) Act as well as the 1956 Industrial Policy Resolution put in place a regime and culture of licensing, protectionism and widespread red-tapism that bred corruption and slowed the growth of the corporate sector. Geo-political developments made the situation degrade from bad to worse in the following decades as corruption, nepotism, ineffectiveness and inefficiency became the hallmarks of the Indian corporate sector. Exorbitant tax rates encouraged creative, dishonest accounting practices and complicated emolument structures to beat the system.

The years since the liberalization of the Indian economy have witnessed wide-ranging changes, in both laws and regulations driving corporate governance, as well as general consciousness about it.

Perhaps, the most important development in the field of corporate governance and investor protection in India has been the establishment of the Securities and Exchange Board of India (SEBI) in 1992, and its gradual empowerment since then. Established primarily to regulate and monitor stock trading, it has played a crucial role in establishing the basic minimum ground rules of corporate conduct in the country. Concerns about corporate governance in India were, however, largely triggered by a spate of crises in the early 1990s – the Harshad Mehta stock market scam of 1992, followed by incidents of companies allotting preferential shares to their promoters at deeply discounted prices, as well as those companies simply disappearing with investors' money. These concerns about corporate governance, stemming from the corporate scandals as well as opening up to the forces of competition and globalisation, gave rise to several investigations into the ways to fix the corporate governance situation in India.

One of the first among such endeavours was the CII Code for Desirable Corporate Governance, developed by a committee and chaired by Rahul Bajaj. The committee was formed in 1996, and submitted its code in April 1998. Later SEBI constituted two committees to look into the issue of corporate governance – the first chaired by Kumar Mangalam Birla, that submitted its report in early 2000, and the second by Narayana Murthy three years later. Table 12.1 provides a comparative view of the recommendations of these important efforts at improving corporate governance in India.

Table 12.1 Governance Measures in India

CII code recommendations (1997)	**Birla Committee (SEBI) recommendations (2000)**	**Narayana Murthy committee (SEBI) recommendations (2003)**
	Board of Directors	
(a) No need for German style two-tiered board. (b) For a listed company with turnover exceeding Rs. 100 crores, if the Chairman is also the MD, at least half of the board should be Independent directors, else at least 30%. (c) No single person should hold directorships in more than 10 listed companies. (d) Non-executive directors should be competent and active and have clearly defined responsibilities like in the Audit Committee. (e) Directors should be paid a commission not exceeding 1% (3%) of net profits for a company with(out) an MD over and above sitting fees. Stock options may be considered too.	(a) At least 50% non-executive members (b) For a company with an executive Chairman, at least half of the board should be independent directors, else at least one-third. (c) Non-executive Chairman should have an office and be paid for job related expenses. (d) Maximum of 10 directorships and 5 chairmanships per person. (e) **Audit Committee**: A board must have an qualified and independent audit committee, of minimum 3 members, all non-executive majority and chair independent with at least one having financial and accounting knowledge. Its chairman should attend AGM to answer shareholder queries. The committee should confer with key executives as necessary and the company secretary should be the secretary of the committee. The committee should meet at least thrice a year – one before finalisation of annual accounts and one necessarily every 6 months with the quorum being the higher	(a) Training of board members suggested. (b) There shall be no nominee directors. All directors to be elected by shareholders with same responsibilities and accountabilities. (c) Non-executive director compensation to be fixed by board and ratified by shareholders and reported. Stock options should be vested at least a year after their retirement. Independent directors should be treated the same way as non-executive directors. (d) The board should be informed every quarter of business risk and risk management strategies. (e) **Audit Committee**: Should comprise entirely of 'financially literate' non-executive members

(Continued)

Table 12.1 (*Continued*)

CII code recommendations (1997)	Birla Committee (SEBI) recommendations (2000)	Narayana Murthy committee (SEBI) recommendations (2003)
(f) Attendance record of directors should be made explicit at the time of re-appointment. Those with less than 50% attendance should not be reappointed.	of 2 members or one-third of members with at least two independent directors. It should have access to information from any employee and can investigate any matter within its TOR, can seek outside legal/professional service as well as secure attendance of outside experts in meetings. It should act as the bridge between the board, statutory auditors and internal auditors with far ranging powers and responsibilities.	with at least one member having accounting or related financial management expertise. It should review a mandatory list of documents including information relating to subsidiary companies. 'Whistle blowers' should have direct access to it and all employees be informed of such policy (and this should be affirmed annually by management). All 'related party' transactions must be approved by audit committee. The committee should be responsible for the appointment, removal and remuneration of chief internal auditor.
(g) Key information that must be presented to the board is listed in the code.	(f) **Remuneration Committee**: The remuneration committee should decide remuneration packages for executive directors. It should have at least 3 directors, all non-executive and be chaired by an independent director.	(f) Boards of subsidiaries should follow similar composition rules as that of parent and should have at least one independent directors of the parent company.
(h) **Audit Committee**: Listed companies with turnover over Rs. 100 crores or paid-up capital of Rs. 20 crores should have an audit committee of at least three members, all non-executive, competent and willing to work more than other non-executive directors with clear terms of reference and access to all financial information in the company and should periodically interact with statutory auditors and internal auditors and assist the board in corporate accounting and reporting.	(g) The board should decide on the remuneration of non-executive directors and all remuneration information should be disclosed in annual report. (h) At least 4 board meetings a year with a maximum gap of 4 months between any 2 meetings. Minimum information available to boards stipulated.	(g) The Board report of a parent company should have access to

(*Continued*)

Table 12.1 (*Continued*)

CII code recommendations (1997)	Birla Committee (SEBI) recommendations (2000)	Narayana Murthy committee (SEBI) recommendations (2003)
(i) Reduction in number of nominee directors. FIs should withdraw nominee directors from companies with individual FI shareholding.		minutes of board meeting in subsidiaries and should affirm reviewing its affairs. (h) Performance evaluation of non-executive directors by all his fellow Board members should inform a re-appointment decision. (i) While independent and non-executive directors should enjoy some protection from civil and criminal litigation, they may be held responsible of the legal compliance in the company's affairs. (j) Code of conduct for Board members and senior management and annual affirmation of compliance to it.
	Disclosure and Transparency	
(a) Companies should inform their shareholders about the high and low monthly averages of their share prices and about	(a) Companies should provide consolidated accounts for subsidiaries where they have majority shareholding.	(a) Management should explain and justify any deviation from accounting standards in financial statements.

(*Continued*)

Table 12.1 (*Continued*)

CII code recommendations (1997)	Birla Committee (SEBI) recommendations (2000)	Narayana Murthy committee (SEBI) recommendations (2003)
share, performance and prospects of major business segments (exceeding 10% of turnover).	(b) Disclosure list pertaining to 'related party' transactions provided by committee till ICAI's norm is established.	(b) Companies should move towards a regime of unqualified financial statements.
(b) Consolidation of group accounts should be optional and subject to FIs and IT department's assessment norms. If a company consolidates, no need to annex subsidiary accounts but the definition of 'group' should include parent and subsidiaries.	(c) A mandatory Management Discussion Analysis segment of annual report that includes discussion of industry structure and development, opportunities, threats, outlook, risks etc. as well as financial and operational performance and managerial developments in HR/IR front.	(c) Management should provide a clear description, description, followed by auditor's comments, of each material contingent liability and its risks.
(c) Stock exchanges should require compliance certificate from CEOs and CFOs on company accounts.	(d) Management should inform board of all potential conflict of interest situations.	(d) CEO/CFO certification of knowledge, veracity and comprehensiveness of financial statements and directors' reports and affirmation of maintaining proper internal control as well as appropriate disclosure to auditors and audit committee.
(d) For companies with paid-up capital exceeding Rs. 20 crore, disclosure norms for domestic issues should be same as those for GDR issues.	(e) On (re)appointment of directors, shareholders must be informed of their resume, expertise, and names of companies where they are directors.	(e) Security analysts must disclose the relationship of their employers with the client company as well as their actual or intended shareholding in the client company.

(*Continued*)

Table 12.1 (Continued)

CII code recommendations (1997)	Birla Committee (SEBI) recommendations (2000)	Narayana Murthy committee (SEBI) recommendations (2003)
	Other issues	
Creditors' Rights	**Shareholders' Rights**	**Special Disclosure for IPOs**
(a) FIs should rewrite loan covenants eliminating nominee directors except in case of serious and systematic debt default or provision of insufficient information.	(a) Quarterly results, presentation to analysts etc. should be communicated to investors, possibly over the Internet.	(a) Companies making Initial Public Offering ('IPO') should inform the Audit Committee of category-wise uses of funds every quarter. It should get non-pre-specified uses approved by auditors on an annual basis. The audit committee should advise the Board for action in this matter.
(b) In case of multiple credit ratings, they should all be reported in a format showing relative position of the company.	(b) Half-yearly financial results and significant events reports be mailed to shareholders.	
(c) Same disclosure norms for foreign and domestic creditors.	(c) A board committee headed by a nonexecutive director look into shareholder complaints/grievances	
(d) Companies defaulting on fixed deposits should not be permitted to accept further deposits and make inter-corporate loans or investments or declare dividends until the default is made good.	(d) Company should delegate share transfer power to an officer/committee/registrar/share transfer agents. The delegated authority should attend to share transfer formalities at least once in a fortnight.	

The SEBI committee recommendations have had the maximum impact on changing the corporate governance situation in India. The Advisory Group on Corporate Governance of RBI's Standing Committee on International Financial Standards and Codes also submitted its own recommendations in 2001. A comparison of the three sets of recommendations in Table 12.1 reveal the progress in the thinking on the subject of corporate governance in India over the years. An outline provided by the CII was given concrete shape in the Birla Committee report of SEBI.

SEBI implemented the recommendations of the Birla Committee to companies in the BSE 200 and S & P C & X Nifty indices, and all newly listed companies, on 31st March 2001; to companies with a paid up capital of Rs. 10 crore (US$2500,000) or with a net worth of Rs. 25 crore (US$6500,000) at any time in the past five years, as of the 31st March 2002; to other listed companies with a paid up capital of over Rs. 3 crore (US$800,000) on the 31st March 2003. The Narayana Murthy committee worked on further refining the rules.

Major emphasis of these reforms has been on the role and composition of the board of directors, and the disclosure laws. The Birla Committee, however, paid much-needed attention to the subject of share transfers, which is the Achilles' heel of shareholders' rights in India.

Among the professions, The Institute of Chartered Accountants of India has emerged as a mature body regulating the profession of public auditors, and counts among its achievements the issue of a number of accounting and auditing standards. Constitution of an independent National Advisory Committee on Accounting Standards has been legislated by the amending Act of 1999. Other professional bodies such as the Institute of Cost and Works Accountants of India and the Institute of Company Secretaries of India have helped in promoting and regulating a well-trained and disciplined body of professionals who could add value to corporations in improving their management practices. The Institute of Company Secretaries of India has also taken a major initiative in constituting a Secretarial Standards Board comprising senior members of eminence to formulate secretarial standards and best secretarial practices and develop guidance notes in order to integrate, consolidate, and standardise the prevalent diverse practices – with an aim to promote better corporate practices and improved corporate governance.

A transitional example of governance

Unlike the US model of corporate governance, that is riveted to investor interests, the South African model of corporate governance addresses the interests of a community of stakeholders.

Good governance means a proper balance between enterprise and accountability, encompassing the two main dimensions of corporate governance: (1) the first dimension concerns active monitoring of management performance and ensuring accountability to the community of stakeholders (in the words of Khanya Motshabi, previous CEO of the National Empowerment Fund, the widest form of stewardship should be demanded through personal and organisational excellence, for the widest set of stakeholders and not just a selected set); and (2) the second dimension, touched on recently in a presentation by Finance Minister Trevor Manual at a University of Cape Town Graduate School of Business function, emphasises how corporate governance structures and processes need to incorporate means for motivating managerial and board behaviour towards issues of enterprise and nation-building, and of increasing the wealth of the business and the country as a whole. This makes the South African model more complex, but highly resilient to excesses of what's commonly called 'corporate greed'. As a template for effective corporate governance, the Institute of Directors in South Africa issued the King Report in 1994, and recently updated this report in March 2002. It is a comprehensive, cutting-edge, principle-based guide for what constitutes effective corporate governance. The King Report outlines seven characteristics of good corporate governance. These characteristics constitute an excellent basis to initiate a reflective audit of companies governance practices, and firmly sets the foundation for the longevity and sustainability of companies in the South African context – a transitional society within an emerging market.

Corporate governance requires diligence on the part of boards and CEOs with their senior leadership teams to create a bond of trust between the company and its community of stakeholders. To prompt a healthy dialogue of how effective your company's current governance structure and practices are in promoting trust, the following discussion amplifies each of the seven characteristics. Table 12.2 summarises the governance characteristics with a checklist for action couched in a question format.

Corporate governance has become an issue of sustainable competitive advantage. Poor corporate governance is now a route to organisational failure. One bad decision, or a right decision poorly explained and communicated, can do untold damage to an organisation's reputation where, only a few years ago, it might have either gone unnoticed or been accepted unchallenged. The freedom of the wider community of stakeholders, to challenge an organisation's decisions, is a sign of a developed civil society – a necessary pillar of sustainable democracy.

An integrated approach

So far, we have looked at the more traditional financial community view of corporate governance, and have also expanded this view to take into account moves in both Indian and South African contexts to broaden the scope and ambition of governance initiatives. In this last section, we will take an exploratory view of how important good governance is to a range of stakeholders and how all of the stakeholders in this expanded view can exercise oversight.

Table 12.2 Characteristics of Good Governance: From Vision to Action in South Africa

Governance Characteristics	Checklist for Action
• **Transparency**: Accurate and timely availability of information to external stakeholders	• **Disclosure**: Are processes in place for timely distribution of financial data such that senior management has adequate time to review reports? • **Communication**: Does your corporate communication plan include clearly defined spokesperson roles (including board members), guidelines to protect competitively sensitive information, and a 'needs to know' distribution list of key stakeholders, especially investors?
• **Independence**: External board members are active rather than passive participants	• **Board Composition**: What is the criterion for board membership? Do your board members present a cross section of your key external stakeholders? Are conflict of interest guidelines in place for board members? • **Company Expectations of Board**: Do boards meet regularly? Are external board members active participants of key committees such as the auditing and compensation committees? • **Risk Management**: Are processes in place to delineate the risk of various key company strategies? Are there employees in place, acting as independent agents, to update and access the risk profile of the company?
• **Accountability**: Role clarity at the board level driven by commitments to company and stakeholders	• **Cascading Accountability**: Can you map accountability from the board to functional managers in the firm, especially in areas of finance, human resources, and marketing/sales? • **Due Diligence**: Are processes in place that encourage board members to know the business and industry? Is there an effective ombudsmen/ombudswomen process in place to protect whistle blowers? Is the board a partner in selecting the external auditor? Can they request the external auditors to undertake an independent assessment on a specific area of the business?

(*Continued*)

Table 12.2 *(Continued)*

Governance Characteristics	Checklist for Action
• **Responsibility**: Clearly defined responsibilities of the board, CEO and senior leadership team	• **Board Expectations of CEO and Senior Leadership Team**: Are performance expectations of the CEO and senior leadership clearly delineated? Is compensation of the CEO and senior leadership team linked to performance outcomes? • **Oversight by the Board**: Are all board members active participants in developing the company's strategic framework? Is there agreement among board members and senior leadership as to the long-term performance indicators such as market share, profit margins, goal commitments to employees, and goal commitments to stakeholder communities?
• **Fairness**: Balance of differing interests of stakeholders	• **Corporate Values**: Is there a consensus between the board and the senior leadership team as to what the core values of firm are? • **Conflict Resolution**: When competing interests create unresolved tension, are there processes in place to resolve these tensions before they become contentious issues?
• **Social Responsibility**: Awareness of external commitments to good corporate citizenship; maintaining ethical standards that build trust	• **Commitment to Ethical Standards**: Is a standard of ethics that addresses the full array of stakeholder expectations in place? Do the processes for adherence to these standards motivate compliance or commitment? • **Balance**: Are both the economic and social responsibilities treated with equal deference?

Source: King Committee Report on Corporate Governance: 7 characteristics of good corporate governance March 2002.

There are internal, mixed, and external methods of scrutiny. There are also formal and informal methods of scrutiny. The purpose of these mechanisms is to 'police and advise'. But what method works best where?

Recent regulations have, unsurprisingly, focused on formal channels. By emphasising board composition and board responsibilities, legislation has brought more outside directors onto boards, and has formalised their responsibilities through the committees. A whole literature exists concerning the effect on corporate performance through these channels. Laing and Weir (1999) reviewed the literature and relationships between 'duality', the separation of the Chairman and the CEO and performance; the presence, and extent of, 'non-executive directors' and 'performance'; and 'Board committees' and 'performance'. Additionally, they test the relationships with a post-Cadbury Report group of companies.

In the case of 'duality', Rechner and Dalton (1991) found that companies perform better with split positions. Others (Boyd, 1995; Donaldson and Davis, 1991) found that they performed worse. Laing and Weir (1999) continue a tradition including Berg and Smith (1978) and Rechner and Dalton's earlier study (1989), that there is no relationship.

Concerning 'non-executive directors' and 'performance', the jury is also out. (Vance, 1964; Ezzamel and Watson, 1993; Pearce and Zhara, 1992; Brown and Caylor, 2004) found a positive relation. Others (Yermack, 1996; Klein, 1998; Agrawal and Knoeber, 1996) find a negative relationship and Daily and Dalton, (1992), as well as Laing and Weir (1999), find none at all.

And so it goes. The presence of 'board committees' and 'performance' is less researched. Klein (1998) found some evidence and, interestingly Laing and Weir (1999) found a significantly positive relationship.

The question for us is *whether the right side of the equation is being measured.* Surely many of these initiatives to restructure boards have more to do with policing than with advising. By measuring performance, is the wrong element being measured? The difficulty, however, is how to measure the opposite – the lack of failure or of 'bad behaviour'.

Spira (2001) partially tackles this issue. The question she poses is not whether board composition prevents bad behaviour, but whether the tremendous emphasis on policing reduces the entrepreneurial spirit of companies by diverting board time and attention with regulatory and compliance activities. While she cites anecdotal evidence of time constraints among non-executive directors, she concludes that there is no evidence that board composition, and the increasing effort for compliance, is related to performance.

Romano (2005) does not focus generally on corporate governance, but specifically on the effect of Sarbanes-Oxley (SOX) compliance in the US. In reviewing the parameters of SOX, she posits that it has had no beneficial impact on governance whatsoever, and instead has create compliance costs which are excessive.

Overall, the picture is not a pretty one. There is little evidence that legislated, formal frameworks for corporate governance prevent misbehaviour, nor is there overwhelming evidence that frameworks improve performance for shareholders.

Corporate governance therefore becomes an area of speculation, as much as of fact. In taking a step away from a formal approach, are there areas where one would believe actions could make a difference? What can help keep a company honest and responsible, and what can help improve a company's performance? And for whom?

Let's start with Board members. If board members are there to police, there are two fundamental requirements. First, they must be conversant in often very challenging aspects of corporate finance. To understand the financial structures of Enron surely required extensive expertise in very difficult valuation challenges for exotic derivatives, questions which were evidently too complex even for the Andersen auditors. Second, the board members must have the respect of the executive directors. If peer pressure and social cohesion are absent, CEOs will not be kept in check. If, on the other hand, peer pressure is extensive, then the ability to block bad behaviour, resign from a board, will have considerable effect.

Broadening this view beyond the boardroom, financial information must be useful for others. Stakeholders do not expect to be inundated with a volume of information from a company. What they do expect is pertinent information that will help them make informed assessments about their own risks. What stakeholders view as transparency translates to effective disclosure processes within companies. To meet regulatory requirements for financial reporting, corporations have maintained reporting processes aimed at meeting deadlines. A complaint often heard by board members is that financial reports often don't reach them in time for adequate review or comment. If board members are to be engaged as active partners in ensuring the overall veracity and coherence of reported information, disclosure processes must build in reasonable time for review. In addition, communication plans and their attendant processes should address how external releases are communicated, so that stakeholders do not feel that they are being manipulated by corporate spin doctors. Public relations and investor relations groups are most effective when they have maintained a list of key stakeholder contacts matched with established internal leaders and board members. Even more importantly, these PR and IR staffs provide an invaluable service by creating opportunities for dialogue between stakeholders and their corporate contacts. Efforts spent in advance, cultivating stakeholder relationships, pay dividends when unexpected bad news develops and must be communicated. Scott (2005) points out that good communication with the financial community is critical to the company's long-term health, and that excessive stock price swings in either direction are dangerous.

A similar need for expertise affects the other purported goal of corporate governance, the goal of strategic support. If board members are to contribute to the development of successful innovation and entrepreneurship, they must surely possess either an understanding of the industry while being non-competitive, or have an understanding of an adjacent industry in which lessons can be learned, or opportunities exist for the company on whose board they serve. Within this remit, respect is critical, and having sufficient, independent insight. Getting insight means having access to information, gatekeepers of information, and networked relationships to information.

In the corporate arena, Paul Desmarais Junior, the CEO of Power Corporation in Canada confirms the challenges. In a discussion that one of the authors had with him in Montreal in 2004, he confirmed that the need for extensive knowledge is paramount, and that he does not sit on boards where he does not understand the business extensively. Additionally, he has a team of researchers working for him to study the companies where he is on the board. He did not think highly of the expanding net of independent board members who represent 'the man in the street' (Desmarais, 2004).

Board members and senior leaders of large global companies rely heavily on a structure of cascading accountability among all the company's managers. This means that directors need to have strategic, rather than operational, foci – they must therefore make the transition from technical/functional expertise, as being their basis of power, to wider influencing skills to manage and motivate people over whom they have no line management authority. This cascading structure is also often only implied, rather than overtly specified. For the board and the CEO to attest to the accuracy of reported information to stakeholders, this cascading structure requires an integrated mapping of accountability, to build the confidence at the board level that their decisions on behalf of the company are based on accurate information. After the fiasco with Andersen, regarded before Enron as a highly respected auditing firm, many US policy makers and investors are calling for external auditors to be engaged on fixed-term contracts, not exceeding five years. This type of requirement can place an undue hardship on a company, because part of effective auditing of large companies is an intimate knowledge of the company and its industry. A feasible alternative is to insure that the auditing firm is responsible to the board, and, if necessary, the board can request specific audits on company practices or its subsidiaries. In order for a company's board members to be active participants, an important means of establishing accountability is to encourage an ombudsmen/women group who sets up a process to raise 'minority' concerns, including whistle-blowing. Another means to support board members is for companies to create forums in which members get a better appreciation for what the company does, and what employees think about the company.

We believe that significant stakeholders in a company are too often overlooked in this debate. Surely, the company's employees have much at stake. They are employed by the firm, and have the foremost stake in ensuring good performance, and in monitoring potential mismanagement. One can make a case that employees are in a good position to influence the development of a successful strategy for the organisation through their on-going, daily efforts.

On the policing front, however, opportunities are mixed. Continental European corporate governance models have often involved works councils, whether representing unionised workers or not, in their management structure. On the positive side, the involvement of employees in understanding the challenges of the organisation are beneficial as they can influence decision-making and diffuse knowledge. On the negative side, employees can place the needs of the entire workforce over the needs of the company as it seeks to transform itself, shed old businesses or locations and invest in new businesses, or new locations. As in the case of the studies looking at the effects of legislation for formal corporate governance at board level, studies are mixed in their assessment of the benefits of formalised participatory governance schemes.

Ironically, one area in which employees should be able to significantly influence corporate governance practice does not seem to be well legislated: the realm of whistle-blowing. As Enron and a range of other scandals have shown, whistle-blowers do not do well personally from letting their conscience rule. This area must surely be better developed if there is a real desire to reform corporate governance reality, rather than corporate governance legislation.

External scrutiny is the area which provides for an increasingly lively area. In the past, a free press and the rule of law have done much to keep an eye on company performance, and to reward good behaviour and punish bad behaviour. This depended very much on formal challenges, however. Good media scrutiny depends on having a free press, but this can be manipulated when the press is owned by the state or by corporate power, as countries ranging from Italy with Berlusconi through to China and Russia have shown all too well.

What is developing, however, is the diffusion of media to a more democratic level, and we believe that this new diversity will be significant in years to come. In an era of mobile phone cameras, personal www sites, blogs, and fast organising protests, one is beginning to see corporate governance changing.

Some organisations are spreading the message of the goals of corporate governance through their entire organisations through the use of the internet as Friedman (2005) notes. In other areas, users are defining which products are acceptable for e-Bay to sell. Judgements are being passed on the behaviour of a whole range of companies by customers and employees, so that governance and reputation management are converging. The highest profile example at the moment concerns Huntington Life Sciences, where animal rights activists have caused the Cambridge, UK firm to flee a London listing and seek a New York listing, which has been prevented by the activists (Berkrot, 2006). That it is possible for a company to be challenged to this extent, is interesting and bodes well for deepening democracy.

The era of the sole voice, with a once-a-year window of opportunity at an AGM, or a pure reliance on formalised corporate governance frameworks from a financial perspective, are being replaced by the ability to scrutinise and diffuse opinion on an on-going basis. While this will not rule out all corporate scandals in coming years, it will certainly go some way to creating more awareness of what listed companies are doing.

Would a broader view have prevented malpractice, and some of the corporate scandals of recent years? Would better monitoring frameworks which included employees, clients, and other stakeholders have helped? Perhaps they would have, and perhaps they would not have. What is clear, however, is that a narrow view which continually increases monitoring only from a financial, compliance perspective, from all evidence, is not solving the problem.

References

Abrahami, A. (2005), 'Business Governance: Sarbanes-Oxley Act (SOA) Compliance', *Management Services*, Vol. 49, No. 3, pp. 28–31.

Agrawal, A. and Knoeber, C.R. (1996), 'Firm performance and mechanisms to control agency problems between managers and shareholders', *Journal of Financial and Quantitative Analysis*, Vol. 31, pp. 377–397.

Berg, S. V. and Smith, S. K. (1978), 'CEO board chairman: A quantitative study of dual versus unitary leadership', *Directors and Boards*, Vol. 3, pp. 34–39.

Berkrot, B. (2006), 'LSRI drops to Pink Sheets amid animal rights action', Reuters News Service, 10 February.

Brown, L. D. and Caylor, M. L. (2004), *Corporate governance and firm performance* (Georgia State University, URL: http://papers.ssrn.com/sol13/papers.cfm?abstract_id=586423, retrieved 25th October 2005).

Boyd, B. K. (1995), 'CEO duality and firm performance: A contingency model', *Strategic Management Journal*, Vol. 16, pp. 301–312.

Cadbury, A. (1992a), *Report of the Committee on the Financial; Aspects of Corporate Governance*, London: Gee & Co. Ltd.

Cadbury, A. (1992b), *Calling firms to account without stifling* (*The Times*, 28th May 1992, pp. 23).

Cadbury, A. (2002), *Corporate Governance and Chairmanship – A Personal View*, Oxford: Oxford University Press.

Daily, C. M. and Dalton, D. R. (1992), 'The relationship between governance structure and corporate performance in entrepreneurial firms', *Journal of Business Venturing*, Vol. 7, pp. 375–386.

Desmarais, P. Jr. (2004), Personal Discussion with Kai Peters at AACSB Annual Conference (Montreal, June 2004).

Donaldson, L. and Davis, J. H. (1991), 'Stewardship theory or agency theory: CEO governance and shareholder returns', *Australian Journal of Management*, Vol. 16, pp. 49–64.

Ezzamel, M. A. and Watson, R. (1993), 'Organisational form, ownership structure and corporate performance: A contextual empirical analysis of UK companies', *British Journal of Management*, Vol. 4, pp. 161–176.

Friedman, T. L. (2005), *The world is flat: A brief history of the twenty-first century*, New York, NY: Farrar, Straus & Giroux.

Greebury, S. R. (1995), *Directors' Remuneration*, London: Gee & Co. Ltd.

Klein, A. (1998), 'Firm performance and board committee structure', *Journal of Law and Economics*, Vol. 41, pp. 137–165.

Laing, D. and Weir, C. (1999), 'Governance structures, size and corporate performance in UK firms', *Management Decision*, Vol. 37, No. 5, pp. 457–467.

Mallin, C, Mullineux, A. and Wihlborg, C. (2005), 'The Financial Sector and Corporate Governance: The UK Case', *Corporate Governance*, Vol. 13, No. 4, pp. 532–541.

OECD (2004), *OECD Principles of Corporate Governance*, last accessed February 24, 2006 http://www.oecd.org/dataoecd/32/18/31557724.pdf

Pearce, J. A. and Zhara, S. A. (1992), 'Board compensation from a strategic contingency perspective', *Journal of Management Studies*, Vol. 29, pp. 411–438.

Rechner, P. L. and Dalton, D. R. (1989), 'The impact of CEO as board chairperson on corporate performance: Evidence versus rhetoric', *Academy of Management Executive*, Vol. 3, pp. 141–143.

Rechner, P. L. and Dalton, D. R. (1991), 'CEO duality and organisational performance: A longitudinal analysis', *Strategic Management Journal*, Vol. 12, pp. 155–160.

Romano, R. (2005), 'Sarbanes-Oxley: Quack corporate governance', *Corporate Board*, Vol. 26, No. 154, pp. 5–11.

Scott, M. (2005), *Achieving Fair Value*, London: John Wiley and Sons.

Spira, L. F. (2001), 'Enterprise and accountability: Striking a balance', *Management Decision*, Vol. 39, No. 9, pp. 739–748.

Toronto Stock Exchange (1994), *Where Were the Directors? Guidelines for Improved Corporate Governance in Canada (The Toronto Report)* Toronto: TSE.

Toronto Stock Exchange (1999), *Five Years to the Dey*, Toronto: Institute of Corporate Directors.

Turnbull, N. (1999), *Corporate Guidance for Internal Control*, London: Gee & Co. Ltd.

Vance, S. C. (1964), *Board of Directors: Structure and Performance*, Eugene, OR: University of Oregon Press.

Yermack, D. (1996), 'Higher market value of companies with a small board of directors', *Journal of Financial Economics*, Vol. 40, pp. 185–212.

Part 4

Creating Reality

Editors' Note: Creating Reality

by Marylou Shockley

There exists, within a post-modern world, a rich marketplace of constructed realities. In this marketplace, variation has come to symbolize the "invisible hand" that encourages suppliers of ideas to keep creating new views – in the hope that some will become "block buster" worldviews. For consumer of these ideas, the "invisible hand" admonishes inspection, debate, and integration. The marketplace of constructed realities is full of the hustle-bustle, excitement, confusing complexity, and dangers of any vibrant marketplace. The *caveat emptor* in this marketplace is alertness; gullibility caused by busyness, apathy, and faddish acceptance is dangerous. Sometimes reliable buying criteria, such as a respected brand name or a trusted endorsement, are not readily available. Thinking and reflection alone are the only reliable buying criteria.

In a corner of the marketplace of constructed realities reside the purveyors of diversity who believe the facets of diversity are robustly varied and are limited only by the human mind's creative potential. Diversity in this context suggests that traditional notions of variations in gender, age, ethnicity, and life styles are only several of diversity's many facets. For this reason, the chapters in this part are eclectic, and for the most part, non-traditional. The authors invite us to ponder and think about diversity in different ways.

Two chapters included in Creating Reality suggest new conceptual frameworks in which to more effectively promote learning and human interaction within organizations and societies. Dave Bond in his paper Reflections on Conscious Communication: a Critical Process for Transitional Societies? introduces the notion concept of conscious communication that builds action and awareness. Bond argues that in transitional societies, where learning is exponential, the construct of conversations requires conscious communication in which not only the *act* of communication takes place. He observes that *awareness* which makes sense of what is being said on several dimensions must also accompany any meaningful conversation.

While Dave Bond synthesizes concepts, e.g., sensemaking, dialogue, appreciative inquiry and complexity theory, Harald Knudsen and Jonny Holbek take us on a historical journey back to ancient Greece to visit the religious festivals, the hub of socio-economic life between villages and cities in Greece. In their chapter Diversity – Creativity – Leadership: A Journey from Ancient Greece to Modern Society Knudsen and Holbek create a learning framework of *theoros* and *theoria* qualities that help mutually reinforce the notions of leadership with those of diversity and culture. They suggest that modern organizations can rely on shared language to instill an "intimacy of communication" to help foster understanding and innovation. However, communications is not enough – leaders must work at cultivating shared values across diverse religious, ethnic, and political beliefs to create "fellows of blood" in an integrated organizational culture.

The final essay by Marylou Shockley entitled Diversity: Not All Are Believers provides a counterpoint. Shockley argues that it is all well and good to discuss the merits of diversity; however, there are many who are non-believers of diversity and have alternative views. She explores the attributes of fundamentalism, both religious and secular. With this backdrop, Shockley then presents observations on why business sees diversity as valuable. She posits that business firms find value in diversity for compliance and opportunistic reasons. Shockley goes on to argue that firms find diversity of value because it is "good for business." Business organizations see that establishing a diverse workforce to match the diversity of their potential client markets is likely to have a positive impact on their profits. Rather than a comparison of fundamentalist and diversity attributes, Marylou Shockley shares her own personal commitments that she feels defines diversity. She challenges readers to reflect on their own thoughts about diversity and create their own personal commitments.

13
Reflections on Conscious Communication: A Critical Process for Transitional Societies?

by Dave Bond

> *Conscious: knowing something with others, knowing in oneself . . . Aware of what one is doing or intends to do . . . Having the mental faculties in an active and waking state*
>
> (*The New Shorter Oxford English Dictionary*, 1993)

Introduction

What kinds of interventions best contribute something of value – to learning and capacity – for people within a transitional society? In the private and public sectors, profit and non-profit organizations, there is a need to promote effective action which leads to sustainable development. This requires complex understandings, vision and strategic design. In this paper, I reflect on issues which I feel are pertinent for people seeking to learn and make a positive impact in periods of transition. I consider links between thought and communication, advocate the need to integrate awareness and action through "conscious communication" and identify three different approaches to communication which have influenced my thinking. In the process, I touch on some overlaps between modern schools of thought on communication and ancient wisdom on conscious action. My purpose is to stimulate alternative, possibly provocative, perspectives in the potentially powerful domain of communication. This potential is often limited by superficial understanding or simplistic formulae. Yet understandings of a more deeply conscious communication open up profound and pragmatic means for actively participating in the reformulation of transitional societies.

"Transition" is about change, risk and uncertainty. In relatively stable conditions, change processes tend to be gradual and unnoticed. By contrast, change in transitional societies is highlighted by forces which make their presence felt at multiple levels of society. The old no longer holds, the new is still emerging, whilst the future is unpredictable. So, transition strips away a sense of constancy, exposing the ground on which we build our sense of self, family, work and life. Sustainable development in transitional societies obliges us to seek out or create new ways of functioning. Perhaps this is part of the gift of transition: it highlights processes of change, compels us to formulate new meaning and understandings, emphasizes the need to reconsider values and behaviour, and encourages us to explore diverse perspectives.

Conscious communication: the link between awareness and action

I would argue that sustainable development, at all levels of society and organizations, needs to be formulated out of two essential, interlinking strands: *awareness* and *action*. To act in the world in new, transformative ways (which do not duplicate redundant habits) requires:

- sharpening and opening up our awareness of what is actually happening,
- considering multiple perspectives,
- making creative use of diversity,
- generating innovative insights, and
- acting on these insights.

Furthermore, I suggest that *conscious communication* serves as a critical link between these strands of awareness and action. In transitional societies, complex and rapid change demands a variety of creative communicative practices. My focus here is particularly on intra-personal and inter-personal communication – conversations – and their critical role in "sensemaking" (cf. Weick, 1995) and action.[1] This may seem a narrow focus for those concerned with broad strategies of society or organizations as a whole. But my concern is with accessing critical points of leverage and encouraging effective implementation. Key processes of strategy, policy formulation, and daily decisions depend on conversations. So, the quality of our conversations and relationships (formal and informal) has considerable impact on our ability to influence others and achieve our goals.

Constructivism

Constructivism relates how we think and relate to how we communicate and act. The starting point is the assumption that each of us is the architect and interpreter of our own meaning. The world which we think of and even see, is *not* a concrete, "reality", seen and understood by all in the same way. We "construct" the world we live in – or at least our interpretations of that world. We can only see things through the lenses and frames which have come to be ours. Based on a range of factors, including our personal experiences and history, belief systems, values and assumptions, we see, hear and feel the world in different ways. Generally, this sensemaking process in the mind is an automatic process, generating a range of thoughts and judgements (usually unconsciously) which then prompt our action. Hence, our perceptions and sensemaking processes shape our knowledge, learning and understanding of the world.

This is an efficient, automatic process of cognition. Yet the very efficiency of this can limit our understanding and learning. Argyris (1986, 1991), a Harvard psychologist, developed a model which helps explain how our automatic sensemaking processes work – "the Ladder of Inference". This model also highlights how the thinking process can come to limit our understanding of the world and others. Its very "efficiency" in selecting and processing data can block us from noticing the underlying assumptions which frame how we see and interpret events. Without a sharpened awareness of these processes, we can be locked into what Argyris and Schon (1978) have described as "single-loop learning". By crafting a picture and language to see and speak of these cycles, Argyris and Schon (1978) helped to create an awareness of these limiting or even destructive habits. This awareness can then be used to create a constructive means of self-change and transformation of our engagement with others – a process they call "double-loop learning".

So I am claiming that the purposeful, skilled integration of a range of mindful communication strategies helps generate influential and sustainable interventions. Here, I would like to mention some significant influences on my thinking. I am referring to a constructivist framework, and three different approaches to communication:

(1) "dialogue",
(2) "appreciative inquiry" and
(3) "complexity".

Dialogue

The notion of "dialogue" has been fairly well publicized in management and leadership development over recent years. I refer here to the work stemming from Bohm (1996), a quantum physicist, who sought ways of linking his insights in physics into the terrains of human interaction. Dialogue is particularly concerned with collective thinking. Bohm's (1996) thesis was that certain communicative practices bring to the surface a pool of common meaning which is not accessible individually. As such, dialogue can be an effective means of considering problems and challenges, as well as a forum for generating novel vision and forms of action. It is possible to see the influence of eastern mindfulness practices here. Bohm maintained an ongoing conversation with the Indian philosopher J. Krishnamurti. These conversations shaped crucial elements of the dialogue process, such as: noticing your thoughts without automatically acting on them (suspension), emphasizing the power and importance of listening; being open to alternative ideas and approaches. These fundamentals, in a systems thinking framework, have been incorporated into very practical measures by writers such as Peter Senge, Richard Ross and colleagues (Senge *et al.*, 1994), as well as William Isaacs (1999) and others.

Additional elements include respecting, voicing, and balancing particular forms of advocacy and inquiry to help reveal assumptions and reasoning.

This is not to say that every form of communication is best approached as an open-ended dialogue. There are practices within the dialogue approach which can enhance the quality of awareness in a variety of communication contexts. A skilful interweaving of simple principles (but challenging practices) generates the capacity to plumb fairly complex depths.

Appreciative inquiry

A more recent, and so perhaps less well known, approach is that of "appreciative inquiry" (Cooperrider and Whitney, 2000). Like dialogue, appreciative inquiry seeks to foster new forms of communication and has its roots in systems thinking. It too focuses on collective inquiry and seeks to avoid adversarial discussions. However, appreciative inquiry eschews problem solving as an unhelpful approach. It strives to reveal and reinforce the positive in relationships and organizations. It operates on the understanding that conversations have a generative power to nurture learning, promote change and to free the human spirit. Appreciative inquiry advocates communication which draws on the emotional and spiritual. As such, appreciative inquiry observed by Barrett (1995, cited in Barge and Oliver 2003: 127) incorporates four particular communicative elements:

(1) *affirmative competency* – the ability to identify positive possibilities by bracketing out imperfections and focusing on past and present successes, assets, strengths, and potentials
(2) *expansive competence* – the ability to challenge existing thinking and organizational practices with an emphasis on stretching the capability of organizational members by having them engage passionately with important personal and organizational values
(3) *generative competence* – the ability to create systems that foster individuals' recognition of the consequence and value of their contribution to the organization and that provide a sense of how they are making progress
(4) *collaborative competence* – the ability to create conversational spaces where members work together and share diverse ideas and perspectives.

Complexity

For those readers who find notions of the spirit irrelevant, unsavoury or, at least, inappropriate in journals of this nature, it may come as some relief that there are alternative approaches to conscious communication. Working within the framework of complexity theory, Stacey (2001) and his colleagues have given considerable attention to communicative practices within organizations. Their perspective or "lens" is that communicative practices are best understood as a form of complex responsive processes – an ongoing process of meaning making and reformulation of meaning in the context of interaction.

In contrast with Bohm (1996), Senge *et al.* (1994), Stacey (2001) explicitly rejects their notions of dialogue as a *process* which somehow surfaces and reveals previously hidden, collective truths. He also takes issue with attempts to contrive *safe* spaces for conversations – an essential element for both advocates of dialogue and of appreciative inquiry discussed above. Rather than prescribing practices to bear the invisible fruit of harmonious meaning, the complexity approach argues, we would do better to understand more fully just how conversations function. Communicative interaction is paradoxical, both creative and destructive, simultaneously competitive and co-operative. Elements which require study include: how people try to cope with the absence of safety in daily life, defensiveness, anxiety, resistance, how power and ideology function, turn-taking, and the dynamics of inclusion and exclusion. What is needed then, is a greater awareness of these processes of responsive relating – a fuller understanding of the complexity of the processes through which we achieve joint action in present time.

In this way, the complexity theory approach argues that we need to gain more understanding of language in action. In doing so, it calls for less action or prescription. Rather than trying to formulate what "should be", we need to develop a deeper sense of "what is".

Conclusion: a return to conscious communication

Which brings me back to the notion of "conscious communication" as a critically important component of the change processes within transitional societies.

Fundamental to such effective communication, are:

- self-understanding,
- reflection,
- a willingness and know-how to learn and change ourselves,
- an ability to surface, interpret and assimilate diverse perspectives,
- a preparedness to broaden our range of thinking and communication practices.

Awareness nurtures new insights which require different types of action – in this case, communicative interaction.

Certain contemplative traditions have known of this cycle for centuries. To increase our ability for spontaneous, open-minded, creative action in the world, these traditions have developed practices for developing a greater degree of "mindfulness". Nairn (1998), a Buddhist meditation teacher, speaks of methods of training people in *mindfulness*, "the systematic training in knowing what is happening, while it is happening", which, in turn, gives rise to *awareness*, "a quality of knowing" (Nairn, 1998: 34). So, the cycle can be described as: practicing mindfulness, generates awareness, which promotes *right action* (including continued mindfulness practices). In some traditions, the appropriate action is understood to emerge as a direct consequence of awareness. In others, there is a more conscious process of using awareness to frame the action.

As mentioned above, both the dialogue and appreciative inquiry approaches to communication make explicit links with notions derived from spiritual practices. Not so the complexity approach. Nevertheless, a complexity approach to communication can generate what sounds like an eastern guide to mindful practice: Stacey (2001) urges us to cultivate a fuller awareness of what is happening in communicative practices whilst they occur; to focus more on observing what is happening in order to understand, instead of prescribing new action. Be fully present and do less! Conscious communication will then emerge from this awareness.

If we take seriously the constructivist notion of sensemaking, then we realize that "knowing what is happening while it is happening", is no simple thing. It requires alertness, sharpness and a willingness to change. This, in turn, requires practices which can expand our awareness of what is happening as well as those which open us to diverse perspectives. Also, what we interpret as true for us, is only partial, and does not incorporate the interpretations and sensemaking of others. If we want to fill out and complement our understandings, we need to be aware that different perceptions exist, and inquire about them. This requires that we nurture a spirit of open inquiry – that we hold open the notion that there are things we do not know. Developing a greater openness refers not only to how we communicate, but also to consciously seeking ways of broadening and diversifying the range of people we communicate with (cf. Cross *et al.*, 2002).

What I am suggesting is that increased attention has to be given to conscious communication: an approach which links how we think, learn and reflect with the ways we communicate and relate. There are many models, guidebooks and consultancies providing input on aspects of communication. My purpose is not to propose one slick new method, or 5-step recipe. Nor is it to offer critique or synthesis of diverse approaches. It is to suggest that we should make conscious choices to develop thoughtfully engaged communication practices – practices which both heighten awareness and contribute to effective action.

Note

1 This has been one of the major concerns of my work as an educator, facilitator and consultant. I have been working with people at varying levels of responsibility, in diverse sectors, and from a variety of cultures and countries. The focus has been at the organizational, team and individual levels. Nevertheless, I see significant links with the broader issues facing society in transition.

References

Argyris, C. (1986), "Skilled Incompetence", *Harvard Business Review*, Vol. 64, No. 5, pp. 74–79.

Argyris, C. (1991), "Teaching Smart People How to Learn", *Harvard Business Review*, Vol. 69, No. 3, pp. 99–109.

Argyris, C. and Schon, D. (1978), *Organizational Learning: A Theory of Action Perspective*, Reading, MA: Addison-Wesley.

Barge, J. and Oliver, C. (2003), "Working with Appreciation in Managerial Practice", *Academy of Management Review*, Vol. 28, pp. 124–141.

Bohm, D. (1996), *On Dialogue*, Nichol, L. (Ed.), London: Routledge.

Cooperrider, D. L. and Whitney, D. (2000), "A positive revolution in change: Appreciative Inquiry", in D. L. Cooperrider, P. F. Sorensen Jr., D. Whitney and T. F. Yaeger (Eds.), *Appreciative Inquiry: Rethinking human organization toward a positive theory of change*, Champagne. IL: Stipes, pp. 3–28.

Cross, R., Borgatti S. and Parker, A. (2002), "Making Invisible Work Visible: Using Social Network Analysis to Support Strategic Collaboration", *California Management Review*, Vol. 44, No. 2, pp. 24–46.

Isaacs, W. (1999), *Dialogue and the Art of Thinking Together*, New York: Currency.

Nairn, R. (1998), *Diamond Mind: Psychology of Meditation*, Cape Town: Kairon Press.

Senge, P., Kleiner, A., Roberts, C., Ross, R. and Smith, B. (1994), *The Fifth Discipline Fieldbook: Strategies and Tools for Building a Learning Organization*, London: Nicholas Brealey.

Stacey, R. (2001), *Complex Responsive Processes in Organizations: Learning and Knowledge Creation*, London: Routledge.

Weick, K. (1995), *Sensemaking in Organizations*, London: Sage.

14

Diversity – Creativity – Leadership: A Journey from Ancient Greece to Modern Society

by Harald Knudsen and Jonny Holbek

Diversity – Creativity – Leadership

The word *journey* seems to be used more and more by leadership consultants and seminar lecturers. It is widely recognised that leadership development is a difficult and challenging task – but you can develop yourself. You may cultivate your leadership capabilities, develop and expand your menu of leadership styles and attributes. This is what your personal *journey* is about: cultivation, development and personal transformation.

It is a journey that sometimes takes you to new environments, new people, cultures, technologies, problems and solutions. It may also take you – through leaps of self introspection – to a closer contact with your own intentionality and your own hidden resources.

A good thing about the journey is that, as you move forward, you not only develop and transform yourself, but you also absorb other aspects of the living world. You become aware of the feelings and orientations of other people. You pick up useful information and make worthwhile experiences. You may even solve problems and find solutions to questions you didn't even know existed before you started on the journey.

It is all about learning. This includes learning about others and about ourselves, about practical skills and theoretical reasoning, about meanings and values. If a story was told about such a journey, it would be several stories melded together into one: the story of your life, the story of your particular project or your particular investigation, and the story of the journey itself and of all the revelations entertained on that journey.

In what follows, we present a metaphorical framework or "model" of learning and development through diversity. It is a model that encompasses the individual search for knowledge, the community of practice and learning through diversity, and the enrichment of the base organisation or base community through the "return" of the innovator. We start with a presentation of an old story – and continue with a presentation of up-to-date research results relating to the same model.

Gazing backwards

For the sake of simplicity, let us assume that there is one object of learning sought throughout the whole journey – some kind of higher level insight. It is the kind of practical insight seldom taught in schools, hardly ever tested during exams, but still a kind which is most decisive for good leadership, for wise judgement, and for creative innovation, personal integrity and respectful behaviour. As a practically-minded reader, you would probably object to calling such an insight anything close to the word "theory". But if we make a sufficiently long leap backwards in history, you will be surprised to find some very practical roots of exactly that word.

Most linguists and philosophers trace the concept of theory back to the Greek verb *theorein*, which is also cited as the origin in most dictionaries. *Theorein* can be translated as "look at" and "behold", but also "contemplate" and "consider". The word *theoria*, which comes from *theorein* and which is the direct origin of the word *theory*, is defined, on the one hand, in terms of *action*: to behold, contemplate or consider; and, on the other hand, as *results of such an action*: an observation, a consideration or assumption. Beyond this, there is little to be found in the standard dictionaries.

So, we need to make an extra journey, going back to ancient Greece, to the time before antiquity, 800 to 1200 years BC. The most important social institution for cultural, economic and political development at that time, was the institution of religious festivals. One such festival formed the origins of the Olympic games, but there were many others. Initially, however, they were small, insignificant religious events, where people from the village and from neighbouring villages took part. Gradually, they grew into large festivals, with visitors from far away. Among these visitors, we find the original "theoretician". A *theoros* was an official representative of a village, a delegate with the mandate of participating in the festival together with other *theoroi*. The group of *theoroi* together formed a legation, the original *theoria*. In the third volume of Grote's *A History of Greece* we find an account of this practice:

> Of the beginnings of these great solemnities we cannot presume to speak, except in mythical language: we know them only in their comparative maturity. But the habit of common sacrifice, on a small scale and between near neighbours, is a part of the earliest habits of Greece. The sentiment of fraternity, between two tribes or villages, first manifested itself by sending a sacred legation or **theoria** to offer sacrifices at each other's festivals and to partake in the recreations which followed; thus establishing a truce with solemn guarantee, and bringing themselves into direct connection each with the god of the others under his appropriate local surname. The pacific communion so fostered, and the increased assurance of intercourse, as Greece gradually emerged from the turbulence and pugnacity of the hero-icage, operated especially in extending the range of this ancient habit: the

> village festivals became town festivals, largely frequented by the citizens of other towns, and sometimes with special invitations sent around to attract **theoros** from every Hellenic community, – and thus these once humble assemblages gradually swelled into the pomp and immense confluence of the Olympic and Phytian games (Grote, 1924: 28–29).

Theoria, then, was a sacred legation, an assembly of delegates, envoys or diplomats from neighbouring villages participating in religious festivals – sometimes as competitors, referees or heralds of the games. The deeper original purpose was to behold God (*theos*) and bring spiritual enrichment to the home village.

The benefits of diversity

So what does the old story tell us about the idea of diversity and learning? Perhaps we need to think back and try to visualise the crowd at such a festival. Again we may turn to the historian, Grote, who observes:

> Nevertheless we may venture to note certain improving influences, connected with their geographical position, at a time when they had no books to study, and no more advanced predecessors to imitate. We may remark, first, that their position made them at once mountaineers and mariners, thus supplying them with great variety of objects, sensations, and adventures; next, that each petty community, nestled apart amidst its own rocks, was sufficiently severed from the rest to possess an individual life and attributes of its own, yet not so far as to subtract it from the sympathies of the remainder; so that an observant Greek, commercing with a great diversity of half-countrymen, whose language he understood, and whose idiosyncracies he could appreciate, had access to a larger mass of social and political experience than any other man in so unadvanced an age could personally obtain. The Phoenician, superior to the Greek on shipboard, traversed wider distances and saw a greater number of strangers, but had not the same means of intimate communion with a multiplicity of fellows in blood and language. His relations, confined to purchase and sale, did not comprise that mutuality of action and reaction which pervaded the crowd at a Grecian festival (Grote, 1924: 15–16).

What we visualise, then, is a multitude of people, characterised by a high level of cultural *diversity*, representing a high level of *variety of experience* combined with a high level of *intimacy of communication*. Such a glimpse of an old society is highly at odds with our normal perception of backward villages and ancient societies. The story tells us that two factors combine to make the high level of diversity useful for learning purposes: *variety of experience; intimacy of communication*. Variety of experience prevents "in-house blindness". Intimacy of communication makes an intimate sharing and exchange of knowledge possible.

In fact, history tells us that if war or weather should hinder participation from other villages in a festival, one would not use the word *theoria*. Instead, the concept *thysia* was used (Rausch, 1982) meaning that the festival was a "local affair" – not offering the diversity and variety of experience associated with *theoria*.

At the level of individuals, in a society without formal education, *variety of experience* is the ultimate basis of learning, subject only to the individual's capacity for absorbing and organising new insight. We may suppose that the capacity for learning is shaped like an inverted U-curve. With a low level of variety of experience, little expansion of knowledge can take place, and the capacity of absorption and organisation will remain underdeveloped. With a higher level of variety, a person's capacity of learning (absorption and organisation) will be enhanced. New insights will be gained in more efficient ways – the brain will be better tuned for learning, and – in fact – there is more to be learnt. But in the farther end of the inverted U-curve, we may imagine a society where the level of variety, complexity, turbulence and chaos is so high, that the capacity for making meaningful experiences, and meaningful inference and learning, breaks down.

At the level of groups and societies, we may assume a similar inverted U-shaped curve for collective learning and innovative capacity. With a low level of collective variety of experience, there is little to be learnt from the others, and the level of communicative ability is not really tested out. With a higher level of variety of experience, there is more to be learnt from the others, provided that the participants are able to communicate with each other. Thus, for a given level of variety, there is more to be learnt, the greater the capacity for intimate communication. And, conversely, for a given level of communication, more can be learnt, the greater the variety of experience. However, at the farther end of the curve, there may be societies and groups where the cultural diversity and variety of experience is so high that it becomes extremely difficult to communicate with other groups. Communication may break down, and individuals may revert to the safety of low variety local groups and communities.

The general tendency of such inverted U-shaped curves, can readily be observed from studies of diversity and efficiency. If we instead of looking at efficiency in general, however, look at problem-solving efficiency and implementational efficiency as separate measures, high diversity groups perform relatively better in the problem-solving and innovative stages and relatively worse at the implementational or operational stages (Smith and Bond, 1998). Because cultural diversity and variety of experience is normally associated both with a more challenging communicative task (communicating something the others do not know anything about) and with a lower level of communicative ability (language problems, other obtrusions), the net benefit of variety becomes marginal. In the early, creative stages of an innovation process, the advantage of variety contributes to a net gain. In the later, implementational stages, the communicative drawback and possible conflicts, contributes to a net loss.

Let us now return once more to the ancient *theoria* paradigm, and take a closer look at the role of the *theoros*. Specifically, let us look at the relationship between "involvement" and "learning".

Involved observation

Our modern concept of theory denotes a type of knowledge that is independent of the person having the knowledge. Whether our theories are of a philosophical or scientific nature, they are typically spelled out and have an existence independent of the "theory-builder". Typically, modern theory is also presented in a positivist framework as a result of objective, non-involved observation. It is frequently assumed, that the greater the detachment of the observer from the object studied, the more reliable is the observation. This should remind us that the word *theoria* at a quite early stage was given two different meanings. The original meaning, however, was a "journey-and-delegate concept", closely linked to the word *theoros*. According to Rausch (1982) the word *theoros* never had more than one meaning, that of being a delegate. Thus, there never existed a passively, observing "*theoros*-theoretician".

According to tradition, the highest ranking of antiquity's seven wise men, was Solon, living 2600 BC. After implementing significant social and political reforms, Solon supposedly set out on a long voyage, most likely to Egypt, Cyprus, and Lydia. About this journey it is said that it was *"for the sake of theoria"* or *"in search of theoria"* (Rausch, 1982: 43–44, referring to Herodot). Tradition tells us that the journey of Solon, therefore, illustrates a model of combined roles – that of researcher, discoverer, explorer, tradesman and seaman, sage and leader.

Later the words *theoria, theorein* and *theoreticos* came to have two different meanings. The original meaning of traveller/delegate was retained, but a new meaning of "observation" was added. The latter was clearly a derivative meaning, used metaphorically by the well educated elite. On the other hand, when these words were used about delegates to the festivals, it was a usage that everybody recognised (Koller, 1958).

We have already noted the distinction between *thysia* and *theoria*, between strictly local, low-diversity games on the one hand and non-local, high-diversity games on the other. A similar distinction can be made between the words *theoros* and *theates*. Rausch (1982: 15) points to an old source, Ammonius, who writes: "*Theoros* and *theates* differentiate from each other, as *theoros* is he who is sent to the gods, while *theates* is a spectator of the games and theater. Those who use the word *theorein* when they say, 'I want to watch the competition', make a mistake. It must be called *theasasthai*". This tells us that the role model of a detached "theoretical" observer is a later construct; one that has little to do with the original meaning of the word "theory". The original meaning of theory and theoretician was that of involved observation and involved observer.

Before we move on to consider practical implications of the old stories for modern management, let us examine one more non-management source. It is a source that is closer to our time, but that definitely relates to a traditional society.

Sagacity philosophy

The Belgian missionary to Africa, Placide Tempels, in 1945 published an important book, called *La Philosophie Bantoue* (in English *Bantu Philosophy*). The question answered in the book, was whether it could be said that Bantu people had a philosophy or not. They had no recognized professional philosophers and no collection of scholarly works describing their philosophy. Nevertheless, Tempels (1945) suggested that they had a philosophy, not written down, but embedded and embodied in the culture. Cultural traditions such as rituals, habits, artifacts, tools, beliefs, values, and behaviours – were all testimonies to a living philosophy, to a higher level guideline for life and society.

Tempels' (1945) understanding of philosophy came to be recognised as ethno-philosophy, a kind of philosophical expression found in all traditional societies – actually in all societies. The logic behind ethno-philosophy is that a "tacit" or "implicit" philosophy surfaces through cultural embodiment. As borne out by later critiques, ethno-philosophy will tend to be local, traditional, in a sense un-critical and to some extent apologetic. What is embodied in culture must in a certain sense be right and legitimate. In a way, it is a very romantic version of philosophy: no scrutinising critical discourses – no long scientific treatises and moral debates. In such a society, there is no source of change, other than through the power of example (internal or external to the local society).

American psychologist and philosopher, William James (1949, 1961), the father of modern pragmatist philosophy, suggested in several works that in a sense we are all philosophers. We all achieve some kind of *primary level* philosophical insight. Through our regular up-bringing we are socialised to accept certain beliefs and understandings, and through personal experience we can add and modify. But James also suggested that there is a *secondary level* of philosophical engagement, achieved when a person is capable of questioning his or her first level philosophy. Due to personal experiences, including education and personal journeys, an individual can mature and adopt new horizons of understanding and belief. We may talk about a journey that involves a major *philosophical leap* of understanding. In psychological terms we may talk about *meta-cognitive experiences* bringing about new perceptions and reasonings. Clearly, such secondary level understanding takes us beyond the scope of ethno-philosophy.

A quite exotic parallel to the Jamesian concept of *secondary-level* philosophy, that also takes us beyond the ethno-philosophical framework without invoking voluminous (European style) philosophical treatises, is the concept of *sagacity-philosophy* suggested by the Kenyan philosopher Henry Odera Uruka (1990, 1991). All the traditional societies had people in the role of sages – people who were intimately familiar with the technicalities and meaning systems of their own culture.

The *cultural sage* is for Henry Odera Uruka a person who is loyal to tradition and to inherited belief systems. It is a person who often can have a great deal of personal power. But it is a conservative power, aimed at the continuation of tradition and power structures, while keeping the community together and pleasing the spiritual world. *Philosophical sages*, on the other hand, are people who make a journey to surrounding societies, who learn about different ways and means, beliefs and values, and who, therefore, are capable of bringing renewal to the home village. The moment of truth – and sometimes of despair – is when the philosophical sage returns home to reveal his new insight. Will there be rejection and stagnation, or acceptance and renewal in the home village?

We may notice the remarkable similarity between the old stories of *theoroi* and *theoria* on the one hand and Odera Uruka's *sagacity philosophy* on the other. Whereas the ancient Greek tradition focuses on the qualities of the festival, Odera Uruka's sagacity philosophy is more concerned with the potential for improvement in the home village.

Theoros qualities and *theoria* qualities

What we have presented here is a rich metaphorical framework for understanding a very basic learning and development model – for small communities and the global economy, for business firms and civil societies alike. But how can the old stories help us to a better conception of leadership and learning – to understand leadership for innovation, involvement and change? And what does modern research tell us that may help us judge the usefulness of the model? The ancient model is extremely simple – is it also valid in our complex modern world?

First, the stories may help us think in concrete terms about the "*theoros* qualities" of a leader. We may perceive three different sets of *personal qualities*, linked to three phases of the journey:

(1) *Making the journey*: Having the personal qualities of being curious, making the search of discovery, being eager to learn, daring and courageous, creative and open-minded.
(2) *Joining the "theoria community of learning"*: Being ready for dialogue and prepared to revise one's opinions in a context of diversity and variety of experience.

(3) *Returning to the home village, spiritually enriched*: Having the endurance and staying power to energize and change the home village, with optimism and ideas for improvement, prepared to meet resistance and ignorance.

Second, the stories help us think in terms of contextual diversity and cultural "*theoria* qualities" for learning. Again, we may perceive three sets of *cultural qualities* forming the contextual framework for optimal learning:

(1) *Variety of experience*: The joining together of people of different backgrounds, climates, ethnic groups, professions, disciplines, and personal experience.
(2) *Communion of interest and identity*: The cultural sharing of objectives and overriding visions – including being "on speaking terms" with the "others" in the context.
(3) *Intimacy of communication*: The commonality of language, reference systems, and ways of understanding in a cultural context.

Of course, we may assume that the two types of qualities (personal and cultural qualities) are mutually reinforcing. On the one hand, people accustomed to high-quality "*theoria*" contexts, are likely to be more apt to develop their own "*theoros* qualities", making journeys, joining communities of learning and bringing back spiritual and cognitive enrichment to the home village. On the other hand, communities of learning and practice that are able to attract people who excel at making journeys, who are engaged in dialogues and who bring spiritual enrichment, are more likely to continue the development of "*theoria* qualities". This can be seen in our global history (which is beyond the scope of this paper to examine), but also in our academic and business research communities.

The two types of qualities are also inter-linked: The journey of the *theoros* – seeking variety, communicating in a context of high diversity, and returning to an uncertain welcome in the home village – presupposes personal qualities that are directly linked to the contextual "*theoria* qualities": variety of experience, communion of interest and intimacy of communication. Thus, in what follows we may focus on three theme areas of modern research: (1) the role of variety and diversity in innovation; (2) the role of shared interests and communication in creative teams; and (3) the challenge of acceptance, implementation and change when returning to the "home village". Let us first take a look at what modern research can tell us about usefulness of our simple model of variety and innovation in our complex modern world. And let us start with the concept of an "innovation system", focusing on the role of variety expansion.

Theme 1: The role of variety and diversity in innovation

The "theoria qualities" of modern innovation systems

The concept "innovation system" was introduced by Lundvall (1985). In general terms, the concept may be interpreted as referring to a semi-autonomous ("*theoria*") arena for interplay between agents ("*theoroi*"), involved in some kind of knowledge production. Innovation systems are open systems and can be of many types, depending upon what kinds of agents and forms of interplay that are involved. They may operate within individual organisations, or within local, regional, national or international business community networks. The centripetal force in the system may be a shared technological interest or a shared problem or challenge having to do with marketing, management or any kind of resource or idea. Of particular relevance to the modern, corporate world, Carlsson (1997: 776) has analysed technological innovation systems defined as ". . . a network of agents interacting in a particular area of technology to generate, diffuse and utilize (knowledge about) technology".

As far as technological systems are concerned, their essential function is ". . . to capture, diffuse, and magnify spillovers of technical and organizational knowledge" (Carlsson, 1997: 776). Empirical research suggests that four features in particular determine the performance of such technological systems: (1) the nature of knowledge and spillover mechanisms; (2) the receiver competence (absorptive capacity of new knowledge) on the part of various agents; (3) the connectivity (ties) between agents of the system, and (4) the vigour of variety creation and selection mechanisms.

Comparing such a modern "technological system" to our previous stories about corresponding "cultural systems" in ancient Greece, we may notice that the first "features" in Carlsson's listing, are essentially the same categories as in the ancient model. The fourth feature, however, presupposes that the agents ("*theoroi*") are active entrepreneurs in variety creation. In the archaic model, variety was a matter of endowment: the Ancient Greek society was characterised by variety, due mainly to topographical-geographical contingencies. Within a small geographical area, people had to learn to cope with a high variety of life-sustaining and life-threatening possibilities. Thereby they developed variety of experiences. When they came together at the "cultural innovation system" of the festival, they had much to share and much to learn. In the modern "technological innovation system", the same learning potential is actively enhanced by vigorously "creating" or "adding" variety through hiring and networking practices. We may presume that the more competitive and the more dynamic the business environment, the greater the need for *active and vigorous variety creation* (Carlsson, 1997).

Thus, we may distinguish between the passive reliance upon tradition and traditional endowments of variety, on the one hand, and the active enhancement of variety, or variety creation, on the other. Traditional societies may be blessed with more or less variety, but we have no reporting that they actively seek to expand the level of diversity through active variety creation. Thus, learning is a happy by-product of existing variety (unless we may presume that some great, ancient strategist pro-actively designed a system with festivals and *theoria*-assemblies for the purpose of speeding up learning in the society).

However, such a category of "incidental learning" is definitely also a part of our modern managerial language. In the modern "technological innovation system" we talk about *knowledge spillovers*, facilitated by the *connectivity* of modern business networks. We may talk about teams and networks as "platforms" for knowledge spillovers (learning and new knowledge creation) through personal interaction. Actually, modern entrepreneurship is to a great extent seen as the active seeking and sometimes the active formation of such platforms.

When we talk about usefulness of "spillovers", we indicate a belief in the value of accidental and incidental learning opportunities. It is like the dog sitting under the table – hoping for food to spill over. Positioning oneself under a table where people are eating, increases the likelihood that food will be available, but it is still a rather indirect way – as compared to a more active and conscious approach to seeking food. In the modern innovation system vocabulary we seek to improve on the situation, and talk about building *receiver competence*. Building receiver competence is both about increasing the learning capacity of the agents in the innovation system – their capacity for absorbing useful information. But it is also about improving the receiver competence of the people in the base organisation. This includes the process of facilitating greater openness to new ideas and greater acceptance of "best practice" in a modern organisation culture. This corresponds to an imagined process of motivating greater responsiveness to spiritual enrichment in the home village of the ancient world. (We will return to the issue of receiver competence towards the end of this chapter, when commenting on the recent work of Debra Meyerson.)

Let us also notice that while we may perceive of innovation systems as open and including several organisations and innovative environments, they are also marked by ". . . some degree of autonomy from their environment with regard to their development, way of functioning, and specialization" (Lundvall, 2001: 44). We noticed the distinction between *theoria* and *thysia* in the archaic world, the idea being that the learning or knowledge derivative of the word *theoria*, is associated with an institutional arrangement that is separate from the home village context. It is a context of deputies, of people making journeys, meeting other people on similar journeys, exchanging information across borders. Of course, we may think of high-quality "*theoria* organisations", continuously sustaining learning and variety expansion, where the organisation as such is an autonomous, learning unit. But even in this case, we need to think of journeys outside the boundaries of the organisation. In order to maintain the viability of the "internal" innovation system, there needs to be a continuous stream of "*theoroi*" doing what the old, wise man, Solon, did – engaging in journeys *"for the sake of theoria"* or *"in search of theoria"* – or what Henry Odura Ureka's philosophical sages do – combining the roles of researcher, discoverer, explorer, tradesman and seaman, sage and leader.

Does it matter?

We have seen that modern concepts of innovation and innovation systems put a premium on variety of experience. But do we have any hard evidence to support our proposition? Is the diversity thesis supported? Does knowledge seeking outside ones local village in fact support innovation?

Most economists have argued that the concentration of economic activity in geographical space stimulates technological advance, and that this stimulus is due mainly to spillovers of new knowledge across neighbouring firms. Spillovers of tacit knowledge make the concentration particularly relevant. However, there has been little consensus as to exactly how these spillovers occur. In the economic literature a broad distinction is made between the *specialisation* and *diversity* of economic activity. While it is generally accepted that economic activity seem to benefit from geographical, or spatial, concentration, it is not clear whether this is due to specialisation or diversity. One argument, supporting a specialisation thesis, implies that knowledge spillovers are limited to occur within the relevant industry (an argument frequently attributed to the so-called "Marshall-Arrow-Romer externality", Glaeser *et al.*, 1992). Another argument, supporting a diversity thesis, implies that important knowledge spillovers occur across boundaries of industries, which means that important sources of knowledge are external to the industry in which a firm operates. Jacobs (1969) provided support for this argument, showing that the exchange of complementary knowledge between diverse firms gave greater returns than specialised knowledge between similar firms.

An important empirical testing of the question was done by Feldman and Audretsch (1999). They set out to answer the question: does the specific type or composition of economic activity undertaken within any particular geographic region matter? Or more specifically, do firms become more or less innovative if they operate in a business environment characterised by a high level of specialisation (all firms producing the same) versus an environment characterised by a high level of diversity (firms representing difference branches of business, different technologies)?

Feldman and Audretsch (1999: 421) studied the distribution of 3969 new manufacturing product innovations in US cities, and found considerable support for the diversity thesis, but little support for the specialisation thesis. More specifically, they say that ". . . innovative activity tends to be lower in industries located in cities specialized in economic activity in that industry". At the same time, "a strong presence of complementary industries sharing a common science base is particularly conducive to innovative activity". They emphasise further that "even after we control for city scale and technological opportunity, specialisation appears to have a negative effect on innovation, while science-based diversity has a positive impact on innovative output" (Feldman and Audretsch, 1999: 422).

A reasonable explanation for this result is that specialisation may more easily lead to in-house blindness and low levels of creativity, while diversity will provide new perspectives, insights, and ideas. This also seems to hold at the level of individual firms. Feldman and Audretsch also tested the effects of specialization and diversity inside individual firms. They found that "diversity in innovation activities (R&D) within a common science base (a crucial qualification) tends to promote innovative output more than does the specialisation of innovation within just one single industry" (Feldman and Audretsch, 1999: 425). The same result was seen across a broad range of industrial sectors (instruments, telecommunications, pharmaceuticals, electrical equipment, and transportation).

What emerges from these findings is that the diversity of economic activity is more conducive to innovation than is specialisation. However, the diversity in question should be relevant. Feldman and Audretsch (1999) describe this relevance or "commonality" in terms of sharing "a common science base". Diverse firms and agents must have some common basis for interaction, and in up-front technological innovation, a common science facilitates the exchange of existing ideas and generation of new ones.

Theme 2: The role of shared interests and communication in creative teams

Cross-functional teams

As we have seen, variety of experience is the cornerstone of modern innovation systems. The joining together of people of different backgrounds and experiences enhances innovation. The macro-economic observations permits us to go a step further and study the micro-level intricacies of how to make diversity work for an organisation.

The roles of a communion of interest and identity, and of intimacy of communication, have received broad research interest, particularly in studies of creative teams. Among such teams, the role of diversity in cross-functional teams has caught particular attention. Cross-functional groups or teams consist of members from different functional areas, such as engineering and technical research (like chemistry, electronics, and metallurgy), manufacturing, and marketing, accounting, etc. The cross-functional project group is particularly interesting, because it is a high-diversity group, increasingly used in order by firms to increase creativity and innovative activity, and thereby cope better with competition. Often employees from upstream and downstream functional areas are brought together, so that they can communicate and bring coordinated knowledge to bear on a project. Indeed, empirical research has shown that a cross-functional project group may be particularly useful when a project is supposed to bring out new and creative product innovations (Olson *et al.*, 1995).

However, the effects of diversity show a somewhat mixed picture. A striking finding from studies of cross-functional groups is that, although diverse groups can have very positive outcomes in terms of innovative performance, they do not always perform well, particularly during the implementation stages. Increasingly, scholars have become concerned about the lack consistency among diversity studies, and there has been an increasing awareness that it is not enough to talk about diversity and innovation. We need to be more concerned about so-called intervening variables – in particular the ability to communicate and the actual patterns of communication.

We recall that the beauty of the ancient Greek story was the commonality of religion and basic cultural values combined with a shared language, facilitating a shared interest and intimate communication. It should not be surprising then, that communication turns out to be a salient factor. Ancona and Caldwell (1992) made one of the first studies focusing explicitly on the intervening role of communications. They investigated 45 new product development groups from high-technology companies. A rather surprising finding was that functional diversity correlated negatively with the level of technical innovation. The reason was that diversity – the fact that people in the teams were so different – made communication and thereby teamwork more difficult. On the other hand, it was also found that functional diversity had a very positive effect upon external communication. Diverse groups had a greater diversity of external networks, that could be drawn upon to sustain innovation. Similarly, Keller (2001) studied 93 research and product development groups from four companies. Again it was found that the main positive effect of functional diversity came through external communication. This also showed up a year later. The main positive effect of diversity was that members with diverse areas of expertise had more varied external network contacts that gave access to important information.

The negative effect of diversity upon team communication and "team spirit" may sometimes take the effect of diversity-provoked conflict. It is well known that conflict may hamper team productivity. In a study of work group diversity, conflict and performance, Pelled *et al.* (1999) distinguished between two kinds of in-group conflicts: task conflict and emotional conflict. Task conflict ". . . is a condition in which group members disagree about task issues, including goals, key decision areas, procedures, and the appropriate choice for action" (Pelled *et al.*, 1999: 2). Emotional conflict ". . . is a condition in which group members have interpersonal clashes characterized by anger, frustration, and other negative feelings" (Pelled, 1999: 2). Studying 45 teams from the electronics divisions of three major corporations, the authors found that task conflict was often a direct result of functional background differences. Accountants and engineers often see things differently, and this leads to conflict at a very matter-of-factly level. However, such conflicts may also serve positively to bring out differences of perspectives and the questioning of "established wisdom". In fact, cross-functional teams may be used for the purpose of creating differences of opinion. Task conflict may foster an exchange of information that facilitates problem solving, decision making, and the generation of ideas.

While functional background diversity drives task conflict, multiple types of diversity (like race and tenure, but also gender, age, religious and ethnic background, marital status, and personality factors) seem to drive emotional conflict. Emotional conflict is a complicated issue, and potentially very destructive. While conflicts may arise whenever people work together, we are here concerned with the potential negative effect of diversity. (Pelled *et al.*, 1999: 20–21) looked in particular at the role of race and tenure, and found that "... because race and tenure attributes are relatively impermeable, people find it difficult to identify with (and easy to stereotype) those of a different race and tenure. Race and tenure differences, therefore, tend to encourage heated interactions in work groups. Given this tendency, managers may want to pay particular attention to group process in multi-race and multi-tenure settings".

However, not all differences have the same effect. Pelled *et al.* (1999: 21) found that while dissimilarities in race and tenure led to increased emotional conflict, differences in age seemed to have an opposite effect: "Any tendency for age differences to trigger emotional conflict appears to be overshadowed by the tendency for age similarity to trigger social comparison and, ultimately, (rivalries and) emotional conflict. Considered together, the findings suggest that "... diverse groups face countervailing forces, such that some forms of diversity increase conflict and other forms do the reverse" (Pelled *et al.*, 1999: 21). Hence, the authors say, managers must be prepared to meet challenges presented by heterogeneity as well as homogeneity in their work group. Further, as Amason (1996) emphasised, the possibility for diversity to create either cognitive task conflict or affective (emotional) conflict or both, makes it important for practical purposes to handle the conflict-creating processes.

Generalised diversity studies

This brings us on from cross-functional to more generalised diversity studies, and the need to look at specific diversities in order to detect positive and negative potential. In a study of 545 employees from one of the top three firms in the household goods industry in the US, Jehn *et al.* (1999) explored three types of diversity: informational diversity, social category diversity, and value diversity.

(1) *Informational diversity* refers to differences in knowledge bases and perspectives that members bring to the group. Differences in educational background, training, and work experience increase the likelihood that diverse perspectives and opinion exist in a work group. Lack of informational diversity undermines the potential for learning, insight, and problem-solving effectiveness. Since naturally formed groups are likely to lack diversity, organisations sometimes proactively create cross-functional groups or teams to enhance the informational diversity available in the group. However, such groups often prove ineffective at capitalising on the potential benefits of their informational diversity. One major reason for this is that disagreements may not only be about task content and the problem at hand – reflecting task conflict – but may also be about how to do the

task or how to delegate resources and duties – reflecting process conflict. Assuming that emotional conflict is avoided, the study by Jehn *et al.* (1999: 758) clearly shows that informational diversity leads to higher group or team effectiveness, particularly when tasks are non-routine.

(2) *Social category diversity* is perhaps what most people are referring to when talking about diversity, including race, gender, and ethnicity. In the study by Pelled *et al.* (1999), we noticed that age diversity might have a moderating influence while race and tenure tended to reinforce stereotyping and conflict. Jehn *et al.* (1999) found value similarity to be a moderating influence. The conflict potential due to variety of social category membership was reduced if people had shared value across categories.

(3) *Value diversity* ". . . occurs when members of a workgroup differ in terms of what they think the group's real task, goal, target, or mission should be" (Jehn *et al.*, 1999: 745). Such differences can lead to task conflict (disagreements about task content), as well as process conflicts (disagreements about delegation and resource allocation). One, therefore, would expect that similarity in group members' goals and values will enhance interpersonal relations and decrease relationship conflict among group members.

Looking at all three forms of diversity, the most consistent finding from the study by Jehn *et al.* (1999), was the importance of low value diversity among group members. Low value diversity (high value similarity) was found to have a positive influence upon most measures of work performance and worker morale. At the same time, the findings also revealed that a high diversity of values was responsible for the biggest problems in communication, performance and morale. "It may actually be that social category diversity results in higher morale in interdependent tasks. Being able to work together successfully, even when the group is diverse with respect to age and gender composition, may result in greater morale because the group has overcome a serious challenge to its effectiveness" (Jehn *et al.*, 1999: 758).

It is also worth noting that the strong importance of value diversity receives support from earlier research: Several early studies in the USA showed that White people preferred working with Black people with attitudes similar to their own over White people with opposing attitudes. "But this effect of value similarity on racial attitudes apparently has been ignored in recent years, as researchers have used similarity in attributes such as race or gender as surrogates for value similarity . . . Unlike demographic characteristics, the characteristics of value and informational diversity are not easily discernible . . ." (Jehn *et al.*, 1999: 758–9). The researchers conclude that in order for a team to be effective in innovation, members should have a high level of information diversity and a low level of value diversity. For a team to be merely efficient, or sustain a high level of morale, or a high level of perceived effectiveness, it should have low value diversity (or high value similarity).

Intimacy of communication

Our archaic model suggested that optimal conditions for learning and innovation prevailed under conditions of high variety of experience, high level of shared interests, and a high level of (intimate) communication. At the ancient Greek festival, all three factors scored positively. The crowd at a Greek festival represented a high variety of practical life experience. And we have already quoted from Grote's *A History of Greece*, describing the participants as "countrymen, whose language he understood, and whose idiosyncrasies he could appreciate" (Grote, 1924: 15–16).

The problem in the modern context, as we have seen above, is that high variety of experience ("functional diversity" or "informational diversity" in the studies reviewed) often is accompanied with a low level of shared interests (high level of value diversity) and lack of intimate communication. There is little disagreement that social interaction among people representing diverse perspectives and viewpoints can lead to new insights, new ideas, and improved decision quality. However, high variety of experience may also tend to make teamwork more difficult. As a general rule, we propose that for a given level of variety of experience, more (up to a certain point) can be gained in terms of innovation, learning and effectiveness, the greater the commonality of interest and of intimacy of communication. Conversely, for a given level of commonality of interest and intimacy of communication, more can be gained the greater the variety of experience.

So far, we have reviewed some of the research bearing upon variety of experience and commonality of interest (value identity). The question is whether there is a communicative solution to the challenge posed by value diversity and relational conflicts?

An overriding perspective on the issue of conflicts is suggested by Hirshman (1970) using the concepts of "exit, voice and loyalty". For instance, Jehn (1995: 276) found that ". . . while relationship troubles cause great dissatisfaction, the conflicts may not influence work as much as expected, because the members involved in the conflicts choose to avoid working with those with whom they experience (emotional) conflict." In other words, people who don't like each other, tend to avoid each other and continue work as usual. This represents an exit or avoidance strategy, which may minimise damage, but definitely also misses out on the benefits of diversity. There is also considerable evidence concerning the detrimental effects of unmanaged conflicts.

A more optimistic approach is to seek compromise or consensus through discourse and dialogue – using voice (Isaacs, 1999). Traditionally, the management literature has made frequent reference to the usefulness of applying *conflict-creating debates* in dialectically styled decision processes. Schwenk and Valacich (1994) found that evaluating and critiquing – engaging conflicts about the task – yielded better decisions in workgroups than when members avoided conflicts or smoothed over their disagreements. Although such debates, like the "devil's advocate" method, have proved to sometimes provide good results, cognitive disagreements can easily slide into rivalries and emotional conflict during debate-driven decision processes. Applying instead a *dialogue-driven* process, the actors or group members involved may be able to make use of the experiences of individual actors, as well as socially constructed knowledge, i.e., knowledge created through a respectful dialogue between the actors.

Mischel and Northcraft (1997) have noted that the success of a workgroup depends not only on its ability to do the task but also on the group's ability to manage its own interactions effectively, including communicating, co-operating, and co-ordinating its collective efforts. In order to achieve this, some similarity in perspective and values among group members is necessary. It seems that without a minimum "common ground" or value identity the technical ability to communicate is never sufficient. This ability to communicate on common ground is captured in the notion of "intimacy of communication", and it seems that a minimum of common ground needed for communication to take place, may be a shared interest in variety. Nemeth and Wachtler (1983) made an experiment involving a problem-solving task. The real subjects of the experiment were exposed to a minority of confederates who consistently proposed alternative solutions to those of the majority. While the majority did not adopt the specific strategies of the minority, in subsequent tests they proved to be significantly more creative than a control group not exposed to a minority. This finding suggests the value of an organisational climate or culture in which members feel able to voice ideas which depart from dominant norms. Apparently, the habit of being exposed to minority views over time made the majority think more critically and creatively about the established ways of doing things. Also, the experiment reveals that even when diversity of information is presented in a rather annoying manner, it may still lead to better decisions or innovations.

While the market for process consultants and conflict resolution seem to be constantly on the rise, our paradigm suggests two main options for creating intimacy of communication. Values may be cultivated, mainly through leadership embodiment. Therefore, organisations and communities of learning should proactively promote values of trust, openness, equity, and the like – necessary for moving the communication from discussion to dialogue, from debate to the seeking of mutual understanding. Secondly, diversity of experience and opinion should be defined specifically as a value, and consistently promoted in the organisation. Organisation members should be taught the appreciation of variety of experience, and they should be trained to revise their presuppositions, prejudices and stereotyping.

This leads us to the final challenge of the journeying *theoros*: arriving in the home village with spiritual enrichment and innovative ideas for change.

Theme 3: The challenge of acceptance, implementation and change when returning to the "home village"

Change and Implementation at the local level

If diversity is going to be conducive to innovation (as suggested by Feldman and Audretsch, 1999), it is not enough to receive new ideas or participate in creating better alternatives. Whatever is new must be implemented; it must be linked to the local conditions before any kind of impact can be made.

This is the theme of an impressive literature on change management, covering strategic, administrative and operational levels in the organisation and a great number of disciplines and theoretical frameworks (political, cultural, psychological-motivational, economic, and ethical). It is certainly beyond the scope of our article to discuss this literature in any detail. What we shall do is to continue our reliance upon the old stories of Greek *theoroi* and African *philosophical sages* and make some brief comments concerning two particular challenges: (1) the "psychological distance" between the ideas brought home and the existing pattern of thought and action in the village, and (2) alternative strategies to "selling ones' ideas" to the home audience. Probably the best description of this problem is the one by Plato in his allegory about the cave. The people who have been able to move outside of the cave, and return to tell the cave-dwellers about life outside, about sunshine and flowers and life, are rejected by the cave-dwellers who have only experienced a shadow world.

Psychological distance

The return of a *theoros* or philosophical sage to the home village is an obvious parallel to the return of a representative of a modern corporation from a benchmarking trip or from work in an exciting innovation system. In both cases, the person returning has acquired some new impressions and ideas, some of which may appear strikingly useful to him or her, but rather odd, threatening or irrelevant to people in the organisation. While new ideas may be welcomed when they do not deviate too much from what is well known already, radical new ideas – with strong implications for current activities – are frequent victims of the "not invented here" (NIH) syndrome. And if the new idea represents a new technology, which threatens half of the work force with redundancy, the reaction may be one of hostility and rejection.

Recent writing has shown that benchmarking, i.e., the comparison of internal, local practice with external, "best practice" should be viewed in a systemic context, because ". . . the context, defined in its economic, technical, geographic, historical and cultural dimensions, has a great influence on what is best practice" (Lundvall and Tomlinson, 2001: 124). This implies that the actual implementation of a radical new idea or alternative must be evaluated with respect to necessary local adaptations. On one hand, it may be possible to adapt the idea to local use – to fit the idea to the existing "system". On the other hand, it may be necessary to modify the existing system – to fit the system to the idea. While the former kind of change is generally preferred in most organisations (firms or villages) the latter may also be necessary, since there is frequently a limit to how much adaptation and reformulation the idea can take before losing its innovative potential.

Returning to the home ground with radical new ideas implies that the *theoros* – or returning manager – to some extent becomes "an outsider within", wanting to rock the boat, yet still stay in it. This may provide an uncomfortable dilemma. If our *theoros* manager speaks out too loudly (suggesting changes that will rock the boat), inter-personal resentment and affective conflict may build up. However, if he or she plays by the local rules and remains silent (wanting to stay safely within the boat), "intra-personal resentment", or personal frustration, may result.

In general terms, it may be suggested that the greater the psychological distance between idea and reality, the greater the potential for change conflict or non-change personal frustration (on the part of the returning manager). This may not always be so, however. Sometimes people are more willing to accept greater or more radical change – 30% improvement instead of 3%. People may be frustrated with the present situation, ready for change, hoping for change leadership. Or they may be "won over" to a new way of seeing things, which is about the way a new idea is being presented and "sold" to the organisation.

Selling one's ideas

Meyerson (2001a and b) has done 15 years of research, studying hundreds of effective managers and professionals, who share the experience of having tried to introduce quite radical changes. What she found was that such managers frequently worked behind the scenes, engaging in subtle forms of "grass-root leadership". She calls them "tempered radicals" because they tended to effect significant changes in moderate, incremental ways. She also observed that they seem to choose between four different, incremental strategies or techniques for creating lasting (cultural) change in their organisations. These four strategies or techniques are: (1) disruptive self-expression, (2) verbal jujitsu, (3) variable-term opportunism, and (4) strategic alliance-building.

(1) *"Disruptive self-expression"* is the most tempered strategy, carrying the assumption that subtle acts of private, individual style, like changes in dress, language, office décor, or behaviour can quietly disrupt others' expectations. Over time, disruptive self-expression may slowly change an unproductive atmosphere at work, as people increasingly notice and emulate it.
(2) *"Verbal jujitsu"* is a slightly more public form of expression. Here, an individual redirects the force of an insensitive statement or action to improve the situation. "Employees who practice verbal jujitsu react to undesirable, demeaning statements or actions by turning them into opportunities for change that others will notice" (Meyerson, 2001b: 96).

(3) *"Variable-term opportunism"* involves spotting, creating, and capitalising on opportunities for change. "In the short-term, that means being prepared to capitalise on serendipitous circumstances; in the long-term, it often means something more proactive" (Meyerson, 2001b: 97).
(4) *"Strategic alliance-building"* is a strategy where an individual joins with others to promote change with more force. By working with allies, tempered radicals . . . gain a sense of legitimacy, access to resources and contacts, technical and task assistance, emotional support, and advice. But they gain much more – the power to move issues to the forefront more quickly and directly than they might by working alone" (Meyerson, 2001b: 99).

By adjusting the four basic strategies to circumstance and organisational characteristics, tempered radicals work subtly but effectively to alter the status quo. "Selling" may take many forms, including sometimes "telling". The innovator becomes a *master of embodiment of change*, understanding radical change for what it is: "a phenomenon that can occur suddenly, but more often than not requires time, commitment, and the patience to endure" (Meyerson, 2001b: 100). It also certainly requires personal qualities and abilities as energiser and relationships-builder.

Concluding remarks

We have presented a metaphorical framework for a very simple and basic learning and development model. It is a framework that is relevant for the understanding of developmental processes of many kinds, in many kinds of organisations, ranging from small communities to the global economy, from business firms to civil societies alike. And we have sought to relate this framework to – and test it against – up-to-date empirical research.

We started out with an identification of three different sets of *"personal theoros qualities"*, linked to three phases of an imagined, modern-day "journey in search of *theoria*". The personal qualities relate to (1) making the journey (being curios, brave, open-minded, eager to learn), (2) joining the "*theoria* community of learning" (being accepting of diversity, ready for dialogue and prepared to revise one's opinion), and (3) returning – spiritually enriched – to the home village (having endurance and staying-power, being optimistic and able to energise and bring about change). This set of personal qualities was again linked to contextual diversity and cultural "*theoria* qualities" for learning, defined in terms of three sets of *"cultural theoria qualities"* forming the contextual framework for optimal learning. The three sets of cultural qualities are embedded in (1) variety of experience (resulting from diversity of people and social strata), (2) communion of interest and identity (resulting from culturally shared values and overriding visions – meaning to be "on speaking terms" with people who are otherwise different from yourself), and (3) intimacy of communication (resulting from commonality of language and reference systems).

We suggested that the two types of qualities are mutually reinforcing, in that people who are used to high-quality "*theoria*" contexts, are more likely to develop "*theoros* qualities", and therefore more able to undertake journeys, join communities of learning and practice, to bring back stimulating ideas to the home organisation. A logical extension is that communities of learning that attract people who are willing and able to make the journey, engage in dialogue and bring home stimulating ideas, are more likely to develop and expand their "*theoria* qualities", something which seems to hold for all kinds of societies, local and global.

Our main concern in this chapter has been to demonstrate, however, the relevance of this learning model to the modern management of diversity, innovation and change. And perhaps the most striking observation from modern research relevant to the model, is the saliency of a shared value structure. The ancient Greek festival hosted a "multiplicity of fellows in blood and language" as well as in variety of experience. Modern organisations and innovation systems marked by high diversity may hopefully rely on a shared language for "intimacy of communication", but cannot assume that they are "fellows of blood" – or religion, ethnicity, or political conviction. The modern organisation cannot take identity of values and communion of interest for granted. It must be cultivated. And – if successfully cultivated – our research result demonstrate excellent opportunities for making good use of diversity.

References

Amason, A. C. (1996), "Distinguishing the effects of functional and dysfunctional conflict on strategic decision making: Resolving a paradox for top management teams", *Academy of Management Journal*, Vol. 39, No. 1, pp. 123–148.

Ancona, D. and Caldwell, D. (1992), "Demography and design: Predictors of new product team performance", *Organization Science*, Vol. 3, Issue 3, pp. 321–341.

Carlsson, B. (1997), "On and off the beaten path: The evolution of four technological systems in Sweden", *International Journal of Industrial Organization*, Vol. 15, Issue 6, pp. 775–799.

Feldman, M. P. and Audretsch, D. B. (1999), "Innovation in cities: Science-based diversity, specialization and localized competition", *European Economic Review*, Vol. 43, Issue 2, pp. 409–429.

Glaeser, E. L., Kallal, H. D., Scheinkman, J. A. and Schleifer, A. (1992), "Growth in cities", *Journal of Political Economy*, Vol. 100, Issue 6, pp. 1126–1152.

Grote, G. (1924), *A History of Greece*, Volume 3, London: J. M. Dent & Co/New York: E. P. Dutton & Co.

Hirschman, A. O. (1970), *Exit, Voice, and Loyalty*, Cambridge, MA: Harvard University Press.

Isaacs, D. (1999), *Dialogue and the Art of Thinking Together*, New York, NY: Doubleday, Random House, Inc.

Jacobs, J. (1969), *The Economy of Cities*, New York, NY: Random House.

James, W. (1949), *Pragmatism – A New Name for some Old Ways of Thinking. Together with four related Essays selected from the Meaning of Truth*, New York: Longmans, Green and Co.

James, W. (1961), *Selected Papers on Philosophy*, Edited by C. M. Bakewell, New York: E. P. Dutton & Co.

Jehn, K. A., Northcraft, G. B. and Neale, M.A. (1999), "Why differences make a difference: A field study of diversity, conflict, and performance in work groups", *Administrative Science Quarterly*, Vol. 44, Issue 4, pp. 741–763.

Jehn, K. A. (1995), "A multimethod examination of the benefits and detriments of intragroup conflict", *Administrative Science Quarterly*, Vol. 40, Issue 2, pp. 256–282.

Keller, R. T. (2001), "Cross-functional project groups in research and new product development: diversity, communications, job stress, and outcomes", *Academy of Management Journal*, Vol. 44, No. 3, pp. 547–555.

Koller, H. (1958), "Theoros und Theoria", *Glotta*, Vol. 36, pp. 273.

Lundvall, B.-Å. and Tomlinson, M. (2001), "Learning-by-Comparing: Reflections on the use and abuse of international benchmarking", in G. Sweeney (Ed.), *Innovation, Economic Progress and the Quality of Life*, Cheltenham, UK: Edward Elgar.

Lundvall, B.-Å. (2001), *Innovation, Growth and Social Cohesion: The Danish Model*, Cheltenham, UK: Edward Elgar.

Lundvall, B.-Å. (1985), *Product Innovation and User-Producer Interaction*, Aalborg, DK: Aalborg University Press.

Meyerson, D. E. (2001a), *Tempered Radicals: How People Use Difference to Inspire Change at Work*, Boston, MA: Harvard Business School Press.

Meyerson, D. E. (2001b), "Radical change – The quiet way", *Harvard Business Review*, October Issue, pp. 92–100.

Mischel, L. J. and Northcraft, G. B. (1997), "I think we can, I think we can . . . The role of self-efficacy beliefs in group and team effectiveness", in B. Markovsky and M. J. Lovaglia (Eds.), *Advances in Group Processes: A research annual*, Volume 14, Greenwich, Conn.: JAI Press, pp. 177–197.

Nemeth, C. J. and Wachtler, J. (1983), "Creative problem solving as a result of majority versus minority influence", *European Journal of Social Psychology*, Vol. 13, Issue 1, pp. 45–55.

Odera Uruka, H. (Ed.) (1990), *Sage Philosophy: Indigenous Thinkers and Modern Debate on African Philosophy*, Leiden: E. J. Brill.

Odera Uruka, H. (1991), 'Sagacity in African Philosophy', in T. Serequeberhan (Ed.), *African Philosophy: The Essential Readings*. New York: Paragon House.

Olson, E. M., Walker, O. C. and Ruekert, R. W. (1995), "Organizing for effective new product development: the moderating role of product innovativeness", *Journal of Marketing*, Vol. 59, No. 1, pp. 48–62.

Pelled, L. H., Eisenhardt, K. M. and Xin, K. R. (1999), "Exploring the black box: An analysis of work group diversity, conflict, and performance", *Administrative Science Quarterly*, Vol. 44, Issue 1, pp. 1–28.

Rausch, H. (1982), *Theoria: Von ihrer sakralen zur philosophischen Bedeutung*, Munich: Wilhelm Fink Verlag.

Schwenk, C. and Valacich, J. S. (1994), "Effects of devil's advocacy and dialectical inquiry on individuals versus groups", *Organizational Behavior and Human Decision Processes*, Vol. 59, Issue 2, pp. 210–222.

Smith, P. B. and Bond, M. H. (1998), *Social Psychology Across Cultures*, 2nd Edition, London: Prentice Hall Europe.

Tempels, P. (1945), *La Philosophie Bantoue*, Trans. to English *Bantu Philosophy* by C. King, Paris: Presence Africaine. Originally published 1945, published in English 1959.

15
Diversity: Not All Are Believers

by Marylou Shockley

Introduction

A celebration of difference, frequently expressed as tolerance and respect for "the other," is the mantra of those espousing the virtues of diversity. Although I too choose to carry the banner of diversity, another pervasive worldview exists whose champions advocate homogeneity, a common set of societal norms reinforced through political, religious, and commercial institutions. This worldview of homogeneous "sameness" is inherently different from heterogeneous "diverseness." As applied to business, who would argue with firms that are successful because, as Peters and Waterman (1982) suggest, they are riveted to a single-minded pursuit; i.e., they "stick to their knitting." Success, as defined by this given attribute, requires focus with an underlying process and implementation homogeneity that excludes many alternate strategic options. Who can argue with Japan's success as the third most powerful economy (as measured by Gross Domestic Product – GDP) in the world? (CIA, 2005) Japan does not encourage inward migration. It prides itself as a people who have a common racial heritage; yet the country has embraced commercial adaptation. Its enterprises have demonstrated time and again an uncanny ability to take what's best in the world and make it even better – it has produced some of the world's best cars, electronics, and animation.

These examples pose a conundrum. It appears that promoting diversity holds no elixir of explanatory powers capable of defining success or curing the ills of the world. Then why do we, champions of diversity, continue to wave its banners? In order to clarify my own thinking on diversity, I have "taken the plunge" into the pool of opposing realities – seeking to understand the position of the "non-believers" who don't hold the view that diversity has no meaningful value. I believe the reality of diversity that spawns creative thought and action must embrace, or at the very least, understand opposing views. After all, the spirit of diversity encourages stepping beyond the world of "like" believers to the uncomfortable realm of those others who see the world differently. To this end, I have chosen to explore fundamentalism, a set of religious and socio-political movements whose worldview is the antithesis of diversity. Fundamentalism, both religious and secular, closes the debate on diversity by building a cocoon around its principles and beliefs to sustain their homogeneous purity as absolutes beyond debate. I want to explore three questions: (1) What are the attributes of fundamentalism? (2) What are the implications for business? and (3) Why diversity? – what is its value to business as well as to my personal belief structure?

Attributes of fundamentalism

Fundamentalism was first used as an "ism" to describe a movement during the early twentieth century in the US. Reacting to the encroachment of modern secularism, especially the Darwinian principles of evolution, a group of Protestant laymen published a set of twelve volumes called *The Fundamentals: A Testimony of Truth* in which several truths were declared, among most notable being the inerrancy of the Bible (Ammerman, 1991; Beeman, 2001). Although first associated with a particular American Protestant movement, fundamentalism has come to describe a wide array of religious and socio-political groups (Armstrong, 2001; Beeman, 2001; Hsu, 2004; Israel and Mezvinksy, 1999; Nanda, 2003). However, some critics, most notably Appleby and Marty (2002) caution against the "labeling of movements" as fundamentalists and choose to use the term to describe religious extremist movements or groups. Most certainly much of the recent literature has focused on rise of religious based fundamentalism, especially since the 9/11 terrorist incident in New York that destroyed the World Trade Center and influence of the Moral Majority[1] in Republican Party politics in the last two US presidential elections (Armstrong, 2001; Hsu, 2004; Nanda, 2003; Sullivan, 2005; J. Wallis, 2005). Even with the caveats of Appleby and Marty (2002), I have chosen in this essay to include both religious and secular based variations of fundamentalism. I believe whether secular or religious based, both types of fundamentalist movements share common attributes. Furthermore, at least in the US, one of the original tenants of the founding fathers was the notion of the "separation of church and state" in which no personal belief was to be prescribed by the state is under assault by some Protestant Fundamental groups (Nielsen, 1993; J. Wallis, 2005). This blurring of the religious and the socio-political spheres fuels the concern, especially as Jim Wallis (2005) observes, of a national religion in which the identity of the nation is confused with religion to support a theology of empire.

Although my reading of the contemporary literature is by no means exhaustive, I have identified seven areas of attributes that capture the character of modern fundamentalism.

(1) Historic context: the golden past, the reviled present and the Utopian future

When chatting with a colleague recently about the relevance of history to modern life, he gave me an astute insight, suggesting that history helps us to understand how the past has shaped life as it has become to be. It is in this spirit that I and others see fundamentalism as extensions of past orthodoxies – it is not new *per se*; it is "awakened" or "revived"(Ammerman, 1991; Armstrong, 2001). I find the historical roots of these various religious fundamentalist movements provide a measure of uneasy comfort, knowing that past generations have had to endure, accommodate, mitigate, and in some cases give way to these movements as the "new order." What religious historians like Armstrong (2001) have shown is that history provides us lessons on what triggered religious groups to put on the mantle of fundamentalism and more importantly, how previous societies have met the challenges of such movements.

Fundamentalism also shares two complementary traits with respect to time. Fundamentalist movements revere the past and see a utopian vision of the future, while reacting passionately to what are perceived as ills of the present (Beeman, 2001). The Nazis glorified the Germanic mythic heroes of the "golden age" as support for its Aryan principles to create the Third Reich. Judeo-Christian fundamentalists look to God's covenant with Israel as the "promise land" whose proportions and plan of occupation were revealed to the great patriarch Moses; it is only when this "restoration" is fulfilled that the "Messianic Age" will commence. Islam extremists hearken back to the golden ages (circa 7th through 14th centuries) where the enlightened rule of Mohamed's believers created a "middle kingdom" between the Christian West, and the Indian and Chinese East; an Islamic kingdom, expressed in today's vernacular as a "Brotherhood," is a reaction to the infringement of Western secularization. Communists glorified the guild and agrarian workers of the pre-industrial era, while extolling utopian virtues like the dictatorship of the proletariat. The point is made. It shows that any "ism" is likely to adopt a fundamentalist overtone when glorifying the past, reviling the present and proposing a utopian future.

(2) Principles: strict adherence to defined precepts

Any institution or movement is in danger of succumbing to fundamental extremism if it holds its principles as absolutes which cannot be questioned. Religions, whose very existences are based upon faith with acceptance of sacred doctrinal principles, are especially vulnerable to fundamentalism. I must make it clear that I am not making a polemic assault on religion. In fact, I strongly believe that religion meets a very human need to know the unknowable, to arbitrate between the world of what's seen and what's not, and to bring meaning to existence. It is when these principles are adhered to *rigidly* with little or no understanding by its believers in why they believe as they do that fundamentalism starts to creep into religion and socio-political social movements. As observed by Kramer and Alstad (1993), religions are socially relevant because in most of today's societies these principles form the basis of moral frameworks that govern behavior.

What then distinguishes, for example, Christian evangelicals from fundamentalists? Or is there a difference? Both most certainly view the Bible as truth inspired by God. However, not all evangelical groups are fundamentalists. The "fundamentals" represents an *interpretation* of biblical traditions and truths by men like Falwell and Robertson[2] – whose views are not necessarily ascribed to by all evangelicals or Christians for that matter (J. Wallis, 2005). The same can be said of fundamentalism in Jewish tradition. The Gush Enumin, a political-religious fundamentalist movement in Israel, whose patron saint according to Shahak and Mezvinsky (1999) is 13th century rabbi Nachmanides and whose recent interpreters of Jewish law are Rabbi Abraham Kook and his son Rabbi Zvi Yehuda Kook; both advocate a religious form of Zionism which proposes sovereignty over the "Promise Land" as a divine mission (Heilman, 1994; Shahak and Mezvinsky, 1999). It's on this basis that Appleby and Marty (2002) refute the myth that fundamentalists are literalists, arguing that indeed the principles or rules espoused by these movements are interpreted and adapted for the movement's needs at any given time.

(3) The other: "non-believers" are objectified

Because fundamentalists have such a fervent sense of being right, all others who hold differing views are considered "misguided" or "evil." At best, those who are not followers of a fundamentalist movement are ignored. More often than not, outsiders are objectified to the point that "others" are legitimate targets for ridicule and even extermination. We are familiar with the examples of genocide when rabid fundamentalism movements – whether religious or secular – have killed people for being "different" and, therefore, a menace. Since the 9/11 terrorist incident in the United States, the bombings in Bali, Spain and the UK, Muslim extremism has crashed onto the world stage. Fundamentalist beliefs among Muslim extremists "objectify" the other, viewing the deaths of both martyrs and non-combatants as acceptable, as they wage war against the US, "the Great Satan"[3] and its allies. Some extremist Christians, whose fundamentalist beliefs look upon abortion as "legalized killing" feel perfectly justified in blowing up Plan Parenthood offices.

I admit these are extreme examples. Other more socially significant examples exist as well. One prominent ongoing battlefront for Protestant fundamentalists has been its campaign against science. The "fight" against Darwinism was one of a major impetus of American Protestants to adopt a fundamentalist stance which culminated in the Scopes trial of 1925 (Ammerman, 1991; Beeman, 2001). In the US, Darwin's evolution theory is at odds with the Christian view of intelligent design. The crux of the argument is that Christian fundamentalism offers certainty of a God-created universe with respect to life and human origin, while science offers an infinite process (Kramer and Alstad, 1993). It is this certainty that prompts fundamentalists to "fight" science, using the classroom as the battleground; in eleven states, the "other theory" of evolution is now being critically analyzed – with a range of views on the origin of life, including "intelligent design" being presented (C. Wallis, 2005).

(4) Leadership: charismatic prophets and gurus

Anderson (1990: 197) argues that our major religions are cults that got lucky, suggesting that "Christ was a cult leader, the Buddha and Mohammed were wandering gurus in their times." In this respect, Anderson's view of cults is not dissimilar to that of Kramer and Alstad (1993: 32) who define cults as groups whose "leader's power is not constrained by scripture, tradition, or any other 'higher' authority." This type of leadership differs from that of many fundamentalist movements – especially religious ones – who generally are *protectors* rather than *creators* of truth (Appleby and Marty, 2002; Kramer and Alstad, 1993). Like the founders of religion, fundamentalist leaders are highly influential – and sometimes charismatic – to the extent that they can inspire people to become believers. Unlike heads of a religious tradition, the mantle of leadership is transferable, i.e., when a leader passes away or is no longer effective, other guardians of a movement's principles can assume the leadership role (Appleby and Marty, 2002). The relatively ease of transferred leadership gives a fundamentalist movement momentum and sustainability.

It seems to me that fundamentalist movements need spokes-people who can take the principles espoused by the group and apply them credibly as relevant truths that capture the hearts of its adherents. More specifically, fundamentalist leaders in order to be successful must vividly portray the golden past, astutely describe the ills of the present, and accurately demonstrate how the movement's principles will create the desired future. Leaders of fundamentalist movements must also define the boundaries carefully for the group as well as be the final arbiter on matters of maintaining the movement's standards of "purity." To fulfill these leadership roles, fundamentalist movement are likely to have a highly authoritarian structure in which the views of the leadership are rarely challenged (Appleby and Marty, 2002).

(5) Enforcement: maintaining purity among believers

Homogeneous practice of belief principles keeps the faithful stalwart and focused. Within the authoritative structure of a fundamentalist movement, individual members are taught to believe, not challenge or question. One of the more benign practices in keeping believers in line is reprimands by both leaders and peers. Harsher penalties include shunning or expulsion from the group. As Shahak and Mezvinsky (1999) have observed, the penalties and in fact wrath of the movement is far more severe for "backsliding" believers than it is for "outsiders." In some cases, membership entry into a movement is "one way;" that is, once in, emotional and physical consequences of leaving make the option of leaving untenable for believers.

(6) Growth and influence: active engagement with society

Not all fundamentalist movements are visible. Many choose to withdraw rather than engage with the world around them. It is not uncommon for these movements to vacillate between periods of withdrawal and those of activism. For such groups, it is generally a crisis, external threat or a prophetic unique window of time that drives a fundamentalist group to action (Heilman, 1994). Other fundamentalist groups feel that it is their duty to be out in the world, sharing their views and winning converts. Muslims in the UK, for example, are recruited by fundamental groups like Hizb-ut-Tahrir (Hizb for short) that offer a vision of caliphate in which Islamic principles prevail; it recruits by sponsoring social gatherings such as all Muslim football matches which appeal to 2nd and 3rd generation of young Muslims (Malik, 2005). Christian fundamentalists share the same goal as other Protestant religions of sharing the gospel all over the world. In Guatemala, for example, Protestant leaders in 1990 estimated that between 30 to 35% of the population was Protestant (Stoll, 1994). Although most Guatemalan claim to be *evangelicos*, Stoll (1994) argues that most of these converts are *fundamentalistas* because many share the same principles of faith and the same spiritual genealogy of the fundamentalists in North America who led the revolt against mainline US Protestant denominations in the early 20th century. Ammerman (1994) disagrees with this portrayal of South American Protestants; indeed they share many traditions of their Yankee counterparts; she, however, sees that these Christians have created their own expression of Christianity that fits their culture. Ammerman (1994) admits that as these evangelical groups become more active to redefine their national identities, they too may become fundamentalists.

As religious fundamentalist groups become active, the lines between religious and socio-political become blurred or nonexistent. In Israel and other countries in the Middle East, religious fundamentalists are politically active and have, in many cases, significantly shaped secular life in their respective countries through social and political activism. It is a misconception to think these fundamentalist movements abhor change; they do not (Appleby and Marty, 2002). In fact, what these groups want is to *transform* the secular world to conform to their world views. Some experts in the USA are concerned about how Protestant fundamentalists movements supported by Falwell and Robertson have hi-jacked the agenda of the Republican Party (Sullivan, 2005; J. Wallis, 2005). The aim of these fundamentalist movements is to curb the excesses of secularism by sponsoring a "Christian agenda" on issues such as abortion, homosexuality, and immorality.

(7) Recruits: who joins?

The believers who make up the rank and file of fundamentalist movements are typically not the poor and down trodden whose focus is on daily survival; they are the educated, but dissatisfied people who seek to remedy the wrongs or injustices they find in the world (Appleby and Marty, 2002). This may be the profile of those who join. It, however, does not address interpersonal dynamics of why people choose to join such movements. In today's post-modern world where the old norms of scientific, rational inquiry are no longer held as the dominant paradigm and where reality itself is viewed as social constructions, the levels of uncertainty and complexity has risen; humans seek shelter from this raging storm of relativism in a variety of beliefs – spiritual or philosophical – that can provide meaning in their lives. For some people, however, fear of the chaotic and the relative ignites a craving for certainty that the purveyors of fundamentalism are eager to provide. English (1996) describes a friend who had become a member of the anti-abortion group called Operation Rescue, an arm of the fundamentalist Christian Coalition. What struck her (English, 1996) was that her friend did not see herself as co-opted by a fundamentalist group with its authoritarian principles; her friend was for the first time passionate about a cause – one that: gave meaning to her life, filled a void of uncertainty and provided an outlet for her creative expression. What psychologists might see as the surrender of self to a higher authority, converts of such movements see as joining a group of like minded people (English, 1996; Kramer and Alstad, 1993). Indeed orthodox religion and secular organizations may instill some of the same zeal; the difference is fundamentalism thwarts any questioning by believers and demands a blind faith in a movement's leaders. The fundamentalist promise of certainty paints the world in black and white; there are no other colors.

Personal reflection: what are the implications for business?

As I reflected on the attributes of fundamentalism, I wondered if businesses themselves could be bitten by the bug of fundamentalism. Certainly Appleby and Marty (2002) would say "no" because secular organizations, by their definition of fundamentalism, are not religious; it is only the religious movements that can fuel the passion for its adherents to make the ultimate sacrifice of martyrdom. History has shown this view to be somewhat blurred. Take, for example, the Japanese *kamakazi* pilots of World War II. It was for both country and Emperor that these pilots made the ultimate sacrifice. I prefer the broader definition of both religious and secular fundamentalism, even if casting a wider definitional net may risk rendering the term meaningless. Adopting such a definition challenges me to look across the full spectrum of socio-political life for institutions or movements whose clarion call is to accept without question, whose leaders champion "one form of right," and most importantly, whose power base is growing. As far as I am concerned, "Business" is not beyond scrutiny.

I can convince myself that adequate checks are in place, through regulation, to prevent business from turning rabid. Anti-trust legislation in most counties is designed to curb the aggregation of power. Yet I remain suspicious. I can think of an "ism" that drives my concern, and that's commercial Globalism. Does this "ism" possess the fundamentalist attributes described above? Not totally. There are no charismatic leaders one can point to as being harbingers of commercial globalization; even the World Trade Organization (WTO), the target for many of the excesses of trade and business power is faceless. However, the principles are well defined. Business is driven by profit – the bottom line is sacred, and therefore, unchallenged. Costs should be reduced; and, if possible, attributed externally whether it is reducing employee benefits, polluting a river, or outsourcing product manufacturing to sweatshops in other countries with cheaper labor costs. Growth, either through acquisition or sales revenue, must be continuous. What CEO would ever stand up in front of his/her stockholders and declare that profits went down, costs went up, and growth was static without fear of loosing his/her job? All who work in business from the CEO to the office clerk buy into these principles of growth and profit . . . they are all adherents. Therefore, the utopian view that "Business" makes for a wealthier and happier world is not likely to be challenged by the business community itself. This utopian view of material wealth creates a collusion of governments (in national or international blocks) with transnational business firms to create powerful oppressive elites who seduce individuals with the prospect of personal wealth (Freire, 1972) and who perpetuate an unbroken cycle of one class with privilege and all others with duties (Engels, 1983).

Do I believe "Business" is evil? Hardly. To put such a label on business and the people who run these firms would make me a fundamentalist. However, I do reserve the right to question and challenge the consequences and motives of business. As both a past practitioner in and observer of business, I believe business firms are too blinded by their zeal for profit performance metrics to be able to see the consequences of their behavior. It takes external pressure driven by consumer advocates, customers, governments, labor unions and other stakeholder groups to "wake up" firms to consider the consequences of their actions. Unlike fundamentalist groups, most business firms embrace the notion of change and have internally established processes to sensitize themselves to their external environments. Companies like Shell have perfected techniques of scenario planning to build future external contingencies into their long-term strategies.

To some degree, businesses are a reflection of the societies and countries in which they do business. Although a powerful block wielding immense power, even the most influential business firms *influence* rather than usurp control of their socio-political environments. As of yet, no business entity or collection of entities has managed to run a country.[4] In some countries business firms have close "partnerships" with their national governments and have been instruments through which these governments implement economic policy. In Sweden, for example, the Social Democrats were able to forge a three-way alliance with their large transnational corporations and their unions that was much credited for bringing Sweden from the backwater of Europe to one continent's wealthiest countries (Korten, 1996).

Why diversity?

As discussed above, firms tend to mirror their socio-political environments. Economists have observed that self-interest drives the market systems in which businesses operate. (Brittan, 1996; Smith, 1993). This self-interest expressed within a firm as profit drives a variety of behaviors from unbridled greed to social altruism. A firm's reflective mirroring is often motivated by enlightened self-interest which converges with the needs of society. Firms, operating around the world, most certainly have complied with government policies that recognize diversity with respect to gender, age, and race as a societal benefit. Many businesses have gone beyond compliance to enthusiastically embrace the ideals of diversity in their workplaces. Enlightened self-interest has made these firms realize that having their workforces reflect their business environments is "good business." A case in point is the 2003 US Supreme Court decision in which the University of Michigan's admission policies were scrutinized for favoring ethnic minorities using a discretionary point system. Large businesses such as Microsoft and General Motors filed petitions with the Supreme Court supporting the University of Michigan's recruiting policies (Crockett, 2003; Schramm, 2003). Their reasons were pragmatic. These businesses as well as many of their counterparts understood the changing population dynamics in the US and knew that both their future employees and perspective customers would continue to come from diverse ethnic, social, and life style backgrounds (France and Symonds, 2003; Schramm, 2003).

Espousing diversity and successfully integrating this value into a firm's culture is not without its challenges. As more diverse groups of employees become established in firms, leadership will find it difficult to balance the varying perspectives as well as "equity" among groups. For example, a special training program for ethnic minorities may be perceived by one group of employees as desirable, while another group of employees may resent such programs as providing special privileges (Dalton, 2003). Research in the area of social identity has shown some cause for concern as employees begin to value their "social" affiliations more highly than their personal identities. This becomes problematic for a firm as the critical mass of groups holding salient values, i.e., fundamentalist religious values or single-issue political values, that are at variance with the firm's organizational values and norms (Dalton, 2003; Herriot and Scott-Jackson, 2002). A business firm, therefore, encounters two challenges: 1) how to balance competing demands of employee groups to maintain a sense of equity for all employees; and 2) how to maintain an overarching set of organizational norms, beliefs, and values as its employee base becomes more socially identified with potentially radicalized movements or causes. I have found that the "business standard" used in firms has been to sanitize the workplace of any religious or politically charged issues with a strong message to employees to keep their personal beliefs at home. This standard has worked because most employees have felt that issues of beliefs were personal;

however, observers such as Dalton (2003) and Herriot and Scott-Jackson (2002) are suggesting that social identities may be held by salient groups of employees who are passionate about their beliefs and who may no longer agree with the tacit arrangement of leaving these beliefs out of the workplace.

"Why Diversity?" is a question not only relevant to business. I have personally reflected on my own views. Through the exploration of fundamentalism, I have come to appreciate the value of diversity. For me, this exploration has reinforced several personal commitments that under gird diversity. These commitments are to:

- *Tolerance* – worldviews and belief structures that support them abound in many variations. These views shape and sometimes construct reality for all of us. Tolerance also implies an absorption capacity – an ability to recognize that standards that define conceptual and institutional boundaries are fluid and that learning can only come through the grafting of new ideas and the sometimes painful shedding of old ideas.
- *Respect for Others* – must be a practice, not an ideal. For me, this means not allowing stereotypes I have created or adopted to be so ingrained as habits that they are beyond my self-awareness. It means putting people and ideas in stereotypic boxes might be efficient, and therefore, comfortable. However, perpetuating this "auto pilot" mode will also isolate me – from both the wonderful and the tragic variety of people and ideas/beliefs that make up the world.
- *Healthy Skepticism* – is a corollary of tolerance and respect for the "Other." It is a challenge to think and study before accepting or trusting. It is a commitment to explore and look at the evidence from a variety of sources and perspectives.
- *Acceptance of the Relative* – as a reality in a pluralistic world. Although uncertainty is painful, the surrender to certainty brings comfort but also closure to the different. This is not a denial of faith or the spiritual, but a discipline to grapple with what I hold to be true and to accept that others may not agree with me.

These commitments are indeed personal. It is by no means a complete list. I challenge you who read this essay to reflect and create your own set of commitments.

Conclusion: a return to the conundrum

I opened this chapter with a conundrum, suggesting that homogeneity at both the business and country levels does lead to success. So why diversity, if homogeneity will do? I have come to the conclusion that homogeneity is but one road to success, and that the "difference" scale from "same to diverse" encompasses a combinatorial array of success strategies. In the case of business, it is what creates "rarity," the basis upon which competitive advantage is perpetuated by successful firms. I have also learned that fundamentalism is a belief structure that is a near perfect antithesis to what I believe diversity to be. To label it as "evil" would be for me hypocritical. I believe various religious and secular fundamentalists provide a benefit, within a forum of public debate, to challenge all who support the status quo or alternative beliefs to defend their views. I also am aware that many fundamentalists are willing to defend their beliefs like anyone else but who find coercively imposing their beliefs on others as despicable. However, when fundamentalist movements become politically militant and socially corrosive, rigorous challenge is necessary to arouse the awareness of a typically neutral public who is busy with the everyday concerns of life rather than of societal debate or politics. For me, I view public activism and debate as only one avenue to neutralize the toxicity of radicalized fundamentalism. An equally important avenue is to actively apply to my personal life the commitments I hold of diversity – tolerance, respect for others, healthy skepticism, and an acceptance of a world populated by a myriad of beliefs with varying degrees of relevance to my own set of quirks that define my reality.

Notes

1 The Moral Majority is a term which refers to a somewhat amorphous voting block in US politics; the movement's spokesman is Rev. Falwell who advocates influencing politics to promote what they consider a "bible-based" agenda (Sullivan, 2005; J. Wallis, 2005; Wuthnow and Lawson, 1994).
2 Both Falwell and Robertson are Protestant ministers in the US who have used radio and television media effectively to extend their views of Christianity widely – beyond the doors of their respective churches.
3 This "label" was created during the Iranian revolutionary war in the 1970s to describe the United States; it's a name that is used, even in Iran today (Kavitha, 2002).
4 Not everyone would agree with me on this point. For example, Korten (1996) argues that US business after the American Civil War became so powerful that in some states they could buy and sell legislation; he also speaks to Corporate Colonialism through which transnational firms exercise significant power of promoting "America first, then the world."

References

Ammerman, N. T. (1991), "North American Protestant Fundamentalism," in M. E. Martin and R. S. Appleby (Eds.), *Fundamentalisms Observed*, Volume 1, Chicago: Chicago University Press, pp. 1–65.
Ammerman, N. T. (1994), "Accounting for Christian Fundamentalism: Social Dynamics and Rhetorical Strategies," in M. E. Marty and R. S. Appleby (Eds.), *Accounting for Fundamentalisms: The Dynamic Character of Movements*, Volume 4, Chicago: University of Chicago Press, pp. 149–170.
Anderson, W. T. (1990), *Reality Isn't What it Used to Be*, San Francisco: Harper Collins Publishers.

Appleby, R. S. and Marty, M. E. (2002), "Fundamentalism," *Foreign Policy, Jan/Feb* (128), pp. 16–22.
Armstrong, K. (2001), *The Battle for God: A History of Fundamentalism*, New York: Ballantine Books.
Beeman, W. O. (2001), "Fighting the Good Fight: Fundamentalism and Religious Revival," in J. MacClancy (Ed.), *Anthropology for the Real World*, Chicago: University of Chicago Press.
Brittan, S. (1996), *Capitalism with a Human Face*, London: Fontana Press.
CIA (20th September 2005), *World Fact Book: GDP Rankings*. US Government – CIA, URL: http://www.cia.gov/cia/publications/factbook/rankorder/2001rank.html, retrieved on 3rd October 2005.
Crockett, R. (2003), *Memo to the Supreme Court: Diversity is Good Business* (*Business Week*, 27th January 2003, p. 96).
Dalton, M. (2003), "Social Identity Conflict," *MIT Sloan Management Review*, Vol. 45, No. 1, pp. 7–8.
Engels, F. (1983), *The Origin of the Family, Private Property and the State*, 4th Edition, Moscow: Progress Publishers.
English, F. (1996), "The Lure of Fundamentalism," *Transactional Analysis Journal*, Vol. 26, No. 1, pp. 23–30.
France, M. and Symonds, W. (2003), *Diversity Is About To Get More Elusive, Not Less* (*Business Week*, 7th July 2003, pp. 30–31).
Freire, P. (1972), *Pedagogy of the Oppressed*, London: Penguin Books.
Heilman, S. C. (1994), *Quiescent and Active Fundamentalism: The Jewish Cases*, Volume 4, Chicago: University of Chicago Press.
Herriot, P. and Scott-Jackson, W. (2002), "Globalization, Social Identities and Employment," *British Journal of Management*, Vol. 13, pp. 249–257.
Hsu, T. C. (18th November 2004), *History of Fundamentalism: How far apart are Al-Queda and Extremist Judeo-Christianity?*, Institute for Research: Middle East Policy, URL: http://www.irmep.org/essays/hf.htm, retrieved 20th September 2005.
Israel, S. and Mezvinksy, N. (1999), *Jewish Fundamentalism in Israel*, London: Pluto Press.
Kavitha, R. (26th April 2002), *The Great Satan*, World Trek: The Odyssey – Middle East Stage, URL: http://www.worldtrek.org/odyssey/mideast/042600/042600kavispies.html, retrieved 4th October 2005.
Korten, D. C. (1996), *When Corporations Rule the World*, London: Earthscan Publications Limited.
Kramer, J. and Alstad, D. (1993), *The Guru Papers*, Berkeley: Frog, Ltd.
Malik, S. (18th July 2005), "The Conveyor Belt of Extremism," *New Statesman*, Vol. 134, pp. 14–15.
Nanda, M. (23rd October 2003), *Postmodernism, Science and Religious Fundamentalism*, Butterfliesandwheels.com, URL; http://www.butterfliesandwheels.com/articleprint.php?num=40, retrieved 18th September 2005.
Nielsen, N. (1993), *Fundamentalism, Mythos, and World Religions*, New York: State University of New York Press.
Peters, T. and Waterman, R. (1982), *In Search of Excellence*, New York: Harper and Row, Publishers.
Schramm, J. (2003), Acting Affirmatively. *HR Magazine*, Vol. 48, p. 196.
Shahak, I. and Mezvinsky, N. (1999), *Jewish Fundamentalism in Israel*, London: Pluto Press.
Smith, A. (1993), *An Inquiry into the Nature and Causes of the Wealth of Nations*, Oxford: Oxford University Press.
Stoll, D. (1994), "Jesus is Lord of Guatemala: Evangelical Reform in a Death-Squad State," in M. E. Marty and R. S. Appleby (Eds.), *Accounting for Fundamentalisms: The*

Dynamic Character of Movements, Volume 4, Chicago: University of Chicago Press, pp. 99–123.
Sullivan, A. (2nd May 2005), *How Fundamentalism is Splitting the GOP*, New Republic Online, URL: http://www.tnr.com/doc.mhtml?i=20050502&s=sullivan050205, retrieved 20th September 2005.
Wallis, C. (2005), *The Evolution Wars* (*Time*, 15th August 2005, pp. 27–35).
Wallis, J. (2005), *God's Politics: Why the Right Gets It Wrong and the Left Doesn't Get It*, San Francisco: Harper Collins Publishers.
Wuthnow, R. and Lawson, M. P. (1994), "Sources of Christian Fundamentalism in the United States," in M. E. Marty and R. S. Appleby (Eds.), *Accounting for Fundamentalisms: The Dynamic Character of Movements*, Volume 4, Chicago: University of Chicago Press, pp. 18–56.

Part 5

Preparing for New Realities

Editors' Note: Preparing for New Realities

by Kurt April

Wishing someone to live in times of change can be a curse, or a blessing, depending on which part of the world you come from, and which cultures influence your belief system the most. In Africa, we find that the duality of new found democracy and ongoing tribal and colonialist identities are causing tensions. In post-Soviet Azerbaijan, the youth are having to simultaneously deal with the pull of their old identities as well as the changes that the consequences of war brings, while trying to forge new identities at the same time. In Europe, many of the accession countries to the EU are finding it difficult to define their new identities that accompany transfer of sovereignty. In China, young and old, rural and urban are all experiencing different forces on their identities. In the USA, disparate parts of the nation seek clarity between living out certain values against its position as the greatest immigrant nation on the planet. And, in our supposed modern world, many women still find themselves oppressed within a male consciousness, and women themselves consciously but mainly unconsciously find themselves party to the perpetuation of such oppression. Such change, may not be at the same pace over similar periods, but has been with human kind since the year dot. And as humankind has experienced over the ages, the new generation's perception of who they are, and who they should be, in all parts of the world, will, in turn, shape the future of these regions and individual countries. The new generation are the ones who, with an appreciation for functional wisdom from the past (as opposed to learning and copying dysfunctional wisdom) are going to bring a very special meaning to the notion of citizenship, because they are the ones who are building these new regions and countries.

Researchers are discovering the extent to which xenophobia can be easily – even arbitrarily – turned on. Apparently, in just hours, we can be conditioned to fear or discriminate against those who differ from us – even by characteristics as superficial as eye colour or height. Traditional social identity groups have to unlearn and unthink their earlier socialised and internalised mental programming and patterns of behavior, build up new mental programs, learn new behaviors, as well as develop new coping mechanisms to adapt to their new and still-changing environments – a type of "cultural intelligence" is needed, both "self-cultural intelligence" and "other-cultural intelligence," and a lack of which results in xenophobic, even racist, overtures. Even ideas we believe are just common sense, can have deep xenophobic underpinnings. Philomena Essed, in her chapter Leadership in Question: Talking Diversity, Walking Homogeneity in the Dutch Police Force, highlights the ingrained way in which people get to perceive things, consciously and unconsciously, and she makes valid points in highlighting the difference between tolerance and inclusiveness (the former being a sophisticated form of discrimination). The drive to completely and quickly divide the world into "us" and "them" is so powerful that some have postulated that it derives from some deep psychological need.

Our authors draw on the work of the late Tajfel and Turner who devised a theory to explain the psychology behind a range of prejudices and biases. Their theory was based, in part, on the desire to think highly of oneself and therefore to continuously seek out positive self-affirmation. One way to lift oneself is to be part of a distinctive group (like a winning team or been singled out for special treatment), and another is to play up the qualities of one's own group ("in group") in a positive light and denigrate others through negative affirmation of those who are not like you or your group ("out-groups"). Kurt April and Amanda April, in their article (Responsible Leadership Ethics) on the moral challenges for leaders in a diverse Europe, raise concern regarding the positivists' claim to have separated out scientific fact from human values – the important benchmark upon which social and leadership action should be measured – and reinforced the now taken-for-granted contingency of existence in which men and women increasingly find their lives manipulated in systematic market oppression and placed outside of their control, in favor of the status quo. Difference, they argue, is indeed, not appreciated, as, organizationally, we find more and more sophisticated ways to continue cloning people in favor of the dominant social group and as Essed asserts, shame at work is used to manipulate people into feelings of lower self-esteem. There is therefore a call for a new focus on diversity through the lenses of intention, shame, identity and power relations.

In many ways, organizations today are standing at a similar threshold to that which framed the practice of Western expansion. Learning underpins the ability to prepare for new realities and is fundamentally consciousness-based, and therefore needs to be viewed as a social process that takes place in the interaction between people, for instance in various communities of survival, communities of interest, communities of practice, communities of spirit, or more generally and exclusively in terms of the so-called social-constructionist view. Engendered curiosity and subsequent learning that takes place, and are influenced through working life and at the workplace, originates in the historosity of technical, organizational and path-dependent social conditions in which the employees are functionally involved. The authors in this section of the book challenge the readers to live consciously in the transformational social realm, and in so doing, continue to reach out for information and perspectives that are relevant and can make them more effective for their own individual purposes, for their organizational purposes, and even for their country. To the extent that they don't, they assume knowledge is unnecessary, that they know all they need to know, or that what they don't know won't hurt them.

Sadly though, the old ways of doing things, even the ones that have brought many successes up to now, may be the very stumbling blocks for forging ahead and leading to new success. The challenge for us therefore is to live consciously, purposefully, with a sense of expectancy – and parallel that with helping others to live consciously too – an almost spiritual requirement. It is Lovemore Mbigi who, in his article Spirit of African Leadership: A Comparative African Perspective, reminds us that we are subjective by nature, and only able to see that which our cultural paradigms allow us to see. He challenges managers to purposefully shift their craft/their art (management) from being a "science of manipulation," to also being a "science of understanding" – this, he claims, quite necessarily requires of us to move from pure rational approaches to also embracing the spiritual.

16

Leadership in Question: Talking Diversity, Walking Homogeneity in the Dutch Police Force

by Philomena Essed

Introduction

Diversity: who can be possibly against it at this time and age? According to the literature, managing diversity – a direction based foremost in the business concern of enhancing competitive advantage – acknowledges multi-identities as valuable resources in the pursuit of company goals. In spite of, or maybe because of the readiness by which the term 'diversity' has been adopted in business and government policy discourses I could not help feeling wary. Diversity resonates with the Dutch self-image of tolerance. At the same time, with the notion of diversity rising in popularity, a number of problems so far insufficiently dealt with, notably discrimination and racism, are being pushed further to the background. Moreover, diversity is often interpreted in essentialist ways. In the name of inclusion different bodies than normative White males are tolerated, as long as there are no cultural changes involved (Essed, 2002). Cultural assimilation serves as a mode for inclusion, while different bodies are problematized, 'othered', perceived as invaders, out of place in spaces originally not meant for them to be (Puwar, 2004). Elsewhere we have argued that the focus on difference, on the 'other' has masked the other side of the same coin, the continuation of preference for sameness. The injustices of preference for sameness, in Charles Tilly's words 'durable inequality' (Tilly, 1998) are embedded in what we have called cloning cultures, the cultures of replica and standardization, consumerism and mass production, homogenization in the name of efficiency (Essed and Goldberg, 2002). Homogenization is at odds with global migration, and the ethnic and cultural diversity of our contemporary societies. The tension seems to be resolved managerially by resisting change, by normalizing existing (White, masculine, dominant) practices within a framework of cultural assimilation. This paradox, between homogenization and diversity, is illustrated with the reappraisal of a case I got involved with in the late 1990s concerning the Dutch Police force.

Conceptual and practical concerns intertwined: Dutch Police force

I had a call, in the late 1990s, from a consultant with whom I had worked before who asked whether I was interested in doing a co-assignment with her in a Police branch located in one of the Dutch municipalities, where the demographic representation of ethnic minorities is 15–30%. Over a period of more than a decade this Police unit had been active in pursuing gender and ethnic diversity. Although there has been an increase in the numbers of (White) women and ethnic minority staff, numerical progress was undermined by high dropout rates. The force was still predominantly White male in structure and in culture. Racial discrimination and discrimination against women continued to maintain glass ceilings and brick walls, preventing gender and ethnic integration from taking place. In order to find alternative ways of breaking through the glass ceiling the Police leadership stated the intention to take a more active leading role in facilitating cultural change. The management appointed a 'diversity project manager', a White female Police officer, who, in her turn, assigned a consultant, a White female, with the request to develop 'a diversity thermometer' – a self-assessment for leaders and managers to qualify and adapt their behavior to facilitate diversity development. The test would be a pilot, to be tried out first among a select number of leaders. The consultant in her turn asked me, a woman of color, to develop and test the diversity thermometer together with her.

I liked the idea of focusing on management and leadership because it was consistent with my theory about organizational change (Essed, 1996) and with my experience in a similar organization. In the early 1990s I had been asked to investigate the causes and nature of increasingly open racial hostilities among the employees of a large Dutch company for public transportation. This was a few years after the introduction and implementation of positive action, a municipal requirement dating from the mid 1980s (Essed, 1993). We interviewed a cross-section of the workforce about their experiences in relation to gender and ethnic diversifying. On the basis of the results, among other things very critical of the management, we conducted a survey complemented by in-depth interviews with the complete middle-management group. Apart from a number of other problems related to the company culture, we found that the middle-management group formed (wittingly and unwittingly) a solid barrier against gender or ethnic change. With few exceptions, all of the managers, White and male, were ignorant, if not indifferent, about discrimination. The majority of the managers were prejudiced against ethnic minority men and women and, as well as against White women. Moreover, the absence of relevant competence to manage a diverse workforce reinforced racist and anti-women sentiments among the workers, the large majority of whom were White men. Among other things we advised anti-discrimination and diversity competence development among the different managerial layers.

I felt challenged by the opportunity to work with managers and leaders, but I did not really like the idea of working with the Police. Diversity development has not only to do with internal dynamics within the workforce, but also with external relations. Here it is relevant to mention the problematic relationship between the Police and Moroccan youngsters in the larger Dutch cities. Clashes have increased and sometimes escalated, thus reinforcing the circle of stereotyping, criminalization and prophecy-fulfilling behavior. In light of the above, the suggestion of a diversity thermometer sounded alarming to me. In my view, a 'hot' or 'cold' indicator would reinforce repression and control of behavior, without nurturing any deeper understanding of learning and growth through dialogue and critical self-reflection. Could I stand idle? I decided to accept the assignment.

Moreover, I knew from other sources of information that the Police force was discursively open to diversity, but in practice the preferred profile remained White, male, heterosexual. Heterosexual, males of color candidates could aspire to become like, but would never be seen quite the same as, the White male Police officers. Socio-cultural cloning of the normative Police officer image starts already in the Police academy. I recalled the news headlines about a case involving a number of racial-ethnic minority students who selected evidence and made a report on everyday racism in the Police academy, which they submitted to the relevant authorities. The critique was badly taken. In personal communication with one of the writers of the report I was told that the school had retaliated. According to this informant, students who had engaged with the critical report got dismissed or pestered away. Those who managed to complete their study anyway are registered on a 'black list' which basically serves to prevent them from ever finding a job at any of the Dutch Police branches. I have not been able to verify this information. To their credit, the Police academy commissioned an investigation and a subsequent study, to find out whether the writers of the report had due cause. The investigation committee, concerned with short-term hearings and evaluation of the problem, rejected the complaints of the ethnic minority students. A subsequent, more thorough study, however, conducted by a Canadian consultant, has criticized the Police academy for systemic racism, thereby confirming the students' complaints (Armour, 1994). Among other things, the recommendations included in the Armour report urge the Police (academy) to diversify in order to fit the requirements of a pluralistic society.

A long-term comprehensive approach to diversity development seemed to make more sense than a diversity thermometer. One could imagine such a project to focus, among other things, at the following research questions:

(1) How does the Police force define diversity (experimental, inclusiveness of the definition, concept of 'other')?
(2) (In which way) is diversity part of the organizational vision, mission, strategic thinking and planning?

(3) Is the diversity process motivated by ethical, business, or legal factors or a combination of those?
(4) (How) is diversity being implemented? What are the main characteristics of this process?
(5) Does the diversity paradigm provide tools to deal with the complexity involved in organizational and management changes?
(6) Which characteristics of the organizational culture are conducive to diversity development, and which ones form barriers? How are barriers, in particular discrimination, dealt with?
(7) What is the role of leadership and management in the implementation of diversity development?
(8) What does diversity mean for the business goals and for the business system (marketing demographics, involvement of employee recourse groups, diversity skills from pre-recruitment through retirement)?
(9) (In which way) is the diversity process meaningful at the level of the individual employee (team-building, education and training facilities) and the individual client (products, services)?
(10) What are the results of the change process in the way the Police force operates, internally and externally, in relation to ethnically diverse communities?

The first obstacles to pursuing these, and other relevant questions, announced themselves immediately: time and budget constraints. We had to restrict our assignment to developing a self-assessment for managers. We decided to highlight one specific dimension, the core values underlying policing as a profession (see question 6). The consultant would take care of the logistics of the test, while I would serve as a resource person and adviser for the methodology of the project. We reformulated the goal of the project as follows: to develop a self-assessment test of leadership and management qualities with respect to the transmission, among the force, of the core values underlying the professional code of the Police work.

Why the core values? We tried to identify an indirect way to deal with discrimination. Could the rejection of rudeness or inhumane treatment of civilians, including racial discrimination, possibly be translated in terms of a violation of the code of professionalism? There are four core values the members of the Police force have to commit themselves to. This is a formal requirement. The fact that police officers have to subscribe to the core values upon being hired, but not to a specific interpretation leaves space for negotiation and discussion around issues concerning difference, discrimination, equality and diversity in the Police force. Police officers are expected to honor the values or *justice, severity, integrity* and *love*. This last value, 'love', a relatively recent addition, has been adopted upon the request of one of the few high-ranking women officials. Arguably, one could see this addition as a 'feminine' touch. At the same time it is increasingly acknowledged that 'love for ourselves, love for others, and love for what we do' (April *et al.*, 2000: 19) are essential needs and values, in particular in organizational settings. 'Love' in this sense means accepting one another as 'legitimate human beings' (Jaworski, 1996, 1998: 11) and '*respecting each other's uniqueness* – the value of our differences that enrich the world we jointly inhabit and so make it more fascinating and enjoyable a place . . .' (Bauman, 2003: 81). Questioning and analyzing interpretations and applications of core values could encourage life-long learning through dialogue and self-critical reflection (Yankelovich, 1999). Self-reflection is a crucial transformational element in learning processes (April *et al.*, 2000). At least three of the core values appeal to humaneness and human respect (justice, integrity, loving). In principle, then, appeal to the core values could serve as an instrument to improve the quality of Police professionalism, by way of critical reflection and reappraisal of the enactment of the core values in everyday practice. Furthermore, dialogue about the 'soft' values, whether love, care, or human respect, can be a tool for questioning the professionalism of officers who abuse civilians on ethnic or racial grounds.

We interviewed a cross-company selection of Police officers, men and women, different ages, White, ethnic minority background, about the meaning of the core values in their everyday professional life. The majority of the sample, 30 in total, involved line managers (in training) at different levels in the Police force. In addition to the line managers, we interviewed a small number of key figures, such as the ombudswoman, the personnel officer, and a few new recruits. The purpose of the interviews was to find out whether the core values are experienced as central, how these values are being interpreted – interviewees were asked to give concrete examples and incidents to qualify their understanding of the values – and whether these values are conducive to diversity development or whether they form a barrier.

We asked the respondents to give examples about how they apply the core values in their daily practice. Interestingly, various interviewees, across age, gender and ethnicity, feel that 'love' does not fit the harsh reality they experience as Police officers. Moreover, they did not receive any coaching as to what 'love' means, why it is important, what it means in daily practice and how it can improve the quality of Police work. This seems to suggest that although the top management has been open to including a non-standard, 'feminine' core value, the daily practice is more resistant to change.

For each value, the interviewees were asked to provide us with two concrete examples of everyday practice, one to show *confirmation* of the respective values of justice, integrity, severance, and love, and the other to illustrate the *violation* of these values. The latter prevailed in the examples the interviewees could think of. This is not necessarily to suggest that violations prevail in reality. It is often harder to recall or imagine decent behavior than to recall offensive or humiliating events (Margalit, 1996). A number of examples of how justice gets to be violated involve gender and/or racial-ethnic prejudice and discrimination. With respect to the value of *integrity*, there are numerous examples of petty corruption in external relations (accepting free meals, snacks etcetera from neighborhood stores).

The examples relating to the value of *severity* revealed an interesting problem. All the examples we got involve situations where rules are applied more strictly against ethnic minorities, both internally (fellow officers) and externally (the public). Internally it has happened repeatedly that White Police officers engage in biographical history analysis of ethnic colleagues. Thus they search, without permission, through Police files to find out whether a colleague of color has ever been involved with the Police. Because the files include reports where a Police officer stops a car in order to ask the driver for his or her driver's licence, racially discriminatory motivated searches are registered and filed too. Thus the likelihood that ethnic Police officers have been in contact with the Police is often higher compared to White colleagues. Next, word gets around that Surinamese officer X or Turkish officer Y are in the files. Rumors are damaging for the reputation of the officer, which can lead to withdrawal from the force. External bias in the application of the value of severity in conduct and appraisal has to do with the zero tolerance policy against Moroccan youngsters, in particular, of whom 50% has been in contact with the Police.

We also found positive examples of active intervention against racial and gender discrimination, but to a large degree the Police force remains to be dominated by macho cultures, where the rule prevails that you have to be able to take a joke – sexist and racist comments and jokes are rampant. Some White women adapt to the degree that they outperform White men in rough and rude behavior. Finally, in relation to the notion of 'care', there are many examples of solidarity and care, for instance for the new recruit, male or female who is confronted with his or her first shooting, first corpse or violent crime.

On the basis of the findings we developed a problem-solving test for the managers. The format consists of sketches of everyday events, most of which were selected from the earlier interviews with Police officers. The sketches appeal to interpretations of the core values in day-to-day work situations. The purpose of the problem-solving test is to find out how managers deal with a dilemma, an everyday predicament, where they are at the same time challenged to deal with diversity and antidiscrimination. In preparation of the test we discussed at length, with a few key officers, whether the sketches were 'realistic' indeed. The test did not have any scientific pretensions – it was primarily meant to serve as a basis for discussion among managers about mentoring, coaching and leadership styles and qualities in dealing with various dimensions of diversity: race, ethnicity, gender, sexual orientation, age disabilities.

Below are a few examples of the sketches we included, all of which drawing from events that happened in the past:

(1) One Police officer is invited to talk in a television program about his being gay. He wants to know from the supervisor whether he could or should not wear his uniform on stage. How would you advise?

(2) A young supervisor is transferred to another department, where a group of older colleagues who have been working together for many years have become largely dysfunctional. The new supervisor is asked to reorganize the department. How do you feel about this?
(3) Two colleagues in your team are competing for the same vacancy. The more competent one who gets the job is a White woman. A few days later she confides in you: a few team members refuse to accept her. How would you go about the situation?
(4) A colleague of Surinamese background files a complaint. She suffers small harassments every day. Each time she confronts her colleagues they habitually respond: 'Sorry, I did not mean it that way', only to continue with the same kinds of things the next day. She cannot take it any longer. How would you intervene?
(5) You are called to intervene in a cafe where a fight has occurred. Upon arrival it turns out to be a Turkish cafe. Your colleague who happens to be of Turkish background switches into Turkish in addressing the problem. How do you feel about this?

The purpose of these and a number of other questions was for managers to make an *anonymous* self-assessment on the basis of points per item, and to generate group discussions about assessments and interventions as supervisors. Anonymity would be helpful in order to prevent stigmatizing. We finalized the self-assessment test and presented in to the diversity project manager, who would organize a workshop with managers for a pilot test of the score list.

My engagement with the project was basically limited to the preparation and development of the leadership self-assessment test. The consultant related the rests of the story to me. Before she could test the score list, the diversity project manager, who had hired her, was made non-active (discharged). After months of delay, the newly hired supervisor of the department, the discharged diversity project manager had worked for, looked at the data we had gathered. Her response was one of great enthusiasm. She put two teams together to discuss the test and in order to keep it on the agenda. Then she proceeded to appoint a new diversity project manager, a woman, who, finally, applied the self-assessment test. The first attempt (with managers in training) went successfully, meaning that it produced constructive dialogue among the selected group. The second application of the test concerned a higher-level group – a number of corps leaders. The test scores turned out to be deplorably low – suggesting low competence in dealing with everyday predicaments around diversity issues and discrimination. The corps leaders got angry and blamed the test. In the meantime, a new crisis swept through the organization when news leaked to the media that ethnic minority Police officers were fleeing the organization – they could not cope with the organizational culture, partly due to racism. White women could not cope well either. This quickly began time for crisis management and short-term interventions: the newly hired diversity project manager got relocated to the personnel department in order to help speeding up the hiring of ethnic minorities. Again, this produced stagnation in the leadership self-assessment project. After a few more months of silence, the consultant contacted another manager to proceed with the project. This manager discussed the test with another corps leader who thought the test was solid and should be very useful, but . . . . . . And so on and so forth . . . . . .

Discussion

The above experiences underscore, that diversity must involve an organization-wide initiative. This was not the case among the Police force, where diversity development was reduced to the size of 'a project' and delegated to one special officer, the diversity project manager. In addition, diversity seemed to be restricted to the recruitment of women and ethnic minorities at the lower levels. There cannot be organizational diversity, however, without diversity among the leadership and management of the organization. In addition, process management is notoriously a weak point in the Police organization. This might mean that, in practice, any renewal, or change project demanding cultural and structural change throughout the organization will be difficult to endorse, because competent management is lacking. Having said this, I would like to end with a point of critical methodological self-reflection.

Although commitment from the top is essential for diversity efforts to take effect, the undertaking can only be successful if the rest of the organization supports the interventions. Here, several experts suggest that diversity efforts must not be directed to women, ethnic minorities or other 'target' groups exclusively, because women and minorities alone cannot make diversity happen (Morrison *et al.*, 1993). The diversity policy must be an inclusive one that empowers the entire workforce, including potential resisters, because their exclusion fuels discontent, whereas inclusion may weaken the potential danger of backlash. Because management approaches seek to change the organizational culture, it is intended that diversity be inclusive throughout the organization: from finance to personnel management, and in particular in the critical business systems and practices, including management practices, communications systems, working assignments and staffing, career development, recruiting, hiring and orientation, performance management, rewards and corrective action, compensation and benefits, education and training (Arredondo, 1996). Moreover, I learned from the Police project that it did not make sense to talk around the issue of discrimination for fear of negative response. After all, discrimination is against the law.

The new European antidiscrimination legislation seems to offer an interesting opening for developing different approaches to the prevention of discrimination. Because it operates through the principle of shared burden of proof, organizations can be challenged directly to 'prove' absence of discrimination in the face of specific charges. In a current action-research project called *Towards a Workplace without Discrimination* (Mannen, 2005) we addressed a question, not dissimilar to the issue of how to measure diversity. Different than the Police force example, we did not target one specific organization, but key figures from a range of organizations, active advocates of diversity. Like the Police force, example, our aims were to generate dialogue among key change agents, irrespective of organizational background, place in the organizational structure, gender, 'race', ethnicity. One of the challenges was how to conceptualize 'free from discrimination'. We opted for an experiential approach focusing on how the work organization is experienced by its members (Essed, 1996). Non-discrimination, in that sense, can be seen as a function of the degree to which members feel seen in their individuality and valued in the organization. Do they feel fairly credited for their input and competencies? And what does it take to identify discrimination? This opened the way to re-link notions of diversity to the necessary insights to counter homogenization, to prevent notions of space invaders, to prevent discrimination, in particular in light of the new European antidiscrimination legislation. At a September 2004 conference, we invited expert speakers from the Dutch Equal Treatment Commission. Participants were invited to engage in dialogue about discrimination cases, hearings from the Equal Treatment Commission, accessible through their website. The discrimination cases were replayed in scene by a theater group, and the public engaged in 'how to rule' about charges made. The conference triggered lots of enthusiasm. This was a major breakthrough in the current political climate where pressures to assimilate into national cultures have become pervasive, while issues of racism and discrimination have been pushed off organizational agendas.

Insights emerging form the conference have been useful for developing a new model for social and cultural sensitivity in work organizations (Mannen, 2005). The real success of the project remains, however, a function of whether or not the model will speak to a larger audience.

References

April, K., Macdonald, R. and Vriesendorp, S. (2000), *Rethinking Leadership*, Kenwyn, Cape Town: University of Cape Town Press (Juta Academic).

Armour, M. (1994), *Diversity and Pluralism at the LSOP (Landelijke Selectie en Opleidingsinstituut Politie – Police Federal Selection and Training Institute)*, Amsterdam and Toronto: Transcultural International.

Arredondo, P. (1996), *Successful Diversity Management Initiatives: A blueprint for planning and implementation*, Thousand Oaks: Sage.

Bauman, Z. (2003), *Liquid Love: On the Frailty of Human Bonds*, Cambridge, UK: Polity Press.

Essed, P. (1993), 'The Politics of Marginal Inclusion: Racism in an Organisational Context', in J. Wrench and J. Solomos (Eds.), *Racism and Migration in Western Europe*, Oxford: Berg Publishers, pp. 143–156.

Essed, P. (1996), *Diversity: Gender, Color and Culture*, Amherst: University of Massachusetts Press.

Essed, P. (2002), 'Diversity Illusions and Disillusions – The Case of the Dutch Police Force', in M. Essemyr (Ed.), *Diversity in Work Organizations*, Stockholm: Nationale Institute for Working Life, pp. 45–69.

Essed, P. and Goldberg, D. T. (2002), 'Cloning Cultures: The Social Injustices of Sameness', *Ethnic and Racial Studies*, Vol. 25, No. 6, pp. 1066–1082.

Jaworski, J. (1996, 1998), *Synchronicity: The Inner Path of Leadership*, San Francisco: Berrett-Koehler.

Mannen, Ann (2005), *Social and Cultural Sensitivity in Work Organizations*, Utrecht: Tiye International.

Margalit, A. (1996), *The Decent Society*, Cambridge, MA: Harvard University Press.

Morrison, A. M., Ruderman, M. N. and Hughes-James, M. (1993), *Making Diversity Happen: Controversies and Solutions*, Greensboro, NC: Center for Creative Leadership.

Puwar, N. (2004), *Space Invaders: Race, Gender and Bodies Out of Place*, New York: Berg Publishers.

Tilly, C. (1998), *Durable Inequality*, Berkeley, CA: University of California Press.

Yankelovich, D. (1999), *The Magic Dialogue: Transforming Conflict into Cooperation*, New York: Touchstone Simon & Schuster.

17
Responsible Leadership Ethics

by Kurt April and Amanda April

Introduction

Getting to grips with the dualistic nature of an emerging, unified Europe is very necessary for incumbent and emerging leaders where, for instance, for the most part Western European countries and companies have opted to either implement the minimum requirements, normally driven through law and legislation in its companies and societies, e.g., implement demographic targets to be achieved, or focused narrowly on context-relevant multi-culturalism. Contrasting with this approach are the newer EU members, like Baltic-located Estonia, for which diversity is a very new concept, and countries on the periphery, like Turkey, for which the concept of the individual is a blurry, changeable one due largely to their experience of heightened individualism as well as communalism throughout their long political and economic history, and finally countries like Romania which are caught in a time-warp of biculturality as they rediscover their historical economic prowess. The fundamental flaw, as we see it, is that too much of the focus has been on how to efficiently box people into certain categories, typically geographic cultural ones, and then seek to lead them through those lenses – as opposed to fully embracing the uncertainty of diversity. In a changing Europe, diversity is an ethical issue, for which leaders have a clear responsibility, if they hope to build a sustainable Europe that works for all – oneself and others. In many ways, the unwillingness by some leaders in Europe – community, organisational and institutional/governmental – to fully engage such discourse and deconstruction is a moral injustice, and erodes the precepts of a free and democratic EU.

Fundamental questions

In the American-dominated global constructs of public, organisational and private life, and particularly its growing influence on business life in the European Union, of which leadership is a key dimension, we notice that the way in which society, and organisations, are structured are treated very differently from the way in which individual, and collective, consciousness is, and is becoming, structured. In American organisation theory, ideas of Weber (1957) and Durkheim (1915; 1938) were reduced to the service of positive science and leading efficient organisational forms. For instance, according to Brown (1978), Weber's notion of bureaucratic rationality, thought of initially as an ideal type, was adopted as a paradigm by American sociologists, in particular Taylor (Merkle, 1980). Brown further argues that in American theory there has been a positivistic emphasis on behaviour, and the behavioural aspects of the rational system, and an ongoing reluctance to look into the "interior" of persons for interests or intentions, and have thus lost sight of the structures of consciousness and society.

Recently within Europe leaders have, and currently still are faced with, intentional and consciousness-laden dilemmas. The dilemmas range in scope and range: some are ethical business dilemmas, some relate to emotional ethnic fervour, others emanate from moral decisions relating to war and terror, still others are induced by the rise of crime in Europe. Additionally, the current perplexing economic issues within Europe fuel new dilemmas, and there is apparent widespread loss of faith in governments in the face of rampant globalisation and paralleled workforce courage/uprising in the face of future labour uncertainty in the region. All of these have, once again, forced a rethinking of the role of leadership in shaping desirable organisations and societies, and the underlying ethical philosophy of such leadership in the presence of, and in collaboration with, the "other". A significant challenge for the next generation of European leaders will be the promotion and advancement of science, technology and business to serve the interest of all of human development, in a knowledge-intensive economic zone. In addition, work, as it evolves, is beginning to induce new upheavals and burgeoning paradoxes in European society – etching at the very fabric of Western society amidst growing indigenous and immigrant influences, traditional versus modern, through the redefinition of work and who is central and "matters" in this new sphere of work and who is marginal, thus raising debate about important and interrelated issues such as meaning, dignity, status, perceived and practiced justice, equity and democracy, truth-telling, life balance and the value of all life, living standards and the virtues of a free society. There is a growing movement within the Euro-zone to incorporate ethical principles and practices pertaining to issues of diversity, transcultural dynamics and human development for all who live in and sustain the multi-variate geographical zone.

Leaders within Europe often find themselves at the forefront of needing to initiate discourse and deconstruction of issues relating to individual and national identity, self-identification and group identity, economic and social benefits that work for all, traditional bastions of power and newer, nebulous forms of power, positivism and constructivism, individualism and collectivism, instrumental reason and commoditisation in the face of community outcries and the seeking of the common good. For Marx (1967), such leadership responsibility, doing the right thing, involves stripping away feudal myths relating to the bureaucratisation of industrial life, to unpack the inherent instrumental rationality for (ab)using people, and lay bare the larger irrationality of exploitative relations that alienate people, which the present evil of formal organisational forms – businesses, in particular, organisations and governments – engender. According to Brown (1978: 366), Weber (1957) would disagree, arguing that leaders are bound to orient and focus the rationality of modern bureaucracies towards solving problems, thus leaders' main tasks are to set goals and organise work so as to create affective human relations that serve the short-term good. The failure of rationality of the Weberian paradigm to manifest itself fully, led to Durheimian thought being invoked (Parsons, 1951; Merton, 1957). Durkheim (1915, 1938), in making sense of the anomie and instrumental reason features of the complex division of labour characteristics of industrial societies, recommended that organisations be humanised through an enhancement of affective relations at the workplace, therefore securing the "self" and "community".

Black (2001: 338) highlights the dispute between the limits of self and community definitions, which European leaders have a responsibility to resolve and provide perspective on. Furthermore, Black warns that discussing such important issues and breaking the tyranny of silence regarding these matters are moral choices. Walzer (1997) argued that identity groups gain power through individuals adhering to their group. As the European workforce demographics have rapidly expanded and changed, we are beginning to see the emergence of leadership-evoked "diversity management" as the magical intonation that absolves the guilt, shame and most significantly, the ethical responsibility for misguided and selfish actions against the left-out, left-behind, unwelcome, different and left-overs of European society – the "others/them". In South Africa, for instance, we would argue that much of the organisational diversity practices are actually attempts by the economically-dominant White minority to both stabilise the issues of psychological emancipation of the majority people of colour and their ongoing struggle for economic equality, as well as appease their Apartheid-induced, guilt-ridden morality which daily erodes their very identities. As a result, "sufficient/minimum processes" and "appeasing practices" are put in place that ensures a form of stability, continuance and comfort. It would appear as if the time is right in the world, but more particularly in Europe, for a different kind of discussion about the intersubjectivity of ethics, diversity and leadership, one that incorporates a compelling European vision of a knitted, collective future that works for all.

We have four fundamental questions that continually intrigue us about organisational and societal life in a globalised world, as regards diversity management and the lack of accountability for action and practice:

(1) Why is it important for leaders to continually focus on issues of diversity management?
(2) Why haven't we got, and why can't we get, diversity management right?

(3) If we can't get it right, why do we keep doing more of the same, just harder and with greater effort? And with the same mental/cognitive and emotional constructs?
(4) When we do eventually get results in diversity management (even though sometimes, not according to some pre-specified diversity plan), what were we actually doing? And what were our individual, and collective, levels of awareness of our practices and behaviours at the time (our discipline of noticing)?

Globalisation is seen in various parts of the world as imposing a hegemonic, Anglo-American-oriented, consumerist culture that uproots and abrogates existing difference in the name of apparent, unexamined progress. According to King (2000: 143) "... such notions of supposed 'progress' prioritise a social ethic of integration that permits no understanding of the culture-systemic character and mode of functioning of 'race' as ideology". Globalisation discourse, for many, has sought to eliminate notions of ethnicity, identity, intention and purpose, and have sought to obscure the contextual application of power and its related, supporting knowledge-infrastructures. Thus, narrowly applied diversity management theory and techniques seek to enable further globalisation, and seek to benefit the "few", not the "many". Gaudelli (2001) argues that some scholars who theorise about the potential outcomes of globalisation suggest that identities will not be lost in this era, only reconfigured. "Local groups often reshape their local identities when they meet challenges related to globalisation processes, but they do not abandon these identities. ... What was 'local' becomes redefined as a modified form of 'local' that can work in conjunction with the supra-local forces" (Stromquist and Monkman, 2000: 21). Others have argued that globalisation does not necessarily forebode the demise of traditional cultures, as individual identity is still a matter of individual development and choice (Parmenter, 2001: 240). Diversity management is already an established theme in the business lexicon, managerial ideology and in the leadership development of leaders in Europe – unfortunately evolving in to yet another resource-leverage through which leaders and managers, and its underpinning maximum-extraction managerialism philosophies, can seek to further exploit human potential and the myriad of possibilities that difference offers us. It is an attempt to capture the elementary experience of "self" and "other" in the sphere of managerial control – therefore treating it as yet another problem to be solved, a pathology (Costea and Introna, 2004; Fluker, 2004), an externality that can, and must, be controlled. Unsurprisingly, women, people of colour, Africans, Eastern Europeans, Southern Europeans, Latin Americans, Asians, disabled people, gays and lesbians are all treated as new phenomena, who only recently entered the workplace in the dominant business consciousness. We are suggesting that in this managerialistic paradigm, people are encouraged, to think of "others who are different" through such narrow lenses, and to act upon such deprived constructs in ways that are automatic, superficial, hurtful, destructive and morally questionable. Typically on a societal level, and highlighted by recent events in The Netherlands, Eastern England, and Central Germany, the appearance of human diversity is quickly and easily substituted for the perception of difference, and with it, assumptions are acted upon about how people think, what they value, and how they are likely to behave based solely on the superficial evidence of how they physically appear (Gaudelli, 2001: 64). Organisationally, more often than not, diversity management is reduced to a set of rules and policies, thereby relinquishing individuals of their ethical responsibility for constructively engaging with others. Our personal experience of diversity, though, is that when done right, it is inclusive, it is gloriously mysterious, it is intensely personal, it engenders the suspension of ego and our narcissistic tendencies, it is the basis for attraction to others, it affects our curiosity and learning outlook, it certainly can be a source of tension, it often takes discipline, but *always* enlarges the possibility of what could be. It is therefore, in our view, not a problem to be dealt with, nor is it pathologic and it does not lead to disorganisation (Costea and Introna, 2004) – rather it leads to, and creates the basis for, new forms of organisation, new potential for leveraging the unexplored "network holes" that diversity presents, sets the stage for broader arrays of ideas and information to be assimilated, provides "licence" for the re-negotiation of new forms of identity and civil alignment, and ultimately in organisations it is the root for higher levels of inventiveness.

Leading Europe in transition

Of particular importance to a high-flux Europe, battling with integrative emergence, is the fact that the American management fraternity, trained and developed in context-relevant Business Schools and which is supposed "role models of development and growth", have continued to supply a steady stream of leadership and management ideas and practices to Europe, and it is the unfortunate unquestioning use of these models that more often than not stifles the incentive to critically examine the real needs of individuals, organisations, and the new European society. The uncritical acceptance of socio-cultural, economic, and political realities in a transitioning Europe cannot be assumed to guarantee any anticipated outcome, because the environment, context, history and desired future of the region is fundamentally different. We would also argue that the complexity and amount of social, political, economic and technological challenges that European leaders have to resolve, as a proportion of the value-added resources available to it at any given time period, is a number of factors different to the USA and, as such, quite naturally demands the embracing of tension, difference and "the other" that comes with the need for new paradigms, the need for integration of geographic consciousness with economic consciousness and the need for infusion with immigrants (mind immigrants, work immigrants, value immigrants, geographic immigrants). Instead, unfortunately and quite predictably in times of great flux, we are reminded by the guru to Tony Blair (Leadbetter, 2000) that strong communities can be pockets of intolerance and prejudice. Settled, stable communities are the enemies of innovation, talent, creativity, diversity and experimentation. They are often hostile to outsiders, dissenters, young upstarts and immigrants. "Community" can too quickly become a rallying cry for nostalgia; that kind of community is the enemy of knowledge creation, which is the wellspring of economic growth.

Chomsky (1996: 107) argued that Americans have been ". . . drowned in 'enduring truths' about our altruism and awesome benevolence, and the ingratitude of a hostile world", which has led to the "othering" of people who appear different, particularly those from the developing and underdeveloped world. The United States, though, is not unique in the creation of identity that marginalises, or who sees the "other" as less-than. Our experience is that, instead of constructively using the well established Anglo-Saxon models existent in Europe, as well as Eastern-European models, the Southern-European approaches, African, Middle-Eastern and Far-Eastern, Nordic and native-culture knowledge and insights to help inform the design of divergent, context-relevant and appropriate constructs and frameworks, many leaders in these parts instead uncritically opt to use convergent, American-styled diversity practices to normalise heterogeneity through active, and purposeful, governance and, as Roberts (2002) describes it, "expert suppression of contradiction", e.g., prescribing organisational values, using standard feedback mechanisms, by using standard job grades and categories to manage people's careers, manage their emotions, and the like – imposing "normality" because of a fear of the unpredicatable. In this leader-developed paradigm, people expend their emotional energy, seek to please other people, play out roles, attempt to please management and leadership, protect themselves, seek self-gratification and engage in power struggles (overtly or covertly). There is no real man (Foucault, 1994), only the organisation of power-knowledge that, through dividing practices, makes each of us a subject of varying sorts. Dividing practices refers to the manner in which diverse individuals are drawn into an otherwise undifferentiated mass, based on a particular commonality (Gaudelli, 2001). This practice tends to victimise the person, leave them in states of dependency or disempowerment of being, as their classification is imposed upon them by others. This dependency, according to Riskas (1997), is often indicative of low levels of moral maturity in leaders, organisations and societies.

Psychological literature indicates that individuals, through social comparison (Bearden and Rose, 1990), may differ in their self-concept, self-knowledge, self-perception and self-thought (Craik and Lockhart, 1972; McGuire *et al.*, 1978; Shavitt and Brock, 1984), which will influence their information processing and emotional responses (Markus and Oysermen, 1988; Wang and Mowen, 1997), which ultimately leads to the activation of their categorisation– a subjectification of self, or self-referencing (Debevec and Iyer, 1988; April *et al.*, 2000). What is fascinating for Foucault (1994) is not the ways that humans sort and are sorted, but rather, the ease by which people allow themselves to be categorically determined and impose categorisations upon others. We would add, what is equally fascinating is the way in which leaders help construct milieus that determine people's self-concepts for encouraging and enhancing, rather than critiquing and deconstructing, such categorisation. Jen (1997: 19), an Asian-American writer, in highlighting the limits she faces in dealing with society asserted: "... a person is more than the sum of her social facts". Self-concept affects our intention, and often our moral courage for publicly acting out/on our intention. Depending on social, economic and political milieus, we tend to exhibit selectivity in our self-perception. Subjectification, unlike dividing practice, is less a process of being acted upon and more a matter of acting upon oneself, that is automatically categorical and self-essentialising (Foucault, 1994; Gaudelli, 2001). According to McGuire *et al.* (1978: 512), "Distinctiveness probably affects the self-concept both directly and indirectly: directly, by our noticing our own distinctive features; indirectly, by others perceiving and responding to us in terms of our peculiarities and our adopting others' views of ourselves ... we are conscious of ourselves insofar as we are different and we perceive ourselves in terms of these distinctive features." The process of self-categorisation involves a process aimed at self-understanding, but reliant upon an external authority figure (Rabinow, 1984: 11) – in the Western world, often a leader. The extent to which these constructions of difference impose a hierarchy of power is particularly disturbing to us. Our research has highlighted the fact that if you alter a person's social or economic milieu so that different physical or intentional characteristics becomes distinctive, within a peculiar context of power and knowledge, we can alter that person's self-concept – empowering some, while disempowering others. Like many contructivists, we disagree with the existence of a permanent truth or permanent categorisation, and argue for truth construction in particular temporal, spatial and power contexts. According to Gaudelli (2001), societies always ascribe to a "regime of truth" about the manner in which they are identified, theorised, and utilised. Leaders in the new Europe therefore have a responsibility to make the emerging discourse acceptable, articulate and put in place modes of enquiry to achieve truth, and should be publicly held to account for declaring truth, thereby establishing a regime of truth that is appropriate to, and congruent with the fluidity of the region.

Dualistic complexity

Within Europe, there is a need for leaders to acknowledge the chaordic mix of complicated social histories *and* simple patterns for forging forward, the ever-present hybrid *and* collectivist values, the embedded social dualisation *and* psychological dualisation, the pressures for individual progress *and* community upliftment, and the complex intertwining of politics *and* business that is inherent to this geographical region. Leaders within Europe also need to consider which leadership and management practices and techniques tend to contradict its combination – this is not a place for "or", but rather as old Sufi wisdom teaches us, it is the place for "and". It is our thesis that, even though many leaders and their organisations/institutions voice common sense visions of diversity in their recruitment, talent management and retention practices, ultimately, through sophisticated 360 degree feedback processes, performance reviews, and cultural-intensive acclimatisation practices, they ultimately seek to clone individuals. It is through these sophisticated practices that they continually clarify what is sought in behaviour within the organisation/community, by making explicit what is not acceptable within the organisation/community and by highlighting the consequences/punishment for not performing as the rest of the organisation/community. Often, that punishment is explicitly overt, but it also can take the form of incentives, like bonuses and financial schemes for towing the organisational line, or citizen benefits for towing the community-line. It is this lust for comfort and doing more of the same, in our view, that make old leadership paradigms irrelevant and morally questionable in the 21st century and ultimately threaten the sustainability of organisations/communities and societies, particularly in high-flux transitional societies in the EU.

The rhetoric, slowly being treated as common sense in Europe, informs us that a free, liberated, emancipated subject is desirable ideologically, but common practice informs us that it is to be treated managerially as a source of tension, conflict and problems – the assumption behind this managerialist thought is that inherent, creative, life-giving tensions driving human systems of activity (in terms of identity and self-worth, collaborations, quality relationships, meaningful work, meaningful living, innovations, knowledge creation, learning, development, etc.) are not desirable, and that they are a pathological manifestation of loss of harmony in social systems, or potential symptoms of dysfunctional social organisms (Brown, 1978; Costea and Introna, 2004). The paradoxical question we are left thinking about is: "How can unique individual potential be truly acknowledged, celebrated and developed if it is at the same time seen as a source of deviancy, a source of tension and/or seen as a potential threat to normality and what has always succeeded around here?" This paradoxical position does not seem to deter anyone either working and researching in the leading-of-diversity domain, or writing about the domain. Researchers, and practitioners alike, appear to just carry on doing more of the same – just harder and faster. In many instances, they are particularly uncritical in moving forward, and one hears the common claims for the inability to critique: "Because that is how things have always been done", "That is how other 'best practice' companies and countries do it" or "That is how much we currently understand, given the narrow and limited time span we have to address the issues at hand". The socially constructed space, or "cognitive space" informing identity as Chomsky (1993: 44) would describe it, therefore remains unchallenged, and therefore the uncritical stance is further embedded.

Multicultural diversity, filled with generalisations about the nature of people in certain groups, is increasingly evident in University and Business School curricula, the training ground for many leaders. Fuelled by such training and education, in order to come to terms with the incomprehensible diversity existent in humanity, we begin to readily and naturally categorise – and once we have established categories, we continue to prejudge on the basis of those constructs (Gaudelli, 2001). Many have raised concerns about the manner in which identity is engaged and its implications for various social phenomena. When speaking of human categories, people most often refer to an essentialising of socially recognisable identity categories rather than saying people are human (higher categorisation) or talking about them as individuals (lower categorisation) (Gaudelli, 2001). More often than not, such categories have implicit degrees of membership that suggests "better representatives" and "worse representatives" of the categories. Gaudelli continues by stating that essentialising people according to broad, social categories, often rejects the uncategorisable as those who do not easily fit within the dominant schema. According to Allport (1954), to consider every member of a group as endowed with the same traits, saves us the pains of dealing with them as individuals. Lakoff (1987: 56) examined prototype effects in human categorical thought, and argued that humans tend to think of "best representations" of categories, adding an evaluative dimension to their groupings. Rationalists argue that identity has social significance because people are, in some ways, reducible to some transcendent, essential facts (Wilkin, 1999). These variable, essential facts, be they culture, race, ethnicity and gender, or a combination of these identities, help organise thinking about otherwise incomprehensible diversity in both individuals and groups, as they change in time. Hirschfeld (1996) reminds us that that there is an innate grasp of these essential facts from an early age, and dominant rationalist motives, fuelled by biological predisposition and bounded reasoning, through schooling, development of leaders and scripting of social forms of organisation rob us of, or banish to our subconscious, such grasp. Rationalist tendencies, according to Wilkin (1999), to universalise human cognition and totalise the individual have been critiqued, particularly by constructivists, who claim they essentialise humanity in a probabilistic and predictive manner that undermines human agency, and humans' limitless capacity for self-invention. Hobsbawm (1996: 1067) wrote "The concept of a single, exclusive, and unchanging ethnic or cultural or other identity is a dangerous piece of brainwashing. Human mental identities are not like shoes, of which we can only wear one pair at a time". There has, and still is, an unease and tyrannical silence, and often unwillingness, by current European leaders to improve conversations that could help us unearth the cognitive tapes (Cialdini, 1988; Lackoff, 1987) and the very presuppositions, more often than not racist presuppositions (Hirschfeld, 1996), that lie beneath the public and private discourse, to shift from categorical thinking and critically deconstruct our models-of-practice. Cialdini (1988) identified some basic social psychological cognitive tapes that are culturally imbued and readily reverted to when information becomes too vast and complex. Hirschfeld (1996: 4) claims that race, for example, is commonly encountered in contemporary discourse as a human categorisation that "encompasses beliefs about inner nature as well as outward appearance". Davidson (1996: 3), critiquing extant identity discourse, argued "Taken to an extreme . . . [racial identity] implies that the meanings, behaviours, and perceptions associated with a specific background are relatively fixed, exerting a constant influence [on an individual]". According to Gaudelli (2001), what separates rationalists from behaviourists in this regard is that while people are inclined to act in a certain way (i.e., to automatically cluster other people on the basis of superficial information), they are not driven to do it. Agreement about which presuppositions are valid is not necessary, as both modes of thinking have value. The answer lies not in having one side "win" the identity debate, but in raising the dimensionality of it within pubic discourse and heightening the awareness of leaders, scholars of leadership and practitioners to confront the ambiguous, make explicit their incongruous assumptions and consider their fundamental beliefs regarding the construction of "identity towards marginalisation", and its relation to power in particular, as they account for identity in their personal, work and societal lives.

There is often an avoidance of tension and a lack of awareness and deep insight into the fact that an "equalisation" will ultimately benefit everyone, of every persuasion toward Giddens (1991) 'democracy of identity'. It does require, though, that we all, and particularly our leaders, have to come clean and acknowledge the ways in which many have been damaged in the past, and unbelievably, still in the present, many have been affirmed in the past and still enjoy the benefits of that affirmation, many were afforded benefits, mainly social and economic, that still persists today and will take a very long time to "equalise". The downside risk is that if nothing actionable is done, we may just end up with social breakdown, possibly modern revolution, where the economically marginalised majority will forcibly take strides towards equalisation. Part of the problem in South Africa, of course, is that because of the country's 300 year history of oppression, it quite naturally and correctly has to focus its efforts on the previously marginalised – and so the more encompassing conversation of "inclusion" (which is both a strategic one, but which more overtly and explicitly benefits all) is postponed for post-2008 – it does not have to be this way, but unfortunately that is also how most companies and countries around the world tend to treat the issue. Similarly in the Baltics, where the influx of East German, Polish and Spanish nationals, for instance, are adding to the already complicated integrative process of EU membership, European countries, in addition, also face tension-filled diversity issues in the broader sense – people from China, Turkey, the DRC, Morocco, Zimbabwe, Ghana, Nigeria, Cameroon, Egypt, Saudi Arabia, Iran, etc., are treated as "problems" or "potential problems". Being focused on minimum, legalistic standards, many organisations/institutions have not even begun to strategise more broadly about an all-encompassing diversity agenda – and so comments such as "we're currently focusing on the issues of equality as far as natural Europeans are concerned" is what a lot of foreign nationals and immigrants are experiencing in their discussions with corporate EU.

Management ideologies, predicated upon a total abhorrence of tension is not new – it forms the basis for much of mainstream management theory, the continued, unfettered reaction against tension. If tension is undesirable, then it must follow that diversity, too, is also undesirable, and the continued dividing of the world is therefore desirable and acceptable. Willinsky (1998: 259), in examining sources of learning, highlighted the fact that the tendency to "other" is a product of a hierarchical Western education, particularly management education, that implicitly, and even explicitly, rank-orders historical and contemporary peoples. He argued that "What needs to be made clear is that, as the schools have contributed to racialised identities, so they need to be engaged in study of their own historical construction". It would appear that one of the roots of our leaders' unwillingness to make responsible, moral choices with regards to diversity is in the formal schooling they receive – and, even though limited, it may be a useful place to start the inquiry and deconstruction process, so as to help them understand what such divisive learning has created, continues to create, and what thinking in efficient categories have come to mean. We need to remind them that the enduring impact of their choices, purposeful or otherwise, or lack of choices, purposeful or otherwise, is not what they eventually get in return, but essentially what they get in return is who they become as people, and so we should seek to mentor, coach and help them to build moral courage before they need to practice it in the world-of-consequences, which has market demands.

Deconstructing instrumental reason

It is the supremacy of instrumental reason and what it entails in the loss of recognition of the intrinsic value of the human being which has produced the greatest split in contemporary Western society (Ruiz and Mínguez, 2001). Public, business and civil society leaders are all under apparent pressure to resonate to market demands, with a seemingly powerlessness to some external force that can not, or more correctly, should not be questioned. Costea (2000: 5) argues: ". . . as a self, the human learns, develops, acts, has agency; it changes its self and the world around it. This is the horizon of everyday practices as they are in the real world of leadership, management and organisations. The reduction of this horizon to functional-economic models leads to the abandonment of the very reality these models purport to represent". Individuals and peoples have unfortunately seen themselves stripped of their identity, being objectified in favour of the market, and ultimately an accompanying loss of the genuine and open anthropological sense that quite naturally exists in human relationships of difference. Instrumental reason has become for modern human beings the overriding, if not the only, principle which determines, justifies and insists on stable and predictable social, political and economic relationships (Ortega Ruiz and Mínguez, 2001). It is our experience, though, that the sense of a difference between "self" and the "other" is a dynamic/temporal phenomenon, and cannot be stabilised in formal, rational and linear categories. Many have raised concerns about the manner in which identity is engaged and its implications for various social phenomena. Identity has been criticised as being essentialised (Allport, 1954, 1979; Appiah, 1992), engaged in a manner that is automatically categorical (Cialdini, 1988; Hirschfeld, 1996) while lacking recognition of the power-knowledge dynamic (Black, 2001; Carneiro da Cunha, 1992; Fiereman, 1990). Identity has also been used to divide and marginalise (Ogbu, 1998; Willinsky, 1998), subsume the individual in a totalising manner (Davidson, 1996; Jen, 1997) and been used to foster an unhealthy individualism (Taylor 1991). Humans are existentially competent, dynamic and complex from birth (Brown, 1978; Costea and Introna, 2004; Stacey, 2004) – and, in relationships, we continually and dynamically negotiate and renegotiate our multiple identities, by confirming and unconfirming self-views (not through self-categorisation, as many "cultural-theorists" would like us to believe). This dynamic process of identity evolution is always defined in dialogue (April, 1999) with, and often in struggle against, the identities of our significant others, e.g., our parents and family, our bosses and organisational leaders, our peers, our community leaders, and so on, want to recognise in us, and that which we would like them to recognise in us (commonly referred to as potential, and we would like to term "potentialitic identity"). According to Taylor (1991), even when we outgrow some of the significant other-defined dimensions of identity (Mead, 1934), like our parents and others who matter to us, and they disappear from our lives, or when we move from geographically-engendered norms, the inner, dialogical conversation (Bakhtin, 1984; Holquist and Clark, 1984; Wertsch, 1991) with them continues within us as long as we live. Classical cultural theorists have attempted, often in unconscious orientation, to use this inner dialogicality as bases for dealing with people through purely culturally defined categories, through shutting out the greater concerns that transcend the self, developing homogenising, narrowing, theories of practice premised on the belief that language, art, gesture, identity, love, relationships and the like are culturally bound and are fairly static throughout an individual's life. According to Gaudelli (2001: 65), "When the incomprehensible diversity of individuals is subsumed under broader cultural headings, the streams of discourse are submerged into what appears to be a broad, homogenous river of culture that is, in metaphorical terms, an intricately constructed levy and dam system created by those who stand to benefit from its operation." In many ways, these cultural categories have replaced the medieval notion of social roles from which it was unthinkable to deviate, even though in modern life their potentialitic identities are no longer sacrificed to the demands of supposedly sacred orders that transcend them and are passed down by anointed leaders – however, the boundedness of such categorisation has not changed, and its commoditised, instrumental significance as well as the heroic nature of leaders who alone have futuristic insights/vision persist even today. In contrast, our research has shown that, in the realities of practice, boundaries between one's "self" and "other selves" are open and expectant; we are often realising their fluidity by realising how feelings of familiarity and unfamiliarity with concrete people, real people, dynamic people we live and have our being with, change in time – the aporetic character (Costea and Introna, 2004) of this dynamism always being mysterious possibilities, resonance, richness and depth in our human interactions and surroundings, and only ever mitigated by notions of power between our selves and other selves. Our identities, shaped by the actions we take as a result of our psychological, cognitive and emotional intent, the roots of our true diversity, are tied in to notions of power, through purposeful alignment with in-groups and out-groups (thereby expanding or shrinking our self-esteem, self-worth and self-confidence).

Patterns of power

Diversity management cannot be, as we commonly find in organisational life, subjucated to mere training programmes that superficially deal with multi-culturalism only, being justified solely for instrumental reasons, and serves to further enhance the continued soft despotism of the embedded managerial dominance over every aspect of people's lives, including civility and morality. It is our considered opinion that we should pay more attention to patterns of power, and the conscious-created contexts within which we find ourselves and our organisations, because power is central to our interaction with each other – and power emerges from the interactions of people. Power is not a thing that some have more of, and some have less of – power is simply just a constraint ("I constrain you, and you constrain me") and also is not equally distributed. Power both enables and mutually constrains (Stacey, 2004). People continuously and unconsciously sustain certain patterns of power relations. It is our observation that power, almost always, is dependent on *needs* (power is a pattern of relating that shifts, depending on how much we need each other) and *intent* (power is given and taken from others, manifesting in in-groups and out-groups, in congruence with our current, and future, intent) (Hogg, 2001). As a result of the mitigating effect of intent on our power, power therefore does not always apply only to individuals; it also affects groupings (an inevitable, conscious or perceived pattern of inclusion and exclusion), and it is those patterns of inclusion and exclusion that give us our very identities. We fear, like some in new Europe, that leaders will gain power by expanding their ethnic base, or dominant culture (perhaps even the culture that best represents America as a role model), and thereby perpetuate the primacy of ethnic identities. Some civil society activists argue that what at first sight appears to be concerned with the maintenance of culture and tradition, is in fact propelled and concerned with unequal distribution of power. Some countries in modern Europe require immigrants and foreign nationals to learn their language, their cultures and their ways of doing things. Ask people who they are, and they inevitably begin explaining which groups they belong to (Stacey, 2004), feel they have to belong to, and want to belong to. The need to maintain an identity base to assert one's power is not unique to plural democracies in the West, but also in places like Africa (Carneiro da Cunha, 1992: 289) and Asia (Hendricks and Huang, 2004). "I" and "we" groups can not be separated out – so we become very passionate about the groupings that we consciously and unconsciously belong to and do not belong to, or groupings that other people, correctly or incorrectly, ascribe to us. These grouping are usually sustained through ideology (norms and values), and ideologies make it feel more natural to operate in certain patterns of power (Stacey, 2004). If we truly want to live in a different world, we must start by being critical about our mental models, become aware, operate authentically, understand our interdependence, engage with others in meaningful ways, and get real about the state we are in. We must get to grips with the repressed historical complexes that have been driving us to collective schizophrenia, and we must consider the need for [collective] cultural psychotherapies (McIntosh, 2002). Fiereman (1990) encountered many instances where individuals' actions contradicted their moral beliefs, as explained in their exegesis of their "culture". Power is often gained by the construction of groups (e.g., "cultures") where previously the discourse to name a group as such did not exist. Organisations need to recover their repressed histories, understand how and why "its being" have been constructed and distorted (in some instances), and notice how it has shaped our organisational ideologies and behaviours. But it is not just a matter of changing the outlook of individuals (hearts and minds), nor is it just a matter of changing organisational understanding (path dependencies and processes), but change, in this domain, will have to be institutional (societies, laws and structures) as well, that requires purposeful action, continual, explicit focus and sustained effort on the part of leaders. Individual citizens also cannot just stay home, enjoy the benefits of societal progress, enjoy the satisfactions of private life, as long as their paternalistic governments and organisational leaders produce the means for these satisfactions and ensure that they are beneficiaries of such "leadership", and therefore contently live disengaged and semi-conscious lives. This, as de Tocqueville (1981: 385) warns, opens the danger of soft despotism in which everything will be run by an "immense tutelary power", a group who constitute the dominant categorisation.

Leadership responsibility

It is therefore our contention that power patterns, shaped by ideology, is what European leaders should focus their attention on, if they stand any chance of disengaging from the dominant American meta-paradigm – to move from "understanding to control" (e.g., the narrow efforts of culture) to "understanding to allow tension, unpredictability and possibility". We would like to debunk and/or question the uncritical, single-minded focus on culture by leaders and their initiated diversity management practitioners. Our observation is that culture is merely one strand of the multiple dimensions that make up individual identities, and thus the multiple identities existent within organisations, institutions and societies. And so we would much rather encourage effort and critical practice in the area of individual identity, work, power, society, context and actioned intent, in moving forward the diversity management agenda. It is, in fact, our rich and varied identities as human beings, and the multitude of ways in which we actually differ (whether that be in gender, socio-economic background, ways of thinking, sexual orientation, life experiences, tenure in organisations, beliefs, ethnicity, ability and disability, religion, values, upbringing, schooling and education, propensity for uncertainty and ambiguity, functional and technical specialisation, heritage, talents, family status, and perspectives) that will allow for the emergence of the required multivariate response in a changing Europe. By prefacing our thinking about diversity through the lenses we have presented above, we can get to a fuller comprehension of the multi-faceted human condition, of which we all are partakers. And, it is our considered belief, that when private organisations can maximise the coalescence of the rich dimensions of diversity mentioned above, they will reap the benefits from sustainable competitive advantage they all long for, and lay the foundations for a sustainable Europe.

Conclusion

Humans are fundamentally hermeneutic creatures, seeking to understand the three fundamental terms of its condition: (1) world (context and meaning) – and the moral prerogative, for leaders, for setting the bases for such meaning for individuals are increasing; (2) finitude (possibility) – and the moral responsibility of leaders to critically deconstruct the reasons, need and continuance of rampant instrumental reason; and (3) individuation (wholeness) – and the purposeful moral choices by leaders to continuously safeguard individuals against the loss of freedom. In many ways, modernity has obscured for us the moral choices to be made. There are many reasons for leaders to continue forward paradigmatically locked in pathways of efficiency and expediency. In summary, individuals seek to critically reflect on the world, and want to be reflected meaningfully and favourably by it – and therein lie the ethical challenge for incumbent and emerging leaders in Europe to demonstrate responsible leadership – as the starting intent, not the guise of humanness post-instrumentality. Through meaningful, critical practice, extended-language, and expanding the metacognitive awareness of individuals, leaders can assist individuals to sense-make their relationships with other people, other perspectives, other practices, other institutions, other landscapes – and the by-product will be a more engaged Europe, that ultimately impacts the sustainability of this exciting region.

References

Allport, G. W. (1954), *The Nature of Prejudice*, Reading, MA: Addison-Wesley.

Allport, G. (1979), *The Nature of Prejudice*, Reading, MA: Addison-Wesley.

Appiah, K. A. (1992), *In My Father's House: Africa in the Philosophy of Culture*, New York: Oxford University Press.

April, K. (1999), "Leading Through Communication, Conversation and Dialogue", *Leadership & Organizational Development Journal*, Vol. 20, No. 5, pp. 231–241.

April, K., Macdonald, R. and Vriesendorp, S. (2000), *Rethinking Leadership*, Kenwyn: Juta Academic Publishers.

Bakhtin, M. M. (1984), *Problems of Dostoyevsky's Poetics*, Minneapolis: University of Minnesota Press.

Bearden, W. O. and Rose, R. L. (1990), "Attention to Social Comparison Information: An Individual Difference Factor Affecting Consumer Conformity", *Journal of Consumer Research*, Vol. 16, pp. 461–471.

Black, L. (2001), "The Predicament of Identity", *Ethnohistory*, Vol. 48, No. 1–2, pp. 337–350.

Brown, R. H. (1978), "Bureaucracy as Praxis: Toward a Political Phenomenology of Formal Organizations", *Administrative Science Quarterly*, Vol. 23, No. 3, pp. 365–382.

Carneiro da Cunha, M. (1992), "Custom is Not a Thing, It is a Path: Reflections on the Brazilian Indian Case", in A. A. An-Na'im (Ed.), *Human Rights in Cross-Cultural Perspectives: A Quest for Consensus*, Philadelphia: University of Pennsylvania Press.

Chomsky, N. (1993), *Language and Thought*, Wakefield, RI: Moyer Bell.

Chomsky, N. (1996), *Power and Prospects: Reflections on Human Nature and the Social Order*, Boston, MA: South End Press.

Cialdini, R. B. (1988), *Influence: Science and Practice*, New York: Scott, Foresman and Company.

Costea, B. (2000), *Existence Philosophy and the Work of Martin Heidegger: Human Diversity as Ontological Problem (Related to Mainstream Management Education)* (Working Paper 2000/034, Lancaster University Management School, UK, pp. 1–55).

Costea, B. and Introna, L. (2004), *Self and Other in Everyday Existence: A Mystery Not a Problem* (Working Paper 2004/020, Lancaster University Management School, UK, pp. 1–24).

Craik, F. I. M. and Lockhart, R. S. (1972), "Levels of Processing: A Framework for Memory Research", *Journal of Experimental Psychology*, Vol. 104, pp. 268–294.

Davidson, A. L. (1996), *Making and Holding Identity in Schools*, Albany, NY: SUNY Press.

Debevec, K. and Iyer, E. (1988), "Self-Referencing as a Mediator of the Effectiveness of Sex-Role Portrayals in Advertising", *Psychology and Marketing*, Vol. 5, pp. 71–84.

de Tocqueville, A.(1981), *De la Démocratie en Amérique*, Vol. 2, Paris: Garnier-Flammarion.

Durkheim, E. (1915), *The Elementary Forms of the Religious Life* (Trans. Joseph Ward Swain), New York: Macmillan.

Durkheim, E. (1938), *The Rules of Sociological Method* (Trans. Sarah A. Solovay and John H. Mueller; George E. G. Catlin, Ed.), New York: Free Press.

Fiereman, S. (1990), *Peasant Intellectuals: Anthropology and History in Tanzania*, Madison, WI: University of Wisconsin Press.

Foucalt, M. (1994), *The Birth of the Clinic: An Archaeology of Medical Perception* (A. M. Shridan Smith, Trans.), New York: Vintage Books (original work published in 1973).

Fluker, W. E. (2004), *Self & The Other* (Personal Conversations, Authenticity Through Ethical Leadership Practices Executive Course, Graduate School of Business, University of Cape Town, August 2004).

Gaudelli, W. (2001), "Identity Discourse: Problems, Presuppositions, and Educational Practice", *International Journal of Sociology and Social Policy*, Vol. 21, No. 3, pp. 60–81.

Giddens, A. (1991), *Modernity and Self-Identity: Self and Society in the Late Modern Age*, Cambridge, MA: Polity Press.

Hendricks, B. and Huang, W. (2004), "The Waking Dragon", *Journal for Convergence*, Vol. 5, No. 3, pp. 63–67.

Hirschfeld, L. A. (1996), *Race in the Making*, Cambridge, MA: MIT Press.

Hobsbawm, E. (1996), "Language, Culture and National Identity", *Social Research*, Vol. 63, No. 4, pp. 1065–1080.

Hogg, M. A. (2001), "A Social Identity Theory of Leadership", *Personality and Social Psychology Review*, Vol. 5, No. 3, pp. 184–200.

Holquist, M. and Clark, K. (1984), *Michail Bakhtin*, Cambridge, MA: Harvard University Press.

Jen, G. (1997), "Who's To Judge?", *The New Republic*, Vol. 216, pp. 18–19.

Jones, M. L. (1989), "Management Development: An African Focus", *International Studies of Management and Organisation*, Vol. 19, No. 1, pp. 74–90.

King, J. E. (2000), "Race", in D. A. Gabbard (Ed.), *Knowledge and Power in the Global Economy: Politics and the Rhetoric of School Reform*, Mahwah, NJ: Erlbaum Associates, pp. 141–149.

Lackoff, G. (1987), *Women, Fire, and Dangerous Things: What Categories Reveal About the Mind*, Chicago: University of Chicago Press.

Leadbetter, Charles (2000) *Living on Thin Air*, London: Penguin.

Markus, H. and Oysermen, D. (1988), "Gender and Thought: The Role of the Self-Concept", in M. Crawford and M. Hamilton (Eds.), *Gender and Thought: Psychological Perspectives*, New York: Springer, pp. 100–127.

Marx, K. (1967), *Writing of the Young Marx on Philosophy and Society* (Trans. Lloyd D. Easton and Kurt H. Guddat, and Eds.), Garden City, NY: Doubleday.

McGuire, W. J., McGuire, C. V., Child, P. and Fujioka, T. (1978), "Salience of Ethnicity in the Spontaneous Self-Concept as a Function of One's Ethnic Distinctiveness in the Social Environment", *Journal of Personality and Social Psychology*, Vol. 36, No. 5, pp. 511–520.

McIntosh, A. (2002), *Europe, Globalization and Sustainable Development* (Keynote Address at the Europe, Globalization and Sustainable Development International Conference, Department of Politics, University of Dundee, 19th–21st September 2002).

Mead, G. H. (1934), *Mind, Self and Society*, Chicago: Chicago University Press.

Merkle, J. A. (1980), *Management and Ideology: The Legacy of the International Scientific Management Movement*, Berkeley, CA: University of California Press.

Merton, R. K. (1957), *Social Theory and Social Structure*, New York: Free Press.

Ogbu, J. U. (1998), "Voluntary and Involuntary Minorities: A Cultural-Ecological Theory of School Performance with Some Implications for Education", *Anthropology and Education*, Vol. 29, No. 2, pp. 155–188.

Ortega Ruiz, P. and Mínguez, R. (2001), "Global Inequality and the Need for Compassion: Issues in Moral and Political Education," *Journal of Moral Education*, Vol. 30, No. 2, pp. 155–177.

Parmenter, L. (2001), Internationalization in Japanese Education, in N. P. Stromquist and K. Monkman (Eds.), *Globalization and Education: Integration and Contestation Across Cultures*, Lanham, MD: Rowan & Littlefield Publishers, pp. 237–254.

Parsons, T. (1951), *The Social System*, New York: Free Press.

Rabinow, P. (Ed., 1984), *Foucault Reader*, New York, Pantheon Books.

Riskas, T. (1997), *Working Beneath The Surface*, Provo, UT: Executive Excellence Publishing.

Roberts, R. (2002), *Religion, Theology and the Human Sciences*, Cambridge: Cambridge University Press.

Ruiz, P. and Minguez, R. (2001), "Global Inequality and the Need for Compassion: Issues in Moral and Political Education," *Journal of Moral Education*, Vol. 30, No. 2, pp. 155–172.

Shavitt, S. and Brock, T. C. (1984), "Self-Relevant Responses in Commercial Persuasion", in K. Sentis and J. Olson (Eds.), *Advertising and Consumer Psychology*, New York: Praeger.

Stacey, R. (2004), *Power & Relationships* (Lecture, Oxford Strategic Leadership Programme, Templeton College, Oxford University, November 2004).

Stromquist, N. P. and Monkman, K. (2000), "Defining Globalization and Assessing its Implications on Knowledge and Education", in N. P. Stromquist and K. Monkman (Eds.), *Globalization and Education: Integration and Contestation Across Cultures*, Lanham, MD: Rowan & Littlefield Publishers, pp. 3–26.

Taylor, C. (1991), *The Ethics of Authenticity*, Cambridge, MA: Harvard University Press.

Walzer, M. (1997), *On Toleration*, New Haven: Yale University Press.

Wang, C. L. and Mowen, J. C. (1997), "The Separateness-Connectedness Self-Schema: Scale Development and Application to Message Construction", *Psychology & Marketing*, Vol. 14, No. 2, pp. 185–207.

Weber, M. (1957), *The Theory of Social and Economic Organization* (Trans. A. M. Henderson and Talcott Parsons; Talcott Parsons, Ed.), New York: Free Press.

Wertsch, J. (1991), *Voices of the Mind*, Cambridge, MA: Harvard University Press.

Wilkin, P. (1999), "Chomsky and Foucault on Human Nature and Politics: An Essential Difference?", *Social Theory and Practice*, Vol. 25, No. 2, pp. 177–210.

Willinsky, J. (1998), *Learning to Divide the World: Education at Empire's End*, Minneapolis, MN: University of Minnesota Press.

18
Spirit of African Leadership: A Comparative African Perspective

by Lovemore Mbigi

Introduction

We are all products of our culture. We can only see what our cultural paradigms allow us to see. Therefore, all managers and employees only see what their cultural paradigms in their organizations allow them to see. The clay material of management is subjectivity. Management is emotional, social, spiritual, political and rational. Therefore, any approach to study management should reflect this complexity and diversity. The current Cartesian scientific paradigm may be necessary, but not sufficient, in understanding management – it only addresses the rational element of management. Ultimately, the challenge of management is to move from being a science of manipulation, to also being a science of understanding. The discipline of management is culturally biased because it is about the issues of how we organize people, and how we manage the work they do. Hence, the management discipline should encompass the great "theory of being".

It is important to explore the role of cultural paradigms in organizational leadership. We are all products of our cultures. Hampden-Turner and Trompenaars (1993) in their book *The Seven Cultures of Capitalism* argue that we can only see what our cultural paradigms allow us to see. Therefore, all leaders and employees can only see what our cultural lenses allow them to see in organizations. This has serious implications on leadership theories and practices. The national host culture determines how the challenge of leadership in organizations is approached. Kuhn (1996) in his book *The Structure of Scientific Revolutions* defines a "paradigm" as accepted examples of actual scientific practice (examples which include, together: law, application and theory, as well as instrumentation). He claims that particular coherent traditions of scientific research emanate from such paradigmatic models, and that people who are committed to the same rules and standards for scientific practice ultimately share paradigms.

His observation of creative thought leaders in the scientific fields was people who understood the prevailing scientific paradigm in their field, and had the courage to think and explore the frontiers beyond it. Organizational leaders should not only be able to understand the culture of the host country in which their organization is operating, but must also have the personal courage to think outside it. At the risk of over-simplifying and over-generalizing, the influence of the four cultures of the four corners of the globe will be examined. It is important to note that every culture has its competencies, strengths and weaknesses. The essence of leadership excellence is the ability to leverage the host African culture and then harness complementary competencies of the distinct global cultures of the four corners of the globe.

Overview of the global cultural diversity for leadership excellence

European North cultural paradigm

Let us start by examining the cultural worldview of the European North and its strategic implications for leadership, theory and practice. The cultural worldview of the North is "I am because I think I am". There is an emphasis on rational and scientific thinking. European leaders have harnessed this competency in planning, as well as scientific and technical innovation. In fact, the stunning achievements of European leadership and civilization have been due to scientific and technological innovations, as well as rational planning techniques. Between 1500 and 1700 there was a dramatic shift in the way people pictured the world and in the whole way of thinking in Europe. The new scientific mentality and the new perception of the cosmos gave our European civilization the features that are characteristic of the modern era. They became the basis of the paradigm that has dominated European culture for the past 300 years (Capra, 1982). Rene Descartes is usually regarded as the founder of the modern scientific paradigm. The belief in the certainty of scientific knowledge lies at the very basis of the Cartesian philosophy and of the worldview derived from it. The Cartesian belief in scientific truth is reflected in the scientism that has become typical of the Western culture. Thus, Descartes (Cottingham, 1996) arrived at his most celebrated statement "Cogito, ergo sum – I think therefore I exist". The European cultural paradigm can assist leaders to plan and create a memory of the future.

Eastern Asian cultural paradigm

The Eastern Asian cultural paradigm is characterized by an emphasis on continuous improvement to attain perfection. In fact, most Asian religions emphasize a pilgrimage into inner perfection. From these religions techniques of personal development and perfection have developed, such as yoga from Hinduism and meditation form Buddhism. The Eastern worldview can be summarized as "I am because I improve". According to the Japanese leadership expert Masaaki Imai: "If you learn only one word of Japanese make it Kaizen. Kaizen strategy so the single most important concept in Japanese management – the key to Japanese competitive success. Kaizen means improvement. Kaizen means ongoing improvement involving everyone: top management, managers and workers". It means much more than that. It means a philosophy that encourages every person in an industry – every day – to make suggestions for improving everything; themselves, their job, their workplace, their factory layout, their telephone answering habits, their products and their services. The giant Japanese electronic company Matsushita receives some 6.5 million ideas from its employees every year. The cultural business strategy of Kaizen inspired the successful Japanese economic revolution because this cultural competency allowed the Japanese to harness mature manufacturing technologies through innovation and team structures such as quality circles. This gave birth to a worldwide revolution in quality through the participatory leadership best practices of Total Quality Management (TQM) and Total Productive Maintenance (TPM).

Western American cultural worldview

America is a young, successful and dominant civilization. Since it is an adolescent civilization, it believes in what Reich (2002) has called the "myth of the individual hero". The Western American worldview puts emphasis on the individual lone hero who, through his or her individual nobility, independence, courage and conviction, saves organizations and communities from their fate. This cultural worldview can be stated as: "I am because I, the individual hero, dream and do". More specifically, this cultural paradigm translates into: "Concentrate on your self-interest and you will automatically serve your customer and society better, which in turn will let you serve your self-interest". The classic representative theorist of the Western American paradigm is Adam Smith whose main thesis is that collective social goals are a by-product of self-interest. Therefore, if each individual pursues their own selfish personal interest, invisibly this will automatically serve the common interests of the larger society. Smith (1991) published his book *The Wealth of Nations* which became a manifesto of American enterprise. Smith (1991) summarized the heart and soul of the Western American cultural paradigm as follows:

> It is not from the benevolence of the butcher, the brewer or the baker, that we expect our dinner, but from their regard for their own interest. [This individual] . . . intends only his own gain, and he is in this, as in many other cases, led by an invisible hand to promote an end which was no part of his intention. Nor is it always the worse for society that it was no part of it. By pursuing his own interest, he frequently promotes that of society more effectually than when he really intends to promote it. I have never known much good done by those who affected to trade in the public good. It is an affection indeed not very common among merchants and very few words need be employed in dissuading them from it.

Another feature of this paradigm is the guts to dream, and the personal courage to put them into action. This cultural paradigm has a visionary enterprising trait which has inspired American economic development and created the largest and most competitive economy in human history. It takes substantial courage and a capacity to dream big and to think of inhibiting other planets in the manner Americans have done and demonstrated.

African cultural paradigm of the South

The African worldview is characterized by a deliberate emphasis on people and their dignity – the emphasis on the collective brotherhood of mankind called Ubuntu, which is the African perspective of collective personhood derived from *muntu* or *munhu*. Ubuntu literally translated means *"I am because we are; I can only be a person through others"*. There is deliberate emphasis on solidarity and interdependence which is a key characteristic of African communities of affinity. The Archbishop Right Reverend Desmond Tutu puts it more clearly:

> Africans have a thing called UBUNTU; it is about the essence of being human, it is part of the gift that Africa is going to give to the world. It embraces hospitality, caring about others, being willing to go that extra mile for the sake of another. We believe that a person is a person through other persons; that my humanity is caught up and bound up in yours. When I dehumanize you, I inexorably dehumanize myself. The solitary human being is a contradiction in terms, and therefore you seek to work for the common good because your humanity comes into its own in community, in belonging.

The key values of African leadership are listed in Figure 18.1 (values from other regions are discussed extensively in Ambassador Kochar's chapter in this book, Geo-Political Diversity, which does not include Africa):

- Ensuring one's security, and the security of others.
- Respect for the dignity of others, and helping then grow into confident people.
- Group solidarity: an injury to one is an injury to all.
- Making your life, and others' lives, count.
- Teamwork: none of us is greater than all of us, and relationships are key.
- Service to others in the spirit of harmony.
- Interdependence: each one of us needs all of us.
- Collaborative meaning and sense-making.

Handy (1997), the British guru on management echoes the same sentiments on collective personhood when he wrote:

> We have to find a personal security in our relationship too. We are not meant to stand alone. We need a sense of connection. We have to feel that

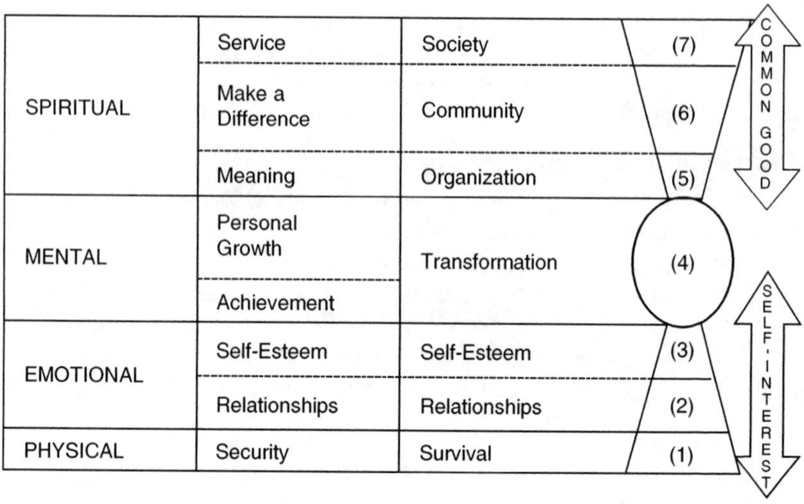

Figure 18.1 The Shift from Self-Interest to Service
Source: Author, and drawing from Greenleaf (in Frick and Spears, 1996) and Barrett (1998)

> it matters to other people that we are there. Because if it makes no difference whether you are there or not then you really begin to feel like a meaningless person. If you have no connection to anybody, you have no responsibility and therefore no purpose.

African cultures stand Adam Smith's premise on its head. In terms of the African cultural paradigm, is the needs of the group or community are considered first, and then the invisible hand will automatically take care of the desires of the individual. Serve your society and stakeholders to the best of your ability and you will automatically achieve your own personal goals, which will allow you to align them with the needs of your relevant stakeholders, including customers. It therefore follows that the African leadership paradigm has a bias towards servant leadership. The practices of the African paradigm of leadership are best articulated by Robert Greenleaf (in Frick and Spears, 1996). These best practices are:

- *Listening:* The servant leader seeks to identify and clarify the will of the group. They seek to listen respectfully to what is being said. Listening also encompasses:
  - Getting in touch with one's inner voice.
  - Seeking to understand what one's body, spirit and mind are communicating.

  Listening with regular periods of reflection is essential to the growth of the servant leader.

- *Empathy*: The servant leader strives to understand and empathize with others. People need to be accepted and recognized for their special and unique spirit. The most successful servant leaders are those who have become skilled empathetic leaders.
- *Persuasion*: Persuasion is the clearest distinctions between the conventional authoritarian leadership style and that of servant leadership. The servant leader is effective at building consensus within groups. The emphasis on persuasion rather than consensus is the heart and soul of African leadership because it is embedded in the ancient African philosophy of Ubuntu. According to President Nelson Mandela (1994):

  Our people lived peacefully, under the democratic rule of their kings . . . Then the country was ours in name and right . . . All men were free and equal, this was the foundation of government. The council of elders was so completely democratic that all members of the tribe could participate in its deliberations. Chief and subject, warrior and medicine man, all took part and endeavoured to influence decisions.

According to Ayittey (1997), African societies have, for centuries, enjoyed a tradition of participatory democracy. The organizational structure of indigenous African systems was generally based on kingship and ancestry. Survival of the tribe was the primary objective. Each ethnic group had its own system of government. These were unwritten constitutions like the constitution of Britain. Customs and traditions established the governance procedures. All African political governance systems in both chiefdoms and kingdoms started at village level comprised of extended families and lineages. Each village had its head chosen according to established rules with checks and balances. The chief was assisted by a small group of confidential advisors drawn from close friends and relatives called the inner council. If he disagreed with them, he would take the issue to the council of elders, a much wider and more formal structure consisting of hereditary headmen of lineages or wards. Their main function was not only to advise the chief but also to prevent the abuse of power by voicing their dissatisfaction and by criticizing the chief. The chief would inform the council of the subject matter to be dealt with. The matter would be debated until a decision was reached by consensus. The chief would remain silent and listen as the councillors debated the issues. He would weigh all viewpoints to avoid imposing his view on the council. The chief did not impose his rule – he only led and assessed the collective opinions of the council. The people were the ultimate judge on disputed issues. If the council failed to reach consensus, the issue would be taken to the assembly for debate by the people. Every person was free to speak and ask questions. Deliberations continued until consensus was reached. Minority positions are heard and taken into account. In a majority rule process minority positions are ignored. The hallmark of African leadership traditions and practices is consensus democracy in order to accommodate minority positions to ensure the greatest possible level of justice and avoid sabotage during implementation process. Compromise, persuasion, discussion and accommodation, listening and freedom of speech are the key elements of the African leadership paradigm. Consensus is difficult to reach on many issues. African political, social and economic leadership tradition is noted for the length of time required to reach consensus and it may take weeks to attain unity of purpose.

Consensus, by its very nature, is the antithesis of autocracy. The problem with the Western American cultural leadership paradigm with its emphasis on individualism, is that it scorns its own origins in the supportive community. The dauntless entrepreneur is a self-made man. According to Hampden-Turner and Trompenaars (1993), these reasons may be good political arguments for keeping the money one has accumulated but, in reality, it is a very dubious claim and one that does not fully acknowledge the many who nurture and shape the individual. The view of the African paradigm is that the nurturant community is the cradle of the individual. Therefore it follows that many changes could be made to transform organizations by shaping them as enterprising communities that could increase rather than decrease the individuality of each member. To focus on individuals only, is to miss all the social and collective arrangements that can be altered to enhance the contribution of the individuals. In African cultures team rewards take precedence over individual rewards; the team is likely to support and reward with their friendship and respect the higher performers and the innovative individuals within the group. If the bonus is paid to individual high performers, or individuals identified as more creative, the group is more likely to gang up on those whom they think are most favoured by management, sabotage their performance and socially punish them for their creativity. Star individual performers will benefit substantially from team rewards, as opposed to individual rewards. They will understand that their success is inextricably related to the success of others, especially their fellow team members. And by focusing on "team", as opposed to exclusively on "themselves", such star individual performers will begin understanding that their ability to be more effective in the workplace and elsewhere, and to be more whole as human beings (i.e., to heal the void/gap of living out one's full potential), relies on them choosing beyond self-interest (choosing to serve something beyond themselves, a more nobler purpose).

- *Healing*: Many people have broken spirits and have suffered emotional hurts. Servant leaders should recognize that they have an opportunity to *help make whole* those with whom they interact. According to Greenleaf (in Frick and Spears, 1996), if the compact between the servant leader and the led entails a co-search for wholeness, then the servant leader will be communicating something quite subtle/deep to the one who is being served and led.

Perhaps President Nelson Mandela can be described as an epitome of African leadership virtues, particularly in terms of healing, compromise and diversity tolerance, as well as his focus on creating racial harmony and consensus democracy. Mandela (1994) states that:

> I am prepared to stand for the truth, even if you all stand against me . . . I am writing my own personal testament; because now that I am nearer to the end, I want to sleep for eternity with a broad smile on my face knowing that, especially the youth, can stretch out across the colour line, shake hands and seek peaceful solutions to the problems of the Country.

He went on to comment on the destiny of Whites in South Africa: "Young Afrikaners had a specific and central contribution to make to the development of the South African nation and had too much potential to allow themselves to be marginalized." Mandela also said that he had always fought against domination of the majority by the minority, as well as the domination of the minority by the majority. This is the essence of African consensus democracy which seeks to accommodate minority groups.

Servant leaders seek to nurture their abilities to "dream great dreams". The ability to look at a problem from a conceptualizing perspective means that one must think beyond day-to-day realities. Servant leaders are called upon to seek a delicate balance between conceptual thinking and a day-to-day focused approach. In other words, in terms of the African leadership paradigm, one of the key functions of leadership is the ability to manage meaning by creating the memory of an attractive future. Leadership has to have the ability to create a shared agenda and vision that is capable of transforming the status quo, as well as the rare ability of enrolling people into the vision and galvanizing support for it. The leaders have to be able to energize people to overcome major obstacles towards achieving the vision of transformation by managing attention to achieve focused excellence. They have the ability to capture their vision in captivating language. Mandela (1994) serve to illustrate this dimension of African leadership practice:

> We have triumphed in the effort to implant hope in the breasts of millions of our people. We enter into the covenant that we shall build the society in which all South Africans, both Black and White, will be able to walk tall, without any fear in their inalienable right to human dignity; a rainbow nation at peace with itself and the world.

Individual social capital is often developed, over time, through specific patterns of self-disciplined behaviour, which then produces the African character and internalized individual serenity. In many instances in Africa, this is often borne out of community struggle and demerited times that forces the individual to collaborate. It is a widely held African belief that such self-discipline produces the necessary moral fabric and mental development of an individual, which is important for engendering the required community-consciousness.

Although, at times, in can be both seen and used in coercive ways, the ultimate purpose of community-consciousness is to facilitate community interaction, and effectiveness, by way of consensus and promotion of collective rules that helps African communities to transcend their struggle.

- *Self-discipline*: Yet another key element is that African leadership practices cherish a warrior tradition. African chiefs and kings were expected to lead their people in terms of war. Management of self-discipline is very important; doing very ordinary things in an extraordinary manner, as well as "walking the talk", thus putting their sincerity on constant display in order to create trust. Management of social capital by creating trust is a key element of African servant leadership.
- *Consciousness*: In terms of the African leadership paradigm, leaders have to be sharply awake and reasonably disturbed. They have to have an inner serenity. They have a high degree of personal consciousness. High consciousness can only be attained through a personal spiritual journey, by reaching into the depths of our spiritual inner resources to transcend our self-interest and attain a high level of personal transformation, to be able to focus on the common good in service of society and the enterprising organizational ability. This also enables leaders to overcome the limitations of their historical circumstances, inspired by a sense of personal destiny, which enables them to infuse spiritual energy into the organization. For this to happen, leaders have to have a sense of connection with both the past and the future. They need a sense of legacy inspired by being rooted in their culture and traditions. In the African worldview, leaders are the custodians of culture and a particular civilization. They have to have a high sense of personal destiny (*dzinza*) by knowing who they are, to become what they know they can become, by knowing their personal and family history, as well as tribal and national history to serve as a compass and a reference point in order to find their paths in a changing world.

Conclusion

The genius of European (North) leadership tradition lies in planning and technical innovation. The genius of the American (West) leadership tradition lies in entrepreneurship and a bias for action. The genius of Asian (East) leadership tradition lies in process innovation to attain quality and perfection. The genius of African (South) leadership tradition lies in Ubuntu – the interdependence of humanity, by emphasizing human dignity and respect through consensus democracy and people mobilization, solidarity and care.

Social learning, it would seem, appears to establish horizons of perception. Therefore, Pascale (1990) was right in stating that leadership is culturally and socially determined, and is not an absolute, or static, but rather dynamic. He asserted that human beings, from all cultures and all societies, are coming together to perform certain collective acts, and in so doing encounter common problems that require culturally-determined direction-setting, coordination and motivation.

References

Ayittey, G. B. N. (1997), *Africa in Chaos*, New York: Saint Martin's Press.

Barrett, R. (1998), *Liberating the Corporate Soul: Building a Visionary Organization*, Burlington, MA: Butterworth-Heinemann.

Capra, F. (1982), *The Turning Point: Science, Society and the Rising Culture*, London: Flamingo (An Imprint of HarperCollins Publishers).

Cottingham, J. (Ed. and translator) (1996), *Descartes: Meditations on First Philosophy, With Selections from the Objections and Replies*, Cambridge: Cambridge University Press.

Frick, D. M. and Spears, L. C. (Eds.) (1996), *Robert K. Greenleaf: On Becoming A Servant as Leader*, San Francisco: Jossey-Bass Inc.

Hampden-Turner. C. and Trompenaars, A. (1993), *The Seven Cultures of Capitalism: Value Systems for Creating Wealth in the United States, Japan, Germany, France, Britain, Sweden and the Netherlands*, New York: Currency and Doubleday (A Division of Doubleday Dell Publishing Group Inc.).

Handy, C. (1997), *Rethinking the Future*, London: Nicholas Brealey.

Kuhn, T. S. (1996), *The Structure of Scientific Revolutions*, 3rd Edition, Chicago, IL: University of Chicago Press. Originally published in 1962.

Mandela, N. (1994), *Long Walk to Freedom*, Boston, MA: Little Brown & Co.

Pascale, R. (1990), *Managing on the Edge: How Successful Companies Use Conflict to Stay Ahead*, London: Penguin Books.

Reich, R. (2002), *The Future of Success: Living and Working in the New Economy*, New York: Vintage.

Smith, A. (1991), *The Wealth of Nations (Great Minds Series)*, New York: Prometheus Books.

Part 6

Realizing New Realities

Editors' Note: Realizing New Realities

by Marylou Shockley

Encounters across cultures often create pell-mell moments of confusion, frustration and helplessness. Yet, such encounters also catapult us into areas where everything is experientially new, producing feelings of childlike wonderment. This cultural diversity, as we travel either voluntarily or because of a work assignment in other countries, challenges our notions of "sameness," for what envelops us is "difference." Different language(s), smells, foods, colors, sounds, weather, people, values, daily rhythms, and modes of behavior assault our senses. No longer do our patterns of behaviors work; we find ourselves in a dilemma that forces us to "swim" by continuously improvising and experimenting with workable routines, or "sink" by cocooning into old patterns of behavior that require others to be flexible, not us.

The impetus behind cultural diversity encounters is globalization. There is a growing realization that this reality is no longer optional as globalization fosters international economic and political development and, consequently, the need to reach out to others around the world. Personal networks are no longer local, but global. Much of the traditional diversity literature is national in scope, while cultural diversity is international in scope. The recognition of new realities propelled by cultural diversity increasingly brings awareness that the wellspring of our own humanity is empathic reciprocality which opens our hearts to a stream of sharing and receiving thus refreshing our own spirit.

This last of the six facets of diversity – realizing new realities – presents papers whose authors provide us with insights on cultural diversity. Several authors in the other five themes of diversity have touched upon this aspect of diversity. These three chapters, however, present several unique observations: (1) countries are not all the same – their histories shape and imbue them with highly unique characteristics; (2) leadership is more than a "standard one-fits-all" paradigm; and (3) exposure to different cultures brings new insight and growth.

Thor Indridason in National Institutions and the Fate of Diversity: What has become of Nordic Corporatism? presents a Scandinavian perspective on cultural diversity by challenging the globalization convergence thesis that argues for the homogenization of socio-economic values and national characteristics among countries as they compete in the world's marketplace. Indridason discusses the dynamics of social, political, and economic histories of three Scandinavian countries – Demark, Finland, and Iceland. He first explains that "Nordic corporatism" is, at one level, normally seen as the archetypical coordinated national economies similar to Japan or Germany in which close cooperation between business, labor and government institutions define governance and public policy development. Indridason then argues that the historical developments in Demark, Finland and Iceland have led to national characteristics that have produced unique approaches to the global competition. He concludes that Nordic corporatism in these countries refute rather than support the globalization thesis of convergence in which all national socio-economic characteristics have been homogenized into to a common Nordic corporatism, leaching out the differences in national profiles.

Through a personal look at culture diversity from a leadership perspective, James Joseph introduces the notion of soft power as a model for international political leadership. In Soft Power in a World of Hard Power: Leadership as a Way of Being, he notes that to think of leadership as a way of being is to embrace the concept of soft power where persuasion and influence rather than coercion and economic muscle define the relationships with others. This way of being influences leaders who practice soft power to become agents of reconciliation who are healers and unifiers. James Joseph suggests that the practice of leadership is far more robust – leadership is situational, yet taps into the full reservoir of "human being-ness" at the mind, heart, and spiritual levels.

The final chapter by Marilyn Thomas entitled An American in Guangzhou, is highly personal. She describes her adventures in Guangzhou, China – a city she is visiting as Professor-in-Residence at Guangdong University of Business Studies. We experience southern China through her eyes. Her essay captures the essence of cultural diversity itself as lived experience. Her respect for her Chinese friends, students and the people she encounters in the market is authentic. Thomas uses the concept of "bao" which means "treasure" to describe her view of Chinese as little containers with treasures of big hearts. Each day the Chinese people she encountered shared some treasure with her that conveyed hospitality and warmth across the barrier of language.

19

National Institutions and the Fate of Diversity: What has Become of Nordic Corporatism?

by Thor Indridason

Introduction: globalisation and the endurance of national diversity

The process of change in Western societies and economies since the late 1970s has been a complex and multifaceted one. Social and economic systems – economic management models, industrial relations, corporate governance, production systems – have undergone alterations that, in some observers' opinions, have been no less than fundamental in nature. Developments in forms and nature of the international competition, underpinned by finance liberalisation, the impressive rise and advances of high-tech industries and geographical dispersion of firms and production regimes, have confronted national economic institutions and organisations with new challenges. These environmental changes have forced them to adjust their structures and strategies in accordance with the new realities of economic globalisation (Turner, 1992). Following Hall and Soskice (2001: 9), institutions here are defined as 'a set of rules, formal or informal, that actors generally follow, whether for normative, cognitive, or material reasons, and organisations as durable entities with formally recognised members, whose rules also contribute to the institutions of the political economy'.

Recent developments in international business systems and the world economy – most notably the rise of Japan as a world-class industrial and exporting nation; the rise of the newly industrialised countries in East Asia and South America; the successful export strategies of firms in the advanced European countries; and the 'multi-nationalisation' or increased cross-border activities of firms – have put new competitive pressures on world markets that have impacted on national systems of economic governance, industrial relations and production (Turner, 1992). Moreover, these global changes have signalled a shift towards 'the competitive state', a definition of the nation-state or the national economy as the primary unit of competition in global markets (Palan and Abbott, 1999). Such a definition puts not only national institutions and historical traditions at centre of analysis, but also diversity among identical national social systems and historically determined conditions.

The complexities of international economic developments, changes in international market structures and competitive strategies have been embodied in the notion of 'globalisation', a concept designed to identify and explain the general currents that affect industrialised countries. These trends tend to sway national economies and social systems towards identical developments that, in the long run, will erase their national characteristics to a significant degree.[1] Changes in social and economic policies, restructuring of industrial relations systems, and streamlining of corporate structures and apparently similar competitive strategies across the advanced industrialised countries have readily been interpreted in terms of the globalisation thesis. Summarising the principal features of such convergence tendencies, Cable (1999: 35) has asserted that globalisation entails that:

> systems of [social and economic] regulation are no longer nationally self-contained but have to be adapted for a world in which financial and human capital is footloose. Instruments of what may once have been exclusively domestic policy – education, social security, labour relations, corporate taxation, corporate governance, utilities regulation, systems of monetary management, law enforcement – all are new ingredients in 'competitiveness' and constrained by it.

More recently the apparent persistence of national diversity has called into question the validity and correctness of such bold generalisations provoking suspicion that they were rather hastily and uncritically formulated, reflecting much publicised Anglo-American experience rather than realities in other countries which, as research has accumulatively revealed, happened to be fundamentally different in important respects. Thus, a basic argument against the globalisation/convergence thesis is that the presence of *similar* challenges of external origin, observed in a number of countries, should not be taken at face value as *evidence* of converging trends towards a single model of economic governance – preferably of Anglo-American style – at national level and 'global best practice' at institutional/organisational level. On the contrary, as a result of different national characteristics and historical institutional traditions, countries tend to develop alternative solutions to common problems and challenges. It lies in the nature of historical traditions and institutions to shape and regulate whatever changes may take place within national economies and civil societies. As Landes (1991: 545) has maintained each country 'develops its own combination of elements to fit its traditions, possibilities and circumstances'. National institutions will, therefore, invariably tend to be reactionary and resist externally imposed changes however flexible they may be within the premises of culture and social values. The new competitive pressures brought about by the forces of globalisation are, for this reason, likely to affect national economies not in any universal manner but in a way that will produce 'a mix of convergence and new and old divergence' (Kitschelt *et al.*, 1999: 428). This line of thought does not conceive national systems and institutions as automatically resisting external pressures for change, but consciously responding to those pressures and adapting on grounds of national traditions, structures and interests.

While national institutions are undeniably of importance in explaining change, external influences are also at work; national economies do not exist in isolation from the outside world nor are they immune from the external challenges that originate from within the international economy. Therefore, changes in domestic structures should not be understood as being solely determined by domestic institutions or entirely externally generated by the forces of globalisation. Instead these changes should be viewed as 'an administered social order' and as such a product of human agency. In this vein, Palan and Abbott (1999: 27) have underlined the necessity of constructively relating the two analytical levels, the international and the national; 'globalisation is a credible thesis only when we can identify the [national] institutions which prescribe and proscribe behaviour associated with globalisation'. The forces of *convergence* therefore need to be explored and understood to no lesser degree than the processes underlying the *continuous diversity* between countries.

This chapter seeks to map recent changes in the social and economic institutions of the small states of northern Europe in light of the two theoretical approaches outlined above. These countries – Denmark, Finland, Iceland, Norway and Sweden – have normally been set apart from other European states and defined in terms of their post-World War II traditions of social democratic politics and corporatist forms of making and implementing socio-economic policies. As such they exemplify unique forms of socio-economic governance and political institutions and thus add to the diversity of European political and social traditions. While Denmark, Norway and Sweden are three of the Nordic countries most frequently referred to (and justifiably so) as 'social democratic' and 'corporatist', their political legacy has (unjustifiably) stereotyped the politics and political culture of the entire region in terms of these concepts. In other words, neither Iceland nor Finland sit comfortably within the confines of such definitions although corporatist arrangements emerged in both countries in the 1970s and social democracy became a leading political form in Finland in the mid-1960s. Thus, within the confines of the vague notion of 'Nordic politics' and 'corporatism' lies a broader spectrum of diversity – five national versions of a socio-political institutional arrangements that share little else than the same definitional label. The Nordic countries make a particularly interesting case with regard to the two theoretical approaches due to their vulnerability which stems from: (1) the openness of their economies; (2) the relatively specialised and un-diversified exports; and (3) the presumed undermining of social democratic ideals and corporatist politics by the forces of globalisation.

For definitional purposes a brief discussion of the two concepts of economic coordination and Nordic corporatism follows this introduction. To adequately comprehend the historical traditions and institutions of Nordic politics and society the chapter will then proceed by briefly exploring the historical developments and economic conditions that have defined socio-political institutions of three of the Nordic countries, Denmark, Finland and Iceland. These three countries are chosen with the diversity of Nordic history, politics and society in mind, which, hopefully, makes the convergence thesis more interesting to test, i.e., *if the institutional structures and practices of economic governance of the three countries are, indeed, becoming more alike*. The chapter then concludes with a brief summary and conclusions.

Economic coordination and Nordic corporatism

Along with the small Rhineland economies (Austria, Belgium, Netherlands and Switzerland), Germany and Japan, the Nordic economies are normally seen as the archetypical coordinated economies. Following Hall's and Soskice's (2001) definition, economic coordination denotes the formation and utilisation of non-market, as opposed to competitive, market based, relationships between political and economic actors in order to secure stable growth conditions and international competitiveness of strategic industries, i.e., provide the principal economic actors with strategic capacities they would not otherwise enjoy. Such relations are embedded in formal as well as informal institutions, promoting extensive networks of cross-shareholding and legal or regulatory systems facilitating trust, cooperation and exchange of information. Economic outcomes in coordinated economies can thus be conceived as the result of strategic interaction between trade unions, employers, political authorities and other important economic organisations to a far greater degree than in economies which prioritise the sovereignty of the market forces and where the principal economic actors deal with each other at arm's-length.

The institutions of a given country's political economy are inextricably bound up with its history in two respects. On the one hand, they are created by activities of political and economic actors that establish institutions and their operating procedures. On the other, repeated historical experience builds up a set of common expectations that allows the actors to coordinate effectively with each other. Among other things, this implies that the institutions central to the operation of the political economy should not be seen as entities that are created at one point in time and can then be assumed to operate effectively afterwards. To remain viable, the shared understandings associated with them must be reaffirmed periodically by appropriate historical experience. The operative force of many institutions cannot, therefore, be taken for granted but must be reinforced by the continuous, active endeavours of the participants (Hall and Soskice, 2001).

With regard to political traditions and structural arrangements of cooperation between governments and organised social interests the coordinated economies of the Nordic countries are generally defined in terms of corporatism, a mode of governance characterised by 'a consensual rather than adversarial approach to policy making' and 'extensive and regular consultation with pressure groups and specialist interests in the consideration of public policy issues' (Arter, 1999: 148). Corporatist politics have been embodied in formal and informal extra-parliamentary cooperation between organised interests and state authorities as well as in various parliamentary committees and commissions. In this respect, the labour market organisations have been of major importance and have, indeed, acquired a status as key actors within the realm of politics. Accordingly, the collective bargaining processes have effectively been integrated as a core element of economic management. High membership levels of unions and employers' associations as well as centralised forms of decision making and bargaining competence have commonly been seen as a prerequisite for the effectiveness of the corporatist arrangements. These characteristics are likely to entail a sufficient level of internal discipline that enables the organisations to deliver and keep their part of the bargain in tripartite cooperation. These are the principal characteristics of the Nordic labour market organisations and to which the success of corporatist politics in these countries has normally been attributed.

Economic management in the Nordic countries has since World War II rested on the rationale and institutions of coordination whether these have been inclusive, cooperative and corporatist in nature as in Denmark, Norway and Sweden, or exclusive and confrontational as in Iceland and Finland before 1970. The late emergence of tripartite institutions in Finland and Iceland, as well as their fragility (Iceland), can be attributed to: (1) different political and industrial relations traditions; (2) the lower profile of social democratic parties and a fragmented political left; (3) organisational characteristics of the labour market actors; and (4) ideology less supportive to cooperative/corporatist arrangements than that found in the social democratic countries. In spite of such differences the five countries are frequently seen to share certain basic similarities in their outlook and institutional settings to a degree that has prompted various authors to encapsulate the specificities of Nordic economic management and industrial relations in a particular conceptual construction – a Nordic model – that supposedly defines a mode of governance and political relations diverse from what is to be found elsewhere in Europe. A fundamental characteristic of the Nordic model is the integration of the two systems of industrial relations and politics:

> At least since the second world war, the trade union movements in all the Nordic countries have worked towards co-operation rather than militancy. The political strength of the labour movement in government and Parliament has created a trade union view that is sympathetic to following the 'rules of the game' at the political level. They have had a positive attitude towards growth policy, productivity increases, structural rationalisation, new technology and the like. The unions have seen these measures as

> essential prerequisites for the expansion of the welfare state, and have attempted to minimise the negative effects [of structural rationalisation on employees]. Thus fixed and stable labour market relations and reformist and consensus policies are further hallmarks of the Nordic model. Within the framework of tripartite co-operation, the Nordic trade union organisations have become well-integrated into government decision-making, and their status in the government apparatus has been generally accepted
> (Bruun, 1994: 18).

End of Nordic corporatism?

Throughout the post-war period high economic growth rates, advanced welfare policies and international competitiveness earned the Nordic countries respect and admiration among policy makers and academics alike. Their success was generally assigned to their models of social and economic governance and reform designed to attain the political goals of efficiency, solidarity and equality (Kettunen, 1998). As greater economic uncertainties set in at the beginning of the 1970s, the apparent success of the corporatist politics of the Nordic states became an example for the non-corporatist countries where some forms of tripartite arrangements were established in an effort to maintain increasingly fragile stability, growth and full employment. However, such 'imitations' proved in most cases to be a forlorn effort; one commentator, comparing British attempts at tripartite income policies with long-standing practices of the coordinated and corporatist economies, was prompted to note: 'there is little point in trying to transplant the entire experience of others, with different traditions and cultures and more centralised and powerfully disciplined trade unions and employer organisations. We can only build painfully from what we already possess' (Taylor, 1981: 157).

By the 1980s the success story of the Nordic economies, and in particular Nordic corporatism, seemed increasingly to be coming to an end. Accordingly, social democratic ideals and policies as well as competitive strategies formulated and pursued through corporative structures were increasingly criticized and denounced as remnants of the past and detrimental to future potential. Such policies and institutions, it was argued, were rigid and unfit to deal with the new realities of a globalised (or globalising) world economy where national success would inextricably be tied to price stability, open markets and deregulation. The presumed disintegration of corporatism in face of the tough challenges of globalisation entailed a change in embedded institutions of political governance and a decline in socio-political relations essential for economic management.

This last notion is of particular relevance for recent experience in the Nordic economies. Since the end of the Second World War extensive regulatory regimes and intervention has characterised the Nordic models of economic governance. In securing full employment, reasonably low inflation and international competitiveness governments relied primarily on three instruments: (1) flexible exchange rates; (2) centralised wage bargaining; and (3) price controls in forms of regulation and subsidies. The aim of these policies, which were primarily formulated in a coordinated manner and implemented through corporatist structures, were to: (1) adjust domestic production costs, in particular wages according to requirements of successful competition in international markets; and (2) secure reasonably high investment levels in the strategically important export industries. Since the early 1980s the effectiveness of the constituent elements of such policies has been undermined due to the practical lifting of domestic exchange controls which has made competitive devaluations more problematic. This has caused the severe erosion of the legitimacy of state support to producers and ailing industries, and greater leverage of industry and enterprise level wage negotiations at the expense of the centralised systems of collective bargaining (Moses, 2000). The implication of these developments seems to lend support to the globalisation thesis; i.e., the regulatory regimes of the corporatist polities and economic coordination in general are, indeed, in a state of crisis and possibly transforming towards more liberal practices and institutions.

The origin of diversity: the formulation and development of national institutions in Denmark, Finland, and Iceland

Because of the seemingly persistent diversity among the advanced industrial economies comparative analysis of current systems of economic organisations, Whitley (1999: 5) suggests, should be based on two interrelated questions: 'given the existence of varied forms of economic organisation, why do they persist and how do they change?' Such an analysis requires first, a consideration of how the various national forms developed in contrasting ways during their formative period and, second, the identification of the processes that maintain or reproduce divergent ways of conducting and controlling economic activities in different institutional contexts.

The traditions of political cooperation and the basic characteristics of the economic management models of the Nordic countries, whether corporatist or not, can be attributed to early developments of the institutions of mass democracy on one hand, and structural characteristics of the economies on the other. Modern democratic politics and political institutions emerged in the Nordic countries during the decades around the year 1900. Despite the relatively late appearance of corporatist institutions they are firmly rooted in the early conditions of Nordic democracy. In particular, the 'corporate channel' of political representation and participation can been seen as a function of: (1) the national multi-party systems and the principle of proportional representation; (2) the organisational characteristics of the national industrial relations systems; and (3) a specific Nordic understanding of the idea of democracy – all features that promoted and facilitated various modes of cooperation between political and economic actors. Economic factors, such as export specialisation and susceptibility to developments within the world economy, also had a major influence on the development and characteristics of the Nordic models of economic governance. Below each of these factors and the conditioning effects of economic structures are briefly examined.

The left in early Nordic politics

Except for Iceland, Nordic social democracy had its parliamentary breakthrough in the period 1884–1908. The rise of the social democrats was most striking in Finland where, in the wake of a new constitution and mass democracy in 1906, they became the country's largest party – and indeed the world's largest party of its kind – with 37% of the vote and two fifths of the parliamentary seats (Arter, 1999). The spectacular rise of Nordic social democracy can be attributed to two intertwined factors: (1) the parties' pragmatic politics of cooperation between the urban working class and the rural population; and (2) the consequent ability to extend their electoral support beyond that of the industrial working class (Esping-Andersen, 1998).

In the wake of the Russian revolution the socialist movement in all the Nordic countries went through a period of internal conflicts over ideology, policy and strategy. In Denmark, Finland, Norway and Sweden radical and pro-Soviet factions splintered off from the social democratic parties to form communist organisations. In Denmark, Norway and Sweden the formation of the communist parties had virtually no or at best insignificant impact on the electoral support of the social democratic parties or their position within the trade union movements. In the case of Denmark, Galenson (1968: 12, 14) has related the early success of the social democratic strategy to the characteristics of the industrialisation process of that country: 'the extremely slow rate of rural proletarianisation in effect hindered the rise of large, destitute *lumpen-proletariat*. . . . some of the conditions most frequently cited for the development of radical leftism or syndicalism were totally absent in Denmark'.

The Finnish experience was, however, markedly different from that of the other Nordic countries and harsher by far. In the aftermath of a bloody civil war plaguing the country in 1918 and fuelled by the highly inflammatory political situation created by the Russian revolution and the subsequent sovereignty of Finland, the Social Democratic Party suffered a split in 1920 when its radical faction broke away to form a new left wing party, the Socialist Workers' Party, in opposition to the moderate reformism of the social democrats.[2] The events of the late 1910s as well as a wave of extreme nationalism and strong anti-socialist sentiments in the late 1920s and early 1930s, led to the marginalisation of the Social Democratic Party in Finnish politics for two decades despite its considerable electoral strength (Kirby, 1986; Knoellinger, 1960; Valkonen, 1989).

The Icelandic social democratic party harboured the radical left until 1930 when it eventually fell out with social democratic reformism and a communist party was formed. Icelandic social democrats suffered a second split in 1938 when the party's left wing broke off to join the communists in a new party impressively strengthening the radical left in Icelandic politics. For the Icelandic social democrats these splits were a major setback as they permanently reduced the party to the position of the smallest of four major parties.

These developments shaped one of the most important features of the Nordic party systems for the remainder of the 20th century. More specifically, in Finland and Iceland the radical left retained its political strength, while in the social democratic countries (Denmark, Norway and Sweden) these radical leftist parties remained relatively weak. In terms of electoral support for the leftist parties, Finland has been on par with the three social democratic countries, the difference being that the vote has been split between the social democrats and a notably strong party of radical socialists. The relative strength of the radical left has also been a characteristic feature of Icelandic politics albeit less so than in Finland. While the combined vote of the two left wing parties in Finland has on average amounted to 45%, in Iceland it has hovered around 30%. The weakness of the Finnish left has thus been the split of the socialist camp into two relatively strong sub-blocks while in Iceland the left has traditionally remained weak *vis-à-vis* centrist and rightist parties. As a result, corporatist politics that were effectively brought to maturity as a feature of the social democratic regimes in Denmark, Norway and Sweden, never enjoyed the same prominence in Finland or Iceland.

Cooperation, political representation and administrative structures

The close relationship between state authorities and various social and economic interest organisations has normally been seen as the main characteristic feature of Nordic politics and forms of interest intermediation. Like electoral representation the 'corporatist channel' is the outcome of the democratisation process in the Nordic countries. Two basic attributes of Nordic politics and political developments seem to have particularly contributed to the early development of corporatist politics – the combined effects of the class-based, multi-party systems and the principle of proportional representation on one hand, and the development of the systems of parliamentary committees and commissions, on the other.

Regarding the first, it can be reasonably argued that proportional representation tends to intensify the competition between political parties and maximise electoral mobilisation, which in turn is more likely than not to promote a closer correspondence between socio-economic cleavages and political parties (Katzenstein, 1987). The links that were created between political parties and economic interest organisations in the early stages of modern politics in the Nordic countries, therefore, tended to be exceptionally strong, enduring and integrative. The important feature of political systems in their formative period was their tendency to 'freeze' the existing balance of power between political parties and, by extension, the form and nature of the relationships between the parties and organised social interests. This tended to generate political predictability and, in the absence of a commanding electoral majority of a single party, facilitated the sharing of power among political opponents.[3] The strong links between political parties and interest groups formed an important feature of the broader context within which such cooperation takes place and may, to a significant degree, translate into a *de facto* representation of interest organisation within parliamentary realms.

The second basic feature of the cooperative approach in Nordic parliamentary politics is the tradition of consultation with vested social and economic interests in the consideration of public policy issues. Government consultation with organised interests and pressure groups is common in all Western societies but a distinctive feature of Nordic polities is the extent, depth and regularity of such consultation as well as its cooperative character and high level of institutionalisation.

Modern forms of extra-parliamentary political cooperation have been traced to the development of the system of parliamentary committees and commissions at the turn of the twentieth century. Participation and representation of organised socio-economic interests in parliamentary committees and commissions provided political authorities with access to expertise and organisational forms of policy implementation and, hence, a pragmatic solution to scarce parliamentary resources and an underdeveloped administrative system (Bloom-Hansen, 2000; Johansen and Kristensen, 1982). However, these early steps hardly amount to what rightly might be described as corporatism. There was no dense or even continuous network of relations in place, but rather relatively few and isolated *ad hoc* initiatives. It took several decades to develop the corporatist political system and bring it to maturity. Three major historical events tended to significantly strengthen cooperative relations between political authorities and interest organisations – the economic depression of the 1930s and the two world wars. These events presented severe and volatile political conditions and economic circumstances prompting governments to promote widespread cooperation between political and economic actors in form of economic coordination. An essential part of this process was substantial increases in the number of corporatist administrative bodies and extra-parliamentary representation.

The labour market organisations

Outside the realm of formal politics, the structure of authority and competence of the labour market parties comprised an elemental feature in facilitating corporatist cooperation. In the social democratic countries employers embarked on highly centralised systems of collective bargaining in order to eliminate wages as a factor of competition, promote peaceful industrial relations, and enhance stability, predictability and competitiveness. In most cases, the trade unions (with the unions in the export sectors as partial exceptions) were fiercely opposed to any such moves although they, under pressure from employers, governments and vital sections of the trade union movement, were gradually forced to give in and cede bargaining and policy making competence to higher organisational structures, national unions or the central organisations. In the longer run, the centralisation of the collective bargaining created an acute awareness among employers and workers of the profound effects of the collective bargaining on economic performance and the state's ability to manage the economy. In fact, this perspective induced the labour market organisations to take into consideration the state of the economy and the export industries as well as objectives of economic policy when formulating their wage offers and demands.

In Iceland and Finland, on the other hand, the authority structure of the labour market organisations did little to facilitate cooperative state-labour market relations of the corporatist type. In both countries labour relations failed to take the route to centralise due to the effective resistance of both local union organisations and employers. In Iceland the tradition of relatively peaceful decentralised local level bargaining was actively supported and adhered to by the local organisations while in Finland the failure to implement more centralised bargaining practices was largely due to the employers' decision to turn their back on the unions as bargaining partners because of their militant behaviour, political radicalism and fierce infighting between the two factions of social democrats and communists. As a result, the central organisations of both unions and employers in Finland and Iceland lacked the authority and organisational competence to enter tripartite cooperation with governments.

Ideology and political resources

Although marked with considerable labour market conflict, the first half of the twentieth century saw the gradual acceptance of corporatist representation in Nordic politics as a legitimate form of the democratic process. To some extent, this can be seen as a continuation of the pre-democratic traditions of representation giving the right to the estates or other major groups of society to be collectively heard. Important elements of such traditions were transmitted to the new era of mass-democracy and confirmed in the new political values in all the Nordic countries where they were consolidated in forms of representation and participation of extra-parliamentary interest organisations within parliamentary systems of making and implementation of state policies. This entailed a feature fundamental to what Einhorn and Logue (1986) have identified as the 'Scandinavian democratic model'; a unique concept of democracy which is specific to the Nordic countries in that it is significantly broader than the Westminster or British version with respect to both political rights and forms of participation. Thus, in the Nordic democracies, interest organisations have come to enjoy a 'semi-political' or 'semi-representative' status as participants in the democratic process. Such a conception of democratic values and processes extends beyond the typical definition of corporatism which is confined to state-labour market relations.

As a result, in the Nordic context the notion of the 'negotiated economy' better encapsulates the actual meaning and characteristics of the corporatist and social systems in the region as,

> an organisational structuring of society, where an essential part of the allocation of resources is conducted through institutionalised negotiations between independent decision-making centres in public administration, organisations and corporations. An essential characteristic of the negotiated economy is the interconnection of institutional and discursive features enforcing compromise and mobilising consensus. It is not only a mechanism for regulation of disputes and mediation of conflicts but also an institutionalised mobilisation of mutual understanding about problems, ends and means
>
> (Nielsen and Pedersen, 1989).

Economic characteristics and structures

The Nordic countries were 'late industrialisers'. By the mid-nineteenth century all five of them had a predominantly agrarian structure and could be counted among Europe's poorest countries with the possible exception of Denmark (Jorberg, 1979). Between 1860 and 1913, the situation had changed markedly and the Nordic countries were among the fastest growing economies in Europe that could be regarded as industrialised. This growth occurred in the context of rapid and remarkable expansion of international economic activities, cross-border trade, capital flows and investments. Between 1870 and 1913, the volume of world foreign trade grew at about 3.4% annually creating a window of opportunity the Nordic countries managed to exploit effectively for their own good.

Given the limited home markets and scarce natural resources for industrial production, economic expansion of the Nordic economies had to rely on a strategy of export specialisation, benefiting from first fairly static comparative advantage and later from dynamic advantages through competitive superiority attained in their respective niches. In each country a single or few industrial sectors were developed as the key engine of growth and economic modernisation, e.g., agriculture in Denmark, timber and wood industries in Finland and fisheries in Iceland. The openness and small size of the Nordic economies combined with the high degree of export specialisation made them sensitive to developments in the international economy and vulnerable to fluctuations in their main export markets. These characteristics have a significant bearing on economic performance, as it is highly dependent on the competitiveness of the export sectors. For a small open economy to ensure competitiveness in international markets, developments in wages, prices and productivity must be in step with that of its main competitors. Under fixed exchange rates and stable prices in international markets, firms and industries in the exposed sector(s) are bound to suffer a loss in profits or a reduction in production when domestic cost increases. Firms in the sheltered sector are less constrained by international price developments and cost increases since these can be passed on more easily as higher prices. Thus, to secure full employment and contain inflation in a small open economy, economic management must keep price/wage developments in the sheltered sector(s) in line with the international constraints imposed on the exposed sector(s). Since international competition determines the scope for changes in wages and prices in the exposed sector(s) employers and unions need to recognise the importance of restrained wage and price increases relative to foreign competitors. By the same token, they share an interest in restraining costs increases in the sheltered industries that necessitates some control over wage growth in those industries and the alignment of wage developments between the two sectors.[4] Also, under these conditions governments find themselves induced to affect the behaviour of the labour market parties through political bargaining and cooperation in order to secure smooth and undisturbed production and stability. The structural characteristics of the small European economies have thus promoted 'a culture of compromise' embodied in corporatist political institutions.[5]

From stability to institutional breakdown? Nordic forms of economic coordination since World War II

Nordic corporatism and post-war models of economic management

Since the end of the Second World War, the maintenance of stable and favourable economic conditions in the Nordic countries has, to a greater or lesser degree, rested on: (1) close integration of the economic management models and industrial relations; (2) a logical continuation of early political developments; and (3) a continuation of industrial relations practices. In the three social democratic countries the tripartite system of collective bargaining proved instrumental in securing international competitiveness by adjusting wages in the exposed sector in accordance with price developments in main export markets. Also, wage development in the sheltered sector was tightly controlled in order to ensure wage stability and prevent wage competition from taking place between the two sectors. In Iceland and Finland, on the other hand, such adjustments were made not through cooperative mechanisms of the corporatist kind (except during the 'war economy' period in Finland which was ended in 1956), but economic policies of a more unilateral and arbitrary nature.

In Denmark the greater prominence of corporatist institutions rested on a continuing process of labour market centralisation. Of significant importance in this respect was an agreement made by the two central organisations in 1951, the General Agreement on Rules for Negotiating Procedure. This agreement assigned to the central labour market organisations the authority to decide, prior to each negotiation round and after consulting their affiliates, the issues that were to be considered 'general' and bargained over by the central organisations and those that were 'specific' to each industrial branch and thus dealt with by the national unions and corresponding employers' organisations. By sharpening the division of tasks between the central labour market organisations and their affiliates, the agreement facilitated the further integration of the two systems of politics and industrial relations, and thus furthered the consolidation of corporatist politics in Denmark.

The principal task of the central organisations in Denmark was to negotiate comprehensive wage agreements which defined scope for further bargaining at lower the levels of the bargaining system, defined by the industry and the enterprise. Due to this arrangement the central organisations were in a position – at least in theory – to determine the average wage level and regulate wage movements within the entire economy. The collective bargaining took place within a broader framework of corporatist state-labour market relations with the integration of socio-economic policy making and wage bargaining. As aggregate wage development was effectively incorporated as an elemental feature of economic policy programmes, so were socio-economic policies made an essential feature of the collective bargaining and internalised in negotiated wage agreements. This reflected both the rationale of the mixed economy and the ideals of the welfare consensus in post-war European politics. It was an optimised rationale based on an understanding of the need to improve living standards not merely by continuous wage increases but also through policy measures in the fields of social security, incomes redistribution, housing policies and subsidies. Public and political authorities were, therefore, brought to the labour markets' negotiating table as *societal bargaining* or political exchanges, became more firmly established as a feature of post-war industrial relations practices.

In the early 1960s this cooperation was underpinned by the creation and work of a specialist advisory body, the Economic Council, that was set up to formulate solutions to current economic problems along the lines of corporatist cooperation by 'improving the coordination between labour and industry, their organisations, and the responsible state organs' (Elvander, 1981: 294). The central organisations of the labour market were thus accorded hitherto unparalleled influence on the management of society. Cooperation between governments and the labour market parties has, however, remained highly informal in nature. Thus, rather than taking the form of proper negotiations between the central organisations and the government in conjunction to general wage negotiations the unions have pursued what can be considered their own voluntary and private incomes policies, denoting adjustment of their wage demands to the state of the economy and objectives of economic management (Due *et al.*, 1994).

With the outbreak of the Winter War in Finland in November 1939, an immediate change in industrial relations and economic governance took place, literally bringing to an end the decentralised wage bargaining system of the pre-war period and the overt hostilities between the organisations of employers and workers. The need for national unity and cooperation compelled the labour market organisations to adopt a more cooperative approach as they assumed new responsibilities as the government's principal partners in administering the war economy. Accordingly, a 'Basic Agreement' was made between the two labour market parties establishing the principle of collective bargaining as the norm of wage determination and defining rules for wage negotiations. Although the war ended in 1944, the war economy regulations were continued in Finland until the mid-1950s as the country dealt with the dire consequences of the war effort.

The conditions created by the war and the war economy regulation were exceptional in Finnish politics and society. Although they gave a strong impetus to the formation of a system of orderly industrial relations based on the principle of collective bargaining, the tripartite cooperation between the labour market parties and the state rested on significantly weaker grounds. As soon as the war regulation was lifted, Finnish corporatism crumbled. Tripartite cooperation between state authorities and the labour market parties as the dominant feature of both economic management and collective bargaining was replaced by more exclusive forms of state-labour market relations; the industrial organisations of unions and employers succeeded the national federations as the most prominent bargaining agents. Thus, despite the major changes brought about by the war, old antagonisms and conflict elements re-emerged to circumscribe the relationship between unions and employers in post-war Finland (Crouch, 1993).

If Finnish employers were less than enthusiastic about inclusive cooperation with the unions, developments within the trade union movement itself did little to promote such forms of industrial relations let alone corporatist state-labour market relations. Political skirmishes between social democrats and the radical left continued relentlessly as the two sides clashed over the union confederation and leading unions. The power struggle within the union movement took the form of aggressive and competitive wage demands as the competing sides attempted to outbid each other in their competition for members and power positions within individual unions. Unions' wage policies were for this reason only to a very limited degree aligned with the state of the economy or the principal objectives of economic management. Towards the end of the 1950s this struggle reached its zenith when, following a split in the Social Democratic Party, a number of unions defected from the central organisation and formed a rival confederation. The split was, indeed, three-sided as significant number of union made the choice to stay outside both federations.

On the other hand, the fragmented party system, relative smallness of the political parties and frequent changes in government coalitions all but weakened chances to construct cooperative state-labour market relations. Finnish governments have since the war been exceptionally volatile and short-lived by Nordic standards; between 1945 and 1970s no less than 23 government coalitions (of which four were non-party 'caretaker' governments) were formed in Finland, ruling for little more than a year on average. The Social Democratic Party was a partner in ten of these governments and a leading party in only five. Thus, government programmes and policy objectives remained inconsistent and subject to changes as one government coalition replaced another, raising criticism among the labour market organisations and causing discord within the union movement (Nousiainen, 1971; Knoellinger, 1960).

Certain conditions of organisational, social and political nature also prevented the formation of Scandinavian-type corporatism in Iceland. Of paramount importance in this respect was the relationship between the labour market traditions that had been established in the pre-war period and the legal environment and the economic policy regime of the post-war era. The labour legislation and the economic management model, both of which were devised at the outset of the war, did not contravene existing labour market traditions. Rather the opposite occurred. By defining individual unions as the primary bargaining units and creating institutions and procedures for the handling of industrial disputes that seemingly had little if any centralising effects, the labour legislation confirmed, if not, strengthened the tradition of *local* level bargaining and consequently the decentralised organisational forms of labour market interests. What made the Icelandic labour law all the more interesting in this respect was the fact that its authors looked to Denmark as a benchmark where a principal aim of the labour law had been to promote centralised wage bargaining.

Besides, political conditions for cooperative or corporatist state-labour market relations were nowhere as supportive in Iceland as they were in Denmark, Norway and Sweden. In addition to the electoral weakness of the Social Democratic Party, the Icelandic trade union movement lacked the social democratic hegemony that might have enabled a central union organisation to form permanent and stable bonds with the party and, more importantly, the government. In this respect, the Icelandic trade union movement was on par with the Finnish one – open to political struggle between rival political factions that almost had led to a split in late 1930s (Indridason, 1997).

Finally, the economic management model followed in Iceland in the postwar period was based on a principle different from that in the three social democratic countries. In Iceland governments prioritised their independence as the makers and implementers of economic policy, free from direct interference of organised economic interests except for consultative purposes. In his assessment of the Icelandic model, Olafsson (1993: 75) has emphasised the qualitative difference between the arbitrariness of the 'enforced' incomes policies of Icelandic governments and the cooperative approach followed by governments in Denmark, Norway and Sweden: 'voluntary incomes policy is likely to be obtained where there is a high-trust relationship between government and unions, while enforced incomes policy is more likely to be applied where antagonism is more prevalent'. Thus a prominent feature of economic management in Iceland and mirroring the nature of state-labour market relations has been the repeatedly 'enforced', adjustments of real wages to economic realities and policy objectives. These have normally taken the form of legislative fiat; currency devaluations, wage freeze or changes in wage indexation systems. Despite the rather hostile approach of the economic management model towards the unions, Icelandic governments were by no means principally opposed to cooperating with the labour market parties and did, indeed, on few occasions, seek to promote some form of cooperative state-labour market relations. However, because of the extremely volatile conditions of the Icelandic economy a form of cooperative economic management was not as easily established as in the three social democratic countries; the scope for compromises and negotiated solutions acceptable to all major interests and actors was narrower in Iceland.

Since the 1970s; demise of corporatism?

Since the early 1970s Western economies have been exposed to changes in their international economic environment that has made it more difficult to maintain the policy aspiration levels of the post-war era – growth, full employment and social welfare. Following the breakdown of the international system of relatively fixed exchange rates, steep rise in prices for raw materials and food products in the early 1970s, and quadrupling of oil prices in 1973–74, the advanced economies of the West experienced job losses to an unprecedented scale, inflation accompanied (and caused) by currency instabilities, and a sharp fall in investments, productivity and profit levels. Although it has been reasoned that economic growth after 1973 remained 'reasonably respectable and it is only against the background of the sustained boom of the 1950s and 1960s that it appears somewhat mediocre' (Aldcroft, 2001: 194) it fell below full capacity potential in many European countries leading to a sharp increase in unemployment; by 1983 10.5% of the labour force was without a job compared to 3.5% ten years earlier (OECD, 1986).

As the 1980s proceeded, the persistent high unemployment was increasingly perceived less as a reflection of cyclical economic recession but more as an indication of deeper alterations in domestic economic and industrial structures. Consequently, developments within the international economy, i.e., integration of national economies on a far greater scale than before in forms of intensified competition in international markets and an increase in cross-border financial flows, have been blamed and praised for the presumed reduction of governments' room for economic manoeuvring and abilities to maintain expensive and extensive regulatory systems in various areas of social and economic governance. In formulating national policies of competitiveness and attracting foreign investments, governments must now pay greater attention to the wider international connotations of their actions and consider their consequences for domestic developments. Structural and institutional adjustments – the creation of advantageous 'framework conditions' – has, in this context, become the main focus of industrial and economic policies of the 'competitive state' (Gassman, 1994).

The implication is rather obvious. National diversity and specificities of historically embedded institutions are on the wane as the key concepts of 'deregulation', 'decentralisation', 'liberalisation', and 'flexibility' have to greater degree than before guided competitive policies and strategies of both governments and firms. However, the general context of the relationship between national economies and global economic and the subsequent impact on business structures conceals certain particularities of that relationship and diverse experience between countries. Despite what may be regarded as similar trends and even growing similarities in their overall industrial structures – most notably diversification and increased sophistication of industrial production – the export sector and the composition of exported merchandise continues to be markedly different between the three countries studied here (Denmark, Finland and Iceland). As a result, they have been prone to different pressures originating from within their external economic environment, which in turn, has posed different problems for governments and has led to different policy responses.

In all three countries state-labour market relations have undergone significant changes since the late 1960s or early 1970s as state authorities have, under increasingly unpredictable and volatile international economic conditions, sought to maintain economic stability and sufficient growth rates through tripartite arrangements, albeit very different in both form and nature. Uneven and contradictory state-labour market relations in Denmark have probably been more consistent with past traditions and institutionalised processes than in Finland and Iceland. As in many other European countries, corporatist politics were more prominent and influential in Denmark in the 1970s than in previous decades. The corporatist tradition in Denmark was markedly strengthened by: (1) continuous process of labour market centralisation, especially on the unions' side; and (2) greater integration of the two systems of social welfare and industrial relations with various social policy measures supplementing stipulations laid out in collective wage agreements.

On the other hand, the greater prominence of corporatist politics can also be seen as a reaction to certain political and economic developments of less positive nature. Thus, following parliamentary elections in 1973, a highly fragmented parliament of ten parties replaced the long-standing four (sometimes five) party system of parliamentary representation. With minority coalitions being 'the rule' in Danish politics (and clearly more so after 1973), this inevitably created some severe governance problems as relative stability and predictability gave way to greater political uncertainties and volatile cooperation between parliamentary parties. In this context, Danish governments came to rely more on cooperation with the labour market parties and less on the highly fragmented parliament. Mounting economic difficulties, in particular rising unemployment, trade deficit and inflation, also tended to make state authorities more dependent on tripartite cooperation for the success of economic management. The economic difficulties experienced in Denmark in the 1970s and 1980s were only partially related to greater instabilities within the international economy. At another level, they reflect the failure of the 'second industrial revolution' in the late 1950s and early 1960s. This 'revolution' was, despite this label, generated not by industrial policies of modernisation and export diversification but expansive fiscal and monetary policies and foreign borrowing (Benner and Vad, 2000).

As perception of the economic downswing as of structural rather than cyclical nature gained recognition among the principal political and economic actors, unions resorted to a policy of wage restraint which, assisted by exchange rate adjustments, proved instrumental in enhancing the competitiveness of the Danish export industries between 1979 and 1982 (Nielsen and Pedersen, 1989). The unions continued their adherence to wage moderation for the best part of the 1980s; however, the liberal-conservative coalition that held power between 1982 and 1993 took a far less favourable stance than any of its predecessors towards the tripartite tradition and, indeed, openly opposed it (Scheuer, 1998). The general understanding in Danish society about the graveness of the economic situation also induced the unions to abide with the governments' interventions in existing wage agreements – wage freezes and restriction of wage indexation – that negatively affected real pay. The unions also accepted the government's recommendation, made at the outset of the 1983 bargaining round, to keep annual wage rises and wage drift within a limit of 4% (European Industrial Relations Review, 1983).

Despite strained relations between the liberal-conservative government and the union movement and the government's determination to significantly play down cooperation with the labour market parties, the main lines of state policies and administration were kept on the rails laid down by social democratic traditions and culture (Amaroso, 1990). In this respect, Due *et al.* (1994: 194) have noted that the framework of political institutions prevented any dramatic political turnarounds during the conservative decade: 'the government could make no drastic changes which would threaten the welfare state or the Danish Model. If the government . . . had wanted to do so, as – to a certain extent – it probably did, it lacked the power to have such changes implemented, as it still had to rely on the support of a number of parties at the centre of the Danish political spectrum'.

In a 'Declaration of intent', signed in 1987 by the government and the labour market parties, it was stressed that domestic costs, and wages in particular, should be constrained and not exceed production costs in the main competitor countries. Unions' wage policies were in this manner integrated into a wider framework of economic policy albeit on purely voluntary and informal grounds (Schulten and Stueckler, 2000). The Declaration constituted an elemental feature of a long-term economic strategy aiming at restoring and maintaining the economy's growth conditions and ensuring international competitiveness. As such it set the parameter followed in wage negotiations for a decade or so, fixing real wage levels and unit labour costs in relation to that of the competitor countries. While wages continued to be regarded a vital factor in determining the state of the exposed sector and the economy in general, the understanding of competitiveness had been broadened significantly since the heydays of the 1970s corporatism:

> In the 1970s competitiveness was generally perceived as equivalent to relative unit labour costs. From around 1980 a new perception gained ground . . . Competitiveness was measured by a composite index including relative unit labour costs, capital costs productivity and exchange rate development.
>
> Over the period 1984–86 a consensus was established around an extended formulation. Product innovation and productivity, technology content, marketing and flexibility on the labour market and in industrial organisation were made part of the concept of international competitiveness
>
> (Nielsen and Pedersen, 1989: 354).

In accordance with a changed perception of competitiveness, the unions supplemented their traditional voluntary incomes policy with an active means of aiming at encouraging investments and creating new investment opportunities and subsequently, new jobs. This has taken cooperation between the labour market parties to a new level, that of industrial development in support of the active industrial policies followed by governments since the early 1980s. On one hand, an inscription into an appendix to the labour market parties' Cooperation Agreement of 1947 stated the unions' willingness to cooperate and contribute to improvements in various areas of work and production (Tarp, 1985). On the other hand, the trade unions established themselves as a major force of industrial modernisation and a staunch partner of Danish business when in 1985 they set up, in cooperation with major financial organisations, what was to become the country's largest venture company. The principal objective was to support particularly risky business projects. Two years later, in 1987, the unions' central organisation took the initiative to change the so-called Employees' Hardship Funds into an elaborative centre of offensive investment strategy and, on request from the Ministry of Finance, set up a fund which provided financial support to R&D projects. This project was also pursued in cooperation with several major financial institutions and industrial organisations.

In spite of such bold initiatives the corporatist arrangement in Denmark was undermined further still in the early years of the 1990s due to organisational restructuring within both unions' and employers' camps which entailed the ceding of bargaining competence downwards to the industrial organisations and the enterprise. The central organisations continue to play an important role in defining the bargaining agenda and coordinating the bargaining policies of their member organisations but they are no longer involved in the actual collective bargaining as before. With the central organisations far less prominent in industrial relations than in the 1960s and 1970s corporatist state-labour market relations have ceased to be the noticeable feature of Danish industrial relations and politics they used to be. (Although the wage bargaining is no longer a matter of high level corporatist politics, tripartite cooperation continues with regard to other social and labour market issues and economic policy matters. In that respect it remains an important feature of Danish politics and industrial relations (Scheuer, 1998)).

However, rather than interpret these developments as a break with long-standing labour market and political traditions in Denmark they are better understood as a return to industrial relations practices and socio-political relations of an earlier era, i.e., before the highly centralised bargaining arrangements of the 1960s and 1970s which, as discussed above, emerged in the context of increased economic and political volatility. With that in mind, recent developments should not be understood as 'transformation' of Danish industrial relations and state-labour market relations or collapse of historically embedded institutions and practices. On the contrary, when contrasted against past experience they are better regarded as a logical continuation of past structures and practices albeit within a context different from that of the past. The most notable example is the continuation of economic coordination which, from an early stage in Danish industrial relations, has been based on unions' voluntary incomes policy approach, i.e., the formation of wage demands with strict regard to general economic conditions and the requirements of international competitiveness.

At the end of the 1960s Finland experienced a major restructuring of state-labour market relations with the formation of a corporatist, Scandinavian-style incomes policy system marking the end of pluralistic (or non-corporatist) state-labour market relations with its rather antagonistic industrial relations. Essential preconditions for the creation of the new arrangement were: (1) the reunification of the trade union movement; (2) the outcome of a parliamentary elections in 1966 in which the Social Democratic Party emerged as the biggest of the political parties and a leading governmental force, a position it has enjoyed to date; (3) a shift towards greater political stability based on strong majority governments (despite relatively frequent changes in the party composition of cabinets); and (4) active support by employers on efforts to unify the trade union movement with an aspiration for more effective and integrative industrial relations. Background factors also contributed to the formation of the new incomes policy arrangement; the maturation of post-war industrial relations practices and the deteriorating economic conditions in the latter half of the 1960s.

The tradition set by the signing of the first incomes policy agreement in 1968 is now regarded as perhaps the most important element guiding politics and industrial relations in post-1970 Finland:

> In conjunction with this agreement was born not merely a new model for the system between the [labour market] organisations and the State but

> also a new model in respect of the wielding of political power. . . . The real decisions in several key fields of economic policy are being made at the new organisational-corporative level. The formal, authoritative sanction for these decisions is given by the traditional system of elections and Parliament. The new model for making fundamental decisions in society has also meant that some of the interest organisations participating in incomes-policy agreements have become comparable in position to official organs of the State
>
> (Helander, 1983: 23).

While most west European economies went into a state of deterioration and instability in the early 1970s, Finland's bilateral trade agreement with the Soviet Union not only shielded Finnish economy and society from experiencing similar ordeals but actually led to an increase in Finnish exports to east European markets. In addition, the Finnish-Soviet agreement was to be in balance by the end of five-year intervals to prevent trade from negatively affecting either country's current account. It, therefore, acted as an inbuilt stabiliser against unexpected price shocks in international markets and subsequently contributed to the exceptionally favourable performance of the Finnish economy in the 1970s and 1980s.

Favourable economic developments and expansion of the Finnish export industries can also be attributed to domestic policies. Thus, decline in price competitiveness of Finnish products in foreign markets was rapidly (and repeatedly) reversed by currency devaluations. Finnish governments also tended to deal with domestic cost increases by occasionally resorting to austerity policies which normally led to temporary rises in unemployment forcing the unions to moderate their otherwise aggressive wage demands and behaviour. Such combination of flexible exchange rate and austerity policies gave the Finnish export industries an edge at a time exporters in other countries found themselves struggling in face of tougher competition in international markets (OECD, 1982).

These favourable conditions came to an abrupt end in the early 1990s when the economy slid into its deepest recession since the war, following overheating in the late 1980s and the collapse of the Soviet Union in 1990. As a result, the early 1990s saw a series of corporate bankruptcies and skyrocketing unemployment, reaching 20% in 1994. The ordeals of the economy put the incomes policy system under pressure, far heavier than experienced before. In addition, the incomes policy arrangement was undermined by a shift in employers' wage bargaining policy towards more decentralised wage bargaining practices. If firms were to deal successfully with the dire economic situation, the argument went, they needed flexibility and some space to act without the restrictions imposed by centrally bargained agreements and incomes policy packages. Employers' demands for greater flexibility were also related to changes in international markets and competition; as competitive industries became more closely integrated into global markets their interests diverged requiring collective bargaining to take their specific situation into account to a greater extent than before. However, employers' stance remained essentially pragmatic and did not aim at dismantling centralised wage bargaining or the incomes policy system on the basis of precedent and principle: 'defining working condition in an appropriate way in different times and situations requires diverse methods. [The Employers' Association] aims to preserve possibilities to alternative ways of acting in its policy of collective agreements' (Nieminen, 1999: 22). Subsequently, the negotiation rounds in 1994 and 1995 took place at a decentralised (i.e., industrial) level outside the premises of the incomes policy system.

Following a major electoral victory in 1995, the Social Democratic Party returned to power after four years of conservative rule. The new government, a broad based left-right coalition, took effective means to revitalise the incomes policy system regarding cooperation with the labour market parties vital for the achievement of its principal objectives of balancing the foreign account, safeguarding competitiveness and combating unemployment. On the government's initiative, incomes policy agreements were signed for 1996–1997 and 1998–1999, the latter being a central feature of the government's decision to join the European Union and the European Monetary Union (EMU). The decision to join the EMU related to the government's effort to restore the credibility of Finnish economic management in the context of the disciplinary effects of the EMU criteria. Joining the EMU ruled out any short-term and opportunistic measures to ensure competitiveness, in the Finnish case, currency devaluations. The burden of responsibility for the competitiveness of the Finnish economy and export industries was therefore shifted to the labour market parties to a greater extent than before. For real wages to be 'competitive' in relation to wages in the main competitor countries, wage demands and negotiations needed to be formulated and conducted within the confines determined by the EMU criteria. In order to prevent serious decline in incomes and living standards during periods of adverse economic developments, the government and the unions agreed to establish 'buffer funds' to cover rises in public expenditure in times of economic recession. The funds were financed by a slight increase in social security contributions paid by both employers and employees (Kauppinen, 1998).

The establishment of the buffer funds and the greater responsibility of the labour market parties in securing favourable economic condition in general entailed greater importance of collective bargaining outcomes for economic management. In this regard, Finland's membership in the EU and the EMU depended on effective coordination of the labour market parties' bargaining policies and the government's economic objectives and management. This coordination has so forth been conducted at central level within the premises of the incomes policy system. At the same time, the decentralisation process – the delegation of certain bargaining issues to industrial level organisations and local actors – that was launched in the 1994 and 1995 bargaining rounds has been continued within the framework set by the subsequent incomes policy deals (Eironline, 1997).

As in the case of Denmark and Finland, the 1970s saw significant tendencies towards labour market centralisation and tripartite cooperation in Iceland. Following a change in government in 1971 close cooperative relations between a new left wing government coalition and the central union organisation were established. In this respect, the tripartite arrangement that was to characterise Icelandic industrial relations and economic policy making for over little more than two decades resembled the formation of the Finnish incomes policy arrangement. However, while the Finnish incomes policy system was characterised by its institutional viability and rested on the strong commitment of its major participants, the Icelandic corporatism remained weak and vulnerable due to exceptional economic volatility, political instability, and decentralised labour market organisation and wage determination practices. Moreover, it was characterised by antagonistic relations between the principal actors, in particular the public authorities and the trade union movement. By the mid-1990s corporatist state-labour market relations had declined to the extent where, despite the presence of tripartite traits, it can be reasonably argued that recent industrial relations and mode of economic policy making have tended to regress to practices more in line with those of the post-war period.

The framework for the collective bargaining and economic policy making in the 1970s and 1980s was set by exceptionally high inflation (46% against a European average of 10.5% between 1973 and 1985). Although inflation was conceived as the most compelling problem of economic management in Iceland, efforts to constrain it took a backseat to other policy objectives; full employment, economic growth and, in the 1970s, progressive modernisation of the export (i.e., marine) sector. These were pursued through flexible exchange rate policies (currency devaluations), accommodative fiscal and monetary policies, and a thoroughly entrenched system of wage and price indexation. High inflation and economic instability in Iceland can be primarily explained by: (1) a high degree of economic openness with foreign trade mounting to more than 90 per cent of the GDP; (2) the external structure of the economy, i.e., heavy reliance on a single natural resource, namely, the fishing grounds characterised by volatile and unpredictable ecological conditions, the one-sidedness of the country's export structure, and significant price and demand fluctuations in dominant export markets; and, (3) domestic policies and mechanisms of wage and price formation that have been instrumental in channelling inflationary shocks through the economy. Because of these economic structural characteristics and policy traditions the Icelandic economy was for a long period locked in a vicious circle of inflationary devaluations (OECD, 1983).

In order to constrain the inflation and stabilise the economy, governments relied on the support and cooperation with the labour market parties. However, due to excessive demand for labour fuelling 'wage drift' unauthorised by collective agreements and, more importantly, the system of wage indexation which tied wages to prices, moderate (i.e., non-inflationary) wage increases proved hard to achieve in practice. Thus, although tripartite cooperation was, at least in principle, made an elemental feature of economic management, the volatility of the economy prevented the tripartite arrangement from becoming integrative as in the other Nordic countries. This was most clearly evident in governments' determination to keep their prerogative and act independently and without regard to bargaining outcomes whenever domestic developments spiralled out of line with the economy's external conditions and thus needed to be adjusted accordingly. Such adjustments, which objective was normally to curtail real wages – using temporary wage freeze, restrictions of wage indexation and currency devaluations as principal means – were not negotiable within the framework of the tripartite arrangement. Through such forceful measures, governments attempted not only to deal with the economic problems at hand but also to bring the labour market parties' behaviour and policies in line with economic reality. The conflicting roles played by governments in industrial relations in Iceland between the early 1970s and mid-1990s go a long way in explaining the precariousness of the tripartite bargaining system, in particular the low-trust and antagonistic relations between the trade union movement and public authorities. On one hand, the government acted as a third party to the collective bargaining, negotiating over the stipulations of collective agreements. Moreover, it typically set the bargaining agenda by referring to economic conditions and its policy objectives. On the other hand, when it came to general economic management it converted to the role of the disciplinarian, acting arbitrarily and without much regard to the labour market parties often invalidating key stipulations of collective agreements.

Following various attempts to stabilise the economy in the 1980s, the breakthrough came in 1990 when the government and the labour market parties with the participation of various other minor union organisations and economic interests managed to reach a comprehensive incomes policy package – the National Consensus Agreement. This agreement marked a break with previous years as it reflected a completely different and more realistic approach among the labour market parties towards the collective bargaining and especially the *real* general framework set by the economy. Besides moderate wage increases, the main concerns of the agreement were price policies, social policies, interest rates, and tax policies. Issues of industrial policy, modernisation or diversification of the export sector were, however, not included and have not been given any significant priority as in Denmark and, albeit to a lesser extent, Finland. The 1990 agreement was based on close cooperation between the central labour market organisations, with the union organisation assuring consensus among the member unions and their adherence to the agreement – which required temporary abolition of local and intermediate level bargaining and hence prevention of the persistent problem of wage increases in defiance of centrally negotiated wage agreements – and the employers' association constraining any tendencies among the member companies to translate wage increases into higher prices. All parties agreed to the first priority of full employment albeit within the premises of economic stability.

Although the institutional mechanism that underpinned the 1990 agreement gradually broke down over the following years, the policies and approaches on which the agreement was based prevailed and continued to be adhered to by the main labour market organisations. Greater stability of the Icelandic economy has also been assisted by greater stability within the international economy and successful efforts of European countries to restore a stable exchange rate system. These developments have markedly eased external pressures for price increases within the Icelandic economy. Relative external stability and more realistic bargaining outcomes than in previous decades have continued to characterise the Icelandic wage negotiation system to date, which in turn has diminished the need for governments to get involved in collective bargaining. Since the mid-1990s the government has for most part kept its distance from the bargaining table of the labour market.

Summary and conclusions

The early political and economic conditions that shaped national institutions and political traditions in the Nordic countries were broadly similar between the five countries but, nonetheless, different enough to warrant significant diversity of their future development. Of the three countries studied in the chapter Denmark was the only one that at a relatively early stage embarked on the route towards economic coordination based on cooperative state-labour market relations and centralised wage bargaining system. In Finland and Iceland pre-war labour market organisation and wage bargaining practices remained decentralised and state-labour market relations were nowhere as integrative as in the three social democratic countries. Consequently, coordination of economic policies and demands and aspirations of the labour market parties in Finland and Iceland were limited. Moreover, in Finland industrial relations were highly conflict based and politicised which led to a complete breakdown of the collective bargaining system in the early years of the 20th century and later the exclusion of the labour movements' organisations, including the trade unions, from politics and society.

While the two interlinked processes of labour market centralisation and strengthening of corporatist politics continued to characterise Danish developments after the war, the Finnish industrial relations system as well as state-labour market relations were thoroughly restructured at the outset of the war with employers' recognition of the principle of collective bargaining and coordination of policies and behaviour of all the principal actors of the economy in relation to the country's war effort. Coordination was also made a central element of economic governance in Iceland at the same time but without any such drastic changes in industrial relations or the relationship between state authorities and the labour market organisations. In the latter countries (with the exception of the war economy period in Finland, which ended in 1956) economic coordination mainly took the form of enforced, non-accommodative state policies without much involvement of the labour market organisations. Early institutions, cultural traditions and, in the Finnish case, past political conflict patterns continued to shape labour market practices and state-labour market relations.

While corporatist politics remained prominent in Denmark throughout the 1970s, Finnish state-labour market relations were again fundamentally reorganised, this time in a highly integrative and cooperative manner, with the formation of the incomes policy arrangement around 1970. In Iceland economic coordination also took the form of cooperative state-labour market relations albeit weak and vulnerable. The Icelandic corporatism was not built to last and may be best regarded as a reaction to the extreme economic volatilities experienced in the 1970s and 1980s.

Since the mid-1990s corporatist state-labour market politics in Iceland have been severely weakened and earlier patterns of wage determination and state-labour market relations reaffirmed although corporatist traits can still be observed. In Finland and Denmark (albeit to a significantly lesser degree) corporatist politics remain strong and viable as ever despite some temporary disruptions and organisational changes; the anti-corporatist attitude of the liberal-conservative government of 1982–1993 and the decentralisation of the wage bargaining in Denmark and the steep recession in Finland in the early 1990s. In both countries corporatist state-labour market politics have been redesigned to a degree as political and economic actors have responded to alterations in global economic structures and processes and revised their policy outlook accordingly. Thus, rather than being primarily focused on redistribute measures, i.e., the integration of the collective bargaining and welfare policies, and competitiveness with unit labour cost at its heart, tripartite cooperation now takes place on the basis of new and significantly wider perception of the notion of competitiveness. Wage moderation, while still a key element, is only one among many factors comprising the competitiveness of the economy and the export industries. In both countries (as, indeed, in Iceland also), the labour market parties have assumed major responsibilities in ensuring and enhancing economic stability and competitiveness by aligning wage bargaining outcomes and aggregate wage development to the requirements of the economy and the export sector. In addition, Danish trade unions have, on purely voluntary grounds, supplemented their traditional voluntary incomes policy with active investment and industrial policies in cooperation with various economic organisations.

A not so unexpected conclusion can be drawn from the evidence presented in this chapter: that the changes observed in state-labour market relations in the three countries are best interpreted in terms of the interplay between historical traditions and institutions, on one hand, and the external dynamics of the present, on the other. However, the Nordic experience appears to be anything but simple and straightforward and the *complicated and diverse developments in the three countries fail to lend much support to the globalisation/convergence thesis discussed at the outset of the chapter*, namely that: (1) the processes of economic integration will invariably lead to the dismantling of centralised social and labour market regulatory regimes and breakdown of corporatist institutions; and (2) the institutional structures and practices of economic governance of the three countries will become, or are already becoming, more alike.

No single pattern of socio-political developments prevails between the three countries: Finland has seen the strengthening of the highly centralised and formal incomes policy system since the mid-1990s; in Denmark corporatist state-labour market relations are still reasonably strong and vibrant although they have become far less prominent in politics and state-labour market relations than between 1960 and 1980, and; in Iceland the corporatist structures that were set up in the early 1970s have virtually been dismantled. While coordination of economic policies and behaviour has been continued to date in all three countries the form this has taken varies from the formal structures of cooperation in Finland to the highly informal and voluntary approach adhered to in Denmark and Iceland. In all three countries, recent experience indicates that in the case of small open economies, traditionally based on high degree of export specialisation, successful adaptation to an integrating world economy is, indeed, highly contingent on effective coordination of economic policies and behaviour whether this takes the form of strong/formal corporatist arrangement or not. In this respect, it is important to bear in mind that the diverse developments in Nordic state-labour market relations merely reflect the different premises on which the corporatist arrangement in each country rested. Given the historical conditions from which they originated, the conditions that maintained them, their status within the political system and, finally, the form and level of institutionalisation they acquired, the corporatist arrangements in the three countries were more than anything an expression of diversity between them, conditioned by different historical circumstances, institutionalised traditions and cultural values.

In all the three countries studied in this chapter, political and socio-economic developments in the last 20 or 30 years exhibit strong features of path dependency or the prevalence of national institutions circumscribed by past political traditions, cultural values and economic structures. Changes in policies and outlook of state authorities and the labour market parties in the three countries, brought about by external economic and political pressures, are not so much a break with past practices and traditions as an indication of incremental adjustments and adaptation to new realities. Besides, when viewed from the point of history, rather than being susceptible to recent and/or temporary shifts in their external environment the socio-political framework of the three countries seem to have developed along historical trajectories regulated by historically embedded traditions, culture and values and thus retained their traditional features.

The failure of the convergence thesis lies in not only its assumption that the inevitable tendency of economic globalisation is to erase national diversity and distinctiveness of national institutions – in the areas of economic governance, industrial relations and business systems – but also in its failure to consider the role of domestic institutions, relations and processes in the context of change. Social systems or institutional arrangements may be resilient but they are not eternally fixed or principally resistant to change. They do, indeed, change but they do so through a selective process of institutional innovations administered by 'a system specific logic' (Hollingsworth, 1998). Consequently, changes in institutional arrangements strongly tend to show consistency with past experience, practices and traditions.

Notes

1 The novelty and magnitude of changes in national institutions and traditions is one of the major issues dealt with in the literature on globalisation. Within the literature two perspectives have been developed, one focusing on the general changes which currently are taking place irrespective of national politics or institutions, the other concerned with the resilience of national institutions and politics and how external challenges are dealt with by national actors. For further reading, see: Boyer and Drache (1998); Berger and Dore (1996); Stopford and Strange (1995); Hollingsworth and Boyer (1998); Palan and Abbott (1999); Kitschelt *et al.* (1999). For studies on the impact of globalisation on industrial relations systems and/or the importance of national traditions in shaping national systems of industrial relations systems see: Turner (1992); Golden and Pontusson (1992); Crouch (1993); Cressey and Jones (1995); Katz and Darbishire (2000); Rigby *et al.* (1999).

2 The split of the Finnish Social Democratic Party in 1920 was preceded by the formation of a communist party in 1918 (after the Civil War) by Finnish refugees in Moscow. As this party, which was illegal and banned from Finnish politics, drew the bulk of its membership from the Social Democratic Party its formation has often been seen as the latter first split.

3 Despite their persistent electoral strength none of the Nordic social democratic parties (nor the dominant Icelandic Independent Party (conservatives and liberals)) has ever gained a majority of the vote except the Swedish party in 1968 when it obtained 50.1% of the vote (Arter, 1999).

4 'In the Scandinavian inflation models, wages in the sheltered and exposed sectors are linked by the assumption of a universal wage. . . . Indeed, because of political and ideological pressures, wage developments in the exposed and sheltered sectors tend to run parallel. Thus, over the long run, exposed sector wage developments set the parameters for wage developments in the sheltered sector. In effect, competitiveness in small open economies is secured by allowing a rather small group (the exposed sector) to restrain the inflationary pressures that originate in the rest of the economy' (Moses, 2000: 66).

5 'The democratic corporatism of the small European states was born in the 1930s and 1940s amidst the Great Depression, fascism, and World War II. In many ways

the domestic structures and political strategies that emerged in these two decades set guidelines for the generation of leaders charged until the 1960s with economic reconstruction and expansion. Economic openness and dependence established a compelling need for consensus, which through complex and delicate political arrangements has transformed conflict among the main social forces in small European states. . . . In the small European states, moreover, political metaphors reinforce the historical memories of the 1930s and 1940s. They emphasize that all members of society are in the same small boat, that the waves are high and that everyone must pull the oars. Domestic quarrels are a luxury that prudent persons will not tolerate in such adverse circumstances' (Katzenstein, 1987: 34–35).

References

Aldcroft, D. H. (2001), *The European economy: 1914–2000*, London: Routledge.

Amaroso, B. (1990), 'Development and crisis of the Scandinavian model of labour relations in Denmark', in G. Baglioni and C. Crouch (Eds.), *European industrial relations. The challenge of flexibility*, Oxford: Oxford University Press, pp. 71–96.

Arter, D. (1999), *Scandinavian politics today*, Manchester: Manchester University Press.

Benner, M. and Vad, T. B. (2000), 'Sweden and Denmark. Defending the welfare state', in F. W. Scharpf and V. A. Schmidt (Eds.), *Welfare and work in the open economy*, Volume 2 (Diverse responses to common challenges), Oxford: Oxford University Press, pp. 399–466.

Bloom-Hansen, J. (2000), 'Still corporatism in Scandinavia? A survey of recent empirical findings', *Scandinavian Political Studies*, Vol. 23, No. 2, pp. 157–181.

Boyer, R. and Drache, D. (Eds.) 1998, *States against markets. The limits of globalisation.* London: Routledge.

Boyer, R. and Hollingsworth, J. R. (1998), 'From national embeddedness to spatial and institutional nestedness', in J. R. Hollingsworth and R. Boyer (Eds.), *Contemporary capitalism. The embeddedness of institutions*, Cambridge: Cambridge University Press, pp. 433–484.

Bruun, N. (1994), 'The transformation of Nordic industrial relations', in T. Kauppinen and V. Koykka (Eds.), *Transformation of the Nordic industrial relations in the European context*, Helsinki: The Finnish Labour Relations Association, pp. 15–43.

Cressey, P. and Jones, B. (Eds.) 1995, *Work and employment in Europe. A new convergence?* London: Routledge.

Crouch, C. (1993), *Industrial relations and European state traditions*, Oxford: Oxford University Press.

Due, J., Madsen, J. S., Jensen, C. S. and Petersen, L. K. (1994), *The survival of the Danish model: A historical sociological analysis of the Danish system of collective bargaining*, Copenhagen: Jurist- og Okonomsforbundeds Forlag. DJOF Publishing.

Einhorn, E. S. and Logue, J. A. (1986), 'The Scandinavian democratic model', *Scandinavian Political Studies*, Vol. 9, No. 3, pp. 193–208.

Eironline (1997), *SAK and TT renew their basic agreement. June: Moves towards local bargaining*, European Foundation for the Improvement of Living and Working Conditions (URL: http://www.eiro.eurofound.eu.int/1997/06/inbrief/fi976118n.html, retrieved 31st October 2005).

Elvander, N. (1981), 'State intervention and economic freedom', in E. Allardt, N. Andren, E. J. Friis, G. Th. Gislason, S. S. Nilson, H. Valen, F. Wendt, F. and F. Wisti (Eds.), *Nordic democracy. Ideas, issues, and institutions in politics, economy, education, social and cultural affairs of Denmark, Finland, Iceland, Norway, and Sweden*, Copenhagen: Det Danske Selskap, pp. 279–307.

Esping-Andersen, G. (1988), *Politics against markets: The social democratic road to power*, Princeton: Princeton University Press.

European Industrial Relations Review (1983), *Denmark. Central pay framework*, No. 111, April.

Galenson, W. (1968), *The Danish system of industrial relations: A study in industrial peace*, Cambridge, MA: Harvard University Press.

Gassman, H. (1994), 'From industrial policy to competitiveness policies', *OECD Observer*, No. 187, April–May Issue, p. 17.

Golden, M. and Pontusson, J. (Eds.) 1992, *Bargaining for change. Union politics in North America and Europe*. Ithaca: Cornell University Press.

Hall, P. A. and Soskice, D. (2001), 'An introduction to varieties of capitalism' in P. A. Hall and D. Soskice (Eds.), *Varieties of capitalism: The institutional foundations of comparative advantage*, Oxford: Oxford University Press, pp. 1–68.

Helander, V. (1983), 'The development of relations between the state and interest organisations in postwar Finland', in V. Helander and D. Anckar (Eds), *Consultation and political culture: Essays on the case of Finland*, Helsinki: The Finnish Society of Sciences and Letters, pp. 11–28.

Hollingsworth, J. R. (1998), 'Continuities and changes in social systems of production: The cases of Japan, Germany, and the United States', in J. R. Hollingsworth and R. Boyer (Eds.), *Contemporary capitalism: The embeddedness of institutions*, Cambridge: Cambridge University Press, pp. 265–310.

Hollingsworth, J. R. and Boyer, R. (Eds.) (1998), *Contemporary capitalism. The embeddedness of institutions*, Cambridge: Cambridge University Press.

Indridason, T. (1997), *Fyrir nedan bakka og ofan. Saga verkalydshreyfingar, atvinnulifs og stjornmala a Husavik 1885–1985*, Volume II, Akureyri: Verkalydsfelag Husavikur.

Johansen, L. N. and Kristensen, O. P. (1982), 'Corporatist traits in Denmark: 1946–1976', in G. Lehmbruch and P. Schmitter (Eds.), *Patterns of corporatist policy-making*, London: Sage, pp. 189–218.

Jorberg, L. (1979), 'The industrial revolution in the Nordic countries', in C. M. Cipolla (Ed.), *The Fontana economic history of Europe: The emergence of industrial societies – 2*, Glasgow: Fontana, pp. 375–479.

Katz, H. C. and Darbishire, O. (2000), *Converging divergencies: Worldwide changes in employment systems*, Ithaca: ILR Press.

Kauppinen, T. (1998), 'The impact of EMU on industrial relations in Finland', in T. Kauppinen (Ed.), *The impact of EMU on industrial relations in European Union*, Helsinki: Finnish Industrial Relations Association, pp. 50–61.

Katzenstein, P. (1987), *Small states in world markets: Industrial policy in Europe*, Ithaca: Cornell University Press.

Kettunen, P. (1998), 'Globalisation and the criteria of "Us" – A historical perspective on the discussion of the Nordic model and new challenges', D. Fleming, P. Kettunen, H. Soborg and C. Thornqvist (Eds.), *Global redefining of working life – a new Nordic agenda for competence and participation*, Copenhagen: Nordic Council of Ministers, pp. 33–80.

Kitschelt, H., Lange, P., Marks, G. and Stephens, J. D. (1999), 'Convergence and divergence in advanced capitalist democracies', in H. Kitschelt, P. Lange, G. Marks and J. D. Stephens (Eds.), *Continuity and change in contemporary capitalism*, Cambridge: Cambridge University Press, pp. 427–460.

Kirby, D. (1986), 'The workers' cause: rank-and-file attitudes and opinions in the Finnish social democratic party, 1905–1918', *Past and Present*, May Edition, No. 111, pp. 130–164.

Knoellinger, C. E. (1960), *Labor in Finland*, Cambridge, MA: Harvard University Press.

Landes, D. S. (1991), *The unbound Prometheus: Technological change and industrial development in Western Europe from 1750 to the present*, Cambridge: Cambridge University Press.

Moses, J. W. (2000), 'Floating fortunes: Scandinavian full employment in the tumultuous 1970s–1980s', in R. Geyer, C. Ingebritsen and J. W. Moses (Eds.), *Globalisation, Europeanisation and the end of Scandinavian social democracy?*, Basingstoke and London: Macmillan Press, pp. 62–82.

Nielsen, K. and Pedersen, O. K. (1989), 'Is small still beautiful? – An evaluation of recent trends in Danish politics', *Scandinavian Political Studies*, Vol. 12, No. 4, pp. 343–370.

Nieminen, A. (1999), *Finnish employer confederations in the 1990s: Streamlining inner organisation and regulating national capitalism* (unpublished paper, received from author during an interview in Finland, 1999).

Nousiainen, J. (1971), *The Finnish political system*, Cambridge, MA: Harvard University Press.

OECD (1982), *Economic surveys: Finland*, December, Paris: OECD.

OECD (1983), *Economic surveys: Iceland*, Paris: OECD.

OECD (1986), *Labour force statistics*, Paris: OECD.

Olafsson, S. (1993), 'Variations within the Scandinavian model: Iceland in the Scandinavian perspective', in E. J. Hansen, S. Ringen, H. Uusitalo and R. Erikson (Eds.), *Welfare trends in the Scandinavian countries*, London: M.E. Sharpe, pp. 61–88.

Palan, R. and Abbott, J. (1999), *State strategies in the global political economy*, London: Pinter, pp. 21–24.

Rigby, M., Smith, R. and Lawlor, T. (1999), *European Trade Unions: Change and Response*, London: Routledge.

Scheuer, S. (1998), 'Denmark: A less regulated model', in A. Ferner and R. Hyman (Eds.), *Changing industrial relations in Europe*, Oxford: Blackwell Publishers, pp. 146–170.

Schulten, T. and Stueckler, A. (2000), *Wage policy and EMU (National Report for Denmark)*, European Foundation for the Improvement of Living and Working Conditions, Eironline, URL: www.eiro.eurofound.ie/about/2000/07/study/itn0007402s.html, retrieved 31st October 2005).

Stopford, J. and Strange, S. (1995), *Rival states rival firms: Competition for world market shares*, Cambridge: Cambridge University Press.

Tarp, A. (1985), 'Denmark', in B. C. Roberts (Ed.), *Industrial relations in Europe: The imperatives of change*, Australia: Croom Helm, pp. 5–44.

Taylor, R. (1981), 'The need for an incomes policy', in R. E. J. Chater, A. Dean and R. F. Elliott (Eds.), *Incomes policy*, Cambridge: Cambridge University Press, pp. 149–167.

Turner, L. (1992), *Democracy at work: Changing world markets and the future of labor unions*, Ithaca and London: Cornell University Press.

Valkonen, M. (1989), *The Central Organisation of Finnish Trade Unions*, Helsinki: SAK.

Whitley, R. (1999), *Divergent capitalisms: The social structuring and change of business systems*, Oxford: Oxford University Press.

20

Soft Power in a World of Hard Power: Leadership as a Way of Being

by James Joseph

Introduction

This is *a* very difficult and dangerous time in the history of our world. We wake up each morning to new challenges and crises. Yet, the conversation about leadership is all too often about yesterday's theories and practices.

I have found it useful to familiarize myself and my students with the best classical thinking about leadership, from Moses, Mohammed, and even Machiavelli, to Robert Greenleaf, James Macgregor Burns, Stephen Covey, John Gardner and a host of scholars whose works are fuelling the new leadership industry. But while each of them has useful observations about the necessary competencies and what appears to be common attributes, I am struck by the insight offered by Hesselbein (1999), the Chairperson of the Peter Drucker Foundation. She sees leadership as not so much a way of behaving as a way of being. Her concern is not so much with what to do as how to be.

Our world might be fundamentally different if we paid more attention to selecting and elevating leaders who see leadership in this way. *To think of leadership as a way of being is to think of the potential of soft power in a world dominated by hard power.* Soft power is the ability to attract and influence through the appeal of cultural, social and moral messages, respect for the traditions of others and acts of compassion in behalf of a distant neighbour. Hard power, on the other hand, is the ability to influence or control through military might or economic muscle. Joseph Nye (2003) of the Kennedy School of Government at Harvard put observes that hard power and soft power are the practice of two different sets of abilities: hard power gets others to do what we want while soft power gets others to want the same thing we do.

We saw the impact of soft power first hand when Nelson Mandela served as President of South Africa. He represented a paradigm of leadership where influence came from something deeper and more enduring than hard power. His moral standing and political stature in the world went far beyond that suggested by the size of the military or the Gross Domestic Product of the nation state. His influence came from the power of his ideals, the strength of his spirit, the elegance of his humanity and the ability to capture the hearts and minds of people in all colours and corners of the globe. Among the many lessons we should learn from Mandela is that winning friends and influencing people depends increasingly on a moral ecology that cannot be found in military or economic power alone. Hard power may lead to more immediate results, but soft power is likely to be far more enduring.

Former US President Jimmy Carter was awarded the Nobel Peace Prize in 2002. While his contributions as President two decades earlier exceeded the credit he has been given, the award was for his work as a private citizen who set an example in the use and impact of soft power. Like Mandela, his influence comes not from economic or military power but because of his willingness to respect local cultures, honour local traditions and elevate local aspirations even as he seeks to introduce new ways of thinking and new ways of being.

In the 20th century, international conflict was modern, ideological and often totalitarian, but conflict in the 21st century is post-modern, non-ideological and often tied to no one definable place or people. Those who seek to engage the world from behind the shield of hard power rather than by engaging it in a collegial manner may soon find their global influence significantly eroded. There has been much commentary about the collage of fractured interests that don't quite cohere, but we will need to learn to live together in a world where cooperation and opposition coexist.

If we have learned any thing from those who are building new societies in Eastern Europe, Africa and South America, it is that the next generation of leaders is not likely to fit the traditional mold, nor are these leaders likely to be found in traditional places. Their styles will be different. Their accents will be different and so will their colour and complexion.

But what about their values? How will they cope with the challenges of globalization? Can they apply ethics to public life without getting caught up in the politics of virtue or the parochialism of dogma? Will these new leaders be able to borrow from the best of the prevailing leadership paradigms while learning to appreciate the differences posed by culture and context? How can they provide hope and healing to a world that is integrating and fragmenting at the same time? These are a few of the questions that leadership scholars and leadership studies should be asking, as they look at leadership in a global context.

Custodians of values as well as resources

Our world desperately needs leaders who see themselves as custodians of values as well as resources. We need to be clear, however, about what values we seek to cultivate. For more than a decade, the conversation about virtue has been dominated by those who have been preoccupied with the micro-ethics of individual behaviour, the private virtues that build character. We who see leadership as a way of being must expand the conversation about ethics to include the macro-ethics of large systems and corporate institutions. Moreover, the religions of the world do a good job of affirming moral absolutes; we need to help set the tone for coping with moral ambiguities.

Far too many of those who talk about good values do so to suggest that someone has bad values. We need to help de-politicize the concept of virtue, to use it in ways that heal rather than hurt, uplift rather than downgrade, open up communities rather than simply appeal to old stereotypes and traditions.

What does it mean to speak of values that build community in a world that is integrating and fragmenting at the same time? The more interdependent our world becomes, the more people are turning inward to smaller communities of meaning and memory. Some observers see this as reason for despair, but it may be that the first phase of the search for common ground is the search for beginnings and that remembering and even regrouping are often necessary preconditions for developing a more expansive sense of community.

As I travel around the world, I hear more and more people saying that until there is respect for their primary community of identity, they will find it difficult to embrace the larger community in which they function. I am, thus, reminded of the statement of the African American mystic, poet and theologian Thurman (1986: xiii) who was fond of saying "I want to be me without making it difficult for you to be you". Can you imagine how different our world would be if more Americans were able to say I want to be an American without making it difficult for Arabs to be Arabs, Africans to be Africans and Asians to be Asians? Can you imagine how different our communities would be if more Christians were able to say I want to be a Christian without making it difficult for a Jew to be a Jew, a Muslim to be a Muslim or a Hindu to be a Hindu? It is only as we develop this sort of discernment and sensitivity that we come to understand how we build the foundation for community, security and reconciliation in a badly divided world.

Agents of reconciliation

There is nothing more characteristic of the notion of soft power than the role of leaders as agents of reconciliation. Responsible leaders are healers and unifiers. They appeal to people's better nature. They seek to bring them together rather than divide them into "we" and "they" camps. The whole world can learn in this regard from efforts in South Africa to reconcile not only racial and religious groups, but also conflicting images of the past and competing visions of the future.

It has been my experience that reconciliation, in order to be effective, must operate on three levels. The first has been described by Kadar Asmal and others as a kind of existential rebalancing of the self. There must be an awareness of the alienation before there can be restoration of what is broken. Bringing back into balance means undoing historical illusions. For as Wordsworth (1959: preface supplement) once said, "To be mistaught is worse than being untaught".

The second dimension of reconciliation is communal. It is a kind of social rebalancing of the community, recognition that we are all members of the human family. There is much that diverse societies can learn from the South African concept of *ubuntu*, the notion that if I de-humanize another person I am de-humanized in the process. If I deny the dignity of another person, my own dignity is denied in the process. As Archbishop Emeritus Desmond Tutu reminds us, anger, hostility and resentment are corrosive of both the personality of the individual and the potential for community.

In the United States, Martin Luther King also emphasized the need to respect the humanity of the adversary. He called it "loving the enemy". This was not to be confused with liking the evil doer or accepting his evil deeds. It was an application of the meaning of love that went beyond romantic or friendly feeling. The Greeks called it *agape*, an attitude of respect for the humanity of the "Other" not because of who he was, but often in spite of who he was.

The third requirement of reconciliation is spiritual and cosmic. It emphasizes our spiritual kinship with the universe. It is recognition of the claims of all religions that we are a part of something bigger and more mysterious than the self. And it may be that despite our different ways of expressing our connection with creation, it is in our common search rather than our different answers that we find common ground.

The impact of personal renewal

Another important dimension of leadership as a way of being is the understanding that personal renewal is not self-indulgent escape, but a necessary part of perseverance on behalf of a cause, a community or a set of values. The needs of our society are so great and the opportunities to make a difference so awesome that many leaders undercut their effectiveness by staying on the front lines too long. The leadership industry, with its hundreds of institutes and proliferating programmes, rarely focuses on how to avoid burnout and what to do for emotional, spiritual and intellectual renewal. Moreover, many of the most committed leaders feel such a sense of urgency about the work they do, they fail to see the need to stop occasionally to sharpen the saw.

I am as guilty as anyone of sometimes neglecting this critical dimension of responsible leadership, but in preparing to teach a course on the subject I rediscovered a wonderful little book that Stephen Covey uses to emphasize the importance of being able to step back and reflect. It was written some years ago by Marcus Aurelius and is called Meditations (Aurelius, 1945). Readers may remember it from their own studies or they may have caught a glimpse of Marcus Aurelius sitting in a tent and writing by candle light in the movie "The Gladiator". Although he ruled a vast empire, this Roman emperor and philosopher used a few moments at the end of each day to try and better understand who he was, and how he should work and live. He kept a journal that he called "To Himself", but which centuries later was re-titled "Meditations".

The example Marcus Aurelius set is worth recalling because it speaks to us about what leaders need to do to avoid burnout. It emphasizes the importance of personal, spiritual and intellectual renewal, the need for moments of serenity when the leader slows down, steps back, withdraws and reflects. The journal reminds us of the hazards of over-immersion, the danger of losing ourselves and our bearings in the performance of busy tasks. If the movie, "The Gladiator", had probed more deeply into the insights of Marcus Aurelius, he might well have asked his generals, his senators and his judges whether they had somewhere in their lives the counterpart of his tent, with its candle and plain table. He would have in mind not so much a physical location, but moments when they could reflect and renew themselves. He reminds us of the need to create a space of quiet, make some time that is genuinely our own not to hide from life, but to renew ourselves in order to contribute more fully to life.

The second lesson from Marcus Aurelius is that he used those moments of serenity to learn from others. In the first chapter of "Meditations", Marcus (Aurelius, 1945) expresses gratitude one by one to more than a dozen people who influenced his life. We learn that to prepare for the challenge of the next day he worked hard to discern what values and insights he could distil from the lives of people he knew and respected. What a difference it would make if the heroes from whom we seek to learn were not simply the giants of history but the quiet leaders who perform the routine tasks that make our societies work.

The third and final example that may be drawn from Marcus Aurelius is the fact that he sought to place his day-to-day concerns in the context of his whole life, and his whole life in the context of eternity. Part of the reason for the enduring value of his advice to himself is its sense of the eternal juxtaposed against the need to live in the moment, to learn from the moment but to understand what it means to be a part of something larger and more enduring.

Hope and healing

The final dimension of soft power that seems especially critical for a world where so many people have grown weary of promises of help and healing is the restoration of reasons for hope. The kind of hope needed is not the same as optimism. As West (1997) reminds us in his book of conversations about the future, optimism adopts the role of the spectator who surveys the evidence in order to infer that things are going to get better. Hope, on the other hand, enacts the stance of the participant who actively struggles against the evidence to change the deadly tides that could lead to despair. I have found a quote from the 'Born to Motivate' website attributed to Havel (2005): Havel puts his finger on the potential of hope when he said "Hope is definitely not the same thing as optimism. It is not the conviction that something will turn out well, but the certainty that something makes sense, regardless of how it turns out".

The time has come for us to remind leaders at all levels that when they provide hope, people are empowered in a new way. They are more likely to accept and support strategies that attract rather than coerce, thus promoting and developing enduring goodwill rather than illusions of influence.

References

Aurelius, M. (1945), *Meditations* (translated by George Long) *Marcus Aurelius and his Times;* Roslyn, NY: Walter J. Black, Inc., pp. 11–133.

Havel, V. (2005), Quotation on Hope found at Born to Motivate website, URL: *http://www.borntomotivate.com/FamousQuote_VaclavHavel.html,* retrieved 27th October 2005).

Hesselbein, F. (1999), *Leader to Leader,* San Francisco: Jossey-Bass.

Nye, J. (2003), "U.S. Power and Strategy after Iraq", *Foreign Affairs,* July/August, Vol. 82., No. 4, pp. 60–73.

Thurman, H. (1986), *The Search for Common Ground,* Richmond-Indiana: Friends United Press.

West, C. (1997), *Restoring Hope,* Boston, MA: Beacon Press.

Wordsworth, W. (1959), *The Prelude; Or, Growth of a Poet's Mind,* E. de Selincourt (Ed.), H. Darbishire (Rev), 2nd Rev. Edition, Oxford: Oxford University Press.

21

An American in Guangzhou

by Marilyn Thomas

Introduction

Often what makes life so intriguing, I think, is that we never know what might be waiting for us around the next corner. In my own life, for example, if a fortune teller had predicted when I was a child that I would enter a convent in Wisconsin at the age of fourteen and then leave after spending 25 years of my life there, that a marriage of 20 years would end in divorce, that my academic career would include fellowships at Yale, Oxford, and Cambridge, that I would teach in China, everyone who knew me would have laughed at the improbability of it all, myself included. I have no idea what is next, but for me, living and teaching in China was a life-changing event. I turned many corners and discovered some wonderful surprises, all of them opening my eyes a little wider regarding cultural diversity and its many dimensions.

Rowing my boat in China

When I was invited by Guangdong University of Business Studies in Guangzhou to be a visiting professor of English, I jumped at the chance, arranging for a leave of absence from Menlo College for a semester. Part of the agreement was that I also teach once a week at a private secondary school, Peiying, a boarding school with 1500 students. Because the university was on the opposite side of the city from the school, a driver from there picked me up every Tuesday morning for the journey. It was a luxury for me to teach there because when I left the classroom at the end of the day, I was done: no papers to grade.

I was fascinated by the school's history. It had been founded by an American, a Christian missionary, in the latter half of the nineteenth century, but had been taken over by the communist government during the time of Mao Zedong when many Christians were expelled from the country. Ironically and beautifully, I thought, its motto had not changed: "Faith, Hope, and Charity."

The students stood and applauded every time I entered a new classroom as if I were some sort of international celebrity. In fact, it was because I was an

American. I introduced myself before asking them to introduce themselves. To do that I taught them a parlor game called "Picnic." I demonstrated: "My name is Marilyn. I'm going on a picnic and I'm going to take marshmallows." I turned to the first student in the row nearest the door. "Now you say your name and tell the class what you want to take on the picnic." The young lady said she had no English name. "May I give you one," I asked. The whole class cheered. So I studied her face for a few seconds and announced, "your name is Sally." She beamed. "My name is Sally. I'm going on a picnic and I'm going to take hot dogs." Everyone laughed. "Sorry," I said, "you cannot take hot dogs." There was consternation in the room, questioning glances, whispering. "It's a game," I said. "The trick is to guess why marshmallows are all right and hot dogs are not." We had gone up and down a couple of rows when I saw a hand shoot up. "My name is Gabriel," he said, "like the archangel in the Bible. I'm going on a picnic and I'm going to take grapes." I clapped, astounded that he had not only chosen a Biblical name, but knew the story created by John Milton in *Paradise Lost.* "You've got it," I said. "Congratulations. Let's play a few more times and see if anyone else catches on." With a little coaching from Gabriel the next person got it. Then I let Gabriel explain to the whole class. Thinking his explanation in need of a little clarification, I repeated. "The first initial of your name and the first initial of the food you plan to take have to be the same."

As a transition between the game and the song I planned to teach, I asked a lanky student with dark-rimmed glasses who had given himself the name Mike to pull a slip of paper from a box of a hundred questions I had prepared ahead of time. "This is an exercise in spontaneous speaking," I said. "Just read the question to the class and answer it if you can. Feel free to say anything. The point is to practice speaking in English." "What do you do when you feel helpless?" That was a difficult question, I thought, wondering how I myself might answer it. Mike thought for a few seconds. Then he spoke in understandable English. "Think of a pyramid. Take care of the source of the problem and everything else falls into place." I couldn't believe the wisdom in his answer, especially when he had had no time to ponder.

Introductions finished, I wrote the lyrics of "Row Your Boat" on the blackboard. I explained that although it is a children's song, the lyrics, if read symbolically, contain a message worth thinking about and applying to our own lives. We are like boats floating down the stream of life. As long as we stay in our own boats and not try to row somebody else's, all is well. It's when we try to live someone else's life that we run into trouble. Life is also good when we accept what we can't change, when we go with the flow and don't try to row against the current. The students must have already been familiar with the tune if not the lyrics because they were singing the song with little trouble in about fifteen minutes. So I thought I would have some fun with them by having them sing in rounds. To that end I gestured toward the first two rows indicating that they should begin. When they got through the first phrase,

I would gesture toward the second two rows, and then the third until all sixty students would be singing. For some reason the boy in the first seat in front of me thought that my gesture to sing was intended for him alone. So he sang. He sang the whole song solo. He sang on key and he sang the lyrics in perfect English. When he finished, the whole class clapped, myself leading in the applause. Then I said, "That was perfect English. You sound just like an American." His eyes got as big as the favorite fruit of the Moon Festival, the pomelo. "Do you mean that?" The expression on his face indicated to me that he thought I was just flattering him. "Yes," I said, "I mean it. I'm not teasing you. I'm serious. Your English is perfect." He beamed, extended his arms as if to embrace the whole class, and yelled, "That's incredible!" An outsider might have thought he had just won a million Yuan. That little incident made my day. Later the regular teacher told me that his spoken English was very good, but he didn't score well on written tests and so would not have the opportunity open to those who did. How sad, I thought, because he was clearly excited about learning. I will always treasure that little incident as one of my special experiences in China.

China: my bao

One morning I decided to wear the pair of slacks I had purchased the day before. I didn't weigh much more than a hundred pounds at the time, but the slacks were a size Large. Women in the South of China, I had realized early on in my stay, have practically no hips and petite bone structures. If New York, London, or Paris were looking for models, all they would have to do is visit Southern China. I couldn't imagine how those women carried their babies throughout pregnancy. Toward the end they must have popped out in front like basketballs. My "child-bearing hips," as a physician once called them, were wasted on me because I had been a nun throughout my childbearing years.

Tucking in my blouse I concluded that my sister, who was visiting me from the States, had been right. "Too roomy in the waist," she had said when I had tried them on in the store. "Just right in the thighs," I had countered, handing the sales clerk my money. That had been the way with just about all the clothing I had purchased in China. If it fitted in the thighs, it was too loose at the waist; if right at the waist, then too tight in the thigh area. In any case, thinking that I would buy a couple of bananas on my way home, I put 3.8 RMB in my pocket and set off for the local tailor shop, which was also the village laundry. A few doors down from the laundry in the other direction was the beauty shop where I had recently had my hair trimmed, no appointment necessary.

Unable to speak the language, I grabbed an inch of fabric at the waist and pinched it. The owner, one of those tiny Chinese women who seemed to be eating all the time but never gaining weight, shooshed me behind a curtain that concealed the drain for two washing machines. Here I removed the slacks that needed alteration and put on the spare pair I had brought with me. The floor was wet so I had to do a clever balancing act or get my socks wet. My slacks, she told me, would be ready "jin tien." That much Chinese I knew. They would be ready that same day. She wrote the number eleven on a scrap of paper. Since it was already after eleven in the morning, I knew she meant for me to return that night. Workers in China put in long days, including weekends. No Sunday rest for them. I expected my bill would be no more than Y10 ($1.25) and so went away whistling a happy tune.

On my way to get bananas at the street vendor's stall outside the campus where I bought them almost every day and where that family quickly knew me, I decided to go on a detour walking adventure into the inner recesses of the market to explore areas I had never visited. I took a detour and went into what they called the "wet market," so called because this area with its dirt-covered cement floor that covered many city blocks was always wet. In one area fish, eels, and other critters, sure to be on someone's dinner table before day's end, splashed around desperate for some kind of escape as they squirmed in their shallow tubs. Some managed to break free only to find themselves gulping helplessly on the muddy cement floor. A customer pointed to a fish splashing around in the water. With a quick, sure eye the vendor grabbed it, slammed it on the head with a knife handle, and slit its belly, disgorging its entrails. Then he scraped off some of the scales before putting it into a plastic bag for her. The whole procedure was done in just a few minutes. Rows and rows of fresh veggies, just washed, were displayed on flat surfaces that served as tables. Vendors were proud of their displays. If a potato was muddy, a buyer might ask to have it washed before it was weighed. Why pay for soil? Many of the veggies I didn't even recognize. Some looked to me like watercress. A popular one had a name that sounded like "sin tai." Or was it "tai sin"? I could never get it straight. There must have been a dozen different kinds of veggies that I didn't recognize but that resembled one another. The carrots, cabbage, cauliflower, squash, rutabagas, turnips, snow peas, regular peas, green beans, cucumbers, yams, tomatoes, potatoes, beets, mustard greens, onions of every kind, peppers in many shakes of red, green, and yellow, and celery bunches were all neatly laid out for inspection. All the produce looked fresh and tasty, better than in the stores. I saw row after row of the same array of things, each vender trying to make a sale by charging a fraction less than his neighbor or by making his display a little more attractive. Food of all kinds was plentiful and inexpensive. Children under school age clung to their elders, some of whom were squatting on the ground where they peeled, washed, cut, or sorted vegetables. I couldn't imagine how they could crouch down flat-footed the way they did. When I tried, I usually lost my balance. Vendors weighed their produce on a primitive balance scale. Everything was weighed in grams and kilograms. I only knew ounces and pounds. So I just handed them money and waited for change if they wanted to give me any. I had a general idea what things cost, so was not totally at their mercy. More than once, however, I gave a merchant what I thought was the correct amount and received change. I appreciated that kind of honesty.

In the meat section men were chopping up chickens, rabbits, and ducks, rinsing the blood off the cutting boards onto the ground. Surprisingly I didn't see too many flies. Large slabs of pork, beef, and lamb hung from large hooks. I saw animal intestines, stomachs, and other organs I didn't even recognize. One could purchase fowl already cooked and ready to eat. Often the heads were left on to assure the buyer that the meat was fresh. Being a vegetarian, I walked through this area quickly, careful not to slip on something raw that might have been tossed on the ground or fallen there accidentally. I assumed some dog or cat would scoff it up when the market shut down for siesta, which lasted from noon until 2 p.m.

I came next to the dry foods section. My eyes grew bigger because I had never seen so many kinds of mushrooms and fungi in my life. In this area one could also buy rice by the sack, a dozen varieties to choose from. I saw all kinds of dried noodles in trays and bags. I moseyed past gunnysacks of dates as well as dried fruits of every kind imaginable. I gazed into a section that looked like a candy store. Unfamiliar with Chinese candy, I sped past because I was getting hungrier by the minute. Of the candy I had tried, much of it was either too dry or too sour for my taste. Having almost no money on me, I was hoping I could find something simple and inexpensive, something I could pop into my microwave and have ready to eat in five minutes or less. As I pondered my choices, I had to keep an eye out for the motorcycles that buzzed in and out, up and down the rows, some delivering, some hauling produce away. A young man wearing a dark polyester suit brushed by me so close I could feel the heat of the motorcycle's exhaust on my leg. Instinctively I jumped, almost stepping on a vendor who was sitting on the ground with five sick-looking chickens that had their legs tied together so they couldn't get away. I assumed that both the chickens and the eggs next to them were for sale. Eggs were sold in plastic bags like everything else. I never saw an egg carton in the wet market. I looked down to see if there was oil on my linen trousers. Luckily my slacks were still clean, even my shoes despite the fact that I had walked through mud. I saw that a motorcyclist was delivering a crate of live chickens and rabbits crowded so closely together in their cages that they couldn't move. They were silent, probably sensing their fate.

The Chinese have a saying. They say that the people in Beijing will say anything. The people in Shanghai will wear anything. And the people in Guangzhou will eat anything. After almost four months of living there, I could attest to the truth of that statement because I had seen steamed chicken feet, deep-fried scorpions, and dried bats though I assume the latter were for medicinal use only. Fowl and fish were generally cooked with their skin, bones, and sometimes heads intact.

In addition to having to look out for motorcycles, I had to dodge a number of bicycles carrying loads that I considered much too heavy and cumbersome for the size of the vehicle. Only once, however, did I see a bicycle tip over, the old man's wicker basket twice as large as he was, dumping a load of deep-fried buns all over the street. He scooped them back into his basket and cycled on.

I strolled through aisles of nuts and fruit. My eyes feasted on walnuts, hickory nuts, peanuts, bananas, apples, pears, grapes of several varieties, oranges, tangerines, kiwis, pomegranates, pomelos, papayas, watermelons, and persimmons. I was sorry I didn't have a camera with me. At night the streets would be crowded with vendors roasting horse chestnuts and peanuts as well as yams and corn on the cob. The makeshift restaurants on the street would be preparing noodle and rice dishes, fish and meat, all with plenty of hot sauce. The aroma from the peppers cooking over the hot flames would almost take my breath away. I would probably stop for a late night snack of roasted peanuts after I picked up my slacks. At the moment, however, I was fingering the bills in my pocket and wondering if I would have to go hungry until I got more money.

I wanted fruit, but returned to the veggie area, grabbed one cob of corn and one medium-sized yam. I showed the merchant 2 Yuan, asking by my body language if that was enough. He nodded, peeled the corn for me, and took the money with a smile. That left me Y1.8 for bananas. Back in the sunshine, I headed toward my favorite fruit stand. On the way I passed another dozen stands. It was December 1 but the climate still felt like mid-summer. When would the weather cool a little, I wondered. Unlike most days, however, today the sky was blue. I silently thanked God for that and the happy faces I saw on the street. All the babies in China, I decided, were beautiful. Many children said hello to me in English as I passed and giggled with excitement when I responded.

As I neared the college gate, I was happy to see that "my fruit stand" was open. I handed the young merchant with the lovely young wife and adorable baby with porcupine hair, the rest of my money. He looked puzzled until I pointed to a bunch of bananas and shrugged my shoulders. He got my message: How many bananas could I get for this amount of money? He put three bananas in a plastic bag and handed it to me with a warm smile. I nodded and smiled in return. With my treasure, my bao, I headed back to my seventh floor apartment. On the way I passed a couple of pregnant dogs and assumed they were strays.

I consumed the yam while I wrote this essay on my laptop computer. Since I knew I wouldn't be able to manage a cob of corn and type at the same time, I turned on the TV for company during that portion of my meal. It was some kind of melodrama involving the life of the aristocracy in ancient times. I enjoyed the elaborate costuming since I couldn't understand the language. For dessert I had a banana. For breakfast the next morning I planned to have the other two bananas and a bowl of oatmeal. What a deal. For less than 50 cents I enjoyed two delicious meals.

The Chinese know that food is more important than anything else. They have an aphorism about it, about how people with full stomachs don't start revolutions. I saw an abundance of food in China. Some restaurants were as many as five stories high. Food was plentiful on the street where the climate is sub-tropical. When we traveled, we could usually find a restaurant even if a village was too small to have a hotel. For the Chinese food is a treasure. In fact the word for "treasure" in Chinese is "bao." And so when a customer wants to take home the leftovers from a meal, he asks for "da bao," a carryout container, a treasure. A steamed bun with filling inside is also called "bao," a bun with a treasure inside. The Chinese people themselves, I decided, are like little containers holding big hearts, their baos. China itself is a bao, a huge container with countless treasures inside waiting to be discovered. Sometimes it was actually to my advantage that I couldn't speak the language, that I must have looked both deaf and dumb to the locals, because in all cases, they at least tried to help even when they failed. Every day they shared some treasure with me, and every day I was more grateful for their warm hospitality.

Part 7

Conclusion

Conclusion: Consequences of New Realities

by Kurt April

A call to responsibility

In concluding this book, which is rich in perspectives, suggestions and affirmations, we would like to close the loop from the introduction by drawing in some (not all again) of the key shifts in diversity understanding and practice around the globe. In doing so, we would like to highlight slivers for provoking further thought on these philosophically-driven shifts.

Are we complying?

During the early to mid-20th century, the focus of diversity was initially driven at a country level, driven by two overriding philosophies: the women's rights and the civil rights philosophies. The women's rights philosophy focused particularly on eliminating sexism with an underlying, principle question: "What can be done to eliminate discrimination against women?" And the civil rights philosophy, mainly driven through the USA, which sought to end discrimination and racism, and was mainly focused at minorities. Its underlying principle question was: "What do broader, equally applied civil rights guarantee our citizens?" These philosophies challenged the status quo of the day, and through legendary actions of individuals and organizations, managed to get these philosophies onto the legal agendas of countries. Countries variously interpreted these legal agendas, e.g., equal treatment infrastructures, affirmative action, equal opportunities requirements, and so on. Citizens, civil society, the private sector and governments thereafter found themselves required to comply with legal requirements that guaranteed citizens certain rights. The movements supporting these philosophies grew so powerful that its spread and got adopted across regions, beyond countries, and in most of the Western world (as well as other, non-Western pockets of the world).

Not long into the lifespan of these philosophies, organizations started complaining about the cost that such compliance was adding to their operational costs. Many internal employees started complaining – those not being affirmed felt left out, claimed reverse discrimination, engaged in confused collaborative-disingenuous relationships with those being affirmed, and some even started psychologically withdrawing from their companies (translating in less effort); those being affirmed felt that their credibility was being put into question, were having to be twice/three times as good as others to feel credible, and were carrying the burden of their entire minority group (i.e., feeling that if they failed, their employees and those not being affirmed would right-off their entire minority group).

Societal reputation

In the last decade of the 20th century, with growing globalisation and cross-regional cooperation and interaction, the shift in focus moved from a legalistic approach, to one of "*valuing diversity*." This socially responsible philosophy was based on a view of the organization, now more international in outlook, operating as a good corporate citizen, and its leadership/management supposedly wanted their organizations to act in ways that benefit society. Its underlying principle question was: "What do the best interests of society dictate that we should do?" A few forward-thinking organizations hopped on the bandwagon, sensing that, in sectors and industries where many products and services are undifferentiated between players in the same/similar industries, responsible behavior that is contextually relevant in regard to these philosophies could, in "moments of truth," lead to competitive advantage. Moments of truth are specific snapshots people take of organizations – and use them to run their own personal "film" (grids of perspectives) of the true intentions of these organizations in their communities and societies. It was believed, by organizations, that visible, socially responsible action enabled organizations to enter into the international arena on stronger footing (Cascio, 1998; Johnston, 1991). More broad-minded organizations, that valued diversity, then actively sought to recruit people who were different from their typical employees, and more local employees where they had an international footprint (private business such as energy companies, airlines, retail outlets, and so on) or international offices (governments and public sector offices which had embassies, consulates, and so on). Diversity was assumed to affect an organization's performance by expanding its ability to serve a broader customer base, acquire more diverse talent pools and procure resources and respond to environmental changes (Roberson and Park, 2004). Recognition for diversity-related programs and initiatives, it was understood, would serve as a powerful signal, improving an organization's ability to communicate its value in capital markets. An added advantage of valuing diversity in this way was that it could provide superior services, simply because it enabled organizations to better understand customers' or citizens' needs (Wentling and Palma-Rivas, 2000), enabled organizations to tap into niche markets (Mueller, 1998), enhanced flexibility through diversifying market segments (Fleury, 1999), and gave them capability to respond to change more quickly (Adler, 1997; Jackson *et al.*, 1992). It was also taken as understood that if an organization did not do well in "valuing diversity," they could actually cause harm to the organization's reputation externally, and internally the harm would be manifested through inefficient communication, high interpersonal conflict and increased employee turnover (Bennett-Alexander, 2000).

Getting ahead of the pack

At the start of the 21st century, the focus shifted from just "valuing diversity" to "managing diversity," and approach based on a humanistic philosophy that viewed the human race as a "sister-/brotherhood," and sought to foster good relations through enhanced tolerance, acceptance, and understanding of "all" – thus shifting from a focus on "others" under the "valuing diversity" paradigm, to a focus on diversity for "all" under a new "managing diversity" mantra. Its underlying principle question was: "What can be done to demonstrate equal valuation and treatment of 'all' that, at a societal level, was good for all peoples of the human species, but which also, at an organizational level, could lead to strategic competitive advantage." Such equal valuation had to be demonstrated around recruitment, selection, placement, succession planning, performance management and rewards processes for all concerned (Cascio, 1998).

To successfully achieve this, organizations were encouraged to move beyond the focus on "some," move beyond the rhetoric of how "all" were benefiting as a by-product of the focus on "some" under the previous philosophy, and provide real resources and real management support for diversity efforts that included everyone. In their early, classical article on diversity as competitive advantage, Cox and Blake (1991) outlined several domains in which competitive advantage should derive from explicitly valuing the diversity of "all" in an organization. These domains include: (1) enhanced skill in entering untapped markets; (2) innovation and creativity flowing from new perspectives; and (3) increased ability to adapt to changing environments. Typically, top management of organizations were encouraged to champion and support such initiatives (Hayes, 1999; Jackson *et al.*, 1992). The diversity business rationale of the time can be summarized as:

- Attracting, retaining and fully developing "all" staff, not just "some."
- Understanding the needs of global customers, by engaging them through local knowledge, local relationships and local employees.
- Maximizing value and productivity by seeking to understand the link between diversity and organizational performance.
- Seizing market opportunities, because broad diversity enhances the organization's sensing capability.
- Being regarded as an employer of choice, because "all" people are valued and the organization reflects the demographies of the regions in which they operate.

- Developing a greater pool of leadership capacity.
- Growth and profitability, resulting from the embedded resilience resulting from the "requisite variety" in the organization.

In practice, this meant that managers had to not only develop an environment which increased the motivation, satisfaction and commitment of diverse people (Subhash, 2003), but furthermore it had to be an equitable work environment where no group had an advantage or disadvantage (Torres and Bruxelles, 1992). To encourage "good practice" of the underlying philosophy, and flavour in the humanistic principle, organizations sought to link human resource management decisions, which flowed from business strategic objectives, to diversity decisions. An example of such linking is listed in the Table I below.

In private businesses, executives were challenged by three recurring questions: (1) "What do I as an executive need to do to ensure the effective and efficient utilization of 'all' employees in pursuit of the corporate mission?";

Table I Linking of Business and Diversity, through Human Resource Strategy

Business Strategy		**HR Strategy**		**Diversity Strategy**
Globalizing	⇨	All cultures working effectively together	⇨	Responding to, and understanding, "all" employees, customers, vendors, suppliers, governments, and other stakeholder groups
Growing the business	⇨	Need more talent	⇨	Attracting and retaining the best possible employees
Innovation	⇨	Generate new ideas	⇨	Accepting and encouraging diverse perspectives
Customer focus	⇨	Develop employee teams close to the customer	⇨	Multi-functional teams operating effectively and creating innovative solutions for customers
Reduced management levels and controls	⇨	Create independent, skilled and motivated employees	⇨	Creating self-directed work teams that leverage differences, and operate with minimal barriers
Reduce costs and improve productivity	⇨	Employees doing more, and developing broader skills	⇨	Maximizing the potential of all employees

(2) "What are the implications of diversity for how I lead and manage everyone?"; and (3) "What is the role of diversity in ensuring the sustainability of the corporation's competitive advantage?" – and, executives began to place priority on unearthing behavior sets that would explicitly keep people accountable for diversity-prioritized behavior. Davidson (2002) points out that leaders cannot excel in today's global economy if they themselves are unable to skillfully lead diverse groups of people. This includes diversity not only within the group of employees, or team members, but also diversity in management itself. Harris (1989) argues that relationships are the key to the individual or organizational performance. In this way, he explains that leaders should be aware of how these relationships affect their own behavior, and may be used to enhance or undermine productivity. Awareness of and skill at human relations, applied to clients, customers, suppliers, and contractors, as well as government and community officials, increases goodwill and productivity (Harris, 1989). Below, we list a set of such behaviors (Figure II), required from managers, which we have collated as common themes, from the numerous sets that we have gathered in our research from various organizations around the world:

The key tenants of these human resource and relationship approaches can be summarized as: (1) treating others with respect and dignity; (2) engendering high trust; (3) fostering open communications; (4) keeping employment systems open and transparent; (5) ensuring that work practices are flexible and innovative; (6) allow for different personal work-life balance approaches; and (7) enabling more cohesive teams.

A number of private companies around the globe began the arduous and complicated work of trying to causally link all of these diversity insights to bottom-line performance measures – measures such as those reflected in Figure III below.

Currently, around the globe, this is ongoing and is where most companies have come to in the evolution of emerging realities of organizational diversity. Some private companies, like Shell International and SABMiller, are well matured in these processes, the latter having initiated its diversity processes with a business-advantage focus during the 1970s. A few public organizations and governments, such as in Canada and Israel, are well matured in understanding diversity in intellectual capital, in preparing their nations for uncertain futures.

But they're so different

All this focus on relationships and behaviors unearthed a new, emerging reality, i.e., that with the "managing diversity" focus on "all," it became apparent that diverse individuals interpreted all of the business imperatives very differently. So, for example, communication in Gabon, communication in China, communication in Denmark, communication in the USA, etc., were all

Require high standards of work performance (excellence) from all employees
Discuss performance difficulties with employees from all backgrounds, and explore approaches for overcoming them
Acknowledge diversity at all levels of work, and encourage expression of divergent views
Align teams with diverse stakeholder goals and diverse visions, and hold them accountable for implementation thereof
Encourage interdependence within, and between, teams of different stakeholders
Work to ensure that diverse candidates are considered for highly visible assignments and other opportunities that lead to access to the informal network (within the organization, and with its partners, vendors, suppliers, customers and the public)
Actively encourage diverse inputs and viewpoints in the development of organizational strategic and operating plans
Provide constructive help to all employees when dealing with problems encountered inside, and outside, of the organization
Encourage people from different cultures, backgrounds, genders, ethnicities, etc., to take responsibility for transferring their knowledge, and acting as positive role models for others in the organization
Signal (through public actions and deeds) the consequences of inappropriate and misaligned action of colleagues, employees, supplies, vendors and partners
Create, sponsor or suggest initiatives to ensure that people are promoted and rewarded in a manner that provides equal opportunity for all, regardless of gender, race, country of origin, educational background, sexual orientation, tenure, socio-economic background, disability, etc.
Break down occupational or divisional barriers, and encourage a multi-disciplinary approach
Pay attention (time, resources, energy, personal commitment) to the needs and potential for development of all people
Give people permission and opportunities to develop skills (beneficial to the organization, their community and society at large) outside of their usual area of work, and extend their experience and capabilities
Provide opportunities for people to demonstrate their differences/differing areas of expertise
Acknowledge and recognize differences as a valuable source of learning in the workplace
Make decisions based on consultation with diverse inputs and people
Make decisions based on job-related qualifications when hiring and promoting, rather than relying on image, fit, feeling, or friendships
Look for instances where people are overlooked, ignored, etc., and take purposeful action to address and correct this
Deconstruct "rank" within the organization and make everyone aware of its effects on relationships and productivity
Openly/publicly recognize the contribution of women, employees from other cultures, people with different capabilities and other significant under-acknowledged groups, to organizational success
Challenge the perception that "less qualified" individuals are hired or promoted, and considered for promotion

Figure II Specific Organizational Behaviors

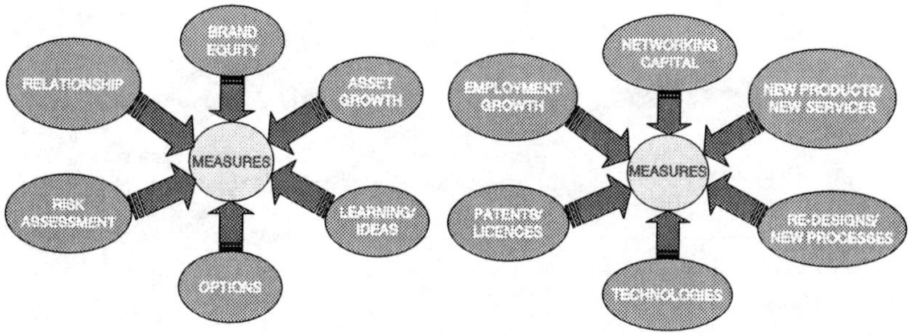

Figure III Business Performance Measures

perceived and practiced differently – dependent on the cultural heritage of the individuals. Sensing, leadership, resilience, and other business imperatives also were perceived differently, and, as a result, the behavior set listed above had varied interpretations and invariably had no single causality path (it dawned that the diversity reality should be more individually focused, reflecting the understanding that relationships are enhanced through heterogeneity). Treating everyone through the same lenses and expecting the same outcomes, became an issue of moral ignorance for many – almost shameful to be doing so.

As a result, a philosophy around moral responsibility began to predominate, termed "inclusion," which challenged people to "do the right thing." Its underlying principle question was: "What do our moral beliefs and standards dictate that we should be doing in expecting and getting the best out of all people?" It is stated in literature that debates between people who believe in "exclusivity" versus those who believe in "inclusion" centre around egalitarian opportunity, a moral view, as the predominant value (Pearpoint, 1990). This philosophy manifested, and still is manifesting, in a new focus on cultures of people, which we aggregated into one figure below (Figure IV). The diagram depicts ten cultural orientations that form the basis for most culturally-focused diversity work in organizations – it is clearly aimed at individuals' perspective-formation.

Pearpoint (1990) describes inclusion as "all welcome," since inclusive communities will utilise the talents of people who would otherwise be discarded and written off – sometimes unconsciously excluded by dominant paradigms and rank. In organizational contexts, "inclusion" seeks to explain the co-existence of employees from various socio-cultural backgrounds, within the organization. Importantly, the cultural work ignited an entire body of work around understanding the grids of perspective, world views/mental models, which now demanded forms of social capability.

Offering the best of me – it's not for sale, it's my choice

More recently, the "inclusion" philosophy has been expanded, beyond a mere cultural focus, to the behavioral manifestations of neurological- and biological

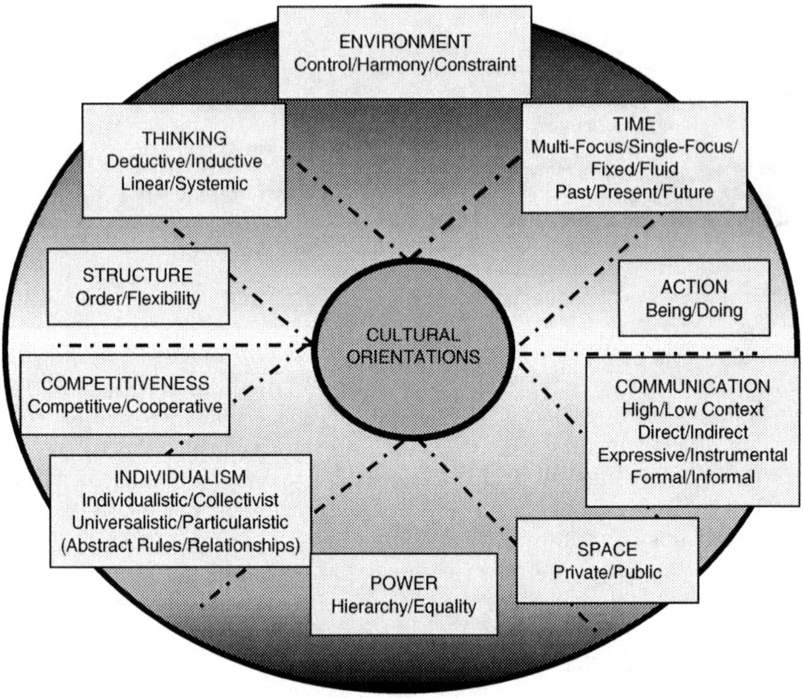

Figure IV Dimensions of Cultural Orientation
Sources: Adapted from: Stewart and Bennett (1991); Rhinesmith (1995); Kluckhohn and Strodtbeck (1961); Hall and Hall (1987); Hofstede (1980); Hampden-Turner and Trompenaars (1997)

circuitry – the "self-leadership" philosophy, which challenges individuals to manage/lead themselves, manage their own prejudices and stereotypes, seek awareness into the ways in which they subtly damage the self-confidence and self-esteem of those with whom they work and live, to understand the influence of their own intentions on lived-behavior, to deconstruct the way in which they negotiate their identities as individuals in networks of power, and constantly expose their own views, and their view of others, to challenge and debate – *metaskills* – a type of cognitive intelligence, as well as emotional intelligence (Goleman, 1998; April *et al.*, 2000). According to Duxbury and Anderson (2000), it is crucial to build on Goleman's emotional intelligence skills related to personal competence (self-awareness, self regulation and motivation) and social competence (empathy, building bonds, cooperation, conflict management, influence, and the ability to catalyze change). According to Schoem *et al.* (1995), diversity increases individuals ways of knowing, enabling them to reread a particular meaning and uncovering new

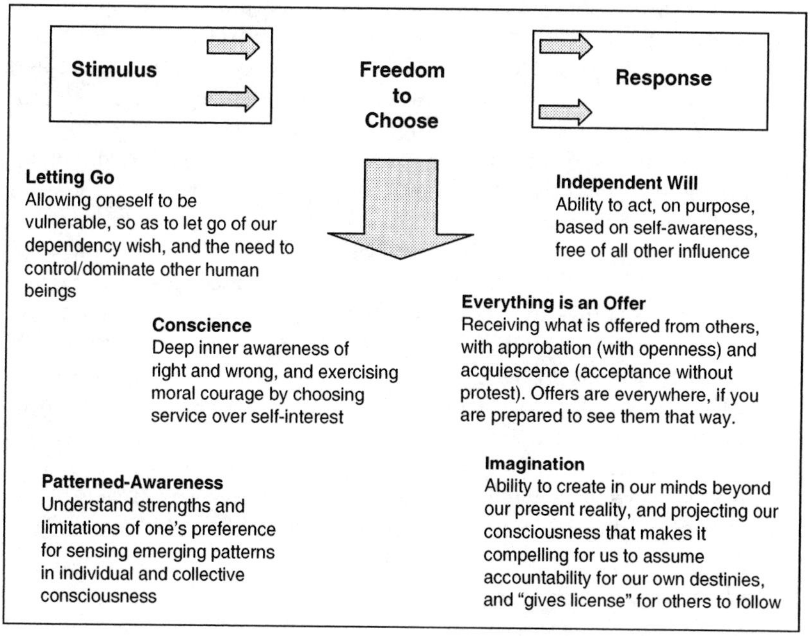

Figure V Every Individual Chooses – Creative Tension of Memory and Possibility

meanings – perspectives that we could not previously see; and these further enable the necessary flexibility, creativity and innovation, so dearly cherished by many organizations. April *et al.* (2000) further assert that progress depends on the extent to which we can harness latent cognitive skills and emotional abilities, motivation and enthusiasm, but we will not achieve this until we recognize our role as either *part of the problem* or *part of the solution*.

Individuals, in the "self-leadership" paradigm, are focused on the self-knowledge and interpersonal knowledge that are required in order to appreciate and cope with diversity. Much of the previous philosophical stances/paradigms emerged as social defenses against anxiety – as all work, relationships and choice entail some form of anxiety. It also, at the same time, creates excitement (opportunity). But anxiety and excitement are closely linked and are present at the same time (it's the balance that is important). And so individuals collectively defend against it (collective defenses) through practices and behaviors. Understanding the power of emotions and cognitive responses, thereby increasing one's sensitivity to them, allows individuals to "tune to the emotions that are the most accurate and most helpful when making difficult decisions" (Cherniss, 2001: 6). It therefore becomes a matter of choice. Covey (1990) related the simple, yet powerful, idea that there is a space between any stimulus and the response to it. And that the key to any personal growth and happiness, including growth in the area of diversity and being open to the "other," depends on how individuals use that space. We have captured, in Figure V, the key mitigating factors (self-awareness, imagination, conscience and independent will) that affect the individual's freedom to choose the desired response, given a set of stimuli (that the individual, often enough, has no control over). The tension ("creative tension" if the individual chooses to see it that way), that the individual is often faced with is the one between "memory" (what life, situations, ideas, views, one's horizon, etc. *were like*) and "possibility" (what life, situations, views, one's horizon, etc. *can be like*).

Although individuals are capable of great creative leaps, most of the time their thinking is pretty conditioned, their ideas follow well-defined, generalized tracks because of inroads in their minds that they have built there through experience, information, knowledge or simple belief. Balancing the tension creatively allows for the unearthing of deeply held, often subconscious, sets of assumptions about how the world works. And if individuals gift this to themselves, they are likely to discover new patterns emerging (Brown and Eisenhardt, 1998) – patterns for shared understanding and reciprocal relationships (Pascal *et al.*, 2000) that would not have been possible if they we not willing to suspend anxiety about diversity, and give themselves the opportunity to "let go."

The call to stewardship and contribution

This book has given lenses through which to view diversity from a multitude of perspectives (captured in Figure VI). Finally, we would like to challenge the reader to positive steps towards *contributing as a steward, to realizing a different world that works for the many*, on individual, local, community and organizational, as well as country and regional levels.

The consequences of all of the presented realities is to challenge people to be more courageous. Covey (1990) developed a framework that highlights the stages of contribution (Figure VII), which we have adapted to link with the motivations from which it emanates.

Stewardship is about living with the tension that anxiety and excitement provokes at the same time, but knowing that leading is not existent in a single individual, but co-created by a group. Stewards are able to "let go" of, and resist, the idealistic belief that they alone can transform things. They understand that idealization rapidly can drop in to denegration. Stewardship emanates from a place of love, a deep love for what it means to be human, and something that has always been understood through the ages (transcending purpose) – but today, we need leaders, at every level of society, who have the courage to be what has always been understood, and to respond to the call of the transcending purpose. Leaders should be willing, at least, to look, but hopefully also engage the questions, presented in this book, and which we are surrounded by – the questions that are happening in the hearts and minds of people all around us, waiting to see what response, what action, those questions will evoke from us. Stewardship is about renegotiating the

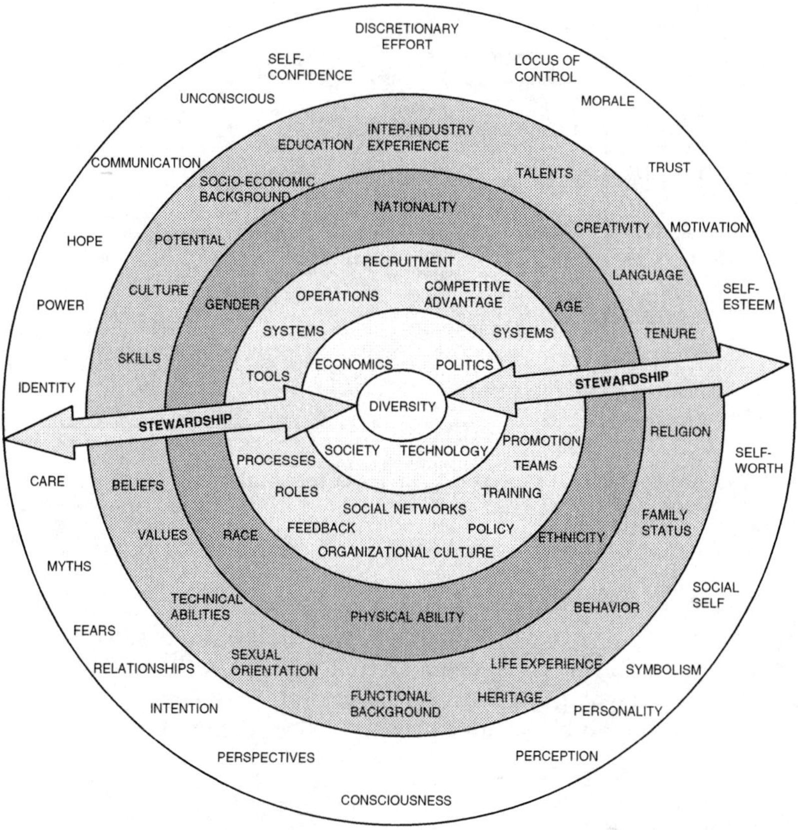

Figure VI Stewardship Across All Levels

social, interdependent contract between people from all walks of life, and all parts of the earth, and redistributing power by affirming a human-democracy. It is our belief that the corrosive effects of not engaging the questions, will keep us locked in anger and fear of the "other." The questions demand your attention.

"People need to act in order to discover what they face, they need to talk in order to discover what they think, and they need to feel in order to discover what it means" (Weick, 2001: 96–7). Stewardship is what facilitates the necessary, respectful, interactive sense-making for the "tension" and "opportunity" that presents itself, moving people lovingly closer together with enhanced trust and self-respect, and which helps to build the stable rendition of what we desire for all of us – it's a choice, a demanding choice.

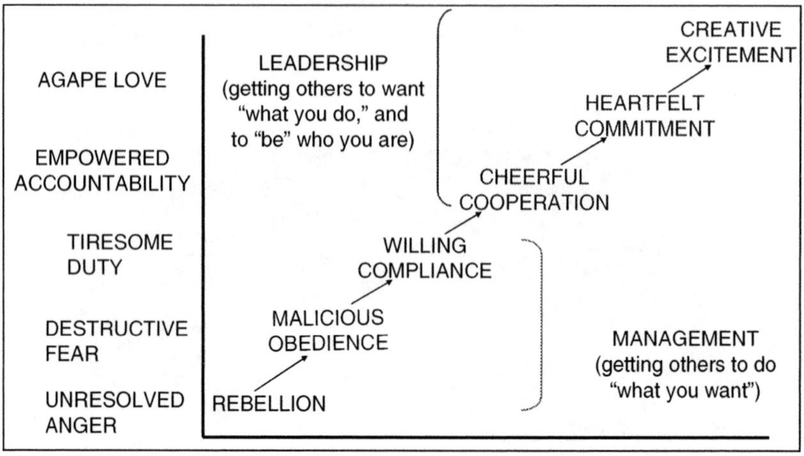

Figure VII Motivation that Determines Levels of Contribution
Source: Adapted from Covey, 1990

We hope this book would have stirred you in some places, evoked some responses in others, angered you in others and engaged you in still others. . . but always towards your choice. You can choose to ignore the choice, or you can choose to respond to the choice – but both have consequences. We would like to end this book with a poem, which we entitle "What If?":

What if you could be whole – truly whole?
What if I am more than you see?

But

If you can't see me, I am unable to engage you
If you think my pain is different to yours
  then you can't see me, and be with me
What if you were truly awake to how you think?
What if?

The lies in your heart and the eloquence of your lips
  betray your true intent,
  when I can actually feel you, your essence
I can connect with the sound of your genuine
Your Spirit
What if you can recognize the other in you?
What if you could see me?

In your silence, my Spirit roused
What if actionable will is released?
What if?

Comparison defeats the Spirit and renders us simply flesh
Common ways defeat our joint possibility
If you can't see the possibility
   then I am forever destined to give less
Your justification of inactivity is tiring
   what if you just acted
Love, beauty, Spirit, connection to God
   you cannot take it from me
What if we could give it to each other?
What if?

But

Imagine if you could really see me
The sound of the genuine in me
What if it could be so?
What if I could offer it to you
   by choice?
What if I really mattered
   so that you could be truly whole?
What if?

Bibliography

Adler, N. J. (1997), *International Dimensions of Organizational Behavior*, Cincinnati, OH: South-Western College, Publishing.

April, K., Macdonald, R. and Vriesendorp, S. (2000), *Rethinking Leadership*, Kenwyn: University of Cape Town Press (Juta).

Bennett-Alexander, D. (2000), "Ten Ways to Value Diversity in your Workplace and Avoid Potential Liability in the Process," *Employee Rights Quarterly*, Vol. 1, No. 2, pp. 57–64.

Benson, J. and Dresdow, S. (2003), "Discovery Mindset: A Decision-Making Model for Discovery and Collaboration," *Management Decision*, Vol. 41, No. 10, pp. 997–1005.

Bogenrieder, I. and van Baalen, P. (2004), "Multiple Inclusion and Community Networks," *Research in Management*, The Netherlands: Erasmus Research Institute of Management.

Brown, S. L. and Eisenhardt, K. M. (1998), *Competing on the Edge: Strategy as Structured Chaos*, Boston, MA: Harvard Business School Press.

Cherniss, C. (2001), "Emotional Intelligence and Organizational Effectiveness," in C. Cherniss and D. Goleman (Eds.), *The Emotionally Intelligence Workplace: How to Select for Measure, and Improve Emotional Intelligence in Individuals, Groups and Organizations*, San Francisco, CA: Jossey-Bass.

Cascio, W. F. (1998), *Managing Human Resources – Productivity, Quality of Work Life, Profits*, Boston, MA: McGraw-Hill.

Covey, S. (1990), *The Seven Habits of Highly Effective People*, New York: Free Press.

Cox, T. H. Jr and Blake, S. (1991), "Managing Cultural Diversity: Implications for Organizational Competitiveness," *Academy of Management* Executive, Vol. 5, No. 3, pp. 45–46.

Davidson, M. N. (2002), "Mentoring in the Preparation of Graduate Students of Color," *Review of Educational Research*, Vol. 71, No. 4, pp. 549–74.

Duxbury, D. and Anderson, P. (2000), "Emotional Intelligence: Fad or Fundamental Skillset," *The Systems Thinker*, Vol. 11, No. 6, August.

Fleury, M. T. L. (1999), "The Management of Culture Diversity: Lessons from Brazilian Companies," *Industrial Management & Data Systems*, Vol. 99, No. 3, pp. 109–14.

Goleman, D. (1998), *Working With Emotional Intelligence*, New York: Bantam Doubleday Dell Publishing Group, Inc.

Hall, E. T. and Hall, M. R. (1987), *Understanding Cultural Differences: Germans, French and Americans*, Yarmouth, ME: Intercultural Press.

Hampden-Turner, C. and Trompenaars, F. (1997), *Riding the Waves of Culture: Understanding Diversity in Global Business*, 2nd Edition, New York, NY: McGraw-Hill.

Harris, P. R. (1989), *High Performance Leadership: Strategies for Maximum Career Productivity*, Glenview, IL: Scott, Poresman & Company.

Hayes, E. (1999), "Winning at diversity," *Executive Excellence*, July, p. 9.

Hofstede, G. (1980), *Culture's Consequences: International Differences in Work Related Values*, Beverly Hills, CA: Sage.

Jackson, B. W., LaFasto, F., Schultz, H. G. and Kelly, D. (1992), "Diversity," *Human Resource Management*, Vol. 31, No. 1 and 2, pp. 21–34.

Johnston, W. B. (1991), "Global Workforce 2000: The New World Labour Market," *Harvard Business Review*, March–April, pp. 115–27.

Kiesler, S. and Sproull, L. (1982), "Managerial Response to Changing Environments: Perspective on Problem Sensing from Social Cognition," *Administrative Science Study Quarterly*, Vol. 27, pp. 548–570.

Kluckhohn, F. and Strodtbeck, F. (1961), *Variations in Value Orientations*, Evanston, IL: Row, Peterson.

Lyles, M. and Mitroff, I. (1980), "Organizational Problem Formulation: An Empirical Study," *Administrative Science Study Quarterly*, Vol. 25, No. 2, pp. 102–109.

McCaskey, M. B. (1982), *The Executive Challenge: Managing Changes and Ambiguity*, Marshfield, MA: Pitman.

Morgan, G. (1980), "Paradigms, Metaphors and Puzzle Solving in Organizational Theory," *Administrative Science Quarterly*, Vol. 25, pp. 605–621.

Mueller, K. P. (1998), "Diversity and the Bottom Line," *Executive Excellence*, December, p. 7.

Nisbet, R. E. and Ross, I. (1980), *Human Inference*, Eaglewood Cliffs, NJ: Prentice Hall.

Pascale, R. T., Milleman, M. and Gioja, L. (2000), *Surfing the Edge of Chaos: The Laws of Nature and The New Laws of Business*, New York, NY: Three Rivers Press.

Pearpoint, J. (1990), "Inclusion vs. Exclusion – Society is at a Turning Point," *Inclusion News*, The Centre for Integrated Education and Community, Canada.

Rhinesmith, S. H. (1995), "Open The Door to a Global Mindset," *Training and Development*, Vol. 49, Issue 5, pp. 34–44.

Roberson, Q. M. and Park, H. J. (2004), "Diversity Reputation and Leadership Diversity as Sources of Competitive Advantage in Organizations," *Academy of Management Proceedings*, pp. F1–F6.

Schoem, D., Frankel, L., Zuniga, X. and Lewis, E. A. (1995), *Multicultural Teaching in the University*, Wesport, CT: Praeger.

Senge, P. M. (1990a), *The Fifth Discipline: The Art and Practice of the Learning Organization*, New York, NY: Currency Doubleday.
Senge, P. M. (1990b), "The Leader's New Work: Building Learning Organisations," *Sloan Management Review*, Fall, pp. 7–23.
Simmons, M. (1996), *New Leadership for Women and Men – Building and Inclusive Organization*, Aldershot: Gower Publishing.
Stewart, E. C. and Bennett, M. (1991), *American Cultural Patterns: A Cross-Cultural Perspective*, Yarmouth, ME: Intercultural Press.
Subhash, C. K. (2003), "Workforce Diversity Status: A Study of Employees' Reactions," *Industrial Management & Data Systems*, April, pp. 1–2.
Torres, C. and Bruxelles, M. (1992), "Capitalizing on global diversity," *HR Magazine*, December, pp. 30–33.
Weick, K. (2001), "Leadership as the Legitimation of Doubt," in W. G. Bennis, G. M. Spreitzer and T. Cummings (Eds.), *The Future of Leadership: Today's Top Leadership Thinkers Speak To Tomorrow's Leaders*, San Francisco: Jossey-Bass, pp. 91–102.
Wentling, R. M. and Palma-Rivas, N. (2000), "Current Status of Diversity Initiatives in Selected Multinational Corporations," *Human Resource Development Quarterly*, Vol. 11, No.1, pp. 35–60.
Wenger, E., McDermott, R. and Snyder, W. M. (2002), *Cultivating Communities of Practice: A Guide to Manage Knowledge*, Boston, MA: Harvard Business School Press.

Index